Assuming the Burden

FROM INDOCHINA TO VIETNAM: REVOLUTION
AND WAR IN A GLOBAL PERSPECTIVE

Edited by Fredrik Logevall and Christopher E. Goscha

1. *Assuming the Burden: Europe and the American Commitment to War in Vietnam,* by Mark Atwood Lawrence

Assuming the Burden

Europe and the American Commitment to War in Vietnam

Mark Atwood Lawrence

UNIVERSITY OF CALIFORNIA PRESS
Berkeley · Los Angeles · London

Portions of this book were published in an earlier form as "Transnational Coalition Building and the Making of the Cold War in Indochina, 1947–1949" in *Diplomatic History* 26, no. 3 (summer 2002): 453–480, and are reproduced here by permission of Blackwell Publishing Ltd.

University of California Press
Berkeley and Los Angeles, California

University of California Press, Ltd.
London, England

First paperback printing 2007

© 2005 by The Regents of the University of California

Library of Congress Cataloging-in-Publication Data

Lawrence, Mark Atwood.
    Assuming the burden : Europe and the American commitment to war in Vietnam/Mark Atwood Lawrence.
        p. cm. — (From Indochina to Vietnam : revolution and war in a global perspective; v. 1)
    Includes bibliographical references and index.
    ISBN 978-0-520-25162-5 (pbk. : alk.)
    1. Indochina—History—1945– 2. Indochinese War, 1946–1954. 3. United States—Foreign relations—France. 4. France—Foreign relations—United States. 5. United States—Foreign relations—Vietnam. 6. Vietnam—Foreign relations—United States. 7. France—Foreign relations—Great Britain. 8. Great Britain—Foreign relations—France. I. Title. II. From Indochina to Vietnam; v. 1. III. Series.
DS550.L385 2005
959.704′12—dc22   2004020239

Manufactured in the United States of America

15 14 13 12 11 10 09 08 07
11 10 9 8 7 6 5 4 3 2 1

The paper used in this publication meets the minimum requirements of ANSI/NISO Z39.48–1992 (R 1997) (*Permanence of Paper*).

*For my mother,
whose memory inspires me in all things,
and for my father,
who made all things possible*

Contents

Preface — ix

Introduction — 1

PART ONE · *Contesting Vietnam*

1. Visions of Indochina and the World — 17
2. U.S. Assistance and Its Limits — 59
3. Illusions of Autonomy — 102

PART TWO · *Constructing Vietnam*

4. Crisis Renewed — 147
5. Domestic Divides, Foreign Solutions — 190
6. Closing the Circle — 233

Conclusion — 276

Notes — 289

Bibliography — 333

Index — 347

Preface

This book, undertaken during one momentous transitional phase in international affairs, looks backward to another. Just as the end of the Cold War confronted nations around the globe with great uncertainty and opportunity, so too did the end of the Second World War a half century earlier. The process by which governments grappled with those uncertainties and opportunities and crafted a new global order holds immense relevance to our own times. By understanding the failures of an earlier generation of Western leaders to take adequate account of the complexity of politics in unfamiliar parts of the world—and by recognizing the consequences that can flow from such errors—perhaps we can make better decisions this time around.

But there is more to the connection between the 1940s and the first decade of the twenty-first century. In both periods, prevailing geopolitical ideas were the work of political elites in many nations. Few would dispute this statement in connection with the current era of globalization, a process defined by the growing interchange of influence across increasingly porous national borders. This book demonstrates that the late 1940s were similar in key respects. Western policies during the Cold War have too often been described as uniquely American in origin, as if U.S. policymakers could sit safely behind impermeable national boundaries, survey the world, and pronounce their decisions. In fact, as this book demonstrates, the United States, in the Cold War era as much as in the period since the fall of the Berlin Wall, should be seen as one participant, albeit an inordinately powerful one, in an international web in which influence flowed in multiple directions. Other actors sometimes set the international agenda by advancing self-serving ideas, constraining choices, and practicing coercion. The ideas that underpinned Western policy for forty years during the Cold War were constructions crafted through constant interaction of decision makers from many nations.

This book seeks to explain the origins of American involvement in Vietnam, but it also endeavors to contribute to a new body of American history that, inspired by globalizing currents, attempts to place the United States within an international context. How, it asks, was the United States affected by the rest of the world even as it was affecting that world in ways that are relatively familiar? Answering this question was a considerable challenge, not least because it required intensive work in the archival holdings of multiple nations—a process that entailed many months of research, a good deal of travel, and mastery of the political cultures and decision-making processes of each government. The outcome, I hope, is nothing less than a fresh way of understanding the roots of America's war in Vietnam and some new ideas about how nations interact with each other to produce policy.

Completing such an ambitious project was possible only thanks to the generosity of numerous individuals and organizations. I am grateful to the Bradley, MacArthur, and Smith-Richardson foundations as well as the Harry S. Truman Library for supporting much of the research. I also wish to thank the Mrs. Giles M. Whiting Foundation for enabling me to complete my writing with minimal distractions. A postdoctoral fellowship from the John M. Olin Foundation allowed me to work on revising and expanding the project during my final year in New Haven. The Yale International Security Studies program also helped me in myriad ways, both tangible and intangible, to achieve my goals. I am grateful to the College of Liberal Arts at the University of Texas for summer funding and a semester of leave that helped me put the finishing touches on this book.

I also wish to thank the Lyndon Baines Johnson Presidential Library and the Lyndon Baines Johnson Foundation, whose ceaseless support has helped make my adjustment to life in Austin such a delight. I am especially grateful to Harry Middleton and Betty Sue Flowers for allowing me and Fred Logevall to live out every scholar's dream—to gather together the world's leading authorities on a particular subject for a long weekend of intensive discussions. I wish to thank those who

Preface   xi

traveled to Austin in November 2002 to take part, especially Laurent Cesari, Chen Jian, Bill Duiker, Lloyd Gardner, David Marr, Lien-Hang Nguyen, John Prados, Kathryn Statler, Martin Thomas, Stein Tønnesson, and Marilyn Young. I learned a great deal from all of them and deeply appreciate their comments on my work. Chris Goscha was unable to attend but nevertheless deserves my heartfelt thanks for hunting down photographs and helping me with questions that only he could answer.

For guidance at an earlier stage, I am grateful to Paul Kennedy, Ben Kiernan, John Merriman, and Gaddis Smith. All four provided a constant stream of insightful feedback despite fierce competition for their time. Moreover, they never lost patience with me despite my occasional scholarly forays into the 1960s and my year-long journalistic foray into the European Union. They are models not only of scholarly excellence but also of kindness, generosity, and good cheer. I owe equal thanks to John Gaddis. Even though John arrived at Yale when my work was nearly complete, he treated me practically as one of his own students and provided enormously helpful comments. His enthusiasm for my ideas gave me a critical dose of confidence at exactly the right moment. I am also indebted to the remarkable collection of young international historians who surrounded me during my years in New Haven, particularly Matt Connelly, Will Hitchcock, Jeremi Suri, and Salim Yaqub.

Since coming to the history department at the University of Texas, I have benefited from the advice and encouragement of an extraordinary collection of colleagues. I am especially indebted to George Forgie, Roger Louis, and Michael Stoff. Their generosity and friendship have meant more to me than I can express, and I treasure their comments on the manuscript. This book also profited from the advice of many others, including Bob Abzug, Caroline Castiglione, Judy Coffin, Tony Hopkins, Ward Keeler, Gail Minault, Joan Neuberger, Bat Sparrow, and David Oshinsky. My research assistants—Tala Gharagozlou and Van Nguyen in New Haven, and Christelle LeFaucheur and Paul Rubinson in Austin—performed routine miracles of proofreading, translating, and library sleuthing.

At the University of California Press, Monica McCormick offered a perfect mix of enthusiasm, patience, and constructive pressure over the many months since we first discussed this project. I am also indebted to Randy Heyman and Marilyn Schwartz for handling my questions and lowering my anxieties at key moments, to Steven Baker for his meticulous work with the manuscript, to Niels Hooper for helping to see the project through to its end, and to two readers for providing comments that immeasurably strengthened the manuscript. Most of all, I owe a profound debt to Fred Logevall, the dean of the younger generation of Vietnam War historians and the person who introduced me to UC Press. Part mentor, part colleague, Fred has influenced my life in countless ways over the years. He is a model for me and someone I am proud to call a friend.

And then there is the small group of kindred spirits who shared my trials and tribulations over the years. Jenni Siegel and Mark Weiner were steadfast supporters and motivated me through their stellar examples. I also value the friendship and wise counsel of Susan Ferber, who knows a thing or two about publishing and expertly coached me through the final stages of this project. Phoebe and Neil Olcott showed me overwhelming hospitality during a particularly memorable month of writing in California. Jolie Olcott was the best proofreader imaginable as well as a true inspiration and an extraordinary intellectual partner throughout the entire process. In Texas, Susan Boettcher, Erika Bsumek, and Carolyn Eastman have been valued companions and confidantes. Stephanie Osbakken gave me boundless support and, most important, told me that the time had come to send the book off into the world. Priscilla, Patrick, Elizabeth, and Jane Melampy lifted my spirits throughout the entire process and helped keep my priorities in order.

Most of all, this book stands as testament to a staggering amount of love and generosity from my parents, Elizabeth Atwood and Robert Lawrence, who long ago shared their enthusiasm for history, taught me to love books, and gave me every advantage in pursuing my studies over the years. That my mother did not live to see the publication of this book is the greatest disappointment of my life. I know how proud she would have been to hold it in her hands, and perhaps to slide it onto the shelf next to her own books. With inexpressible gratitude, I dedicate this book to her and to my father.

Introduction

> . . . the end of all our exploring
> Will be to arrive where we started
> And know the place for the first time
> T. S. Eliot

Cold War tensions weighed heavily on U.S. secretary of state Dean Acheson as he wearily climbed aboard the presidential plane *Independence* on May 6, 1950. Recent months had brought little but bad news. In August 1949 the Soviet Union had shattered the nuclear monopoly enjoyed by the United States by detonating an atomic device. Two months later Mao Zedong's armies swept to final victory in China, pushing the world's most populous country into the communist orbit. Meanwhile, U.S. efforts to build a robust anti-Soviet front among West European nations lay in doubt as old animosities between France and Germany threatened to block cooperation. It was, Acheson later recalled, a "long, strenuous, wearying" time.[1] The secretary's trip to Europe promised a crucial opportunity for face-to-face discussions with his French and British counterparts to forge common positions on a vast array of problems. "They have been talking about the 'Atlantic Community' for over a year," the *New York Times* pointed out. "Now they are going to try to give it substance."[2] Mostly, the Western powers faced questions about European security. How could the Western allies put more military muscle behind the North Atlantic Treaty, the mutual-defense pact they had signed a year earlier? How could they overcome lingering suspicions within Western Europe so as to create a more unified, integrated bloc?

The most urgent question of all, however, concerned not Europe but Indochina, the distant territory where the French military had been waging a costly war against Vietnamese revolutionaries for more than three years. Would the Western powers be able to submerge their differences over colonialism and find a basis for common action in a part of the world that seemed increasingly to be threatened by communist advances? For years, the status of Indochina had deeply divided the Western allies and provoked bitter, inconclusive debates among U.S. policy makers. Now Acheson was ready to tell the French and British governments what they desperately wanted to hear: Washington would provide military and economic aid to bolster the French war effort. The United States was prepared to extend the principle of transatlantic cooperation all the way to Southeast Asia, to assume part of the burden of waging war in Vietnam.

Acheson's trip, culminating in his assurances to French foreign minister Robert Schuman on May 8, marked a landmark moment in the development of U.S. policy toward Indochina. Less than a decade earlier, the territory had barely registered in American consciousness. To be sure, the United States had become increasingly concerned with Southeast Asia over the previous half-century as burgeoning American industries fueled a drive for markets and raw materials in the Far East. U.S. trade with British Malaya and the Dutch East Indies grew in the early twentieth century as rubber and tin became commodities of major importance to the U.S. economy. But trade with the Indochinese territories of Vietnam, Cambodia, and Laos lagged far behind, excluded by an uncompromisingly autarkic French imperial system.[3] Although Vietnam's rubber and oil drew the covetous eye of U.S. firms, Americans could do little to gain a foothold. Nor did Indochina attract much attention from U.S. diplomats or journalists. The State Department operated a tiny consulate in Saigon, and only a handful of Americans, mainly Protestant missionaries, resided in the French territories. For most Americans, as the Asia scholar and travel writer Virginia Thompson observed in 1937, Indochina had been "largely lost to view."[4]

Within a few years after the Second World War, everything had changed. "Indo-China Has Become Vital Cold War Front," trumpeted a *New York Times* headline on February 12, 1950, three months before Acheson's trip. Proclaiming Indochina the "Greece of the Far East," the *Times* described the French territory as the battleground where Asia's destiny appeared about to be decided, just as Europe's seemed to depend on the outcome of fighting between Greek communists and the pro-Western Greek government, the major focus of America's Cold War anxieties at the time.[5] Many policymakers in Washington spoke in equally drastic terms. If France were defeated in Indochina, the Central Intelligence Agency warned, "the forces of International Communism would acquire a staging area from which military operations could be launched against other countries in Southeast Asia, whether on the mainland or across the South China Sea."[6] There was no telling where the communists would stop once they had gained control of Indochina. In the most alarmist scenarios, Mao Zedong's victory seemed to open the floodgates to communist expansion all the way to India or even the Middle East, areas of great value to the West. The fate of Vietnam seemed directly connected to crucial geopolitical priorities of the United States.

The decision to throw American aid behind the French war marked the first definitive American step toward deep embroilment in Indochina affairs, the start of a long series of moves that would lead the administration of Lyndon Johnson to commit U.S. ground forces to Vietnam fifteen years later. But if 1950 signaled the beginning of that process, it marked the end of another. As U.S. officials began shipping weapons, aircraft, and other military supplies to Vietnam and as they set up the first U.S. military mission in Saigon, many had already embraced the set of fundamental assumptions about Vietnam that would guide American involvement over the following twenty-five years. They now believed that the fate of Vietnam carried heavy implications for the destiny of Asia. They saw Vietnamese insurgents as the agents of international communism and assumed that their success would serve the interests of Moscow and Beijing. And they embraced the idea that the United States, through the proper application of material aid and political guidance, could play a key role in establishing a new Vietnamese political order reconciling the nationalist aspirations of the local population with the requirements of Western security.

To be sure, U.S. thinking about Vietnam continued to evolve in significant ways in the 1950s and 1960s, and policymakers had opportunities to change course in those years.[7] It would be going too far to argue that patterns of thinking established in the early Cold War years made a U.S.-Vietnamese war inevitable. Yet the pattern is unmistakable: basic ideas conceived in the late 1940s had remarkable staying power. To understand America's war in Vietnam, one must reckon seriously with the years before 1950, a period that figures only marginally in most Americans'—and even in many historians'—perceptions of the U.S. experience in Southeast Asia.[8]

How did U.S. policymakers come to think of Vietnam as they did during those years? How did a faraway corner of the French empire acquire such significance that Americans saw fit to intervene with economic and military aid? Why were other roads not taken? Unsurprisingly, these questions, like so many connected to Vietnam, have drawn a good deal of interest from historians over the years. The resulting body of scholarship, although little accounted for in general histories of the war, is large, complex, and contentious. Fundamentally, historians have offered three explanations for American behavior—one stressing geostrategic calculations, another highlighting U.S. economic objectives, and a third focusing on the imperatives of domestic politics.

The first line of argument emphasizes that Vietnam acquired urgency in American minds in the late 1940s because the situation there increasingly seemed to conform to a global pattern of communist aggression against the West and its interests. In the early postwar years, according to this interpretation, American alarm about Soviet expansionism had focused on Eastern Europe and the eastern Mediterranean. Following the communist victory in China in 1949, however, Truman administration policymakers came to view the threat as global. Under these new circumstances, it was only natural that they extended their solution to communist expansion in the European theater—the containment of Soviet power within its existing bounds—to Asia. Scholars, then, have seen the 1950 decision to support the French war effort as just one prong of a global effort to check communist expansion. That effort began with the Truman Doctrine in 1947 and continued through a long chain of worldwide interventions calibrated to squash challenges from the Kremlin and its allies wherever they arose.[9]

A second explanation for Vietnam's emergence as a major U.S. concern stresses American calculations about the region's economic value. Few scholars, it is important to note, contend that Americans were guided by a belief that Vietnam's natural resources and markets were critical to U.S. prosperity. Unquestionably, American business wished for greater access to the French territories, and U.S. officials occasionally fretted that a communist victory in Vietnam would deprive the United States of raw materials potentially useful to the American economy or to U.S. national security. But these considerations were minor since Vietnam offered little that could not be obtained elsewhere. Indochina's economic assets were, as the CIA put it in 1950, merely "desirable," not "absolutely essential."[10] Still, several historians have argued that economic considerations drove U.S. policy. Many U.S. officials, they argue, concluded by 1950 that Indochinese resources and markets mattered to the economic health of crucial U.S. allies, especially

Britain and Japan. Vietnam's economic significance lay not in the territory's contribution to the American economy but in its potential contribution to industrialized nations that American policymakers regarded as crucial to the establishment of a new global order. In helping to keep Vietnam embedded in the Western orbit, Washington sought to enhance not a bilateral relationship of limited importance so much as a system of global economic interaction in which it had a colossal stake.[11]

A third explanation for Vietnam's emergence as a major U.S. preoccupation emphasizes domestic politics. In this view the Truman administration fixed its attention on Southeast Asia and began pumping U.S. material assistance into the region to fend off critics at home. Central to this interpretation is the contention that Harry S. Truman's narrow reelection victory in 1948 left a frustrated Republican party searching for an issue it could use against the president. The administration's failure, despite years of effort and vast expenditures, to prevent a communist victory in China provided the cudgel the president's enemies sought. As Mao Zedong triumphed in 1949, Republicans assaulted Truman and the Democrats as weak willed and demanded vigorous action to prevent the further spread of communism in Asia. Truman, the argument runs, had little choice but to go along. The president not only feared political damage from charges of being soft on communism but also saw no alternative to bold policies in Asia if he was to secure congressional support for his most cherished objective abroad, the construction of a strong transatlantic relationship. When Congress insisted in December 1949 that the administration spend $75 million to fight communist insurgency in Asia, the White House accepted the task without quibble as the price of attaining its Eurocentric priorities.[12]

All three arguments hold merit, and none excludes the others. Taken together, this body of work leaves little doubt that several reciprocally reinforcing considerations helped propel the Truman administration toward supporting the French in Indochina. Nonetheless, this scholarship falls short of offering a satisfactory explanation of American behavior. Above all, it fails to reckon with the fact that Washington, as it crafted policy toward Vietnam, was merely one participant in a complicated, decidedly international dynamic in which other governments usually held the initiative and set the agenda. Historians have largely treated U.S. policymaking in isolation, removing the Truman administration's deliberations of geostrategy, economics, and politics from the complex transnational interchange in which those calculations were embedded. This approach has generated two problems. First, it has attributed too much autonomy to the United States and overlooked crucial ways in which other governments shaped U.S. choices. Second, the conventional approach has reified the alleged distinctiveness of American consideration of colonial questions, making it impossible to discern the ways in which U.S. policymaking fit into broad patterns of debate that cut across nations. In fact, toward the end of the Second World War and in the immediate postwar period, several governments engaged in far-reaching deliberations of what should become of European empires. U.S. policymaking involved nearly constant interplay among representatives of various nations.

This book offers a fresh look at the origins of U.S. involvement in Vietnam by treating the United States as just one participant in a complicated transnational deliberation over the destiny of Indochina. In part, the innovation lies in the simple matter of sources. This study makes sustained and rigorous use of archival material from the three nations that most determined Indochina's postwar destiny—France, Britain, and the United States. Other scholars have occasionally drawn on material from more than one of these countries in attempting to elucidate Indochina's emergence as a Cold War battleground. But they have almost always isolated one leg of the Washington-Paris-London triangle (usually, in the case of American historians, the Washington-London leg). The French diplomatic record has received little attention in English-language studies. Scholars, moreover, have usually focused on relatively narrow periods of time, usually the months around the end of the Second World War or the months in 1949 and 1950 following the communist victory in China.[13] By contrast, this book rests on extensive reading of diplomatic, political, and military records in all three countries—in more than a dozen archives stretching from the French colonial archive in Aix-en-Provence to the Truman presidential archive in Independence, Missouri. And it covers the entire period from the middle years of the Second World War until the U.S. decision to aid the French war effort in 1950, encompassing the whole span of time over which U.S. attitudes changed so dramatically.

In examining material from several nations, this study does more than write three stories where there was only one. It explores the complex patterns of interplay over Vietnam among the three key Western governments. For the first time, we can see the transformation of American perceptions of Vietnam as the result of efforts by policymakers in Paris and London as well as Washington to recast the Vietnam problem in a way that would overcome disagreements over colonial questions and permit common military and political action to suppress the Vietnamese revolution. In this analytical context, it becomes clear that American deliberations over Vietnam were hardly unique. To the contrary, American debates paralleled—and were affected by—discussions in other nations. Washington's decisions were only one part of a series of decisions taken in capitals around the world as various governments sought to shape Indochina's future.[14]

The risk, of course, is that geographical breadth comes at the expense of analytical depth. This book aspires to avoid that danger by delving into the inner workings of each government as it grappled with Indochina. Through deep research into the U.S., French, and British foreign-policy bureaucracies, it examines decision-making currents not just at the level of presidents, premiers, foreign ministers, and ambassadors but also at the equally important level of ministry desk officers, embassy staff, and midlevel military and intelligence personnel. Although Indochina sometimes held the attention of high-level national leaders in France, it rarely drew the gaze of their counterparts in the United States or Britain. During these years when the attention of the Western powers was fixed on matters of profound significance—among others, the status of Germany and Eastern Europe, the reconstruction of Western economies, the control of atomic weapons—Indochina ranked as a minor issue at best. To appreciate policymaking in Washington and London (and often Paris as well) therefore requires careful attention to the obscure bureaucrats who actually managed the issue. For this reason, Harry Truman, Clement Attlee, and even Charles de Gaulle appear only occasionally in the pages that follow, while individuals such as James O'Sullivan, M. Esler Dening, and Philippe Baudet receive sustained attention. These were the sort of men who counted most in recasting Indochina as a Cold War crisis by 1950. The development of their views and, more important, the debates that they carried on within their own bureaucracies as well as with their foreign counterparts form the central focus of this study.

Taking an approach that is both global and national, I argue that the transformation of American thinking about Vietnam occurred as part of a grand, transnational debate about Vietnam in particular and the fate of colonial territories in general following the Second World War. As the book's first half demonstrates, each capital became deeply divided over Vietnam during the war or in its early aftermath, torn between contradictory impulses to reestablish French colonial rule and to acknowledge the legitimacy of Vietnamese nationalism and permit at least a degree of self-determination. Although the precise dynamics of the debate differed among the three countries in question, the basic contours were the same. Each policymaking establishment wrestled with the same set of fundamental problems that faced Western nations as they confronted colonialism in the mid-twentieth century: Should they attach higher value to the stability of their own political and economic interests or to the desires and grievances of colonized peoples? Should they seek the near-term benefits of continued Western domination or the potential long-term advantages of harmonious relationships with Asian peoples? Should they take Asian nationalist movements seriously as legitimate negotiating partners, even protogovernments, or dismiss them as irresponsible minorities unprepared to lead their nations? Contestation only intensified in the first months and years following the end of the Second World War as Western governments gradually became aware of the enormous anticolonial discontent brewing in Southeast Asia and the difficulty of finding satisfactory compromises. By mid-1947, Paris, London, and Washington were deeply split over what course to follow—divided from each other but also divided internally, with different groups of policymakers advancing conflicting preferences. To the considerable extent that Vietnam's political destiny lay in the hands of the Western powers, its future remained highly uncertain.

Between 1947 and 1950, as the book's second half reveals, division and hesitancy gave way to decisiveness and, finally, action. In 1950 the three governments came together to form a coalition aimed at destroying the Vietnamese revolution. They agreed to hold military talks on the defense of Southeast Asia, and the Truman administration promised to supply military and economic support to resist communist aggression. The intensification of the Cold War between 1947 and 1950, especially the triumph of communism in China in 1949, helps explain this convergence of Western policy. Amid an increasingly threatening global and regional environment, policymakers who advocated a firm multilateral response stressing the need for short-term stability in Southeast Asia were bound to attract support. The intensification of Cold War pressures is not sufficient, however, to explain U.S., French, and British behavior. The shift in Western policymaking rested not only on a reappraisal of the broader geopolitical environment but also on a reconceptualization of the political situation within Vietnam. Decision makers who advocated a bold, concerted Western effort to suppress Ho Chi Minh's Democratic Republic of Vietnam faced a difficult task, more difficult than most accounts of the early post–Second World War years in

Vietnam have suggested. Even as the Cold War intensified, influential officials in each bureaucracy clung to a nuanced view of events in Vietnam and questioned whether the perilous situation there could be resolved through the relatively blunt methods conceived for waging the Cold War in Europe: Western partnership and military preparedness. These skeptics cautioned against hasty repressive action that might alienate Vietnamese nationalists permanently and create the very outcome that Western governments wished so much to avoid. It might, in other words, drive Vietnamese radicals further into the arms of Moscow and Beijing.

To overcome this skepticism, supporters of a bold Western policy in Vietnam worked in the late 1940s to reconfigure the political situation in Vietnam so that it would conform more closely to the Manichean vision that had given rise to Western solidarity and activism elsewhere around the globe. Like-minded U.S., French, and British officials worked together to recast Vietnamese politics in a way that would promote international consensus, as well as bureaucratic harmony, sustaining an activist policy in each of the three key capitals. In constructing Vietnam as a Cold War battleground, the three governments jointly undertook to demonize Ho Chi Minh and the Viet Minh movement as full-fledged communists, to advance the idea that the future of Southeast Asia depended on the outcome of the conflict in Vietnam, and to promote the possibility of establishing a viable alternative to Ho Chi Minh's leadership to satisfy legitimate Vietnamese nationalist demands and preserve a high degree of French influence. Only after establishing a common set of rationales and assumptions could the three governments find a solid basis for the partnership that would draw the United States into Indochina and open a new phase in Vietnam's postwar history, the period in which Vietnam's political struggles would be seen principally as expressions of the global confrontation of Soviet communism and Western liberal capitalism.

In arguing for this process of construction, this book rests partly on the theoretical insight that "reality" is established through social interaction. Simply put, the situation in Vietnam acquired new meaning between 1945 and 1950 partly because powerful policymakers said it did and because they took actions that gave substance to their coalescing representations of reality. The enormously complex Vietnamese political situation defied easy categorization, as nationalists, communists, royalists, and many other elements jockeyed for power in the turbulent years following the Second World War.[15] Viewed from Western capitals, the situation seemed to clarify over time as government officials brought to bear assumptions and fears generated by menacing developments in the larger geopolitical environment. The Cold War was, as political scientist Alexander Wendt has phrased it, "a structure of shared knowledge" that gave meaning to international politics for more than forty years. This book explores how a particular set of ideas about a particular country took shape during a transformative phase of the twentieth century—a case study that can help us to understand, in Wendt's words, "how agency and interaction produce and reproduce structures of shared knowledge over time."[16]

This analysis also rests on a more literal notion of what it means for policymakers to have "constructed" Vietnam. Even as "construction" has acquired a particular meaning for theorists such as Wendt, it has retained a simpler definition that is central to this book's claims. To construct something—whether a house, a bridge, or a policy—can simply refer to the process of assembling an integrated, functioning whole out of disparate materials that might have been combined to create something different.[17] So it was with Vietnam. Before 1948 the U.S., British, and French governments were stymied by the complexities of making policy toward Vietnam, especially the contradictory needs to give rein to Vietnamese nationalism while maintaining order and stability in the region. Division and uncertainty prevailed in Western capitals, with no clear solutions in sight. Thereafter, factions within each government worked in a reciprocally reinforcing fashion to craft solutions that satisfied each and enabled them to move jointly toward a common approach. Over three years or so, participants in this complicated interchange assembled an edifice that contained elements of French, British, and American origin. The end point of this process, the agreement in 1950 to proceed in unison to wage a counterrevolutionary war in Vietnam, represented a compromise that made no one entirely happy but provided a basis on which Western governments could respond to what they perceived as a deepening crisis. In later years the problems and contradictions inherent in the 1950 solution would begin to show. First the French and then the Americans would confront the impossibility of allowing full expression of Vietnamese nationalism while keeping Vietnam securely within the Western economic and political order.

Beyond this concern with elucidating the circumstances of America's first Vietnam commitment, this study has two other aims. For one thing, it sheds light on the origins of the Cold War in the colonial world (the "Third World") more generally. In retrospect, we tend to see the Cold

War as a global phenomenon, a conflict that touched places like Indonesia, Guatemala, and Angola as much as the nations on either side of Europe's "iron curtain." But there was nothing inevitable about the Cold War's global scope. U.S.-Soviet tensions erupted during the Second World War and in the war's aftermath because of conflicts over the future of Europe and contiguous areas of southwestern Asia—places where Soviet political and territorial ambitions were relatively easy to see. Although we can fairly criticize Western leaders for overreacting to Soviet assertiveness, we can surely understand why they responded as they did. In the Third World, the range of options was much broader and the difficulties of choosing which path to follow much greater. It falls to historians to explain why Western policymakers extended assumptions and policies developed in the European theater to parts of the world where social and political tensions emerged from a different set of causes. The misapplication of the Cold War paradigm produced little but horror and tragedy for forty years.

The pages that follow offer insight into the process by which the Cold War came to the Third World. While diplomacy connected to Vietnam has generally attracted scholarly attention because of the turmoil of the 1960s and 1970s, it is worth recalling that Vietnam was in fact one of the first parts of the Third World to attract sustained American and international attention after the Second World War. Even if Vietnam had never emerged as a major issue for the United States in later years, the controversies surrounding it in the late 1940s would merit careful attention. It was there as much as anywhere that Americans first confronted the need to craft a response to surging anticolonial passions after the Second World War. It was there that Americans confronted the difficult choice between supporting nationalists seeking self-determination—the course that their oft-professed anticolonial convictions dictated—and supporting the neocolonial objectives of France, the course suggested by their determination to promote a new global order built on cooperation among Western states.

The solution to this conundrum, an awkward compromise that paid lip service to America's anticolonial principles while leaning toward the interests of France, established a pattern that would play out repeatedly in the Third World over the course of the Cold War. From Vietnam to Indonesia, Guatemala to the Dominican Republic, Ethiopia to South Africa, American policymakers would invoke dedication to liberal, democratic solutions and sometimes would take concrete steps in that direction by sponsoring elections, pushing the pace of reform, or attempting to build popular bases of power for the regimes that they preferred. Almost always, however, Americans set the highest priority on the protection of short-term U.S. economic and geostrategic interests and embraced policies geared to limit the scope of social reform and the expression of genuine nationalism if those developments seemed to threaten American objectives, as they often did. The United States, then, often invoked liberal principles and sometimes even insisted on concessions to those principles while carrying out illiberal policies. Vietnam provides a telling case study of the pressures that helped establish this pattern in the aftermath of the Second World War, a period of unique fluidity in the history of U.S. foreign relations that might have yielded a different outcome.[18]

This book also offers insight into the nature of the transatlantic partnership between the United States and Western European countries that came into existence over the five years following the Second World War. Above all, it demonstrates that European governments sometimes held the initiative in their relationship with the United States and dictated policies ultimately embraced in Washington. The Western economic and security system was, in other words, the work of government officials in multiple nations, not a unilateral imposition of U.S. preferences for remaking the world. In making this case, I offer new evidence for a view of transatlantic alliance that has gradually gained currency over the last fifteen years—a vision of the alliance as a complicated partnership in which power and influence ran in all directions across permeable borders, not just outward from Washington. The North Atlantic partnership, we now know, allowed for substantial give-and-take among its members.[19] While confirming this basic idea, this study also elaborates on it in various ways. To begin with, it shifts the focus of transatlantic discussions from European problems to colonial problems. Most of the existing scholarship arguing for European agency in the formation of Western policy concentrates on European controversies, especially economic reconstruction and the postwar status of Germany and Eastern Europe. But how successful were European governments in influencing American behavior in the non-European world, where the Soviet menace was anything but obvious and where the U.S. rhetorical commitment to self-determination tended to divide Washington from, rather than bond it with, Western Europe? This study reveals the more difficult challenges the Europeans faced in trying to build a common front with the United States and the strategies necessary to overcome them.[20]

It also builds on previous scholarship by showing that France—in its Gaullist wartime guise and then during the Fourth Republic—successfully influenced U.S. behavior. That Britain wielded influence over U.S. thinking about colonial problems is hardly surprising given the enormity of British power in 1945 and the long tradition of close Anglo-American cooperation. But in the French case, historians have long painted a picture of a hopelessly divided, ineffective, and even clumsy nation where cabinets came and went with astonishing regularity and where policymakers could maintain little consistency. Scholars have suggested that most of the time, the U.S.-French relationship was wholly dominated by American power and influence. Although the French policy establishment frequently suffered from division and that division sometimes produced disastrous results in Vietnam, key French officials were nevertheless remarkably successful in the overall strategy they pursued in connection with Indochina—to internationalize the problem and thereby to put foreign resources to use in the service of French objectives. French competency and consistency in connection with Vietnam suggests the need for a new understanding of the French role in crafting the postwar international order.[21]

Finally, this study identifies precisely how governments with divergent aims and interests came together around a specific policy in Vietnam, providing a case study that might help illuminate similar processes related to other issues of contestation within the Western alliance. In his controversial narrative of the Cold War *We Now Know*, historian John Lewis Gaddis suggests that Western cooperation was built upon shared democratic principles and practices. Governments, he contends, understood the need for bargaining and compromise and frequently managed to submerge their differences in the interest of the common good. This book offers a much less exalted view of how Western nations crafted policy. After carefully examining intragovernmental disputes over policy toward Vietnam, I argue that hawkish factions in each country—those who viewed the turmoil in Indochina as an expression of binary Cold War tensions—made common cause with one another to recast Vietnam, to assure the triumph of their policy preferences, and to marginalize those with different ideas. In each country, dissenters against the extension of Cold War thinking to the colonial world represented a serious threat to those who wished to pursue a vigorous anticommunist war in Vietnam. By working together and drawing strength from one another at critical moments of decision, factions in each country favoring a bold Cold War posture were able to have their way by 1950.[22] The policy embraced by the three leading Western powers in that year represented not the triumph of democratic principles or processes but the victory of thinking that lacked subtlety and sensitivity to the peculiarities of Vietnamese history and society. This victory, achieved more through maneuvering and manipulation than democratic deliberation, marked a moment of great tragedy. Over the following twenty-five years, the Western powers would reap what they sowed in 1950.

PART ONE

Contesting Vietnam

CHAPTER 1

Visions of Indochina and the World

The Second World War ended one epoch of Vietnamese history and launched another. For half a century France had dominated the territory collectively known as Indochina—the Vietnamese provinces of Cochinchina, Annam, and Tonkin, plus neighboring Cambodia and Laos. Vietnamese nationalists had periodically challenged colonial rule, but French authorities had squelched demands for change in every case, reaffirming their nation's supremacy through a mix of armed repression, economic subjugation, and cultural domination that had characterized colonial rule in Indochina since its beginnings in the nineteenth century. Nationalist agitation aggravated the colonial administration but did not threaten its control. Nor was French rule much challenged from beyond Indochina's borders. The Western powers, respectful of French claims and excluded by formidable trade barriers, took little account of the area. China, for centuries the main Asian aspirant to power in the region, remained too weak and divided during the decades of French rule to interfere. For its part, Japan steadily emerged as a regional power during the early twentieth century but posed no direct threat to European dominance in Southeast Asia until 1940.[1]

The events of that year changed everything. In May Nazi armies launched a crushing attack against France and, a month later, forced the French government into a humiliating armistice that shattered the country's pretensions as a global power. The defeat had immediate consequences in the Far East, where the Japanese government eagerly exploited French weakness. Seeking to bolster its war effort against China, Tokyo demanded that the colonial administration close the Chinese-Tonkin border, thus sealing off an important channel of Western supplies for the beleaguered Chinese army. Severed from Paris, hopeless of challenging Japanese military power, and doubtful of receiving support from Western nations, French governor-general Georges Catroux capitulated. Over the next eighteen months, the trickle of French concessions grew to a flood as Catroux's Vichy-appointed successor, Admiral Jean Decoux, struggled to appease Tokyo and avert an outright Japanese takeover. First Japan demanded airfields in northern Indochina and the right to transport troops across Tonkin to fight in China. Then in summer 1941, as the Japanese military prepared to attack southward toward the Dutch East Indies and Singapore, Tokyo insisted on establishing bases in southern Indochina. By the time of Japan's assault on Pearl Harbor, the French administration had become a virtual accessory to the Japanese war effort.[2]

In a sense, Catroux's strategy was successful. In return for French cooperation Tokyo permitted the colonial administration to remain in place at a time when Japanese forces were uprooting Western regimes in Malaya, Singapore, Burma, the Philippines, and the East Indies. Even in its hour of humiliation France nominally remained master of its Southeast Asian empire, a privilege that the colonial administration struggled to protect over the following years. But this arrangement—really an expedient that served Tokyo's interests by relieving it of administrative and military burdens—could not mask the underlying reality of French impotence.

To Vietnamese nationalists the crumbling of French power signaled an unprecedented opportunity to overturn the colonial order. They understood that their goal would not be realized quickly. There remained not only the matter of ending what was left of French control but also that of evicting the Japanese. Still, the rapidly changing international situation generated hope. Amid surging optimism Ho Chi Minh and other Vietnamese nationalist leaders gathered in a damp mountainside cave near the Chinese border in northern Tonkin to begin laying the groundwork for revolution. The delegates agreed to submerge clashing agendas within a broad patriotic coalition—the Viet Nam Doc Lap Dong Minh Hoi, or Viet Minh—and chose guerrilla warfare as the principal method of struggle against foreign occupiers. With those matters settled, Ho Chi Minh appealed to Vietnamese patriots to join the fight. "The hour has struck!" he proclaimed. "Raise aloft the insurrectionary banner and guide the people throughout the country to overthrow the Japanese and the French!"[3]

The Viet Minh's unalloyed enthusiasm contrasted sharply with the deep anxiety that prevailed among Western policymakers concerned with Indochina's future. Events that inspired optimism and boldness in the Tonkin mountains generated fear and discord among Free French, British, and American officials charged with settling Indochina's destiny following Japan's defeat. Above all, the evisceration of French control raised the vexing question of how—and, at least in Washington, whether—colonial rule should be reestablished. In the early months of the Pacific war, Allied deliberations amounted to little more than academic exercises since Japan totally dominated the region. As the tide of war turned toward the allies in 1943 and 1944, however, Indochina's postwar status became a steadily more pressing issue. Small clusters of French, British, and U.S. policymakers focused on a full slate of questions: Who should govern Indochina after the war? How should the aspirations of local nationalists be taken into account? What would be Indochina's place in the postwar international order? In attempting to answer these questions, the three Western governments laid down patterns of thinking and debate that would underlie policymaking for the next half decade.

FREE FRANCE AND THE RECOVERY OF INDOCHINA

As Allied victory grew more certain in 1944, the Free French organization under General Charles de Gaulle became increasingly anxious about Indochina. To be sure, the matter ranked below the most pressing national concerns—the reestablishment of the French state, economic rehabilitation, and the war against Germany. Consumed by these challenges, ordinary citizens, the Free French media, and the renascent political parties showed little interest in the fate of a territory on the other side of the world. For the small leadership group concerned with recovering France's traditional role as a global power, however, the issue did not lag far behind the nation's top priorities. These men—bureaucrats, diplomats, politicians, and military officers—shared a conviction that their country's long-term prospects rested on its ability to preserve the empire, not least Indochina. François de Langlade, a one-time rubber planter who became one of de Gaulle's chief delegates for Indochinese affairs, succinctly stated the group's thinking in early 1945. "Without Indochina," he wrote, "France is no longer a world power."[4]

The equation of French *grandeur* with imperial prowess ran deep in French history. Since the early nineteenth century, French colonial ambition had swelled during times of national crisis as leaders strove to compensate for setbacks in Europe with victories overseas. It was no accident that the most active phase of French conquest followed the humiliations of the Franco-Prussian War in 1870–1871 or that French determination to maintain the empire soared during the Second World War. Indeed, the necessity of preserving the empire was as plain to Vichy officials as to Gaullists. Both regimes struggled desperately to preserve a glimmer of French independence following the debacle of 1940. "The colonial peoples represented the best reason for France to believe and to hope," the Vichy colonial minister, Admiral Charles Platon, asserted in fall 1940. De Gaulle, employing remarkably similar language, proclaimed the empire "a strong ray of hope," offering France "trump cards in the game where its destiny will be decided."[5] For both regimes, Indochina held special significance. Although less directly tied to French national identity than Algeria and perhaps other African possessions, it surpassed any other imperial holding in conferring great power status on France. The farthest-flung of major French territories, it rivaled India, the jewel in Britain's imperial crown, and entitled France to a major role in Far Eastern affairs.

French determination to hold Indochina also stemmed from a pervasive, if less explicitly stated, belief in the territories' economic value. To be sure, Indochina had not yielded the returns that French colonial enthusiasts had hoped for over the years. As one U.S. study remarked, French fiscal, tariff, and wage policies since the late nineteenth century had been "unfortunate" at best, failing to generate a healthy colonial economy or to bring many benefits to the metropole. A small group of white planters and the Banque de l'Indochine reaped most of the rewards, while French consumers paid high prices for colonial goods. So questionable was Indochina's economic value that one U.S. study suggested in 1944 that France might simply be better off without it.[6] Still, the French economy had become dependent on Indochinese exports, especially rice, tin, and rubber, before the war, making the territory the second most important source of French imports (after Algeria) within the empire. In addition, Indochina represented a source of food and labor for other French possessions and served as a hub of the French colonial economy in the Far East and Pacific.[7] All in all, Free French leaders had reason to believe that Indochina, however weak its prewar performance, could play a valuable role in metropolitan recovery.

While officials agreed on the need to recover Indochina, they differed over precisely how French rule should be reconstituted after the war. A conference of colonial administrators in Brazzaville, the capital of French Equatorial Africa, in January 1944 revealed a wide range of views about the possibility of postwar colonial reforms. Formally, the Brazzaville meeting dealt only with Africa. But discussions reflected thinking about the empire in general—its structure and the degree of self-rule that should be permitted within it. On one side, the embryonic Gaullist colonial ministry based in Algiers offered relatively ambitious proposals.[8] Henri Laurentie, head of the political section of the Commissariat aux Colonies, laid out plans not only to liberalize administrative practices but also to reconfigure the empire as a federation allowing greater autonomy for the various component territories. Laurentie stopped well short of proposing self-government. "If there is to be self-government," he insisted, "it can come only at the end of a fairly long and strictly controlled evolution."[9] But there was no mistaking that Laurentie's proposals envisioned significant change.

This view encountered stiff opposition from the assembled colonial governors, most of whom had risen to positions of influence under a prewar system that eschewed federalism and emphasized the assimilation of colonial peoples into a unified French empire. Under their sway the meeting accepted only minute steps to improve *indegène* opportunities and coldly rejected Laurentie's guarded language about self-determination. To the conservatives, talk of "*le* self-government"—a phrase so alien that it was always rendered in English, as historian Martin Shipway has pointed out—flew in the face of the hallowed Jacobin principle of "France One and Indivisible." The conference's final declaration, though only an advisory document, left no doubt where the conservatives stood. The French "civilizing mission" in the colonies excluded "any idea of autonomy [and] all possibility of evolution outside the French bloc," the statement asserted. "Also excluded," it added, "is the eventual establishment of self-government in the colonies, even in a distant future."[10]

These opposing viewpoints laid out the parameters of a debate over Indochina's future that would percolate within the Gaullist bureaucracy for the remainder of the war and would, in later years, break into the open. For the time being, however, deliberation over postwar reforms remained muted. Far more pressing was the challenge of assuring that France, rather than some other power, would make the decisions when the moment came. On this score French officials of all political stripes were united in anxiety. While every other part of the prewar French empire had rallied to de Gaulle by 1944, Indochina floated in precarious limbo, nominally under the control of a French administration loyal to the Vichy regime but vulnerable to Japanese takeover.

From 1940 Gaullist leaders had done what they could to show their determination to recover Indochina and to reclaim for France a prominent role in the Far East. Free France declared war on Japan immediately after the Japanese attack on Pearl Harbor in December 1941 and a month later began planning for the eventual dispatch of forces to fight alongside the allies in the Pacific. De Gaulle's Comité Français de la Libération Nationale stepped up its efforts in 1943, approving creation of an expeditionary force in North Africa for use in Indochina and requesting British and U.S. permission to post an officer to the Allied headquarters supervising the war in Southeast Asia. In December the French National Committee condemned Vichy's collaboration with Japan and proclaimed its intention to recover the territory. "In partnership with the United Nations, [France] will pursue the fight until the aggressor's defeat and the total liberation of all the territory of the Indochinese Union," asserted a declaration.[11]

None of these acts held more than symbolic significance, however, for Free France lacked any capacity to challenge Japanese domination. Distasteful as it was, Gaullist policymakers saw no alternative during 1943 and 1944 to Vichy's accommodation with Japan. Any attempt to coax the Vichyite administration into the Gaullist camp or to push the sixty thousand or so French-led troops in Indochina to take up arms against Japanese control seemed certain only to compound the problems of recovering the territory by provoking a Japanese takeover. Under the circumstances, asserted René Massigli, a prominent Free French diplomat, it was "better to leave things alone."[12] Convinced of this logic, the French National Committee contented itself with planning for a military effort that would come when more auspicious conditions developed in the Far East.

That moment seemed to draw nearer in late 1944. French officials took note in October when American military successes in the Philippines seemed to clear the way for Allied operations on the Vietnamese coast—a prospect that French officials viewed as a mixed blessing. On one hand, it would presumably bring closer the day of Indochina's liberation. On the other, it would disrupt the fragile administrative status quo in Saigon and place Indochina's destiny in the hands of foreign armies with unpredictable objectives. Gaullists worried that U.S. advances in the Pacific would provoke Tokyo to end French rule altogether. But the prospect of U.S. or Chinese forces operating on Indochinese soil, unaccompanied by French troops, caused almost as much alarm. The best way out of this bind was to introduce Free French military forces into Indochina ahead of any Allied operation in order to defend French interests. "It is in our fundamental interest to supply our own troops in Indochina so they will be *in force* in order to welcome [the allies] with dignity and *in force*," advised General Zinovi Pechkoff, the battle-scarred foreign legionnaire who served as Free French ambassador to the Chinese Nationalist government in Chungking (Chongqing).[13] The problem was that France, depleted by four years of war and still burdened with fighting in Europe, utterly lacked the troops, warships, and other equipment to reinforce its position over such great distances and in the face of the still-formidable Japanese occupation. "Unfortunately," a Foreign Ministry study asserted with notable understatement, "the resources available to France today are too limited and it will be years before they can be reconstituted."[14]

Of the two nations most likely to challenge French sovereignty in Indochina, China represented the lesser threat. French officials were keenly aware of long-standing Chinese designs on Indochinese territory and worried that any Chinese incursion into Tonkin might prove impossible to dislodge. They also feared that Chinese patronage of various Vietnamese political organizations during the war would lead to dangerous cross-border meddling in Indochinese politics after the fighting ended. Nevertheless, these dangers seemed manageable. Chinese Nationalist leader Chiang Kai-shek repeatedly assured Ambassador Pechkoff that his government had no territorial ambitions in Indochina and even suggested that he was willing to help restore French rule. While the possibility remained that rogue Chinese military officers might have ideas of their own, Chiang's assurances eased fears that the Nationalist government would interfere as a matter of state policy. French observers also drew confidence from the growing likelihood that China, consumed by internal rivalries and rapidly descending into civil war, would have little energy for peripheral adventures. Foreign Ministry experts even speculated that Chiang might steer clear of Indochina out of a desire to cultivate French cooperation with his anticommunist fight inside China.[15]

The United States represented a much more serious threat. For years, both Vichy and Gaullist leaders had watched anxiously as Franklin Roosevelt had grown increasingly vocal about his desire to grant independence to colonial territories after the war. In August 1941 Roosevelt and British prime minister Winston Churchill had proclaimed the Atlantic Charter, whose third article, pledging to "respect the rights of all peoples to choose the form of government under which they will live," seemed to promise postwar independence to any nation seeking freedom from foreign rule.[16] During 1942 Roosevelt focused his anticolonial agenda on the British empire, demanding especially that London promise independence for India. By 1944, however, Roosevelt had fixed his attention on Indochina. In a stream of pronouncements to aides and foreign leaders, the president advocated plans to bar the return of French colonialism and to establish an international trusteeship that would prepare the territory for eventual independence.

To make matters worse, Americans of all political persuasions appeared to share the president's agenda. "The colonial problem is one of the few issues on which American opinion is not divided," Foreign Ministry analysts wrote in a survey of U.S. attitudes in early 1945. "For different reasons, emancipation of European colonies is desired as much by Republicans as by Democrats, by conservative industrialists and radical intellectuals, by the *Chicago Tribune* as much as the *New Republic*." Both ideology and self-interest seemed to propel U.S. anticolonialism. French views on this matter echoed widely held stereotypes of Americans as simultaneously naive and materialistic. In its analysis of U.S. ideology the Foreign Ministry despaired of changing American minds. "The American people, born of an anticolonial revolution, are hostile to colonies by tradition," asserted the report, adding, with questionable historical insight, that the United States had always sought to avoid acquiring colonies of its own and had secured those it had merely "by accident." The American "penchant for crusades" compounded the problem. "Of the two wars that [the United States] fought before 1914, one was carried out to achieve its own emancipation, the other for that of black slaves," wrote the ministry, adding that in their latest war Americans naturally sought a new ideological aim to endow their sacrifices with ennobling purpose. Liberal internationalists, Europhobes, and Protestant moralizers, the study added, were filling the void by reviving Wilsonianism and promoting decolonization as the latest variation on the American commitment to self-determination for oppressed peoples.[17]

Much as it decried such zealotry, the Foreign Ministry worried even more about a narrower segment of U.S. society allegedly motivated by avarice. The study contended that American businessmen, backed by a compliant political and military establishment, were cleverly exploiting anticolonialism in pursuit of less lofty objectives. "The people of the United States barely perceive these influences," the report stated. American businessmen seemed to support decolonization partly out of eagerness to exploit previously inaccessible raw materials. At the same time, the study asserted, American entrepreneurs were anxious to open new markets in the hope that new overseas customers for their goods would help maintain the pace of wartime production in the United States and minimize postwar unemployment. The overall aim seemed to be "an open door for merchandise as well as capital," contended the report, whose authors had no doubt as to who would win once colonial areas were opened to all comers: "The open door would favor powerful Americans over European competitors."[18]

By 1945 French officials suspected that Americans were already busily exploring economic opportunities in Indochina. Diplomats in Washington and the Far East sent numerous reports to Paris warning that agents of the U.S. Office of Strategic Services (OSS) seemed to be operating on behalf of American oil companies. From Chungking, for example, Pechkoff alleged that an American agent in Vietnam was busy not only gathering intelligence about the Japanese military but also collecting information on the region for Texaco. Still more alarming, these corporate agents sometimes seemed determined to bypass French authorities and make contact with Vietnamese nationalists in hopes of securing concessions. Speculation about such activity was fueled by a belief that Americans had already begun taking a keen interest in the region in the years just before the war. The statistics suggested a worrying trend. In 1933 the value of Indochinese exports to the United States had totaled 20.8 million Indochinese piastres, while imports from the United States had amounted to a mere 3 million piastres. In 1940 the figures jumped to 64 million piastres and 24 million, respectively. It was hardly a bold leap to believe that Americans would attempt to exploit wartime conditions to tap further into Indochina's resources and markets.[19]

French officials also suspected Washington of exploiting anticolonialism to mask its plans to extend U.S. military power around the globe. "It is possible that the American government favors independence in certain colonial territories only in order to gain possession of bases," asserted the Foreign Ministry's postwar planning committee. This theory rested on a widely held belief that U.S. leaders were determined, no matter what the objections of their own people or of foreign governments, to establish a new global order tailored to U.S. commercial and strategic interests. The postwar planning committee suspected that the U.S. military, bristling with power and convinced of its unique ability to keep the peace after the war, desired the means not only to defend the Western Hemisphere but also to project power into the Far East. Zealous assertions of anticolonial principle were, in this view, mere cover for illiberal designs on various Pacific islands and possibly even on the Asian mainland. The committee alleged that Washington policymakers suffered from a "guilty conscience" over these cynical plans and hoped to conceal them within idealistic language that would "satisfy the public's appetite for progress and new ideas."[20]

All these anticolonial motives—ideological, economic, strategic—seemed to converge on Indochina. "The appetite for power that the dominant U.S. role in the war has excited in Washington, concern about security in the Pacific, the defense of American commercial interests in the Far East, and the Methodist ideology determined to liberate oppressed peoples have combined to create an attitude strongly unfavorable to the maintenance of our position in Indochina," Ambassador Pechkoff wrote from Chungking. Aware of the quickening pace of Roosevelt's assertions of hostility to French rule, the provisional government feared the worst. "There is no longer any doubt that the Americans now envisage depriving us of our sovereignty, or at least greatly constraining it," Henri Hoppenot, one of de Gaulle's chief emissaries in Washington, reported in November 1944. "President Roosevelt," Hoppenot added, "is personally the author [of a trusteeship scheme] and has sketched an outline for some of his intimates."[21]

For all this anxiety, however, some French officials detected cracks in the American anticolonial facade. The Foreign Ministry's office for Asian affairs, for example, judged that behind routine expressions of hostility to French rule the U.S. position on Indochina in fact remained "extremely fluid."[22] Washington's policy seemed vague and contradictory. Exactly how would a trusteeship work? Who would take supervisory responsibility? Would China, the United States itself, perhaps even France take the leading role in preparing Indochina for independence? On these questions, French observers noted, U.S. policymakers appeared to have few answers. Imprecision in the U.S. position became especially obvious in February 1945, when Roosevelt, meeting with his Soviet and British counterparts at Yalta, seemed to backtrack on earlier pronouncements, agreeing that trusteeships would be established only with the consent of the imperial powers concerned.

Three further considerations inspired confidence that Washington would back down. First, as Foreign Ministry officials repeatedly emphasized in internal correspondence, U.S. diplomats had offered several assurances early in the war that the French empire would be fully restored following Germany's defeat. Ministry personnel acknowledged that those promises may have been desperate bids to maintain French fighting spirit, but they nevertheless expected that Washington would honor explicit commitments. Second, French officials speculated that Americans would ultimately back away from policies predicated on the inherent rights of colonized peoples—a principle that, if generally accepted in international affairs, might expose the United States to criticism for its treatment of its own minority populations. "Above all," asserted the Foreign Ministry's study of American anticolonialism, "the condition of blacks in the United States leaves the Americans open to easy counterarguments from their European interlocutors." Third, French officials doubted that Washington would push its anticolonial agenda at the risk of alienating France and Britain, countries whose cooperation the United States would obviously need in constructing a postwar order. "The American government," the ministry report insisted, "cannot ignore the resistance that [trusteeship] would encounter among European governments and public opinion."[23]

Washington's unpredictability exasperated French officials, who privately railed against U.S. behavior. Even the Foreign Ministry's normally cautious reports indulged in vituperative language on the subject, with one paper decrying the "disconcerting amateurism" and "inexperienced zeal" of U.S. policymaking. Almost any flip-flop seemed possible.[24] For all the aggravation it caused, however, the muddiness of U.S. policy also represented an opportunity. As long as U.S. policy remained in flux, the door would remain open for the restoration of French rule. No other power, after all, was likely to block the way. French diplomats judged that Chiang Kai-shek and Soviet premier Josef Stalin, despite verbal support for Roosevelt's trusteeship scheme, had little interest in pressing the matter. The only other nation with authority over the postwar colonial settlement, Great Britain, resolutely supported French objectives. Hoping to exploit this disunity to their advantage, the small group of French cabinet ministers, bureaucrats, diplomats, and military officers concerned with Indochina intensified their effort over the last months of 1944 and the first weeks of 1945 to reestablish their nation's claim.

One method of strengthening the French position was to involve French troops in a military campaign to liberate Indochina. With the war obviously entering its closing stages, Free French officials calculated by the end of 1944 that fighting in and around Indochina, whatever the short-term risk of destroying the Franco-Japanese condominium, would strengthen French claims over the long term by demonstrating that French people were willing to fight and die for their possession. After that, it would presumably be more difficult for other governments to deprive France of its territory. "I was not distressed by the prospect of taking up arms in Indochina," de Gaulle recalled in his memoir, adding:

> Measuring the shock inflicted on France's prestige by Vichy's policy, knowing the state of public opinion throughout the [Indochinese] Union, foreseeing the outbreak of nationalist passions in Asia and Australasia, aware of the hostility of the Allies—particularly the Americans—in regard to our Far Eastern position, I regarded it as essential that the conflict not come to an end without our participation. Otherwise, every policy, every army, every aspect of public opinion would certainly insist upon our abdication in Indochina. On the other hand, if we took part in the battle—even though the latter were near its conclusion—French blood shed on the soil of Indochina would constitute an impressive claim.[25]

On this logic, de Gaulle and his advisers believed it was essential to organize forces capable of waging a military campaign against the Japanese. In July 1944 the general's personal emissary, Major de Langlade, parachuted into Indochina to establish contact with Gaullist sympathizers and to organize resistance. Several more agents of the provisional government followed soon after. Meanwhile, the provisional government stepped up its effort to move fresh troops from Algeria to Indochina. Above all, French diplomats pressed their demands for Allied help to transport the Corps Léger d'Intervention, a force of twelve hundred men designed to fan out across Indochina and to lead guerrilla operations against the Japanese.[26]

Efforts to organize resistance within Indochina went hand in hand with a diplomatic campaign to convince Washington to allow regular French units to participate in the broader Pacific war. French leaders hoped that such forces might take part in an eventual liberation of Indochina, but they understood that any insistence on the point might result in Allied rejection and therefore proposed only that French units serve as the U.S. and British commands wished. In September 1944 the provisional government formally offered to send a naval task force as well as an expeditionary force of as many as thirty thousand troops to the Far East as soon as fighting had ended in France. Half the force would join the U.S. campaign in the Western Pacific, while the rest would serve under South East Asia Command, the British-dominated headquarters in Kandy, Ceylon, that supervised the war in Burma. So urgent did de Gaulle's top military aide, General Alphonse Juin, consider these initiatives that he urged taking equipment away from forces in Europe if necessary to demonstrate a powerful presence in the Far East.[27]

French hopes foundered not on equipment shortages but on U.S. hostility. Despite intense French pressure the Roosevelt administration blocked French forces from the Far East and excluded French officers from Allied war-planning councils. Such opposition underscored the importance of obtaining political support for French aims from other foreign governments, another major feature of French diplomacy in late 1944 and early 1945. One focus of French hopes—ironically, in view of later developments—was the Soviet Union. Foreign Ministry experts predicted that Moscow, at the end of the European war, would reassert traditional Russian dominance in northeast Asia while also trying to extend its influence in China by supporting the communists there. Yet French experts believed that Soviet ambitions stopped at China's southern borders. In Southeast Asia, they anticipated that Soviet leaders would welcome the restoration of European colonialism as a valuable stabilizing force. "The USSR does not wish to see Chinese influence or American imperialism gain predominance in that strategically important region," asserted one study prepared for the foreign minister. "France, strong enough to resist foreign ambitions and sufficiently disinterested to constitute a precious element of stability in the Far East, seems to them best qualified to protect and administer Indochina."[28]

If French diplomats hoped to gain from benevolent passivity in Moscow, they looked to fellow Southeast Asian colonial powers for active help. "We must not miss a single chance to remind London and The Hague of common interests based on the similarity of the situations of France, England, and the Netherlands in Asian matters," the cabinet's foreign affairs committee asserted. "Without doubt," it added, "the British and Dutch governments will wish to see the French government's national and international standing ever more firmly established." French officials saw strong parallels between their nation's position in Indochina and the Dutch predicament in the East Indies, where American anticolonialism raised similarly annoying questions about the future of European rule. To bolster their colonial positions, the two countries' colonial bureaucracies routinely shared information and sought common diplomatic positions. Nevertheless, French officials doubted that the Netherlands could offer decisive assistance. The Hague obviously lacked equipment or ships to help France achieve its objectives in Indochina. Moreover, the Dutch government seemed unlikely to risk its relationship with Washington by advocating the French cause.[29]

The provisional government expected much more from Britain, which possessed far greater resources and infinitely more influence over postwar settlements. On the whole, the British government gratified French hopes. René Massigli, the French ambassador in London, found "no reason to doubt" British dedication to French interests by January 1945.[30] As with the Netherlands, however, French officials saw limits to Britain's capacity to help. For one thing, British resources, while considerably greater than those available to the Dutch, were still badly depleted by years of war, and it was obvious that little could be spared to assist a foreign ally. Moreover, French officials suspected that they could not depend on London much more than The Hague for help in recovering Indochina if doing so risked a rupture with Washington. As Pechkoff put it, "England depends too heavily on the United States for us to rely on London to support us openly against the wishes of Washington." Ultimately, then, there was no escaping the fact that Indochina's postwar fate rested with one country: the United States. "Some might say," Pechkoff asserted, "that once we have British support in Indochina, we can ignore China and the United States. No illusion," he warned, "is more dangerous." However annoying the conclusion may have been, Washington obviously bore the brunt of the fighting against Japan and would dictate postwar arrangements in the Far East. "Nothing will or can be done in Indochina without their agreement, at least tacit," wrote Pechkoff. Even the French embassy in London, a strong proponent of Anglo-French cooperation, recognized the danger of overreliance on Britain. "It is the Americans who will have the last word at the moment of decision," advised Ambassador Massigli. "The Pacific war is above all an American war, a fact which the British themselves recognize with bitterness."[31]

Inescapably, the only sure method of restoring French control over Indochina was to change American minds and obtain U.S. support. Only Washington, it was clear, possessed the authority to approve French ambitions and, just as critical, the resources to fulfill them. Only with access to American material power—shipping, military equipment, and economic aid to rebuild the Indochinese economy—could France recover its prewar position. The indeterminacy of U.S. policy left space for optimism that it might be possible to change American views and harness U.S. strength, but there was no obvious way to do it. Consequently, French political leaders, diplomats, and military officials embraced a range of strategies to convince, cajole, and if necessary, coerce the United States into backing French aims in Indochina.

In a quickening series of bilateral meetings devoted to Indochina, French representatives in Washington worked hard to persuade Americans to abandon their hostility to colonial restoration. Above all, French diplomats strove to appeal to American sensibilities by stressing their country's good intentions toward the Indochinese population. The provisional government, of course, had no detailed plan to reform French rule in Indochina. Deliberation of postwar colonial problems had not proceeded very far. But in contacts with U.S. officials and in public pronouncements, French officials hinted otherwise, promising repeatedly that Indochina would be allowed a greater degree of autonomy after the war. In its December 1943 declaration proclaiming its determination to reestablish colonial rule, the French National Committee pledged that Indochina would be given "a new political status" involving new governing arrangements of a "liberal character." De Gaulle reiterated that pledge during a July 1944 trip to Washington, although he provided no details. A diplomatic note handed to the U.S. ambassador in Chungking, Patrick Hurley, similarly promised that a revived French republic, "together with the populations concerned," would work out new arrangements providing Indochina "autonomy within the framework of the French Empire."[32]

Officials also sought to appeal to Americans by recasting the historical record of French imperialism in Asia. Diplomats had orders from Paris to emphasize the metropole's accomplishment in promoting economic development and bringing advancement to the Indochina's twenty-four million inhabitants. This was no difficult task for French leaders accustomed to touting their nation's accomplishments in Southeast Asia. For decades colonial enthusiasts had pointed with pride to the symbols of modernity that France had created: a rationalized agricultural system, Western-style schools, advanced hospitals, and a network of roads, railways, and port facilities. Thanks to these accomplishments, French officials could proudly trumpet Indochina's transformation by the eve of the Pacific war from a subsistence, single-crop economy to a rich polyculture that produced vast exports. Grateful for such progress, "*les indigènes*" genuinely supported the French presence, according to French officials steeped in the Orientalist assumptions about the docility of Asian peoples. "The population of our colonies has always had confidence in us," Colonial Minister René Pleven told foreign journalists in October 1944. "The mass of the natives want us to help and protect them," added Pleven, rebutting American charges that only elite profiteers supported French imperialism.[33]

French officials also attempted to shape American perceptions of Indochina by appealing to presumed U.S. ambitions to penetrate the region economically and militarily. They understood that their country's long record of exclusionary economic policies made it impossible for France, even more than for other colonial powers, to pose as a champion of economic liberalism. The provisional government's relative inattention to colonial matters also made it impossible to state with any specificity the types of economic reforms that might ensue after the war. Nevertheless, discussions with American interlocutors often included vague promises to open the Indochinese economy to foreign trade and investment. In its December 1943 declaration the French National Committee pledged to overhaul Indochina's "economic status" by granting local authorities autonomy over fiscal and customs policies. New promises, though still vague, followed a year later. The note given to Ambassador Hurley pledged that Indochina "will be granted an economic regime enabling her to profit greatly from the advantages of international competition." Similarly, French leaders hinted that they were prepared to satisfy the other material objective they believed Americans held in Indochina: access to military bases. De Gaulle himself indicated willingness to allow foreign use of Indochinese airfields and ports as long as French sovereignty remained unchallenged.[34]

This persuasion campaign formed a central part of French contacts with American counterparts through the second half of 1944 and the first weeks of 1945. French officials were not, however, naive about their chances, at least in the short term, of overcoming entrenched anticolonialism through this means alone. Another, more forceful current also ran through French diplomatic activity—an attempt to coerce the United States into backing French objectives. Above all, French officials hoped to gain leverage from possession of two commodities that they believed U.S. authorities coveted—intelligence and rubber. They correctly judged that the OSS, the American intelligence agency, hoped to obtain information about Indochina in order to plan bombing operations against Japanese forces and to recover U.S. airmen shot down over the region. For French officials the American need for information represented an opportunity to exact a price. "On this point, as on others, it is necessary to apply pressure in order to obtain vital cooperation from the Americans," the interministerial committee in charge of Indochina affairs concluded in January 1945 while turning down a U.S. request for data concerning Indochinese beaches. De Gaulle had already set a precedent for such a refusal in September 1944 by ordering French intelligence agents to suspend cooperation of all kinds with the OSS in the Far East so as to make clear French exasperation over American attitudes toward Indochina. Although information continued to flow to U.S. authorities, cooperation was strained and a total breakdown remained possible. Threats to cut off rubber supplies were bound to be less impressive to American officials, partly because of rapid wartime advances in production of synthetic rubber. Still, Massigli proposed in early 1945 that France exploit its potentially important role in global production to demand that Washington agree to permit French recovery of Indochina after the war.[35] So great was the French predicament that he precluded no avenue of applying pressure.

GREAT BRITAIN AND THE REGIONAL IMPERATIVE

British policymakers backed the restoration of French colonialism for three reasons. First, they anticipated that a successful American challenge to French control in Indochina might lead Washington to question British rule in other parts of Southeast Asia that had been occupied by Japan, including the economically vital territories of Hong Kong, Malaya, Singapore, and Burma. Those possessions had played important roles in the British economy before the war and promised to offer crucial advantages, especially the capacity to earn foreign exchange, during the inevitably difficult reconstruction period following the war.[36] Most alarming to British observers was the seeming ease with which Washington contemplated radical solutions that carried potentially devastating consequences for its allies. "We'd better look out," Alexander Cadogan, the Foreign Office's permanent undersecretary, warned in early 1944 after Roosevelt had complained of the "hopeless" French record in Indochina. "Were the French more 'hopeless' than we in Malaya or the Dutch in the E[ast] Indies?" he wondered. Like his French counterparts, Cadogan judged that imperial solidarity in the face of such dangers was vital. "In view of the well-known American attitude towards the restoration of colonies generally, there is much to be said for the Colonial Powers sticking together in the Far East," Cadogan advised Churchill.[37]

The second reason for Britain's support of French colonialism was a belief that France stood a better chance than any alternative source of authority to maintain stability in Indochina. This was no small matter given the critical importance that British policymakers attached to Indochina as the linchpin of all Southeast Asia. Already in 1944 strategists in London viewed Indochina as a principle barrier between Chinese power to the north and the chain of territories to the south that included several British possessions. The loss of Indochina to a hostile power, Foreign Office officials conjectured, prefiguring what would later be known as the "domino theory," might set off a chain reaction across Asia. The pattern of Japanese aggression during 1940 and 1941 offered a model of how such a process might play out. "The potential threat to Australia, New Zealand, India, Burma, Malaya, and the East Indies Archipelago resulting from Indo-China being in the hands of a weak or unfriendly power," asserted one April 1944 Foreign Office study, "has been sufficiently demonstrated by the action of Japan in this war."[38] To be sure, doubts abounded about the capacity of France, badly weakened by the war, to defend the region. But British officials trusted that with adequate foreign assistance France could once again exert reliable control.

In any case, there existed no promising alternative to continued French rule. British officials shuddered at what they considered to be the most likely alternate scenario: Chinese control. Chinese Nationalist forces might, with U.S. blessing, simply invade Indochina and establish puppet regimes in Vietnam, Cambodia, and Laos. Or China might gain control under the cloak of international trusteeship. Either way, London foresaw nothing but chaos. An invasion carried the nightmarish prospect of fighting between French and Chinese troops, while a trusteeship would undoubtedly, in the cabinet's scornful words, "open the door wide to Chinese intrigues." Instability, in turn, promised to invite intervention over the long term by other powers—a renascent Japan or perhaps the Soviet Union. "We should expect the Japanese to start fishing in the troubled waters at the first opportunity," the cabinet's postwar planning committee asserted in a January 1944 memorandum. As for the Soviet Union, British planners saw no likelihood of direct interference in Southeast Asia. Nevertheless, they found it impossible to predict the extent of Soviet ambitions in Asia and could not exclude the possibility that within several years Moscow might exert significant influence in the Far East through a Japanese puppet state or through construction of a substantial Pacific fleet.[39]

Beneath British anxiety about foreign meddling lay an assumption that the Indochinese people were unprepared to resist such intrigue if left to their own devices. Some British observers sharply criticized the French record in Indochina, blaming Paris for harsh repression, underdevelopment of the economy, and heavy-handed administrative techniques that left little space for indigenous involvement. But British officials also had a degree of sympathy for the French. "In judging the achievements of a colonial administration, some consideration must be paid to the material it has to work upon," the Foreign Office's research department asserted in a study of Indochina. Reflecting widely held Western notions of Asian societies, the report depicted the Indochinese population as stunted by centuries of war, poverty, and oppression as well as the "extremely debilitating" effects of a tropical climate. The study went on to quote American author Virginia Thompson, whose 1937 book on Indochina criticized the Vietnamese for their deep-seated "apathy, insensitivity, and placidity" as well as their taste for "ruse and intrigue." If granted self-rule, such people would, in the British view, unleash political and economic havoc, with potentially devastating consequences for the region as a whole. Above all, many officials feared mass starvation across Southeast Asia if Indochina's rice industry fell under indigenous supervision.[40]

The third reason that Britain supported French claims to Indochina was the consensus among London policymakers that they must do everything possible to restore France as a robust partner in European affairs. No matter what scenario played out in the postwar years—German revival, Soviet expansionism, U.S. withdrawal, general social and economic collapse—British officials agreed that a reliable France was essential. Winston Churchill stated the matter grandly in a 1944 speech, telling the House of Commons that his government, as well as the entire Commonwealth and empire, wished "to see erected once more, at the earliest moment, a strong, independent, and friendly France." Behind such altruistic bluster lay hardheaded calculation of British national interests. "It is strategically essential in Europe, so long as there is any possibility of aggression by a European Power against the British Isles, that our policy should aim at maintaining a strong and friendly France," asserted one paper for the cabinet. Even if France remained feeble, the report added, "she should at least be friendly"—willing to play its part, in other words, in British-centered defense arrangements in the postwar period.[41]

No one doubted that losing Indochina would be a grievous blow to France. In material terms, British observers believed it would deprive

France of economic advantages as the country embarked on what would inevitably be a difficult recovery from war and occupation. More often, they cited the likely damage to the French national psyche if Indochina were taken away. The loss would "cause bitter resentment in France," asserted one Foreign Office paper. The postwar planning committee sketched a horrific scenario that might follow such a setback. Combined with the material and psychological damage already afflicting France after years of national humiliation, the loss of Indochina might push Paris to look to the East, rather than to Britain and the United States, for postwar cooperation. Franco-British partnership, the committee worried, "would be jeopardized if it could be represented to the French that we had willingly connived at a plan to despoil their Empire during the period of temporary weakness." Paris might respond by forging an alliance with Czechoslovakia or the Soviet Union—the Eastern option that had tempted France in earlier decades. "One way to keep the French loose from such a bloc," the Foreign Office committee asserted, "would be to give them as far as possible a sense of common interest with this country as an overseas colonial power."[42]

As vital as British policymakers considered the fate of Indochina for all these reasons, their deliberations remained hypothetical until the second half of 1944. With the U.S. arrival in the Philippines, British officials, like their counterparts in France, sensed that decisions could no longer be put off. Although French demands often exasperated officials in London, most were convinced that the moment had come to demonstrate sympathy for French objectives. Fearful of antagonizing the United States, the British government had not done much to promote French interests during earlier stages of the war. Now some in London understood French restlessness. "[The French] suspect, not without reason, that we are not putting ourselves out to give them a substantial military part in the reconquest of Indo-China," asserted L. H. Foulds, a Southeast Asia specialist in the Foreign Office. Among other risks was the alarming possibility that the French would give up on cooperation with Britain in Asia. The British commander in Kandy, Lord Louis Mountbatten, predicted a "disastrous effect" on the "whole British position in the Far East" if Franco-British cooperation in the region broke down. Only by demonstrating clear determination to protect French interests could Britain secure crucial French cooperation in the future, he maintained.[43]

More immediate considerations also encouraged British policymakers in summer and fall 1944 to seek decisions about Indochina's postwar status. For one thing, they knew that South East Asia Command would benefit from clearer planning as it began contemplating more intensive military operations in Southeast Asia. Firm decisions to restore French sovereignty would obviously encourage greater French cooperation with those activities while also eliminating the danger that U.S. and British propaganda would clash. The cabinet worried that any contradiction between U.S. emphasis on self-determination and British stress on restoration of colonial rule could confuse potential resistance forces in Southeast Asia and create long-term political problems with local nationalists. The danger of rice shortages following the war in the Far East also suggested a need for quick decisions. Early 1945 estimates predicted a major shortfall in regional production, due largely to an anticipated two-thirds drop-off in Indochinese production from 1940 levels. Fearing the political consequences of starvation in India and other British territories, experts in London hoped to establish a regional approach to the food problem as quickly as possible. Any such scheme clearly required decisions about postwar authority in Indochina, the world's second largest rice exporter before the war.[44]

Motivated in all of these ways, the British government provided a good deal of military and diplomatic assistance for French efforts to recover Indochina. To some extent, London was committed under its basic wartime agreement with Free France, the Anglo-French Protocol of Mutual Aid of February 1944, which called for cooperation not only in Europe but also overseas. But British support went beyond formal commitments. Officials repeatedly took up the French cause in meetings with U.S. counterparts, hoping to coax the Roosevelt administration into accepting a significant French role in the Pacific war. Although the British Chiefs of Staff were reluctant to give French officers any part in war planning until the liberation of Indochina was imminent, they persistently argued in favor of French requests to send a liaison mission to South East Asia Command and to involve French forces in the Far East as soon as possible.[45]

Meanwhile, the British military did what it could to support French ambitions, often exploiting American ambivalence in order to go beyond what U.S. policy formally allowed. At the end of 1944, the British Chiefs of Staff, after failing repeatedly to win U.S. backing to attach a French military mission at South East Asia Command headquarters, went ahead anyway, welcoming General Roger Blaizot and his fifty-member staff on a mission thinly disguised as a "personal visit."[46] Eden told French officials that he hoped the move would make the

United States "less difficult than earlier," apparently by forcing Washington to accept the inevitability of French involvement in the Far East. For his part, Mountbatten provided extensive air support for Free French agents in Indochina throughout 1944 and encouraged cooperation between the British intelligence apparatus in the Far East and the Gaullist intelligence organization. In December 1944 alone, British forces carried out forty-six air operations and succeeded in establishing a radio network among resistance cells in Indochina, building up stores of military equipment for use in a possible future campaign against Japan, and occasionally transporting French agents into and out of the region—all acts undertaken without U.S. approval and arguably in violation of Anglo-U.S. agreements about the boundaries of operational theaters in the Far East. All in all, British diplomats impressed themselves with their accomplishments. "I do not think the Americans realize anything like the extent to which our penetration of French Indo-China jointly with the French has already progressed," one Washington-based diplomat confided to the Foreign Office.[47]

London policymakers held no illusions, however, that these efforts, even if successful, would be sufficient to accomplish British objectives in Southeast Asia. Merely winning U.S. tolerance of a larger French role in the Far Eastern war would not come close to accomplishing the larger purposes of restoring France to its prewar position and reconstructing a stable political and economic order across the region. To achieve those aims, British officials recognized as clearly as their French counterparts that they had no choice but to obtain active, material support from the United States. Britain by itself was simply too weak to undertake the job of restoring the prewar order. Even before 1941 British leaders had foreseen that their country would have great difficulty maintaining a leading role in the Far East while fighting a major war in Europe. Four years of draining warfare proved them right. By 1944 British resources were badly depleted, leaving London with limited capacity for independent action.

By any measure, the disparity between British and U.S. power was gargantuan. While the United States tripled its production of manufactured goods between 1940 and 1944 and expanded its fleet to three times the size of the Royal Navy, Britain lost about a quarter of its national wealth and became overwhelmingly dependent on the United States for war matériel of all sorts. By fall 1943, for instance, Britain relied on the United States for 88 percent of its landing craft, 60 percent of its tanks, and nearly all of its transport aircraft.[48] Such imbalances undercut London's influence around the globe but carried particular meaning in the Far East, where Britain was least likely to share U.S. objectives but had the fewest resources of its own to spare. Keenly aware of these problems, Churchill warned de Gaulle in November 1944 that Britain faced a "manpower crisis" and could not offer the kind of assistance that France needed most in Indochina: ships to transport French troops to the area as well as aircraft and other equipment to support future French military operations.[49] Nor did British officials see much hope that the French government would obtain necessary assistance as long as Washington remained hostile to the entire colonial enterprise in Southeast Asia. "The hard fact is that the Americans have got us by the short hairs," wrote Mountbatten's chief of staff, Lieutenant General Sir Henry Pownall, who added that Britain could do little in Southeast Asia without U.S. approval. "Who pays the piper," Pownall lamented, "calls the tune."[50]

British policymakers thus confronted the same conundrum as their French counterparts: the nation most hostile to their objectives was the one whose cooperation had to be obtained at all costs. In the near term, no other country could provide the military and economic power that Britain lacked to accomplish its objectives in Southeast Asia. "Our Service and Treasury advisers both assure us that it is essential to carry the Americans with us," wrote Neville Butler, head of the Foreign Office's American department. Over the longer term, American support of European objectives seemed even more crucial. The British cabinet agreed that only full U.S. participation in the establishment of a chain of Anglo-American military bases in the Pacific and Southeast Asia could adequately safeguard Britain's Asian possessions as well as Australia and New Zealand. Colonial Office policymakers similarly believed that only the United States, with its massive productivity and technological prowess, could provide the economic aid and technical expertise necessary to restore colonial economies badly damaged by the war. All in all, the cabinet agreed in 1944, "in order to provide a greater measure of security in the Far East, it is essential to have United States participation."[51]

The challenge for the British government was, then, to lead the United States to drop its hostility to French control and to play a role on the Indochinese stage scripted for it in London. At moments, some British policymakers despaired of the possibility of pulling off such a feat and feared that they might ultimately be forced to choose between France and the United States. If that happened, postwar planners had little doubt which way London would tilt. "If it becomes clear that the

United States are determined to insist on the termination of French sovereignty as the price of their participation in security measures, and that their attitude is approved by the Dominions," asserted one cabinet study, "we should acquiesce in this, particularly if French sovereignty over her other overseas territories is allowed to continue." Meanwhile, the Foreign Office took seriously the notion that administration of Indochina should be handed outright to the United States as a way of guaranteeing that Washington would have no option but to concern itself with the postwar stability of Southeast Asia. If France would not play that role, London would make sure that the United States did.[52]

Few, of course, were enthusiastic about these extreme solutions. But the mere fact that they arose as possibilities suggests the fog of frustration that shrouded the Indochina issue during 1944. In private, British officials excoriated the United States for placing them in such a bind on behalf of what London regarded as simpleminded idealism.[53] Echoing their French counterparts, British policymakers castigated Roosevelt for clinging to a trusteeship idea that they saw as irresponsible. "This is one of the president's most half-baked and most unfortunate obiter dicta," Permanent Undersecretary Cadogan wrote in early 1944, while Dening wondered whether Roosevelt suffered from the same "megalomania" that had driven Woodrow Wilson's grandiose efforts to remake the world after the First World War.[54] Others fretted that the problem ran far beyond the president's opinions. Indeed, British analysts attributed American anticolonialism to the same hypocritical combination of idealism and self-interest that French officials detected deep in the fabric of American society. In one scornful survey of U.S. public opinion, the Foreign Office denigrated American sentimentalism as "a potentially excitable and clamorous factor" in international affairs. Even worse, American businessmen seemed to be maneuvering cynically behind the screen of idealism. The British ambassador in Washington, Lord Halifax, reported that anticolonialism found favor not only with "missionaries and educators and almost every kind of league and association seeking to regenerate Asia" but also, more quietly, with "American imperialists and American commercial and financial leaders."[55]

Many British policymakers saw reason to believe, however, that they would not ultimately have to choose between the U.S. and French partnerships that they hoped to forge. Like their French colleagues, British officials detected sufficient ambiguity, division, and flexibility in the United States to believe that U.S. policy on Indochina might yet change. The Americans "had not really made up their minds" about Indochina,

Eden told Ambassador Massigli in August 1944. The Foreign Office's November 1944 report on U.S. opinion found a glimmer of hope that American anticolonialism was outweighed only by American ignorance about colonial issues—a calculation that seemed to leave space for change if the U.S. population could be educated properly. As for Roosevelt himself, British diplomats also saw some reason for optimism. At a meeting in early 1944, Halifax took comfort in the fact that the president seemed not to be "taking it all too seriously," while Eden asserted that Roosevelt's statements on Indochina seemed to result from his tendency to "throw out ideas" without much regard for their consequences. Churchill concurred with this view, calling the president's comments "chance remarks."[56]

British observers also drew encouragement from increasingly apparent divisions within the U.S. bureaucracy. While Roosevelt and his supporters maintained their hostility to French colonialism, British diplomats watched with satisfaction as another body of opinion gathered strength. In Chungking Ambassador Sir Horace Seymour found that Americans with practical experience dealing with colonial problems thought more realistically. "There is," Seymour reported, "among a considerable proportion of thinking Americans who have acquired some first-hand knowledge of dealing with 'dependent peoples,' a growing realization that the complexity of the problem of the 'Imperialist' Powers has not been fully appreciated at home." From Washington Ambassador Halifax similarly reported "a few encouraging signs." He wrote that "well-informed opinion" in the United States—a category that apparently did not include the president—was "moving towards a realization that . . . problems of the treatment of dependent peoples cannot be disposed of by wholesale liberation or by a mere statement of liberal principles, but are complex and difficult of solution." Among the most encouraging trends seemed to be the growing realization among U.S. policymakers that China, in the throes of worsening internal chaos, would be unable to play a stabilizing role in Southeast Asia after the war. With China weak and unreliable, Americans seemed increasingly inclined to accept that European rule should be restored as the only way to preserve peace and stability to the region.[57]

The task for the British government, as for its French counterpart, lay in exploiting the ambiguities and divisions within the United States so as to change Washington's position. Like Paris, London developed a series of strategies to accomplish this aim. Most important, British officials sought to persuade the Americans to accept the restoration of

French sovereignty in return for certain concessions to the U.S. point of view. Specifically, British policymakers proposed that France be allowed to recover its control over Indochina on the condition that it accept "international"—meaning, in practice, U.S.-dominated—bases on Indochinese territory, as well as any other obligations, including a commitment to international consultation in times of crisis, placed on colonial powers under a worldwide security system supervised by the new United Nations. Foreign Office officials recognized that they might have difficulty convincing the provisional government to accept such a scheme since it departed from French insistence on unconditional return of colonial rule.[58] But they had no doubt that France would have to surrender something to American sensitivities. Even Dening, a staunch defender of French prerogatives in Asia, accepted that Paris must make political and economic concessions. "In the ultimate settlement," he wrote, "the French should be required to fall into line with the general concept of ultimate autonomy and ... should abandon their exclusionist economic policy in Indo-China."[59]

British support for international bases in Indochina formed part of a broader approach advocated by the Foreign Office to blunt U.S. hostility to French colonialism by embedding both French and American involvement in Southeast Asia within regional integrative mechanisms that would provide at least the veneer of international accountability. In particular, the British government called for establishment of "regional councils" to oversee development in various colonial areas. Such consultative bodies, though holding no enforcement powers, would coordinate food, health, labor, and other policies across regions such as Southeast Asia or sub-Saharan Africa. The Colonial Office had already taken the lead in establishing a Caribbean Council, an exercise that had won U.S. approval and participation. Establishing additional commissions, Cadogan confided to French colleagues in late 1944, might help satisfy Washington's desire for liberal reform in a way that did not threaten the principle of European sovereignty—precisely the sort of compromise British leaders desired.[60]

While trying in these ways to accommodate American anticolonial sensitivities, British diplomats also embarked on a multifaceted effort in 1944 to convince Washington that it had a strong interest in supporting active French participation in the Far Eastern war and in restoring French sovereignty in Indochina. Eden and other British policymakers lost few opportunities to press the issue in meetings with U.S. counterparts. It was Britain's task, as Dening phrased it, to "stimulate American thinking" to reconsider naive ideas about Asian nationalism and to embrace a policy "not openly and widely divergent from that of Great Britain." British efforts were calculated to appeal to what they considered to be key American desires—to end the Pacific war as quickly as possible, to promote postwar stability in the Far East, and to gain access to Indochina's natural resources. On the first theme, British diplomats stressed that involving French forces in the war against Japan would help tie down Japanese forces in the Far East and save American lives. To assuage American concern that French involvement would foreclose political decisions on Indochina, the British embassy in Washington even promised that all options would remain open—an assurance that clashed with secret calculations that greater involvement of French troops in the Far Eastern war would vastly improve chances of restoring French colonial rule.[61]

More significant, British diplomats sought to convince Washington that restoration of French sovereignty would serve U.S. strategic and economic interests by ensuring stability throughout Southeast Asia. Only the colonial powers, they argued, could maintain a peaceful and stable climate where U.S. aims—presumably economic penetration and the maintenance of regional peace—could be achieved. Premature independence would inevitably expose Southeast Asian states to "military and economic dangers," Eden argued before senior U.S. officials in November 1944. Taking account of apparent U.S. fondness for Asian nationalist movements, British diplomats emphasized that such dangers would come not from the Indochinese peoples but from foreign aggressors attempting to exploit the power vacuum that would inevitably result from the removal of French control.[62]

Although China loomed as the power most likely to threaten Southeast Asia, the Foreign Office stressed risks from sources more likely to provoke alarm in Washington—a revived Japan or an expansionistic Soviet Union. By spring 1944 some British policymakers recognized that mounting American anxiety about Soviet expansionism in particular might have a helpful impact on U.S. policy toward not only Europe but also Asia. To be sure, this was not a unanimous view. Halifax, for one, speculated that a Soviet threat in Asia was just as likely to lead Washington to withdraw entirely from the region, with devastating consequences for Britain. But most British officials expected that anti-Soviet sentiment would help their cause: American fears of Soviet assertiveness in the Far East would lead Washington to commit itself to Asia and to accept partnership with the colonial powers. So intriguing was this possibility that one Far Eastern specialist in the Foreign Office, J. Thyme Henderson, mischievously proposed that Britain encourage Soviet assertiveness in northeast Asia in order to demonstrate the hazards of removing colonial control elsewhere. "We shall only convince the U.S.A. of the value of continued existence of the British Empire as an element of stability in Asia if we let the Russians have their [way] a little in the North," he mused.[63]

A sense of foreign menace seemed likely to help advance British objectives mainly because it would crack the alliance between anticolonial idealists and hardheaded businesspeople that British observers believed underpinned American enthusiasm for decolonization. London officials suspected that although Americans might wish for Indochinese independence in an ideal world, the most powerful elements in the United States would much prefer continued European rule to control by a hostile power that would bar access to the region's raw materials and markets. The Foreign Office recognized that the United States had become practically self-sufficient in rubber production through synthetic processes developed during the war and might no longer rely to any meaningful degree on natural rubber from Indochina, Malaya, and the East Indies. But there was no alternative to natural tin from the region, and Foreign Office analysts reckoned that the United States, which had consumed two-thirds of the world's tin ore before the war, could not tolerate any threat to the flow of that mineral. British officials hoped such considerations would weigh heavily with hardheaded American industrialists, whom they, like the French, credited with strong influence over U.S. policymaking. In contrast to the French, however, British policymakers believed the answer to European problems lay in encouraging American economic entanglement in the area, rather than resisting it. The task was to urge the United States to act unhesitatingly on its presumed capitalist inclinations. Again, Henderson wrote most explicitly: "It would seem [best] not to discourage American attempts to acquire vested interests in China and the Far East generally, because there is nothing like vested interests for improving the education of American businessmen in foreign affairs. The fact that the United States had so little external trade in comparison to her internal trade before the war was one of the reasons why the American people are so uneducated as regards international affairs."[64]

To help educate Americans, many British officials also urged an aggressive public-information campaign to point out to Americans the positive results of European colonialism. If U.S. opinion, media, and policymakers were deeply hostile to imperialism, Foreign Office officials sometimes blamed themselves as much as ignorant Americans. Dening wrote that Anglo-American tension over colonialism was attributable "basically to our failure to convince the world in general and the United States in particular that we are not materially and morally bankrupt as a Far Eastern power." To resolve the problem, officials suggested various strategies, including efforts to extend special hospitality to U.S. dignitaries throughout the empire. The Foreign Office summed up the basic approach in a September 1944 report:

> [It is] not at all a matter of giving way to the Americans, but rather a question of dealing with them in such a way as to obtain from them the maximum of support for our objectives. During the war with Japan, it [is] necessary to let Americans know the great part we [are] playing. If we could do this, and could convince them of our cooperation and of its essential contribution to their security in the future, we should do much to ensure a better opinion of the Empire and encourage American cooperation with us.

While no single, coordinated publicity campaign resulted, British diplomats paid closer attention in the war's final year to U.S. public opinion and press coverage of colonial issues.[65] Ultimately, they understood, British interests would be safe only if Americans embraced them as their own.

THE UNITED STATES AND THE IMPERIAL DILEMMA

By the end of 1944, rough consensus about Indochina prevailed within French and British policymaking circles. In Paris, policymakers, whatever their latent differences over the long-term restructuring of the empire, agreed on the need to recover undisputed rule over Indochina and to obtain U.S. support to achieve that objective. In London, officials similarly concurred on the need to win U.S. support for French rule in order to protect crucial British interests. In the United States, no such agreement prevailed. As the Europeans themselves understood, the U.S. foreign policy bureaucracy was split on Indochina. Without doubt, many American officials appreciated the growing urgency of decisions about the territory's future. But the central dilemma that Washington confronted with respect to colonialism during the Second World War stymied U.S. policymaking. Should Washington support the ambitions of its European allies or seek a new global order based on self-determination and free trade? Americans could not decide.

On one hand, some U.S. officials, most notably Franklin Roosevelt, advocated ending French colonialism in Indochina and setting the region on the road to independence. The president repeatedly expressed strong feelings on the subject during the course of the war.[66] "Indochina should not be given back to the French Empire after the war," Roosevelt characteristically declared at a 1943 meeting of Allied war planners. "The French had been there for nearly one hundred years," the president growled, "and had done absolutely nothing with the place to improve the lot of the people." Early the following year, he spoke out even more strongly in favor of trusteeship, telling Ambassador Halifax that the French had "milked Indochina for a hundred years" and must not be allowed to return. Roosevelt's hostility probably sprang from numerous sources, including his dislike of de Gaulle, his contempt for the French performance in the face of Axis aggression, and his view of France as a decadent society that would require years to recover any international standing. France, he asserted in a relatively charitable moment, "would certainly not again become a first-class power for at least twenty years." If the French protested the Indochina trusteeship, he declared, "so what?"[67]

While the president spoke most acerbically on the subject, many other American officials shared at least parts of his critique, a fact that has sometimes been obscured in scholarship focusing narrowly on Roosevelt.[68] Without question, the president's views carried far more weight than anyone else's, and his opinions set a tone hostile to French colonialism throughout the U.S. bureaucracy. Yet many U.S. officials shared the president's opinions, if not necessarily his specific trusteeship scheme, and continued to advocate plans to constrain French sovereignty following Roosevelt's death in April 1945. These officials—principally State Department policymakers concerned with Asian affairs but also OSS analysts, Asia-based diplomats, and Anglophobic military officers—shared an elaborate set of views about colonialism in Southeast Asia that exceeded the president's thinking in sophistication and persuasiveness.

This set of ideas about Indochina might be called the "liberal" viewpoint. This term is not meant to imply anything especially praiseworthy or perceptive about officials who advanced these views. Indeed, liberal-minded officials held deeply paternalistic views of the Indochinese peoples and were driven by the perception of American self-interest far more than any sense of altruism. Nor is the term meant to imply that a fixed group of individuals held a static set of views. In fact, different elements of liberal thinking about Indochina ebbed and flowed at different moments, and different policymakers, depending on their particular decision-making roles, promoted different strands of the broader set of ideas. Those who advocated liberal opinions, in fact, constituted not so much a defined policymaking bloc as a loose collection of officials from different bureaucracies who followed different paths to the same basic conclusion—that the United States needed to promote Indochinese self-determination, at least in the medium term. Rather, the term *liberal* is apt because it captures two general characteristics of these individuals. First, they perceived of themselves as stewards of a new, Wilsonian world order based on free trade and self-determination, a complex of ideas that historians have sometimes dubbed "liberal internationalism." Second, these policymakers believed that the United States had to promote moderate change in the colonial world in order to head off a possibly dangerous explosion of revolutionary change later. In this way, *liberal* corresponds to the way American historians have often used that term—to denote political movements that seek to promote gradual change through existing political and economic structures.

The most important element of liberal thought was the idea that the United States would have tremendous interests in Southeast Asia after the war and that the best way to protect them was to promote at least a degree of self-determination for colonial territories aspiring to overthrow European domination. Above all, as European observers suspected, American anticolonialists were motivated by the desire to gain freer access to the region in order to exploit it economically. State Department and OSS studies carried out during the war identified Southeast Asia—Indochina as much as any other area—as an unrivaled source of raw materials "essential to both our wartime and peacetime economy," as one State Department memorandum put it.[69] Among other Indochinese resources, Americans coveted rubber, tin, oil, and minerals including tungsten, antimony, and phosphates. Although the United States held only a small economic stake in Indochina before the war and possessed alternative sources for everything that might come from the area, U.S. officials, perhaps recalling the economic chaos of the 1930s, calculated that the opportunity should be seized, at least as a hedge against sudden shifts in the availability of other markets. "The [global] situation may change in the future," one OSS report asserted in early 1945, "and vital commodities may be more accessible or available to greater advantage when acquired from [Indochina] rather than from other countries."[70]

The area also held strong appeal as a potential market for American goods at a time when American policymakers and public opinion were increasingly alarmed by the prospect of postwar overproduction and its frightening corollary, unemployment. Obtaining Indochinese resources and markets clearly required freer access for American trade and investment—hardly developments that the French government, with its long record of exclusionary economic policies, could be expected to encourage. "We must demand that American goods be admitted to the Southeast Asian market on a basis of full equality with those of all other nations, and that the undeveloped potentialities of this market be realized by all possible measures designed to raise the native standard of living and increase the purchasing power of the masses," insisted Hawley Oakes, a State Department specialist in Southeast Asian affairs. The department's Foreign Economic Administration (FEA) was more specific about the changes that had to be made. "The United States has a genuine interest in the removal of the pre-war French restrictive trade and investment practices, including tariffs, quotas, and legal devices designed to monopolize trade for metropolitan France under the so-called 'assimilationist policy,'" the FEA asserted in an August 1944 study. With colonial practices eliminated or sharply curtailed, the report went on, there would be "considerable potential demand for American imports." The administration acknowledged that developing the Indochina market would require significant rehabilitation assistance and steps to improve local purchasing power through development of light industry. But that too seemed to represent an opportunity for Americans. "The United States," the FEA concluded, "would be in a strong competitive position to participate in such a development program, including projects for the improvement of technical training, transportation facilities, agriculture, and manufacturing, provided, of course, the restrictive barriers of pre-war colonial exclusiveness have been removed."[71]

Policymakers who advocated ending or loosening the bonds of colonialism also invoked a strategic rationale. Especially within the State Department, officials concerned with Asian affairs asserted that the Indochinese peninsula promised to be vital to the United States because of its position commanding shipping routes between the Far East, Australasia, and the Indian Ocean. A friendly Indochina fully integrated into a U.S.-oriented global security system seemed essential to preserving American access to the markets of East and South Asia. "Of all the dependent areas of the world, only the Caribbean is of greater importance to the United States than ... Southeast Asia," wrote Abbot Low Moffat, chief of the State Department's new Division of Philippine and Southeast Asian Affairs. The region's importance, Moffat added, was likely only to grow over the next "several decades at least" as American trade and investment expanded into regions acquiring their independence from Europe.[72]

Moffat rated Indochina the most valuable of all Southeast Asian territories, explaining that "its geographical position on the southern flank of China, with its potential naval base at Camranh Bay, halfway between Hong Kong and Singapore and the same distance due west of Manila, gives Indochina great significance." Like Roosevelt, Moffat doubted whether the United States could rely on France to ensure stability in such a crucial area. "France, whose major interests are in Europe and North Africa, was never and can never be in a position to protect Indochina," wrote Moffat, who also doubted French willingness to participate in any new U.S.-organized security arrangements for the region. Simmering tensions between U.S. and Gaullist officials in New Caledonia, a French colony where Washington had established a major wartime military base, seemed to bode ill for future cooperation. "Even in those regions nominally Free French there has been not only serious lack of cooperation in the war effort, but even interference," Moffat complained.[73]

While liberal officials fretted that restoration of French rule would place Indochina in unreliable hands, they worried too about the impact on the indigenous population. If Washington permitted recolonization, they charged, it would ensure decades of resentment against the West and lay the seeds of political turmoil that might prevent establishment of a stable Southeast Asia open to cooperation with the United States. "Unless substantial modification of prewar colonial policies takes place, continual unrest and instability will be inevitable," asserted a January 1945 memo prepared by Moffat's Southeast Asia division. Most frightening was the prospect that unrest could spread into a full-fledged race war between Asia and the West if the legitimate desires of Asian nationalists were frustrated by the Western powers. "Japanese occupation of these areas may ... leave a residue of influence which might conceivably serve as a foundation for a future Pan-Asiatic movement directed against the Occident," asserted the Southeast Asia division, noting the possible effect of four years of intensive Japanese propaganda emphasizing "Asia for the Asians." Already U.S. intelligence had reported that most Indochinese people believed the era of colonial domination was over. "There is a nationalistic ferment brewing in Asia which nothing will stop," Moffat wrote.[74]

The key objective for liberals was to assure that U.S. policy swam with and not against the tide of history. Joining Britain and France in opposing the new racial energies of the East would lead to certain danger. Nothing less than the long-term willingness of Asians to cooperate with the United States economically and politically seemed to be at stake. "American influence among Asiatic peoples will suffer if the status quo ante is re-established in Indochina," asserted one State Department paper. "The United States, as the dominant power in the Pacific War, cannot in their eyes escape a major responsibility for postwar arrangements in the Far East." Liberals noted that Washington was partly responsible for creating high expectations among populations clamoring for self-rule. "During the war, through the Atlantic Charter and other statements, we have proclaimed our recognition of the aspirations of people throughout the Far East as well as other parts of the world," the State Department's Liberated Areas Division asserted. If Washington took no steps to prevent restoration of prewar conditions, the division insisted, "not only will our prestige suffer on the ground that we are but a catspaw of the imperialist powers, but also because our public statements will have been found to be platitudes which raised men's hopes and then proved meaningless."[75]

The United States had already failed once in this regard, the argument continued. After the First World War, Washington offered "high-sounding phrases" about self-determination, only to disappoint aspiring nationalists in the colonial world by permitting the continuation of imperial rule and then withdrawing from international affairs in the 1920s and 1930s. "We now have declared the Atlantic Charter which is an appeal to the peoples of the East as well as the peoples of the West," contended Moffat. "If we again refuse to accept the responsibility which in fact is ours, we will be laying the foundation for further trouble in the East." Liberal policymakers also worried that reneging again on U.S. principles would disappoint another, even more important group: ordinary Americans. If disillusioned by a second failure to follow through on high-minded wartime declarations, Americans might choose to make another unceremonious exit from the world stage, a development that, most wartime policymakers agreed, spelled certain disaster for U.S. prosperity and world peace. State Department aide Hawley Oakes suggested that Washington exploit this nightmare scenario as leverage with the European colonial powers, which were obviously eager for full U.S.

engagement in the postwar world. Oakes proposed that U.S. officials spread the message in European capitals that the United States would be able to justify a policy of close transatlantic cooperation only if the Europeans permitted change in the colonial world.[76]

Liberals exuded confidence that the Indochinese were capable of establishing successful states if given their independence in the near or medium term. This optimism resulted partly from a conviction that no one could do worse than the French in administering the region. Roosevelt asserted that opinion most strongly, but virtually the entire U.S. bureaucracy shared his view of French colonialism in Southeast Asia as especially brutal and corrupt—an idea that, as historian Mark Bradley has shown, ran far back into prewar scholarly and diplomatic commentary about Indochina.[77] "It is generally conceded that Indo-China is the most exploited of all Far Eastern colonies," the Liberated Areas Division asserted in early 1944. Whenever the Vietnamese had shown any initiative, added an OSS report, the French administration had immediately "smothered" it, exercising a repressive vigilance that had prevented the emergence of a capable indigenous elite. The report found anti-French sentiment in Vietnam understandable. "The attitude of the natives in Indo-China toward the French," it asserted, "[is] that which one might expect of a people downtrodden by their master."[78]

But U.S. optimism also rested in part on a genuinely hopeful view among liberal policymakers of the capacity of the Indochinese people, above all the Vietnamese, for development. Policy papers advocating trusteeship or sharp curtailment of French control, while deeply patronizing in tone, gave the Vietnamese (called "Annamites" at the time) credit for significant levels of intelligence, cultural sophistication, and vigor. Kenneth P. Landon, assistant head of the State Department's Southeast Asian division and one of the few U.S. officials who had spent much time in Asia, went furthest in a June 1944 memo declaring that the Vietnamese had "a highly sophisticated, well-developed culture." Blaming the French for stunting their progress, Landon found "every reason to believe that the Annamites are as able as the Thai, their independent neighbors to the west, and as the Filipinos and that if given an opportunity the Annamites, together with the various minority people within the country, could become a self-governing nation." Similarly, Melvin Knight, a historian of Asia who served on the State Department's Subcommittee on Territorial Problems, one of the main forums for discussion of colonial issues, predicted in late 1943 that an independent Vietnam would stand "good chances for survival," pointing out that the country's people would benefit from rich political traditions that, together with foreign tutelage, would provide the basis for a functioning state. Few U.S. policymakers hazarded guesses about exactly how long a trusteeship in Indochina might last, but no estimate was longer than fifty years—not coincidentally about the same span as the United States had held the Philippines when that territory became independent in 1946.[79]

If the United States failed to align itself with the legitimate aspirations of the Indochinese peoples, liberal U.S. officials feared that another nation might do so, possibly with disastrous results. U.S. studies noted that Japan would inevitably remain dependent on Southeast Asian resources, especially minerals and rice, and therefore would likely seek influence in the region. Another possibility was Soviet meddling. Few Americans detected any immediate Soviet interest in Southeast Asia, yet officials responsible for Asian affairs took the long-range threat seriously, asserting that communist ideology would give Moscow an advantage in seeking the loyalty of ordinary Asians tired of colonial domination. "Soviet Russia's policies and ideologies have gained a real hold over many progressive leaders in Asia and nearby areas," wrote Max Bishop, the U.S. consul at Colombo, Ceylon, where he watched as South East Asia Command prepared to restore colonial rule throughout its region. "A feeling of sympathetic receptivity toward Soviet Russia's leadership is widespread." Bishop hastened to add that U.S. and Soviet interests in the area might not be irreconcilable, and he even held out hope that the two nations might cooperate by promoting self-determination. The Cold War in Southeast Asia, after all, lay in the future. But for Bishop, the best way to avoid risks was for Washington to declare itself clearly on the side of Asian nationalism.[80]

Ranged against this cluster of liberal views stood a set of "conservative" ideas that favored allowing France to regain sovereignty over Indochina. As with *liberal,* the term *conservative* is not intended to imply the existence of a rigid or static set of views among a fixed group of decision makers. Rather, the term is useful because it aptly captures two important characteristics of the loose grouping of policymakers who favored restoring French control—principally State Department officials concerned with European affairs, but also War and Navy Department personnel and some OSS officials. In contrast to the liberals' vision of a Wilsonian order based on self-determination and free trade, conservatives believed, first, that the United States could best protect its interests through more traditional means of exerting power:

close partnerships with like-minded industrial powers and the maintenance of geographical strongpoints from which power could be projected. Second, conservatives, in contrast to liberals' determination to channel revolutionary energies in moderate directions, detected no danger so great that it could not be managed by reestablished colonial regimes. Thus old forms of colonial control were still appropriate in the postwar international environment.

The two strains of thinking about the Indochina problem reflected different currents in U.S. foreign policy thinking that ran far back into the past. It is true, of course, that officials' views of Indochina were driven in part by their differing immediate concerns: policymakers responsible for Asia unsurprisingly showed greater sensitivity to developments in that part of the world, while those responsible for Europe emphasized U.S. interests there. But the clash between progressives and conservatives was more than a simple contest between bureaucracies with different geographical portfolios. Officials on both sides situated their arguments within broader, long-standing sets of ideas about how the United States should go about defending its interests in the international arena. On one side, liberals tapped into Wilsonian discourse about spreading republican practices and the principle of equal economic opportunity. By accommodating demands for self-determination and ending exclusive economic practices, the liberals hoped to establish a postwar order with fewer sources of conflict and greater possibility of universal prosperity. On the other side, conservatives harkened back to Wilson's internationalist critics, who had argued after the First World War that Washington needed to avoid overcommitting itself on behalf of vague principles and to protect its right to distinguish between primary and secondary interests. Conservatives did not reject the desirability of the Wilsonian vision so much as argue that it was impractical in a complex world where immediate necessity conflicted with the pursuit of larger ideals.[81]

Many conservatives shared Roosevelt's antipathy toward de Gaulle and bitterness over the French performance against Nazi and Japanese aggression, but they disagreed with his assessment that France could not be a major power again for many years. On the contrary, those who backed French recovery of Indochina anticipated that the United States would depend heavily on French cooperation in the postwar period in rebuilding Europe and creating a new international system. Like their liberal counterparts, conservatives wished to sustain booming American productivity and protect U.S. economic interests over the long term. They differed, however, over the precise method to achieve this goal. Liberals sought to promote American prosperity by establishing a new free-trade regime that would break up exclusive colonial arrangements and permit equal access to resources and markets. Conservatives considered such a vision unrealistic, at least in the short term, and emphasized the necessity of preserving colonial arrangements in order to prevent economic chaos and the weakening of the powerful industrial economies of Europe that, once rebuilt from the war, could provide the United States with far more advantages than tiny, relatively undeveloped areas such as Indochina. For conservatives, French recovery trumped self-determination for Indochina as a U.S. policy objective, not only because of the value of France as an economic partner but also for the crucial role that Paris might play in the establishment of a new Western economic and security system that served U.S. interests around the world.

Conservative policymakers consequently opposed any initiative likely to engender resentment in Paris, especially as anxiety mounted in 1944 about Soviet assertiveness in Eastern Europe. With new tensions coming into view, the State Department's Division of Western European Affairs put the matter starkly in a June 1944 memorandum warning that any attempt to force a trusteeship on Indochina would jeopardize U.S. interests. "We must determine," the memo stated, "whether it is of more interest to us and the world as a whole to have a strong, friendly, cooperative France, or have a resentful France."[82] U.S. policy, the European specialists wrote on another occasion, must be aimed at helping France "regain her strength in order that she may be better fitted to share responsibility in maintaining the peace of Europe and the world." Depriving France of Indochina would do precisely the opposite. "French resentment will be such as to impose a very serious strain upon our relations and thus tend to defeat basic elements underlying our policy towards France," asserted the June 1944 memo. "A disgruntled, psychologically sick and sovereign-conscious France will not augur well for post-war collaboration in Europe and in the world as a whole."[83]

The West European division had no doubt that French resentment would fall squarely on the United States, since no other power, with the possible exception of China, seemed likely to help enforce trusteeship. Chiang Kai-shek had indicated support in principle during his meeting with Roosevelt in Cairo in 1943. But Chiang had also made clear that the Chinese government had no interest in taking the lead in such an endeavor. Soviet support for trusteeship also seemed weak. In a

December 1943 conversation with Roosevelt in Teheran, Stalin stressed the degeneracy of the French ruling classes and argued that France must be made to pay for its collaboration with Germany, in part by losing Indochina. But he also made clear that Soviet support for such a move would be passive at best.[84]

Other considerations strengthened the conservatives' fears of damaging U.S. interests. The West European division contended, for example, that establishing a trusteeship under full or partial U.S. supervision would mean assigning to the overstretched Washington bureaucracy "a social and administrative problem of the first magnitude." Although no U.S. agency grasped the complex political situation in Vietnam, American experts had sufficient information to predict great uncertainty after the war. Conservative policymakers insisted that France, for all its irresponsibility as a colonial power, at least promised to offer a degree of stability in an area of inevitable turmoil. This view of French colonialism emerged as a corollary to a growing sense among many U.S. officials that British imperial control, though objectionable in many ways, would play an important stabilizing role in postwar Asia, at least in the short term. Crucial to this attitude was mounting conviction that China, consumed by internal crisis, would be unable to play the dominant role in Asia that the Roosevelt administration had assigned to it in earlier stages of postwar planning. Lacking any realistic alternative, restoration of the old imperial order held obvious advantages.[85]

The keen desire within the Navy and War departments to establish permanent U.S. military bases on various Pacific islands also dictated acceptance of European colonialism. As French and British observers knew, uniformed as well as civilian U.S. officials were eager to establish military bases in the Mariana, Caroline, and Marshall islands, territories formerly administered by Japan. Advocates of this plan believed that the United States needed a network of bases to guard its growing interests in Asia and protect against the kind of aggression that had occurred in the 1930s. Some of these officials opposed outright annexation of the islands and hoped that international approval could be obtained through the United Nations. But few were willing to tolerate any limits on the permanence or totality of U.S. control. For this reason, Secretary of War Henry L. Stimson and Navy Secretary Frank Knox strongly opposed trusteeship. Just as it would complicate French, British, and Dutch control in Asia, they understood that it would complicate U.S. ambitions in the Pacific by inviting the involvement of other powers and creating expectations of independence.[86]

Conservatives also made their case by heaping doubt on the idea that Indochinese nationalism amounted to an irresistible force of history. Like their liberal counterparts, conservatives lost few opportunities to denigrate French colonialism. But they differed in their appreciation of the nationalist movement seeking to end foreign rule. Where liberals saw a vibrant, powerful movement, conservatives saw a weak and selfish cabal of Vietnamese elites. According to the West European division's June 1944 assessment, the Vietnamese nationalist movement had never involved more than 5 percent of the population and had no support whatever beyond urban intellectuals. The "great mass of the people" was "unaffected," the report asserted. Nationalism had not percolated more deeply, it continued, partly because of French repression but partly too because nationalist leaders had little regard for the grievances of ordinary peasants. They seemed to be motivated only by personal resentment against French policies that excluded them from wealth and power. Conservatives also discounted liberal insistence that nationalists, if frustrated by the West, might turn to more radical solutions, including Soviet communism. The European division's report asserted that communists had bid for control of the nationalist movement in the 1920s but had been driven underground by French repression and no longer posed a significant threat.[87]

Early in the Second World War, the liberal viewpoint prevailed in Washington. Roosevelt encountered little resistance as he proclaimed his ideas in a series of meetings with his advisers and foreign officials. Meanwhile, most specialists on Asian affairs shared the president's deep skepticism about French colonialism and, although they did not always endorse trusteeship per se, advocated serious efforts at least to constrain French sovereignty in a way that would promote Indochina's development toward independence under a degree of international supervision.[88] During 1944, however, the tide began to turn. Developments in the broader international environment help explain this trend. First, as British and French observers understood, the decline of American confidence that China would play a major stabilizing role in Asia after the war diminished the appeal of phasing out European colonialism. Through the early years of the war, Roosevelt had hoped that China would emerge as one of the "four policemen" (along with the United States, Britain, and the Soviet Union) that would manage international affairs in the postwar era. By mid-1944, however, the president and his advisers had lost confidence in that plan because of mounting turmoil in China. Conservative arguments in favor of restoring European colonial rule in Southeast Asia grew more convincing as European rule seemed increasingly to be the only possible source of stability in the region.[89]

The deterioration of U.S.-Soviet relations in 1944 also undercut the liberal position. As the Red Army pushed Nazi forces westward, Moscow aroused suspicion among U.S. officials by tightening its hold over Poland and other parts of Eastern Europe. Roosevelt believed he could manage Stalin's ambitions in Eastern Europe without destroying the U.S.-Soviet partnership, but many of his advisers were less sure. Toward the end of the year, many observers voiced fear that the Soviet Union represented a major threat to the establishment of a postwar order tailored to American interests. "Our relations with the Soviets have taken a startling turn evident during the last two months," the U.S. ambassador in Moscow, W. Averell Harriman, reported in September. While focusing his worry on Soviet behavior in Europe, he also suggested that Moscow might someday pose a danger in the Far East. Asserting that the Soviets were becoming a "world bully wherever their interests are involved," Harriman warned that Soviet meddling "will reach into China and the Pacific as well when they can turn their attention in that direction."[90] In these circumstances conservative arguments for rebuilding France into a bulwark of Western power in Europe and Asia gained new persuasiveness.

None of this, however, is to say that Washington had embraced a pro-French position by the end of 1944 or that that outcome had become inevitable, as some scholars have suggested.[91] To be sure, conservatives achieved significant breakthroughs in the first weeks of 1945. They convinced Roosevelt to accept the participation of French operatives in clandestine activities within Indochina—a climbdown from his previous unwillingness to countenance French involvement in the Far Eastern war. Next, at the Yalta conference, Roosevelt accepted the principle that, except in the Japanese-mandated territories, trusteeships would be established only with the consent of the colonial power concerned. But these shifts should not be taken as evidence of anything more than a gradual and incomplete evolution of American attitudes—more an evening of the playing field than a victory for the conservatives. Roosevelt remained deeply uncomfortable with the idea of French forces operating in Indochina and approved Allied support for limited clandestine activities in strict secrecy, hopeful that the decision would not set a precedent. Indeed, the president vetoed other proposals for greater French involvement in the war around the same time.

Nor did the decision on trusteeships mark a decisive break in U.S. policymaking toward Indochina. Few Americans beyond the president, after all, had ever strongly advocated international trusteeship as the best solution in Indochina. Most liberals preferred the restoration of French sovereignty on condition that Paris promise sweeping reforms and set a date for Indochina's independence. Even as the president dropped the trusteeship scheme, that somewhat less draconian but far more practical alternative held strong appeal for many policymakers. Roosevelt himself endorsed this approach in the final month of his life, telling his aid Charles Taussig that France could have Indochina back as long as Paris accepted the obligations of a trustee, including setting a date for independence.[92]

Other evidence, too, suggests that the liberal ideas remained persuasive to many American officials. Most obviously, civilian and military officials with responsibility for the day-to-day conduct of the war continued to oppose steps that would bolster French chances of recovering Indochina. After Roosevelt permitted Allied support for French sabotage activities, the plan was vetoed by U.S. commanders in the Far East, who opposed the reassertion of European colonialism as much as Roosevelt and deeply distrusted British and French motives. Meanwhile, other bureaucracies took steps to fight any drift of American policy toward permitting French recovery. The State Department's Office of Far Eastern Affairs, fearing any close association between U.S. policy and European colonial objectives, rejected proposals to send U.S. political advisers or civil-affairs personnel to South East Asia Command headquarters, and U.S. military officers in Kandy received orders to avoid all political questions in discussions with British counterparts. In Chungking the U.S. general in charge of China Command, Albert C. Wedemeyer, stoutly resisted British pressure to revise the boundaries of the Far Eastern military theaters in a way that would have permitted greater British activity in support of French activity in Indochina. For his part, U.S. chief of staff George Marshall, fearful that U.S. representatives might be implicated in European activities, ordered the OSS in February to tighten its control over agents in Southeast Asia.[93] Liberals were digging in for a fight as the end of the war drew closer.

CHAPTER 2

U.S. Assistance and Its Limits

By the start of 1945, General Yūichi Tsuchihashi, commander of Japanese troops in Indochina, faced severe problems. Indochina remained as important as ever to Tokyo's war effort—no longer as an avenue of expansion but now as a corridor of escape for 700,000 Japanese troops facing defeat in Indonesia, Burma, Malaya, and other parts of Southeast Asia. From every direction threats abounded. The U.S. Navy had destroyed most of Japan's biggest warships in fall 1944, leaving Indochina vulnerable to Allied assault. Although no invasion came, U.S. aircraft devastated Japanese shipping in the port of Saigon and in the South China Sea, sinking twenty-four ships and damaging thirteen others during January 1945 alone. To the west, British imperial forces in Burma, despite their material shortcomings, steadily rolled back the three-year-old Japanese occupation. But the most immediate threat to the Japanese position seemed to come from within Indochina itself. Japanese intelligence picked up enough clues to know that Gaullist agents were increasingly active in the region. Tsuchihashi sensed, too, that he could no longer trust Governor-General Decoux's promises to adhere to the Franco-Japanese understanding that had held French authorities in check since 1940.[1]

This rapidly evolving situation set the stage for a momentous event that generated sudden urgency in international deliberations about Indochina. On the night of March 9, 1945, Tsuchihashi's troops acted boldly to end the French threat, executing a coup d'état that destroyed the colonial administration in a matter of hours. Japanese authorities ordered some low-ranking French bureaucrats to remain at their posts to manage day-to-day affairs, but Tokyo left no doubt that it intended to put an end to a half century of French rule. Some twenty-one hundred French troops died or disappeared in brief fighting, and the Japanese threw another twelve thousand into prison, where many would die of malaria, typhoid, and other diseases. Only in Tonkin did elements of the French Indochina Army put up sustained resistance. From the Japanese standpoint, however, that fighting amounted to little more than a brush fire to be stamped out in the days ahead. On March 10 Radio Tokyo declared "the colonial status of French Indochina has ended."[2] Japanese authorities moved quickly to establish nominally independent governments in Vietnam, Cambodia, and Laos. On March 11 Emperor Bao Dai, heir to the Annamese throne, abrogated the 1884 protectorate treaty with France and declared Vietnamese independence. King Norodom Sihanouk of Cambodia followed suit on March 13, followed by King Sisavong Vong in Laos on April 8.[3]

For Vietnamese revolutionaries the collapse of French power created golden opportunities. On March 12 the Indochinese Communist Party's Central Committee, the key decision-making body within the Viet Minh, declared that Vietnam had entered a "preinsurrectionary period," with conditions for national uprising ripening quickly. The optimal moment would come, the Central Committee judged, when Allied landings took place—an event that would destroy Japanese authority and create a power vacuum that the Viet Minh could exploit. For the time being, the Vietnamese revolutionaries contented themselves with preparing for the decisive moment. Over the spring and early summer, the Viet Minh merged its guerrilla forces into a single People's Liberation Army, recruited new troops, and extended its control over most of Vietnam's mountainous north. Politically, the Viet Minh concentrated on expanding its influence into lowland areas, an effort that achieved rapid success as disgruntled workers and peasants, many facing starvation, rallied behind the movement. Within three months of the coup, the Viet Minh had established a six-province "liberated zone" of more than one million people in northern Tonkin and set up a provisional administration under Ho Chi Minh. To the south, revolutionary activity was less intense, but the Viet Minh, capitalizing on Japanese apathy as the war neared its end, made significant inroads in the Saigon area and much of Annam by midsummer.[4]

Policymakers in Paris and London also viewed the coup as an opportunity. The Japanese takeover caused deep anxiety by overturning

French sovereignty. Many European observers believed, however, that the coup might strengthen long-term prospects for restoring French control by encouraging a more sympathetic view in the United States, the country whose support both French and British policymakers considered essential to all their plans in the region. By imprisoning Decoux and drawing French colonial forces into open resistance, after all, Japan helped the provisional government in Paris demonstrate precisely what its diplomats had been claiming to Americans for some time: the French community in Indochina had no reservations about fighting and dying for the Allied cause. At last, they hoped, France would be able to lead Americans to a more sympathetic view of French colonialism in Southeast Asia and tap into U.S. material power. Whether they would succeed depended on decisions in Washington.

THE U.S. POLICY SHIFT

As soon as the full extent of the coup became clear on March 12, the French provisional government launched an intensive diplomatic effort to capitalize on the suddenly changed situation. The ambassador in Washington, Henri Bonnet, and other embassy staff met urgently with State and War Department personnel to request U.S. air support for struggling French forces in Tonkin. Hoping that the new circumstances would cast old demands in a new light, they also renewed their requests that the United States help ship French troops to the Far East and recognize General Blaizot's mission in Kandy. In those meetings and in a declaration handed to Undersecretary of State Joseph Grew, French officials hammered away on a single theme: France had proven its fidelity and should now be accorded the respect due a full member of the Allied coalition against Japan. The declaration asserted that pro-Allied French officials in Indochina had provoked the coup through subtle acts of resistance and insisted that the French fight in Tonkin amounted to a full-fledged "resistance movement." If properly assisted by the U.S. Air Force based in China, the statement continued, French fighters could offer "effective assistance to allied military action in the Far Eastern theater."[5]

The following day in Paris, French leaders resorted to more strident appeals after learning that U.S. authorities in China had rejected initial French requests for aid pending guidance from Washington. The provisional government's colonial minister, Paul Giacobbi, in remarks to the cabinet that were immediately relayed to the U.S. embassy, claimed that with American help French resistance in Tonkin might form nothing less than "a new front . . . capable of completely isolating the Japanese forces in Burma, the Malay Peninsula and the Netherlands Indies." De Gaulle took an even more extreme tack, warning U.S. ambassador Jefferson Caffery that a weakened France might slide into the Soviet camp if deprived of U.S. help in Indochina. "What are you driving at?" de Gaulle asked Caffery. "Do you want us to become, for example, one of the federated states under the Russian aegis?" The general asserted that the Soviet army was "advancing apace" toward France. "If the public here comes to realize that you are against us in Indochina there will be terrific disappointment and nobody knows to what that will lead," he ominously asserted. "We do not want to fall into the Russian orbit, but I hope that you do not push us into it." The next day, de Gaulle took his case to the French people, telling a radio audience that France had done everything it could to obtain Allied help. "It was not her fault," he said, if nothing had been done.[6]

The British government also escalated pressure, albeit of a more nuanced sort, on Washington. Keenly aware of their declining capabilities in the Far East, British policymakers understood that they had little to offer in response to desperate French pleas for assistance. Manpower, equipment, and shipping shortages, as well as long distances between British stores and the battlefield in Tonkin, ruled out any help beyond what the British headquarters in Kandy was already providing. "We have every sympathy with the French desire to play a greater part in the Far East," wrote J. C. Sterndale Bennett, chief of the Foreign Office's Far Eastern department, on March 12, "but the French must realize that, with the best will in the world, equipment and transport difficulties are very great and that priorities must be arranged accordingly." True to the approach it had developed during the months of debate and planning, London looked to the United States to compensate for its weaknesses. The coup offered a glimmer of hope that the United States might finally play the role Whitehall had scripted for it. "Painful as the new development may be to the French Government, it may in the long run work out in their best interests," wrote Sterndale Bennett. "It puts an end to an uncertain and anomalous situation, and [provides] the best propaganda that the French could have in the United States."[7]

Some British officials feared irritating Washington by pressing too hard on an issue that U.S. leaders obviously wished to avoid, but most advocated diplomatic intervention in Washington at the highest level. On March 19 the British Chiefs of Staff instructed their representative in Washington, Field Marshal Sir Henry Maitland Wilson, to insist that the U.S.-controlled China Command begin sending supplies to French resistance fighters in Tonkin. If Washington did not comply, he was told to say, in an ultimatum that was largely bluff, that Mountbatten's South East Asia Command would begin doing the job by itself. Churchill suggested a different approach in his instructions to Wilson. While the Chiefs of Staff proposed threats, Churchill indulged in sentimentality. "The Prime Minister feels it would look very bad in history if we were to let the French forces in Indo-China be cut to pieces by the Japanese through shortage of ammunition, if there is anything we can do to save them," Churchill's aides wrote in a telegram instructing Wilson to seek a meeting with senior U.S. commanders.[8]

All this pressure, combined with sheer uncertainty about events taking place in Tonkin, left American policymakers befuddled and frustrated. In Chungking a few sympathetic U.S. officers prepared supplies to be airlifted to Tonkin in case Washington approved. But no such permission came, and the 14th Air Force refused French pleas for help. French pressure, in fact, may have been counterproductive in the short term. So hard did French diplomats press that several U.S. observers doubted the seriousness of the situation in Indochina and suspected the French government of merely exploiting the coup to influence U.S. behavior. "The French are making a great fuss over the Indo-China resistance for political reasons only and in an effort to smoke out our policy," complained James Clement Dunn, the usually strong Francophile who served as undersecretary of state for European affairs. Assistant Secretary of War John J. McCloy chastised François Lacoste, the senior counselor of the French embassy in Washington, for insisting too strenuously on decisions "which were very difficult to make at the present time." To gain time, the State and War departments referred the problem to the Joint Chiefs of Staff for further study.[9]

Some conservative American officials, however, responded to European pressure much as the French and British governments hoped. Citing de Gaulle's warning about the Soviet menace and his speech condemning American ambivalence, newly appointed secretary of state Edward R. Stettinius, an Eastern patrician who strongly advocated European interests, warned Roosevelt that the French were successfully spreading the view that Washington was failing an ally in its moment of desperate need. "It appears that this Government may be made to appear responsible for the weakness of the resistance to Japan in Indo-China," Stettinius wrote in a memorandum to the president. "The

British," he added, "may likewise be expected to encourage this view." Much as Stettinius may have wished to reposition U.S. policy squarely behind French objectives in Indochina, though, he understood the limits of what was possible within a deeply divided bureaucracy led by a president who remained determined to avoid the reimposition of unconditional French rule. An able bureaucratic tactician with skills honed as head of the Lend-Lease administration, Stettinius proposed a nuanced solution aimed at gratifying immediate European demands—thereby releasing the United States from a difficult bind—without explicitly abandoning principles dear to the president and other liberals in Washington. The key, the secretary advised, was to give the Europeans military assistance while insisting that such aid in no way prejudiced U.S. policy regarding the future of Indochina. Stettinius proposed that the administration issue a declaration asserting merely that the United States, "in accordance with its constant desire to aid all those who are willing to take up arms against our common enemies, . . . will do all it can to be of assistance in the present situation."[10]

Roosevelt, still wary of any encouragement for French colonialism, rejected Stettinius's proposal. The president's precise logic is not clear from available documentation, but it is plain that liberals had long opposed compromises such as the one the secretary of state proposed. Back in 1944 Max Bishop, the U.S. consul in Colombo and an outspoken critic of European colonialism in Asia, had warned against any solution that attempted to decouple short-term military problems from long-term political questions in Southeast Asia. "It is difficult to understand how action taken by a government or its officers on one 'level,' such as the 'military level' or the 'political level,' can be expected not to affect other 'levels,'" Bishop wrote. Southeast Asia division chief Moffat had issued a similar warning, asserting that "compromises all too often are dangerous, the weakness of each policy becoming dominant."[11]

Still, Stettinius's proposal held inescapable attractiveness as European pressure for decisions mounted. The Joint Chiefs of Staff (JCS), the institution charged with considering French demands, readily seized on Stettinius's formula and made it the centerpiece of a plan that gained momentum despite the president's initial opposition. The JCS drafted orders for the U.S. headquarters in Chungking to begin supplying military assistance to French forces in Tonkin. Moffat, Bishop, and other liberals, apparently resigned to some sort of compromise, registered no opposition. On March 19 Admiral William D. Leahy, the Joint Chiefs' chairman, authorized General Wedemeyer, the U.S. commander in

China, to send whatever assistance could be spared without detracting from the main thrust of the U.S. war effort there.[12] Although no record exists of the president's response to the Joint Chiefs' order, it is likely that he communicated his approval to Leahy, his close confidant and recent chief of staff. One is left to imagine Roosevelt's frustration as he recognized that Paris, London, and their sympathizers in Washington had successfully forced his hand.

In providing military assistance for French forces operating in the Far East, Washington crossed a threshold where it had balked in earlier months. Compromise, though an obvious solution to the dilemma with which European pressure presented Washington in March 1945, involved a significant break with the principles underlying the liberal viewpoint in Washington. Most important, it raised the possibility, as Bishop and Moffat had warned the previous year, that the United States would have difficulty preserving the fuzzy line between military and political support. The March 19 decision marks a significant moment for another reason, as well. For the first time, European pressure achieved decisive results in Washington. Without intense French and British advocacy U.S. policy would not have changed in response to the coup; the Roosevelt administration, satisfied to avoid painful choices, would have persisted in indecision and inaction. European efforts to sway U.S. policymakers placed Washington in an impossible bind and furnished conservatives like Stettinius with a hard-to-refute case in favor of giving ground. With French and British diplomats and American conservatives all pushing in the same direction, Roosevelt and his liberal allies could not hold the line.

Even so, the European victory brought few results. Many U.S. officials showed deep reservations about the new policy and worked successfully to minimize its significance. To be sure, the U.S. 14th Air Force in Chungking began supplying the Tonkin resistance within a few days. By March 30 U.S. aircraft had carried out thirty-five bombing and resupply missions. But those numbers fell far below American capabilities, as French officers repeatedly pointed out to the War Department. Air Force personnel were quick to assert the limits on American help, stressing bad weather, long distances, equipment shortages, and poor intelligence.[13] In Washington, meanwhile, liberal officials did their best to prevent the decision for military support from taking on unintended significance. In the official reply to the French declaration of March 12, the State Department asserted that the provisional government must understand that "no commitment can be given with regard to the amount or character of any assistance which may be provided." Meanwhile, Archibald MacLeish, the famed poet serving as assistant secretary of state for cultural and public affairs, rejected a request from the Office of War Information to change U.S. propaganda policy in the Far East and begin broadcasting material favorable to France. "The most authoritative sources," wrote MacLeish, presumably referring to Roosevelt, remained "quite rigid" in opposing any such move.[14]

The American attitude disappointed French leaders, who sulked back to the drawing board to devise new schemes to influence U.S. policy. The French military tried to sweeten its offer of assistance to the Allied war effort as a way to pry loose additional concessions from the Joint Chiefs of Staff. De Gaulle's military representative in Washington, Admiral Raymond Fenard, offered U.S. and British forces access to the Diego Suarez naval base in Madagascar and new intelligence information about the Indochina coast in return for an assurance that French forces would be involved in the eventual liberation.[15] Increasingly, however, the French leadership recognized that inducements based solely on promises of military cooperation would not produce results in Washington. The United States, waging a massive assault against Japan in the western Pacific, clearly had no need for French assistance in such a remote location, and U.S. officials were apt to regard French offers as mere annoyances. French policymakers concluded that the U.S. position would change in meaningful ways only if they could overcome entrenched skepticism among U.S. leaders and public opinion about long-term French intentions in Indochina.

Accordingly, the provisional government made new efforts to change American perceptions of the French empire. Some officials concentrated on influencing the attitude of the American press, which they believed to be dangerously naive and Francophobe. The Foreign Ministry ordered Ambassador Bonnet to lodge complaints with the State Department about offending reporters and welcomed Dutch proposals that the two nations' information services step up cooperation to combat U.S. anticolonialism.[16] Most French officials believed, however, that Paris needed to do far more than to improve information management. In the days following the coup, a critical mass of French leaders concluded that nothing less than a new declaration of French policy toward Indochina would be necessary to curry favor abroad. "The moment has come," as Ambassador Massigli put it, "to arouse greater interest in our colony with British and especially American opinion." The Brazzaville declaration and other previous attempts to persuade foreign observers of the French commitment to colonial reform "do not suffice today," Massigli insisted.[17]

Persuaded of that view, the French government on March 24 launched its most aggressive appeal to international opinion to date, issuing a declaration making unprecedented, if still vague, promises of autonomy for Indochina. The statement, authored by Henri Laurentie, the leading liberal voice in colonial affairs, pledged to establish a federated "French Union" in which the Indochinese, like indigenous populations of other French territories, would acquire significant new rights. Although a French governor-general would continue to sit atop the administrative hierarchy in Indochina, his cabinet would include both Indochinese and French ministers. In addition, the French government promised to set up an elected federal assembly with authority over economic and fiscal policies. The declaration reverberated with democratic rhetoric. "Freedom of press, freedom of association, freedom of assembly, freedom of thought and of belief and democratic liberty in general will form the basis of Indochinese laws," the statement asserted.[18]

Other sections emphasized economic liberalization—always a central feature of French promises aimed at foreign opinion. While calling for "full agricultural, industrial and commercial development," the statement pledged to allow Indochina "to develop without discrimination her commercial relations with all other countries." None of this, of course, committed France to any specific course of action in the near term. Despite the declaration's sweeping promises, debate within the French political establishment over imperial matters had hardly begun. But that was not the point. Increasingly desperate for foreign help following the coup, the most important matter for the Colonial Ministry was to ensure that French diplomats in the United States took special care to publicize the paper and underscore its liberality.[19]

In so doing, French diplomats found a strong ally in the British government. As significant American help failed to materialize by the end of March, disappointed British authorities scraped together modest new support for France. To do otherwise, British officials feared, would have risked damaging Franco-British relations. "If we fail to implement support at this juncture ... without one cogent reason to give the French, our position will be little better than that of the Americans," wrote Colin MacKenzie, commander of British guerrilla operations in Indochina. While MacKenzie struggled to increase deliveries of medicine and other supplies to the Tonkin resistance, London offered new help to broadcast French propaganda into Indochina and invited the French government to send colonial administrators designated for postwar duty in Indochina to attend special training centers in England and Ceylon.[20] As before, however, British policymakers hoped that such pittances would soon be overtaken by U.S. assistance as Americans took over the main burden of supporting France in the Far East. The March 24 declaration gave them new hope that U.S. policy might soon move in that direction. "These proposals," wrote one Asia specialist in the Foreign Office, "might help reconcile the U.S. to the French view that Indo-China is a French concern." With the French government moving to alleviate U.S. reservations, Sterndale Bennett, head of the Far Eastern department, judged that the moment was ripe "to grasp this Indo-China nettle and to tackle the Americans squarely on the whole issue. I cannot see that they can well resist us."[21]

In Washington, however, little changed as March gave way to April. Certainly the Joint Chiefs of Staff, free since March 19 to make judgments about Indochina based on military advantage, continued to make small concessions. First, the chiefs dropped their long-standing opposition to Blaizot's presence in Kandy and approved the stationing of a comparable French liaison mission at China Command headquarters in Chungking—a necessity in order to ensure efficient distribution of what little aid U.S. aircraft dropped into Indochina. The Joint Chiefs then approved proposals to integrate a small number of French ships into Allied naval forces in the Far East and, in principle, to move the Corps Léger d'Intervention from North Africa to Ceylon.[22] On political questions, though, Washington conceded little. In his final comments on Indochina before his death, the president told aide Charles Taussig that although he might be willing to see France recover Indochina, the French government must accept "the obligations of a trustee," including a commitment to independence as "the ultimate goal." Neither dominion status nor self-government within a federated empire would suffice, the president insisted. Liberal solutions to the Indochina problem also continued to find strong support within the State Department. A Far Eastern division memorandum surveying various options for Indochina in early April gave as much attention to trusteeship and conditional restoration of French control as to unconditional French recovery.[23]

Only Roosevelt's death on April 12 cleared the way for significant change. The advent of the Truman administration brought to power a group of men with substantially different attitudes regarding colonial problems. The political tenor in Washington had already shifted in more conservative directions as the businessmen and technocrats brought into government during the war began to achieve positions of greater prominence, displacing liberal-minded New Dealers who had controlled the administration's agenda in earlier years. But the biggest shift came at the top. Truman himself, largely kept in the dark about Roosevelt's foreign policy plans, probably had no idea of his predecessor's qualms about French colonialism or the concept of trusteeship. Additionally, he showed no patience for complexity and little desire to come to grips with the background of thorny issues.[24] The new president's top adviser on foreign affairs, James F. Byrnes, the former congressman, Supreme Court justice, and director of war mobilization, gave similarly little thought to colonial nationalism—hardly a surprise, perhaps, in view of his dedication to white supremacy. New personnel immediately created new possibilities. Sensing that the new administration represented an opportunity to break the policy logjam and to move in the direction they favored, conservatives pushed for a thorough review of U.S. policy toward Indochina. The State-War-Navy Coordinating Committee, the interagency policy board that predated the National Security Council, decided the day after Roosevelt's death to take up the issue and make recommendations to the new president.

If conservatives skillfully exploited the new atmosphere in Washington, they also made careful use of European pressure. Assistant Secretary of War Robert Lovett, the chief proponent of the policy review, stressed that the lack of U.S. policy on Indochina was a mounting "source of embarrassment" to U.S. officials confronted with daily French pleas for help. U.S. indecision, Lovett continued, had given rise to "suspicions" in Paris that could damage Franco-American relations. Furthermore, he warned that without a clear policy, Washington risked losing control over its own decision making. "Admiral Fenard has been using the technique of submitting a series of questions to various agencies of the United States Government and by obtaining even negative or non-committal responses thereto has been in effect writing American policy on Indo-China," Lovett told the committee. Apparently persuaded by Lovett's arguments, the panel ordered the State Department to prepare a "prompt clarification of our policy on Indo-China."[25] The resulting process pitted conservatives against liberals for control over U.S. policy amid an altered policymaking context. The outcome represented Washington's most important policymaking shift with respect to Indochina before 1949.

Over the second half of April, the Far Eastern and West European offices debated the issue with unprecedented thoroughness. On some points, they found easy agreement. Disburdened of presidential pressure, they concurred most importantly that France should not be singled out among colonial powers and forced to submit its territory to international trusteeship. In fact, the Roosevelt administration's concessions at the February 1945 Yalta conference, specifying that trusteeships would be implemented only on a voluntary basis, had already seemed to eliminate the possibility of subjecting Indochina to that destiny. But Roosevelt had continued to speak vaguely of trusteeship, and it was only during the mid-April policy review that the idea was unequivocally put to rest. Underlying that agreement was a shared sense of the steadily increasing value of France as an ally in Europe, where the Soviet Union continued to defy Western governments by tightening its hold over Poland, Bulgaria, and Romania. Under those circumstances Far Eastern specialists recognized as clearly as their Europeanist colleagues that outright humiliation of France was not an option. The growing power of the French Communist Party also encouraged consensus on this point. Municipal elections held in spring 1945, the first round of voting since France's liberation, confirmed that the Communists would emerge from the war as the nation's most powerful political party. State Department policymakers of all persuasions agreed that blocking French efforts to recover Indochina would likely further the Communists' advantage by discouraging partnership with the West.

Beyond this area of agreement, however, crucial differences persisted. Conceding on trusteeship did not mean that liberals threw their support behind the conservative idea of simply permitting France to recover Indochina without quibble. On the contrary, liberals asserted a position that many of them, increasingly skeptical of the trusteeship idea, had advocated for months or even years: Indochina should be restored to France subject to stringent conditions involving the liberalization of French rule and the establishment of a date for full independence. The defeat of trusteeship, a mere formality by April 1945, left in place this more nuanced alternative. This idea, not trusteeship, formed the nub of controversy during the spring 1945 policy review. Specifically, the two State Department offices clashed over whether the United States should require the French government to make concessions to Indochinese nationalists before Washington would formally drop its objections to French restoration or provide meaningful aid to French forces in the Far East.

A draft policy paper by the Office of West European Affairs recommended that the United States "exert its influence" with French leaders to give the Indochinese peoples greater political and economic rights. A positive response from Paris would not be required, however, in order for Washington to adopt the pro-French policy that the paper urged. Regardless of French behavior in Indochina, it asserted, the United States "should neither oppose the restoration of Indo-China to France . . . nor take any action toward French overseas possessions which it is not prepared to take or suggest with regard to the colonial possessions of our other Allies." The paper's authors knew that the latter qualification carried little meaning, since the great powers, despite various high-minded wartime proposals, had made little progress toward an agreement specifying the obligations that colonial administrations would have to fulfill. Meanwhile, the paper struck a tone of enthusiasm about French offers to participate more fully in the Far Eastern war. It stressed that French requests for Allied help in mounting operations in the Far East should continue to be evaluated on the basis of military merit. But the paper departed from the mood of ambivalence around the policy established in late March by insisting that French offers to contribute to the war against Japan "should be regarded as desirable in principle." It went still further: "The fact that acceptance of a specific proposal might serve to strengthen French claims for the restoration of Indochina to France should not be regarded as grounds for rejection."[26] The West European office thus accepted the possibility that military decisions could, over time, become the basis of a political fait accompli.

The Office of Far Eastern Affairs had little patience for this approach, insisting instead that the United States preserve all possible leverage to compel France to liberalize its rule in Indochina. In its counterproposal to the Europeanists' draft, the Far Eastern office acknowledged that it was "established policy" to help France "in order that she may be better fitted to share responsibility in maintaining the peace of Europe." But in contrast to the European office, the liberals insisted that Washington must avoid jeopardizing its considerable interests in Southeast Asia. To safeguard those, the Far Eastern office urged that Washington withhold any promises of material or political support until the French government embraced policies more liberal than anything it had announced so far. Even the most far-reaching French proposal to date, the March 24 declaration, was, in the liberals' opinion, "vague" and "when examined with care" stopped short of offering "genuine self-rule for the Indochinese." They argued that the French would go further only if the United States maintained strong pressure. The French government seemed, after all, to have taken past steps toward liberalization only when it believed that

American acceptance of French recovery depended on it. "Any indication at this time that the United States will not oppose French restoration in Indochina would negate American influence in securing French policies consistent with American interests," wrote Edwin Stanton, a key Far Eastern specialist, in a memorandum explaining his office's position. "Merely exerting influence to achieve such a result will not prove adequate," he wrote, criticizing the Europeanists' toothless proposal to communicate American desires without attaching any quid pro quo. The liberals insisted that Washington require France to accept American or international bases in Indochina, end discriminatory economic practices, and establish a democratic form of government "so that within the foreseeable future Indochina may be fully self-governing and autonomous" within the French Union. Without such steps, the Far Eastern office predicted a grim future. "If really liberal policies towards Indochina are not adopted by the French," its paper asserted, "there will be substantial bloodshed and unrest for many years, threatening the economic and social progress and the peace and stability of Southeast Asia."[27]

The clashing drafts touched off a war of words between the two State Department offices. Dunn, the conservative assistant secretary of state insisted that "it would be better just to let the matter drift rather than to base our policy on the [Far Eastern office's] version of the Indochina paper." Dunn declared that it was time "to cooperate wholeheartedly with France" and pointed to the danger of losing France as an ally. "We should attempt to remove the sources of friction between France and the United States and should try to allay her apprehensions that we are going to propose that territory be taken away from her." Dunn even embraced the hyperbole of French leaders, quoting Foreign Minister Bidault's "fears for western civilization as a result of Russia in Europe" if France were weakened by losing Indochina. On the other side, liberals complained of their rivals' heavy-handed tactics. The Asianists believed that Dunn was trying to force a dramatic change in U.S. policy without any effort to explain the dilemma to the new president. The European office's paper amounted to "a complete reversal, without even letting the president have background," Moffat later recalled. "I thought that was a little improper."[28]

Confronted with conflicting positions, Acting Secretary of State Joseph Grew ordered the two offices to negotiate a compromise that could be passed along to the president. The result was an impossibly muddled document that resolved little. As the Far Eastern office wished, the compromise paper paid lip service to "the dynamic forces leading toward self-government" in Indochina and warned that further French repression might provoke unrest that would threaten "the peace of the Far East and the world." The March 24 declaration, it added, was "vague" and "showed little progress toward the establishment of genuine self-rule for the Indochinese or of an open-door economic policy in Indochina." The compromise also gratified the Asianists by directing that the U.S. embassy in Paris should communicate U.S. concerns to the provisional government. An accompanying draft telegram to Paris instructed Ambassador Caffery to seek "some positive indication" of French intentions and to raise the various desiderata enumerated in the Far Eastern office's original draft. The problem was that neither the compromise paper nor the telegram specified whether those desiderata were demands or suggestions. Was the French government, in other words, required to make any particular commitments before Washington would accept restoration of French sovereignty or would further open the aid spigot for the French military in the Far East? The two offices simply ignored this question.[29]

The U.S. policy reconsideration during spring 1945, undertaken to clarify the U.S. position and deprive French policymakers of the ability to drive U.S. policy, resulted, then, in precisely the opposite. Still unable to choose between its liberal and conservative impulses, Washington fell into renewed disarray on the question, while U.S. policymakers looked to the French government for decisions that would help bring clarity. A "final determination" of U.S. policy, as H. Freeman Matthews, director of the Office of West European Affairs, put it, would "probably involve and depend upon discussions with the French government."[30] Neither side was happy with this outcome. For his part, Dunn was apparently so incensed by the inclusion of the Far Eastern office's concerns, even in their watered-down form, that he torpedoed the entire policy review process, refusing to pass the compromise paper to the president or to send the proposed telegram to Caffery, even though both documents had the approval of the Far Eastern and European departments.[31]

In retrospect, however, it is clear that the liberals had more reasonable grounds for complaint. By dropping the trusteeship idea without specifying any conditions for French recovery of Indochina the review effectively abandoned much of the leverage that the United States possessed over Indochina's postwar destiny. The failure to agree on any policy at all meant that U.S. officials enjoyed considerable latitude to do as they saw fit. Since most of the American officials in close contact with the French provisional government held conservative views, U.S. reassurances of support for the French position in Indochina became increasingly likely. As so often in the course of U.S. policymaking between 1944 and 1950, ambiguity left openings that policymakers with clearly defined agendas were able to exploit to their advantages. In this way, incremental movement within the bureaucracy became decisive, transformative movement at the level of international diplomacy.

Stettinius and Dunn found their opportunity in early May 1945, even as the policy review was sputtering to an end in Washington, at the inaugural meeting of the United Nations in San Francisco. In a meeting with Georges Bidault, the Americans endured a verbal barrage as the foreign minister unloaded his resentment against the United States on a range of subjects and insisted on closer Franco-U.S. cooperation. On Indochina Bidault lashed out at the American media for spreading "utter rot" about the French role there and reiterated his country's liberal plans. But he insisted that the provisional government had "no intention" of placing the territory under trusteeship and even excoriated the voluntary provisions agreed upon at Yalta because, he claimed, they would likely embolden anticolonial nationalists. In response Stettinius and Dunn, apparently confident that the policy review in Washington left them free to do as they wished, offered unprecedented reassurances about American intentions. With remarkable disingenuousness, Dunn insisted that "no official policy statement of this Government... has ever questioned even by implication French sovereignty over Indochina." Anxious to obscure the Roosevelt administration's long record of hostility to French rule, Dunn pinned the blame on "certain elements of American public opinion" for stirring up all the trouble over Indochina. However roundabout and even bizarre his comments, Dunn surrendered the leverage that the United States might have used to force thoroughgoing reform. Formally, the United States remained without a policy on Indochina. But persistent French officials and cooperative conservatives within the U.S. bureaucracy, operating within the more permissive atmosphere following Roosevelt's death, had succeeded in bringing about significant change anyway.[32]

THE LIMITS OF AMERICAN SUPPORT

French leaders had good reason to be pleased with the changed attitude in Washington, especially when the president offered reassurances of his own on May 10. Truman told Defense Minister René Pleven that "no one in the United States wanted more than him personally to see France restored to all its power." Speaking specifically about Indochina, Truman then confirmed the statements of lower-ranking officials, telling Bidault that the United States did not oppose French rule and declaring publicly that French participation in the Pacific war "would be welcomed" as long as it did not distract from primary U.S. objectives. By the beginning of summer 1945, such comments had generated unprecedented optimism among French officials. A Foreign Ministry report noted that Truman, in sharp contrast to his predecessor, seemed "well-disposed toward our country." Even in Chungking, home of some of the most Francophobe Americans, Ambassador Pechkoff observed a "notable change" among his American counterparts. U.S. diplomats were, he reported, "now ready to talk about [Indochina] and to give precise answers and assurances that were once very difficult to get." All in all, Foreign Ministry experts believed that France could "without doubt profit from this in the weeks and months to come."[33]

French officials could take satisfaction that their efforts had helped produce this favorable shift. The Indochina issue might have lain in abeyance indefinitely if not for relentless French pressure. It is true that the advent of the Truman administration opened the way for change in the American attitude, but neither the new president nor the senior officials he brought with him to the Oval Office had any particular interest in Southeast Asia. On the contrary, they cared far less about the region than the Roosevelt administration and would surely have been content to let the matter alone if the French government had let them. It required persistent French requests for help and warnings about the danger of inaction to activate the new potential in Washington for pro-French decisions. French pressure was shrewdly calculated to achieve this result. By insisting that U.S. indifference was damaging prospects for the revival of France as a reliable partner for the United States, French diplomacy tapped into mounting Cold War anxieties within the early Truman administration and equipped sympathetic U.S. policymakers with an argument they could use in fighting bureaucratic battles in Washington.

Impressive though their achievement may have been, however, French officials understood that in practical terms they had as yet accomplished little. A major challenge remained: to assure that the shift in the U.S. attitude resulted in active material aid for the French position in the Far East—the sine qua non of French ambitions in Indochina since planning had begun in earnest in 1944. So far, Truman administration officials had indicated only that they had no principled objection to a French recovery of Indochina. The real meaning of Washington's apparent willingness to provide military aid for the French Far Eastern war effort, always carefully qualified by the need to avoid detracting from Allied operations elsewhere, remained unclear. In fact, early indications were not promising. In the weeks after the administration's shift, American military authorities showed little eagerness to increase aid for French forces in Tonkin or to recognize France as a full combatant in the Far East. The Foreign Ministry acknowledged that U.S. aircraft had carried out more than two hundred sorties by mid-May, but it complained that these missions had mainly dropped food, medicine, and other relief supplies that would help the six thousand Tonkin resistance fighters struggle across the border into China but would not enable them to mount effective military operations. Resentful of the American tendency to treat French troops as mere charity cases, General Blaizot charged that it was "nothing more than an illusion" to count on the United States for meaningful assistance. He expressed greater confidence in the willingness of "certain Americans" in Chungking to help on their own initiative than in the possibility of concerted U.S. cooperation approved by Washington.[34]

French observers also feared that the shift in U.S. policy had not put an end to U.S. meddling in Indochinese affairs. Anxiety on this score seems, in fact, to have increased following the Truman administration's reassurances about French sovereignty, perhaps because of suspicions that Americans would be even more motivated to find informal ways to influence the local situation. Foreign Ministry analysts remained convinced that Washington would push to establish military bases on Indochinese territory—bases that, as French critics had long pointed out, might serve as bridgeheads for American economic, political, and cultural influence. More alarming, ministry observers suspected that many Americans, including some who had recently spoken reassuring words about Indochina, remained dangerously sympathetic to Asian nationalism and hostile to France in ways that could bar further evolution of the American position on colonial questions. Indeed, Franco-U.S. tensions increased markedly in mid-1945 as the two countries sparred diplomatically over the postwar status of French territories in the Middle East—Syria and Lebanon—as well as the Rhineland and the Franco-Italian border area known as the Valle d'Aosta. The French embassy in Washington reported to Paris that ordinary Americans were disappointed that France did not seem to be living up to their vision of it as a "sister democracy." With respect to Southeast Asia French diplomats worried that Vietnamese nationalists might be able to exploit American sentiments in ways that would undercut French interests. Just as U.S. ambivalence created opportunities for French diplomats to influence American behavior, it also created chances for others. French intelligence in Indochina rightly suspected that the Viet Minh hoped to secure U.S. assistance in its independence struggle.[35]

The British government was similarly disappointed by the U.S. failure to translate the policy shift of May 1945 into substantial aid for French political and military objectives. Like their French counterparts, British officials expressed satisfaction with U.S. reassurances that Washington would not block a French recovery of Indochina. The Colonial Office's top delegate to the San Francisco conference, A. H. Poynton, noted with relief that the U.S. contingent was "as firm . . . as anybody in opposing schemes for compulsory internationalization of colonial areas." Still, British observers were keenly aware that much remained to be done to assure French recovery of Indochina. Americans had given "no positive assurances" of support for France, as Poynton put it. Ambassador Halifax went further, expressing anxiety that even the partially changed American attitude might prove fleeting. "Generally speaking," a gloomy Halifax wrote in July, "the signs at present are that any American intention to impose some arrangement in Indochina irrespective of French wishes has lapsed for the present and that France's position there has ceased to be singled out from our and Dutch positions in the Far East for special treatment." Over the long term, Halifax was evidently uncertain which way Washington would go.[36]

The United States disappointed British officials especially by its obstinacy over a relatively technical issue that carried enormous significance for Indochina's future: the boundaries between military theaters in the Far East. Washington and London planted the seeds of controversy in 1943, when they established South East Asia Command (SEAC) under British leadership to manage the war in Burma and Malaya. The problem lay in the two sides' failure to specify the status of two territories further to the east—Indochina and Siam. Although those areas remained within the U.S.-dominated China Command, SEAC officials claimed that the boundary was permeable and that British forces, under an informal agreement with Chiang Kai-shek, had the right to conduct operations in Indochina and Siam as they wished. Initially, British insistence on this point hardly mattered since neither headquarters stood any chance of launching operations in the area. By spring 1945, however, things had changed. With British forces advancing across Burma and French forces fighting in Tonkin, SEAC commander Mountbatten began to insist upon his right to act in Indochina as he saw fit. Nothing less than the survival of the French resistance—and possibly, therefore, the survival of French colonialism in Indochina—seemed to be at stake.

Mountbatten's political adviser, Esler Dening, saw grounds for optimism after the Japanese coup. "The recent change in the position of Indo-China, where French troops are now fighting the Japanese, seems to offer a good opportunity of getting a decision [in Britain's favor]," he wrote.[37] But Albert Wedemeyer, the senior American commander in Chungking and a staunch opponent of European colonialism, firmly resisted British overtures. He disputed Mountbatten's interpretation of the earlier boundary agreements and insisted that SEAC could carry out operations only with China Command's specific approval—a formula likely to result in American vetoes of British proposals. With neither side willing to back down, the dispute mushroomed into a full-blown diplomatic confrontation.

British officials could hardly miss the implication of American stubbornness: commanders charged with day-to-day military decisions would not necessarily take heed of the more permissive atmosphere in Washington and use the new flexibility available to them in ways that would benefit the French cause. Indeed, just as matters seemed to be improving on the highest level, British and American authorities in Asia dug in for one of their sharpest disputes to date over Indochina. Frustration percolated through the British bureaucracy. Sterndale Bennett, head of the Foreign Office's Far Eastern department, complained that Wedemeyer had "behaved very badly" on the theater issue and detected persistent hostility to European aims in Southeast Asia behind the uncompromising U.S. position.[38] While Wedemeyer clung to his insistence that China Command review every proposed SEAC operation in Indochina, Mountbatten vowed to resist U.S. demands "tooth and nail." The confrontation grew uglier as the two theater commanders accused each other of undermining the war effort. Wedemeyer charged Mountbatten with diverting essential resources to support insignificant and "mercurial" resistance bands in Indochina, while Mountbatten accused his counterpart of overstepping his authority and violating the spirit of agreements reached at a higher level.[39]

British and French frustrations in the middle months of 1945 reflected the fact that the United States was gradually settling into a policy of neutrality regarding Indochina. The U.S. government would not obstruct French recovery. Truman and others had made that much clear in May. But neither would it offer active, material support for European ambitions. The United States would provide assistance for French forces strictly on the basis of military necessity—a principle that American officials emphasized repeatedly in the final months of the Pacific war. Significantly, no policy document ever spelled out the American approach. Instead, it took shape as the logical consequence of indecision and unwillingness within the bureaucracy to risk another confrontation over questions that remained highly sensitive. If both liberals and conservatives recognized drawbacks to neutrality, both, it seems, could live with them, especially perhaps because liberals such as Wedemeyer could interpret the policy one way and conservatives such as Dunn could interpret it another way.

One can surmise other reasons for the relative bureaucratic tranquility that prevailed in mid-1945. Liberals surely recognized neutrality as a victory in their struggle to prevent the abandonment of trusteeship from sliding into support for European objectives. Conservatives, meanwhile, likely calculated that they had eliminated the danger that the French government could claim that Washington had blocked one of the renascent French republic's most cherished objectives and damaged prospects for bilateral cooperation in the postwar period. Conservatives could also rest assured that they had achieved another central aim: by jettisoning trusteeship, they had eliminated any danger that Indochina's treatment would establish a precedent interfering with the imposition of U.S. control over Pacific islands coveted by the military as postwar bases. Important conservative constituencies—the War and Navy departments—thus lost a good deal of their earlier interest in Indochinese affairs.

If neutrality eased tensions between conservatives and liberals, it also carried the advantage of insulating Washington from the sort of European pressure that had influenced American decision making earlier in the year. Between March and May, the French and British governments successfully forced senior U.S. decision makers to confront difficult political questions about Indochina by repeatedly requesting military assistance. The sheer lack of policy guidance, as well as the urgency created by desperate fighting in Tonkin, meant that demands at the technical level inevitably posed sensitive political questions that could not be deferred. By the middle of the year, the Europeans enjoyed far less leverage of this sort. For one thing, Japanese suppression of the last large-scale resistance in Tonkin by the end of May deprived Paris and London of one of their best arguments in favor of supporting France. But the neutrality policy also helped to lessen European leverage by decoupling military decisions from the broader political issues. Initially, this approach had been the brainchild of Stettinius and other conservatives who saw it as a way to move in a pro-French direction without overstepping Roosevelt's basic hostility to French restoration. Liberals had regarded it warily, fearing that the formula would prove difficult to maintain over the long term. But by the middle of the year, following the policy shift in the conservatives' direction, both sides backed it as a way to deal with persistent European demands without confronting the bureaucracy with impossibly difficult decisions at every turn. By giving the military the flexibility to do as it saw fit, Washington could safely put the issue on the back burner.

For Paris and London neutrality brought little but disappointment. Since Southeast Asia obviously ranked as a relatively minor area of concern, U.S. calculation of military necessity and efficiency was likely to cut against European interests in most cases. Indeed, American authorities provided little of the military equipment or shipping that the French most desired. To be sure, U.S. decisions sometimes went in favor of the Europeans, especially when Americans saw the possibility of easing U.S. burdens. In late July 1945 the U.S. Joint Chiefs of Staff, concerned with reducing U.S. obligations as they began contemplating 1946 operations against the Japanese homeland, agreed in principle to involve French forces in the Asian war and to permit them to benefit from the Lend-Lease military assistance program—a concession of potentially great significance for French ambitions in Southeast Asia.[40] The resolution of the theater controversy around the same time also favored the Europeans. At the Potsdam meeting of Allied heads of state, the Joint Chiefs agreed to cede all of Indochina south of the sixteenth parallel to British control, meaning that British forces would occupy the area and preside over the restoration of civilian rule. The Joint Chiefs might even have been willing to concede all of Indochina to SEAC had it not been for the lingering possibility that the northern part might prove a useful staging area for American attacks against Japan contemplated for the fall of 1945.[41]

From the European point of view, however, even this concession was a mixed blessing. On one hand, it meant that British occupation forces would be well positioned to facilitate the return of French control in the south, a beachhead from which French authorities could reclaim control over the remainder of the country. On the other hand, American abandonment of responsibility for Southeast Asia was hardly the first choice of French and British officials. On the contrary, they had worked for months to encourage deeper U.S. engagement and understood the possible results of failure. French authorities clearly recognized the drawbacks of reliance on Britain. British officials themselves held no illusions on the matter and fretted around the time of the Potsdam agreements over whether they had the resources to manage new occupation duties in Indochina and the still-vaster Dutch East Indies, also placed under British control as the U.S. military sought to cut its commitments. The British request at Potsdam to incorporate Indochina reflected not so much a cherished hope of acquiring control over new territory as a rueful acknowledgement that the United States had failed utterly to support France in any of the ways that London had hoped it would following the March coup. Lack of American cooperation left the British government with no alternative but to take charge of restoring French power by itself, a duty that hardly generated enthusiasm in London.

The French and British governments were also frustrated by another aspect of the neutrality policy. By insisting that decisions would be made strictly on the basis of military efficiency, Washington inadvertently ensured that liberals, who continued to hold key positions in the military and intelligence bureaucracies in the Far East, would effectively write U.S. policy on day-to-day matters, at least in the near term. By failing to spell out a clear Indochina policy, in other words, the policy-making bureaucracy left space for motivated individuals to do as they saw fit. During May Dunn, Stettinius, and other conservatives had benefited from this situation and provided French counterparts with unprecedented assurances. A few weeks later, however, opponents of European colonialism showed that flexibility in the American position could work the other way, too. Wedemeyer, for one, exploited the leeway left to him by imprecise instructions from Washington. Invoking the need for an efficient division of labor between theaters, he took advantage of ambiguities and technicalities in the agreements establishing South East Asia Command so as to block British activities that would have strengthened French claims.

But the best example of individual Americans exploiting the ambivalence of U.S. policy to frustrate European aims is the OSS "Deer" team that parachuted into Tonkin in July 1945 to make contact with Viet Minh leaders and to initiate cooperation on various tasks that would serve U.S. military objectives in the region—intelligence gathering, anti-Japanese sabotage, and recovery of Allied pilots shot down in the area. The two flamboyant leaders of the OSS mission—Archimedes L. A. Patti and Allison K. Thomas—were deeply impressed with the Viet Minh and stepped beyond their official instructions by offering encouragement to Ho Chi Minh and promoting the Viet Minh cause with their superiors in Chungking. In a series of lengthy interviews with Ho in July, August, and September, Patti and Thomas showed sympathy for Viet Minh objectives and, by their own admission, probably gave meaningful encouragement at a key moment in the development of the Vietnamese revolution.[42]

In later years former French officials and other commentators would charge that this support formed part of a plan orchestrated in Washington to undermine French influence in Indochina. Jean Sainteny, the senior French official in China during the closing stages of the Pacific war, insisted in an interview published in 1978, for example, that Patti regarded France as a "deliberate enemy" and acted on "general directives issued much higher up" when he supported Ho Chi Minh's anti-French ambitions. Other critics alleged that the Deer team armed and trained Vietnamese guerrillas with the expectation that they would not only resist the Japanese but also help the United States prevent a French reconquest.[43] Such accusations are groundless. Washington had already given assurances of nonopposition to the restoration of French colonialism, and no evidence suggests that anyone in Washington gave secret directives to a different effect. Nor is there evidence that the OSS supplied Ho Chi Minh with significant quantities of arms or military training, much less that it encouraged the Viet Minh to use these against the French. The Deer team disbursed only modest amounts of equipment and spent perhaps two weeks training small numbers of Viet Minh fighters before Japan's abrupt surrender ended the program.[44]

Rather than demonstrating an anti-French conspiracy in Washington, the OSS team's support for the Viet Minh reveals the extent to which senior American policymakers, satisfied with neutrality, turned away from Indochinese affairs in the final weeks of the war. Content to leave the matter in the hands of lower-ranking officials, Washington decision makers cleared the way for individuals like Thomas and Patti to use their immediate authority to undermine French rule. Given the views that prevailed among many U.S. officials in the Far East at this time, their activities are hardly surprising. Some of these Americans, lacking information about policy deliberations in Washington, probably assumed that Roosevelt's hostility to French rule still prevailed. But most also acted on personal anticolonial convictions that coincided with the late president's opinions.

French policymakers knew little of the Deer team's activities until after the end of the Pacific war. But they did not need to know all the details of American behavior in order to recognize the ominous bottom line in the final weeks of the Pacific war: American policy was unlikely to evolve beyond neutrality. With U.S. forces closing in on Japan, French officials therefore increasingly feared that the war would end without French troops being involved in Indochina's liberation. Any delay between Japan's surrender and the reassertion of French authority seemed riskier than ever. The old danger—that other powers would decide Indochina's postwar fate—was now compounded by a new one: the possibility that the surging nationalist movement in Vietnam would step into a postwar power vacuum and complicate any restoration of French authority. "Any delay will be serious because of the possible actions of foreign countries . . . and because of the independence movement, which is highly developed in the country," advised one Foreign Ministry paper prepared for Bidault. In Washington Ambassador Bonnet concurred, asserting that "in view of the weakness of our forces" the success of French policy in Indochina still depended wholly on the attitude of other governments. Any failure to be included in the liberating force, Bonnet wrote, "could have a serious and even decisive effect on our rights and interests both with our allies and with the natives."[45]

The French response to this increasingly dire situation reflected a logic that had prevailed for many months: France would fall back on Britain's help in the short term while continuing to seek American assistance over the longer run. In Kandy General Blaizot pressed for stepped-up British air support of French resistance bands inside Indochina, while French military representatives in Paris and London continued to push for British assistance in transporting French troops to the Far East—the single most important objective in the middle of 1945. The Foreign Ministry, realizing that Britain's shipping shortage would prevent the arrival of significant French forces before the end of the war, increasingly focused on obtaining an agreement with Britain to ensure the quick revival of French colonial administration even if that administration depended for some time on the presence of British, rather than French, military forces. For that reason, Ambassador Massigli renewed his government's plea to London to open negotiations on a civil-affairs accord spelling out procedures for reestablishing civilian rule.[46]

The British reaction to these requests, like the requests themselves, reflected mounting resignation among the Europeans that the United States could not be counted on in the short term to shoulder any of the burden in Indochina. While South East Asia Command increased material support for French troops—now mainly congregated in refugee camps across the border in China—military authorities in London began to study the possibility that Britain alone would have to manage the sealift of French troops to the Far East. The Chiefs of Staff showed the same grudging acceptance of French requests for cooperation on postwar civilian administration of Indochina. The Foreign Office agreed in principle to negotiate a civil-affairs accord, although it insisted that uncertainties about theater boundaries had to be resolved before it would be possible to hold detailed discussions. The Colonial Office was quicker to approve proposals to expand the number of French personnel admitted to British training centers in India that prepared colonial officials to accompany SEAC troops into areas liberated from Japan. That request, unlike most of the others, squared perfectly with the British government's determination to minimize its obligations in Indochina as far as possible. "It is urgently necessary," wrote Mountbatten, "to prepare a firm phased plan for reception of French administrators."[47]

French observers in the Far East knew as well as Mountbatten that British resources were dwindling quickly and amounted to a mere fraction of what the United States could offer. General Gabriel Sabattier, who had fled into China with remnants of the Indochina Army, reported to the provisional government on June 21 that Britain's ability to equip French forces was "far below requirements." Not only could the United States potentially supply far more, but, Sabattier asserted, it would likely provide it on far better terms once the U.S. commanders in China made up their minds to help. As an example of potential American largesse, Sabattier noted that while bedraggled French troops in southern China generally had to pay for British assistance with Chinese dollars or Indian rupees, Americans would most likely provide unconditional assistance through Lend-Lease—"a considerable financial advantage for us," as Sabattier put it.[48] The rewards promised to be vastly greater if new French troops were introduced to the Far East, since they would unquestionably be equipped with U.S. gear supplied to metropolitan France under Lend-Lease in the European theater. Under these conditions French officials saw no alternative but to persevere with—even to intensify—the multipronged diplomatic campaign to influence U.S. perceptions of the Indochina issue.

In the late spring, French officials endeavored especially to capitalize on Washington's oft-stated determination to end the war against Japan as quickly as possible. "American opinion is extremely sensitive on this point and is becoming more and more so," noted French defense minister René Pleven during a May trip to Washington. In China the ebullient Pechkoff insisted as always that the Tonkin resistance—in reality petering out by that point—formed a potentially crucial part of the anti-Japanese effort, and he resorted to ever more extreme hyperbole in describing its exploits. French fighters were single-handedly preventing Japanese forces from attacking southern China, he told foreign reporters, claiming incomprehension that U.S. commanders could not recognize this accomplishment. In Washington, meanwhile, French military officials made their most sweeping proposal yet to the Joint Chiefs of Staff for full involvement in the Far Eastern war, a formal offer to place two elite divisions of French ground troops under American command. "Thus France affirms its determination to participate energetically in the defeat of Japan and to open a new battlefield in solidarity with the United States," Ambassador Bonnet told Joseph Grew, the acting secretary of state. To create a "psychological climate more favorable to an affirmative response," French representatives stressed that the troops could be used for any operations against Japan, not just for the liberation of French territory. Bonnet argued that Truman had already settled the matter in principle during his talks with Bidault and demanded that the U.S. government issue a public statement accepting full French participation in the Far Eastern war.[49]

French officials also reemphasized their commitment to a liberal colonial policy. The Foreign Ministry instructed the French delegation to the San Francisco meetings to stress that the "French empire" no longer existed and was steadily being transformed into a "community of nations" based on individual dignity and equal opportunity. "We must appear to the United States," as one diplomat in the Washington embassy put it, "to be the European democracy par excellence, or they will lose interest in us." The French delegation that accompanied de Gaulle on a visit to Washington in August dwelled on the same theme. Georges Peter, a senior Colonial Ministry official who led the Indochina portion of the talks, declared to U.S. officials that "the Rudyard Kiplings" who had once run the empire had been replaced by "younger men" who "propose to move toward increasing autonomy for colonies in political as well as economic matters." Under pressure for greater specificity Peter insisted that the provisional government could not yet spell out details of future political arrangements because the situation in Indochina was constantly changing. In the meantime, the best French officials could offer was assurances that the Indochinese themselves were content with the pace of French reforms. In Chungking Pechkoff painted an especially rosy picture, telling reporters that the Indochinese were "showing themselves faithful to the cause of France" in the struggle against Japan. "The real 'trusteeship,'" he announced, "is in our hearts—it is the mutual confidence which exists between Indochinese and French."[50]

Aware of American skepticism about such vague promises of political reform, French diplomats sprinkled their assurances with relatively concrete pledges of economic liberalization. The interministerial committee that supervised Indochina policy assumed that the most influential group of Americans remained motivated principally by a desire for access to the Indochinese economy and could be won over to active support for French objectives through carefully calculated concessions. "In order to inspire the Americans to meet our demands," the committee concluded, "it is vital to offer them economic advantages for the future in Indochina." At a July meeting, the committee proposed various guarantees that could be offered to the United States. Paris might, for example, give Americans new details about French plans for establishing Indochina's economic autonomy or nondiscriminatory customs arrangements, both of which had been promised in the March 24 declaration. In addition, Paris might offer "supplementary guarantees" about freedom of investment in Indochina for American capital and the rights that American companies would enjoy in Indochina.[51]

Over the following month, the Foreign and Colonial ministries drafted additional proposals that were unveiled during de Gaulle's trip to Washington in August. The plan contained few details about when and how the new policies would be implemented. But the four basic stipulations exceeded the March 24 declaration in their specificity. First, the paper proposed abandoning discriminatory duties against non-French trade. It observed that this step would inevitably be "harmful to metropolitan interests" but was "dear to the Americans" and therefore desirable. Second, the paper proposed allowing the Indochinese piastre to fluctuate freely against the franc, although the paper added that such an arrangement would not rule out an undefined "solidarity" between the two currencies. The third proposal, repeating the central point of the March 24 declaration, called for granting "economic autonomy" to Indochina or its component states, meaning essentially that they would be permitted to establish their own decision-making institutions. Finally, the paper suggested assurances of "economic equality" for foreign investors, a step that the document asserted would bring France into compliance with the spirit of the Atlantic Charter and Bretton Woods accords, both cherished by Washington.[52]

In its discussion of the need for such concessions, the paper offers a remarkable glimpse into French anxieties and objectives in the weeks around the end of the Pacific war. The goal of economic concessions, the paper asserted, was to "create a favorable climate at a time when the French government is concerned with gaining Allied recognition of its full sovereignty over Indochina." It was increasingly clear that French forces would not be involved in Indochina's liberation and that shipment of troops to reestablish French rule thereafter would depend on Allied cooperation. It was equally clear that France would depend totally on foreign assistance for the resources to rebuild the Indochinese economy, badly damaged by four years of war. "It is the Allies, especially the United States, that will provide the necessary supplies, since the Metropole is unfortunately unable to satisfy immediate needs," the paper asserted. Everything seemed to hinge on obtaining adequate resources from abroad. The paper insisted that whatever country showed the capacity to tend to Indochina's material needs would reap immeasurable prestige in the eyes of the indigenous population. If France were to be that power, its ability to supply Indochina's needs would "depend essentially on American good will." Active American support seemed vital for another reason, as well. If the indigenous population saw evidence of U.S. support for French aims, it would be inclined to accept the return of France as inevitable. "If not," the paper warned, "they will seek to open direct relations with our allies." Economic concessions may be painful, the paper concluded, but they were an unfortunate necessity and were much preferable to political reforms that might undercut the principle of French sovereignty. "It is necessary to assure ourselves of the moral and material support of the Americans and, in order to do that, to take certain economic measures that will enable us to avoid political concessions."[53]

As the French delegation had hoped, some conservatives in Washington picked up on French promises of reform and tried to exploit them within the U.S. bureaucracy to nudge American policy in a pro-French direction. Following de Gaulle's visit to Washington, Walter Kahn, a legal expert at the State Department, went furthest by asserting in an internal memorandum that, based on French assurances, it was "entirely clear" that Paris intended to establish a new economic regime for Indochina and "welcomed and encouraged" American trade and investment. Although Kahn conceded that future political reforms were "not indicated precisely" and that there remained "much to work out," he insisted that Paris had demonstrated its intent to establish democratic institutions in Indochina and to expand opportunities for the indigenous population throughout the public and private sectors. "It is clear," he wrote, "that a new policy is being proposed and will probably be tried; that Indo-China is to be given a large degree of economic autonomy and thrown open to the world for trade and development; and that the interest of the U.S. Government and U.S. private enterprise is warmly solicited."[54]

The very vehemence of Kahn's language, however, betrayed the fact that many Americans held a sharply different view of French promises—a fact that became clear as de Gaulle's visit, combined with uncertainties created by the sudden end of the war against Japan, forced Washington to revisit the Indochina controversy in a way it had not done since May. Liberals made abundantly clear that their thinking had changed little since the springtime policy review. On the day of the Hiroshima bombing, an OSS report prepared in Washington cautioned against accepting French promises at face value and urged that the U.S. administration preserve its leverage over French behavior. "Unless pressure is brought to bear, the situation vis-à-vis the natives and the U.S.A. will revert to that of before the war," the paper asserted, adding that "suppression and exploitation will be the watchwords, as in the past." The State Department's Southeast Asia division expressed much the same view in a combatively worded memorandum drafted for Truman just before his meeting with de Gaulle. Showing few signs of any climbdown since May, the division urged the president to stress that the United States might abandon neutrality in favor of outright opposition to the restoration of French sovereignty if Paris did not take concrete steps to accommodate Indochinese nationalists.[55]

The Southeast Asia division's proposal probably never made it to the White House, and even if it had, President Truman and his closest aides had no inclination to issue such an ultimatum. The logic that had prevailed in the spring of 1945 only became more convincing as time passed and the uncertainties of postwar European politics grew more troubling: to demand bold reforms in Indochina would risk alienating a French government whose cooperation with U.S. priorities in the postwar period seemed ever more vital. To be sure, the Truman administration deeply resented French behavior during 1945 in many parts of the world—

Germany, the Franco-Italian border, and the Middle East even more than Indochina, which remained, as always, a secondary issue. Most U.S. policymakers nevertheless increasingly regarded France as an indispensable participant in Western economic and security arrangements in the postwar era. Soviet moves to tighten communist control over Poland, Romania, and Bulgaria highlighted the importance of France, a country that had once been—and might again become—a major political, economic, and military power harnessed to a Western-leaning, democratic group of states. The emergence of the French Communist Party as the nation's largest and most dynamic political force also contributed to American caution about alienating de Gaulle's government. With the Communists apparently well positioned to benefit from political and economic chaos within France, the Truman administration had little interest in antagonizing the center-right political forces that, whatever their drawbacks, at least seemed open to partnership with the United States.

Even as this logic guided U.S. policymaking toward France, however, the Truman administration made no move toward embracing a pro-French policy in Indochina. That remained as much as ever the French government's central objective in the early postwar weeks. "What we need in order to assure [recovery of French sovereignty]," insisted one Foreign Ministry report on August 24, "is active and rapid support from our allies, especially American aid." But liberal concerns about alienating Asian opinion remained sufficiently strong within the U.S. bureaucracy that any bold departure in that direction was out of the question. By the time of Japan's surrender, Washington had done nothing to help France "either by a decisive assurance or by an accord," as the ministry report put it.[56] Nor would Washington change its approach over the rest of the year. In fact, the epic events of the late summer and fall of 1945—the end of the Pacific war and the climax of the Vietnamese revolution—further solidified American neutrality and put the French goal of active support, if anything, further out of reach.

The end of the war harmed French prospects by depriving the French government of the only effective argument it had made to obtain U.S. backing: the need for military cooperation to bring about Japan's defeat. That argument had hardly produced impressive results. Beyond a smattering of food, medicine, and other humanitarian supplies for the defeated resistance fighters in southern China, the French military had received little that it requested from the United States—a failure that was all too obvious to the Foreign Ministry as analysts looked back over the previous months. Resistance against Japanese forces in the closing stages of the war had "failed to boost French prestige noticeably," much less convinced the United States to move French troops to the Far East, asserted a paper by the ministry's Asia department. But now even the possibility of attracting American support on the basis of shared military objectives had evaporated in the mushroom clouds over Japan. All that remained to the French government was the weak reed of diplomacy to protect its colonial interests. "France, without sufficient military means to reconquer Indochina by itself, must use all the resources of its diplomacy to overcome the biases or the apathy of foreign governments on whom now depends the future of this territory," the Foreign Ministry report gloomily asserted.[57] Even worse, the ministry anticipated that the United States might slip back toward overt hostility at precisely the moment when French leverage was on the wane. American attitudes, after all, seemed to have changed little since 1944. "Every American is anti-colonial by instinct and because he owes his existence to an anti-colonial reaction," the ministry paper lamented. Americans' cynicism also seemed to be coming to the fore now that the fighting was over. "With its growing economic potential, the U.S. is more and more disguising its expansion with terms like 'civilizing mission' or 'educative mission,'" the paper stated.[58]

Fears of American backsliding toward Roosevelt-era hostility were mistaken, but the Foreign Ministry judged correctly that the end of the war would bring no positive change. The U.S. response to new French demands in the days following the Japanese surrender made this much clear. Immediately after the surrender, Ambassador Pechkoff asked Wedemeyer to help move French troops from southern China into Tonkin to help disarm Japanese troops there. The matter held great symbolic importance since accepting the surrender of the seventy thousand or so Japanese troops in Indochina would naturally bolster French claims to sovereignty over the area. True to form, Wedemeyer refused the French request, claiming that only Chiang Kai-shek, the ultimate authority over China Command, could make such a decision. The United States, Wedemeyer wrote, "did not want to be involved either politically or militarily in Indochinese complications." Wedemeyer also showed that he had lost none of his earlier sensitivity about theater boundaries, refusing to permit British aircraft to supply the ragtag collection of French resistance fighters north of the sixteenth parallel. As the alarming prospect of unaccompanied Chinese troops entering northern Indochina grew more imminent, French diplomats repeated their requests, while also launching a desperate, last-minute bid to overturn the Potsdam decision giving China occupation duties in the north. All Indochina, they insisted, should fall under British command on the principle that, in order to avoid confusion and wasted effort, any single political entity should fall under a single occupation authority. Again, however, Wedemeyer, apparently with approval of the Joint Chiefs of Staff in Washington, refused French demands.[59]

Stung by these failures, the French government requested U.S. support for the principle that France, as the territorial sovereign if not the prevalent military power, should at least play a token role in Japanese surrender ceremonies. The acceptance of French officers at both SEAC and China Command headquarters in the closing months of the war encouraged some optimism that French representatives would be involved in the ceremonies. On August 14 de Gaulle ordered diplomats in Washington, London, Moscow, and Chungking to take the initiative in seeking approval for full French involvement, while also instructing the ambassador in The Hague to arrange a common position with the Dutch government, which faced a similar problem in the East Indies.[60] To French relief, Secretary of State James Byrnes told Ambassador Bonnet five days later that the U.S. government had approved French requests to participate in the main Japanese surrender to take place in Tokyo harbor.

This concession amounted to a minor victory at best, however. It clearly stemmed more from the Truman administration's general desire to see France revived as a global power than any specific calculation concerning Indochina's postwar destiny. Indeed, even relatively Francophile U.S. officials in Washington and Paris showed little interest in assuring French representatives a role in Japanese surrender ceremonies in Indochina. Jefferson Caffery, the generally sympathetic U.S. ambassador in Paris, told Bidault on August 15 that the United States, largely to demonstrate that the division of Indochina had been approved strictly for operational reasons, would support French efforts "to have representatives present" at ceremonies throughout Indochina. But this lukewarm assurance led nowhere. Caffery offered no details about what the function of those representatives might be. Meanwhile, the State Department insisted that the French government take up the issue directly with British and Chinese authorities. In the British occupation zone, of course, the French government had few worries. But without U.S. backing, French officials feared total exclusion from the surrender of Japanese units in the Chinese zone—a fear that was borne out in the weeks that followed.[61]

CEMENTING NEUTRALITY

If the end of the war seemed to bring nearer the nightmare scenario of exclusion from Indochina, or at least half of it, another development in the weeks around the end of the Pacific war—Vietnam's August Revolution—made the situation more worrying still for French policymakers. By demonstrating the hazards of close association with the French cause, surging Vietnamese nationalism further cemented American attachment to neutrality. The effect on American policy was, of course, hardly the only way in which the revolution threatened French interests. We can see now that the momentous events of August and September served notice that France, regardless of its fortunes in obtaining foreign help, would face determined and organized resistance to any bid to restore colonial rule. The revolution resounded, after all, with hostility to French colonialism. Recent scholarship on the August Revolution has de-emphasized this point, stressing instead the fortuitous confluence of circumstances that led to the Viet Minh's triumph: widespread rural grievance caused by persistent famine in northern Vietnam, agile leadership in parts of the country isolated from centers of revolutionary power, and especially the vacuum of power created by the rapid collapse of Japanese authority and the slow arrival of British and Chinese occupation troops. There was, as historian William J. Duiker has argued, "a distinct aura of spontaneity and improvisation" to it all.[62] Yet there was also an unmistakable ideological center to the revolution— burning resentment against French rule that rendered any attempt at relegitimation of French colonialism, with or without foreign assistance, extremely unlikely. Ho Chi Minh made the revolutionary outlook clear in his famous declaration of independence in Hanoi's Ba Dinh Square on September 2. Following his invocation of the American Declaration of Independence, Ho devoted the bulk of his speech to a scathing catalog of abuses committed by the French. "Their deeds run counter to the ideals of humanity and justice," Ho proclaimed, charging that France had "shamelessly exploited our people, driven them into the worst misery and mercilessly plundered our country." The Vietnamese, he vowed, "are determined to fight to the death against all attempts at aggression by the French imperialists."[63]

Despite such warnings the French government regarded Vietnamese nationalism as a problem that could be solved by obtaining sufficient international support. In part, it did so because it lacked alternatives. General disdain for the nationalists also contributed to the French fixation with diplomacy by encouraging the belief that the reimposition of colonial authority was simply a matter of obtaining adequate material strength. But French officials also viewed the revolution as a problem of great power relations because they understood that the Vietnamese leadership attached a high priority to attracting foreign support. As historians have frequently noted, Ho Chi Minh was keenly sensitive to the international context as he and the rest of the leadership of the Democratic Republic of Vietnam plotted the revolutionary course.[64]

French policymakers at the time also appreciated that the Viet Minh hoped to achieve its objectives by influencing international opinion, especially that of the United States. Ho's invocation of the 1776 Declaration of Independence at the outset of his own independence address may have been an attempt to cast the revolution in ways that would appeal to Americans. At other points, Viet Minh attempts to curry U.S. favor were more explicit. In a declaration released in Kunming on August 15 and intended for an international audience, for example, the Viet Minh leadership proclaimed its desire "to make known to the United States Government that the Indo-Chinese people first of all desire the independence of Indo-China, and are hoping that the United States, as a champion of democracy, will assist her in securing this independence." The declaration then requested that Washington help by "prohibiting" or, failing that, "not assisting" the French to reenter Indochina, keeping Chinese occupation forces above the sixteenth parallel "under control," assisting the revival of the Indochinese economy by sending technical advisers, and even placing Vietnam under American tutelage. Similar appeals to the Truman administration, both public and secret, followed over the ensuing months.[65]

Worried that these appeals might find a receptive audience in the United States, French authorities struggled during the late summer and fall of 1945 to control international perceptions of the Vietnamese revolution. Lacking military force to destroy the revolution physically, the French government attempted to contain it perceptually by exploiting an extensive diplomatic and intelligence network that the revolutionaries could not possibly match. Part of this strategy involved a concerted effort to close down sources of information that could challenge the French version of events taking place in Vietnam. Foreign Ministry officials had suspected since the spring that nationalist agents were traveling secretly to the United States and trying to open contacts with the American government, perhaps even by posing as journalists covering the inaugural UN meeting in San Francisco. Ambassador Bonnet had not thought at that time that the threat required an elaborate surveillance operation, but by the fall, things had changed.[66] The ministry took increasing care to monitor the activities of Vietnamese organizations in the United States, many of which, indeed, had begun peppering the U.S. government with anticolonial appeals. On at least one occasion, French officials took their concern straight to their U.S. counterparts. When rumors circulated in late October that a Viet Minh agent carrying documents potentially damaging to France was traveling to Washington, François Lacoste, the French embassy's senior counselor, warned Moffat that any U.S. welcome for the Viet Minh mission would be considered an "unfriendly act" and leave a "very bad impression" in France.[67]

Contacts between the Americans and Viet Minh officials in Tonkin posed more serious problems since Chinese occupation authorities, once they began arriving in September, made it impossible for French observers to monitor what was taking place above the sixteenth parallel. Lacking detailed information, French officials assumed the worst. The newly appointed French high commissioner for Indochina, Admiral Thierry d'Argenlieu, revived the old suspicion that Americans were secretly scouting for economic opportunities and currying favor with Vietnamese elements that might help them. "Americans in the Sino-American theater, especially OSS agents, more concerned with immediate economic gain than world peace, have given the Viet Minh material and moral support on every possible occasion," charged d'Argenlieu, a devoted Gaullist who had bickered constantly with the U.S. military during his tenure as wartime high commissioner in New Caledonia. New hints about the activities of OSS agents in Tonkin also encouraged French fears of continuing U.S.–Viet Minh contacts in Hanoi. One Foreign Ministry study in October charged that the OSS had attempted—and possibly was still attempting—to carry out a "secret but real" plot to prevent France from recovering its sovereignty. On the international level, the paper stated, the United States vowed to respect French sovereignty. Meanwhile, however, it had given "no practical assistance to help us exercise our rights" while introducing OSS agents to cooperate with the Viet Minh and to "fight against our influence." To resist these American activities, French diplomats complained strenuously to the State and War departments, especially after Major General Philip E. Gallagher, the senior U.S. military adviser to Chinese occupation troops, told reporters that the Allies had not yet recognized French sovereignty over Indochina. Lacoste demanded that Washington send "very strict instructions" clarifying U.S. policy on Indochina.[68]

French diplomats also responded to the revolution by attempting to belittle and even demonize the Viet Minh in American eyes. One line of attack was to vilify the Viet Minh as a mere puppet of Japan. Philippe Baudet, the head of the Foreign Ministry's Asia department, joined d'Argenlieu and the Ministry of Information in Paris in instructing French representatives around the world to accentuate what the high commissioner called the "Japanese nuisance." Diplomats were to stress that the Viet Minh had been created by Japanese occupation authorities and owed all its strength to Japanese support. When the Pacific war ended, according to this version of Vietnamese history, well-armed and unrepresentative Viet Minh forces turned to "piracy" and "brigandage" unrelated to any legitimate political aspirations. In the interests of law and order, then, the Viet Minh had to be suppressed by force of arms. D'Argenlieu and Baudet believed this to be a potentially effective line of argument, probably because it rested on more than a grain of truth. The Viet Minh had benefited from the benevolent passivity of Japanese occupation forces during the final weeks of the war, and many Japanese troops—perhaps a few thousand—either deserted to the Viet Minh or surrendered their weapons to Ho's forces once the war came to an end. Additionally, as political tensions mounted in southern Vietnam in the first weeks of the British occupation, Viet Minh political agitation was increasingly accompanied by street violence and an escalating series of reprisals that involved conspicuous brutality on both sides. General Jacques Philippe Leclerc, the newly designated French military commander for Indochina, could thus claim to Admiral Mountbatten with some legitimacy that mounting "disturbances" in Vietnam "were provoked more by looters and brigandage than by political aspirants."[69]

Despite the risk of inconsistency, French officials also attempted to besmirch the Viet Minh as communists—as the agents of the Soviet Union rather than Japan. Exploiting anticommunism was a tricky matter in French policymaking circles in fall 1945. On October 21 the first nationwide legislative elections in France following liberation confirmed the Communists' status as the nation's largest political party. It was therefore somewhat awkward to vilify the Viet Minh as "communist" as part of any overt campaign to attract foreign support. Nevertheless, the French Communist Party held little influence over foreign or colonial policy, which remained thoroughly under the control of parties further to the right as well as a conservative civil service and diplomatic corps. To these groups anticommunism had strong appeal not only for its diplomatic advantages but also as a deeply held personal conviction.

Baudet, head of the Foreign Ministry's Asia office, hit the theme hardest. Although he admitted to the U.S. ambassador, Jefferson Caffery, that the Viet Minh was not a "communist organization" per se, Baudet insisted that there was nevertheless cause for grave concern. Communists occupied key leadership positions within the Viet Minh movement, he told Caffery. Baudet also expressed worry that Vietnamese communists had established contact with the Soviet mission in Chungking. In a message endorsed by de Gaulle, Baudet advised the embassy in Washington to dwell on similar themes in conversations with Americans. "In your commentaries," Baudet instructed Ambassador Bonnet, "you should not hide that the preponderant influence of communist elements at the heart of the Viet Minh is a subject of great concern for the French government."[70]

Despite French efforts to manipulate foreign perceptions of developments within Vietnam, U.S. officials gradually grasped the basic outline of events. Earlier in the year, it is true, State Department analysts had complained repeatedly of their difficulty obtaining information. Washington lacked its own sources and, as the OSS suspected, may have suffered as well from French efforts to hinder the flow of information to the West. Even as late as August Moffat complained that he had "no information from inside the country" and that it was impossible to distinguish fact from propaganda.[71] By the following month, though, most U.S. appraisals of the situation in Vietnam called attention, with reasonable accuracy, to the seriousness of the situation. As early as June a State Department appraisal prepared at the request of Secretary of War Henry L. Stimson noted that the "Indo-Chinese Independence League" was attracting a broad following of committed nationalists "who are neither apathetic nor supine and are willing to fight." The French, the report added, would encounter "serious difficulty" in defeating the nationalists by force of arms. In the days following Ho's declaration of independence, the OSS provided detailed reports on the revolution's progress, noting on September 5 that the "Provisional Annamese Government" was "in full control and so well organized that several attempts by French from Calcutta to parachute into the country have been frustrated." On September 20 General Gallagher reported from Hanoi that the Viet Minh was "definitely in the saddle" and willing to fight to resist French reconquest.[72]

The problem for U.S. policymakers lay not in understanding the scale of the upheaval occurring in Vietnam but in appreciating its long-term significance and in choosing the appropriate policy response. As usual where Indochina was concerned, policymakers offered a range of views. For their part, liberals saw the revolution largely as an expression of legitimate nationalist grievances that, if denied, might contribute to a race war between Asia and the West. "The United States cannot afford to risk a second Greater East Asia war by remaining indifferent to the affairs of the dependent Asiatic nations," the Office of Far Eastern Affairs wrote in an early September memorandum. "Indifference is almost as bad as actually cooperating in the re-imposition of imperialism," it continued, "for we are linked with our Allies, and the Asiatics would take our silence as tacit approval." Already, liberals claimed, close Franco-British cooperation in Southeast Asia was creating the impression among Asians that Western powers were united against them. Moffat pointed to an example of how U.S. prestige in Asia was crumbling while the United States remained passive: although South East Asia Command continued to function under the formal control of the Anglo-American Combined Chiefs of Staff, the U.S. military, desperate to avoid political complications, had withdrawn all but one liaison officer, who had strict orders to avoid meetings unless they had direct bearing on military operations involving U.S. forces. Under these conditions British and French commanders in Kandy had been able to settle on "a strong anti-Annamese policy" and then to present it publicly as an "Allied" decision. The use by British occupation forces of U.S.-manufactured military equipment also caused worry that the United States was being implicated in colonial repression despite its efforts to steer clear of the Indochina and East Indies controversies.[73]

As political tensions mounted in Indochina during September and October, liberals in the State Department sensed an opportunity to retake the upper hand in formulation of U.S. policy toward European colonialism. British complicity in the reimposition of French control south of the sixteenth parallel sparked a wave of fighting that seemed increasingly capable of exploding into a full-fledged crisis pitting Asians against the Western powers. "Conditions in Indochina indicate ... that a continued hands-off policy by the United States may result in a 'Syria-Lebanon crisis' in the Far East on a large scale," asserted John Carter Vincent, chief of the State Department's Office of Far Eastern Affairs, referring to the diplomatic crisis that erupted in March over the postwar status of the two Middle Eastern territories. Vincent noted that even those French officials inclined toward a liberal approach were determined to reimpose full French control in Indochina before making any concessions. "Lack of Annamese faith in French promises under such circumstances, the danger of [a] massacre of French residents in Indochina when French troops arrive in force and the danger of a subsequent bitter military campaign by the French against the Annamese make it of utmost importance that the powers concerned endeavor to bring about negotiations now between the French and moderate Annamese elements," Vincent wrote to Undersecretary of State Dean Acheson on September 26, two days after newly arrived British forces overturned Vietnamese rule in Saigon in preparation for the return of French authorities.[74]

During October Vincent, Moffat, and other liberals repeatedly proposed that the United States, either alone or at the head of a small group of interested governments, promote negotiations between France and the Viet Minh, as well as between the Dutch government and Indonesian nationalists, to lay out plans for immediate reform and eventual independence. Instead of its current posture of passive neutrality, the United States should "work directly with the colonial powers," one report urged. On Indochina, Vincent laid out the basic idea in late September as the Franco-British crackdown against Vietnamese revolutionaries went forward: the United States would call together an international investigating commission made up of representatives from the United States, China, Britain, and France to study the situation and issue a report that would serve as the basis of negotiations between France and Vietnamese nationalists. In the meantime, no new French forces would be introduced into Indochina. Vincent conceded that this plan would inevitably spark French resentment. "However," he added, "this disadvantage would appear to be far less dangerous to the future of French-American relations and to the position of France and all the Western powers in the Far East than a further explosion of Annamese nationalism and French resort to military force in order to re-establish their control over the Annamese."[75]

European desk officers and other conservatives within the State Department opposed the proposal and urged caution in taking any action that would imply opposition to French policy. James Bonbright, the European office analyst charged with studying that plan, admitted on October 2 that such a scheme might be desirable if the situation in Vietnam got "further out of hand," but at the moment, he saw no need. Fundamental to his position were two long-standing tenets of the conservative outlook on Indochina. First, Bonbright had low regard for Vietnamese nationalism. Despite the information that had poured into Washington about the Viet Minh's strength, Bonbright asserted—

without marshalling evidence to support his claim—that he was "not convinced that it will necessitate a major military operation by the French to put down the revolt in their area." He warned that international mediation might ultimately harm the Vietnamese by giving them more authority than they could handle. "To my mind, the setting up of an international commission can only lead to one result—the eventual ejection of the French from Indo-China," Bonbright asserted. "In addition to being bad for the French and the Western powers generally, I think this would also be bad for the Indo-Chinese themselves." Second, Bonbright repeated old worries that any challenge to the French position in Indochina would invite dangerous meddling by other powers. By late 1945 the Soviet Union had replaced Japan as the most worrisome aspirant. Any move to set up an investigating commission would inevitably provoke a demand by Moscow to be included, Bonbright warned. Since American commitments to the United Nations would leave Washington little choice but to support such a request, he advised that it was best to prevent the entire issue from arising in the first place.[76]

The communist issue was becoming increasingly central to the conservative outlook on Indochina. Early reports on the Vietnamese revolution often noted the prominent role of communists among the Viet Minh leadership. OSS director William J. Donovan reported in August, for example, that the Viet Minh was "a 100% Communist party," and he told Truman early the following month that the Viet Minh was "composed of strictly left-wing elements," having excluded the Vietnamese Kuomintang (the Vietnamese Nationalist Party, or Viet Nam Quoc Dan Dang) and other "republican factions." In earlier months concern about communist inroads in Indochina had not always amounted to arguments in favor of supporting French restoration. Indeed, during 1944 it had been the liberals, more than conservatives, who worried about communist advances in Indochina, usually arguing that French repression would fuel communism and that sensible steps toward independence would lessen its appeal. In the final weeks of 1945, however, conservatives began to challenge liberals for control over the communist issue, arguing that the Viet Minh might represent a threatening offshoot of Soviet foreign policy. From Moscow embassy analyst George Kennan honed the argument that the Soviet Union favored independence for Indochina in order to open the region to communist penetration. "We are of the opinion that the USSR now entertains a greater interest in Indochina than it did during the course of the war," wrote Kennan, noting that Mao Zedong's advances meant that the forces of international communism might soon arrive at China's southern border and exert direct influence in Indochina. Kennan explained away the utter lack of evidence of Soviet interest in Indochina by surmising that Moscow wanted to keep its direct involvement in Indochina to a minimum and to rely instead on the Chinese and French communist parties to act on its behalf.[77]

Sudden sensitivity to communism in Indochina stemmed partly from the Truman administration's surging anxiety about Soviet expansionism in the last quarter of 1945. As historian Marc Trachtenberg has shown, many U.S. leaders turned dramatically against the Soviet Union at precisely this time. To be sure, American policymakers had already come to regard the Soviet Union as an expansionist power by the middle of the year, but most had also concluded that Washington and Moscow could avert a direct clash by respecting spheres of influence in Eastern and Western Europe. This relatively harmonious situation came to a crashing end, Trachtenberg argues, in the fall as the Soviet Union began probing for opportunities in Iran and Turkey, countries that Americans were unwilling to concede to Soviet hegemony. By January 1946 Truman lamented that a Soviet invasion of Turkey—and worse—seemed imminent. "Unless Russia is faced with an iron fist and strong language another war is in the making," he wrote.[78] Under these circumstances, it is hardly surprising that Americans would overgeneralize their fears and see dangers even in remote places like Indochina.

Washington's mounting sensitivity to communism in France and the Far East had the effect of weakening liberal schemes for American mediation in Indochina. In this way, the conservatives succeeded in defeating liberal bids in the wake of the Vietnamese revolution to turn U.S. policy back in the direction of internationalization schemes that might ultimately challenge the principle of unconditional French sovereignty. Bonnet seems to have understood Washington's basic reliability on this point by late September. "It seems fairly clear," the ambassador reported to Paris, "that the current administration is, at bottom, favorably disposed toward the restoration of our sovereignty in Indochina even though it also wants to remain as far as possible, in the eyes of colonial natives as much as American anti-colonialists, free from the charge of having contributed actively ... to restoring colonial rule over territories that the war had momentarily liberated."[79] Bonnet's confidence was borne out a month later when Vincent, head of the State Department's Far Eastern office, delivered a speech to the Foreign Policy Association in New York—the first public statement of U.S. policy toward Southeast

Asia since the end of the Second World War. "This government does not question French sovereignty in that area," Vincent asserted, though he hastened to add that Washington had "no intention to assist or participate in forceful measures for the reimposition of control by the territorial sovereigns" in Southeast Asia. Most significant, Vincent unveiled a toothless mediation proposal, a far cry from the plan he had suggested a few weeks earlier. The United States, he said, would intervene diplomatically in Indochina only if asked by the parties directly involved.[80] Since Paris had no interest in such mediation, Vincent's proposal carried virtually no meaning.

The French government could take some solace, then, in the fact that the August Revolution had not provoked any dangerous new initiatives in Washington. Mounting Cold War tensions insulated them from any dramatic turn of U.S. policy against French interests. But the larger problem—American refusal to contemplate active support for French policy—remained and had, if anything, been exacerbated by the events of the autumn of 1945. Even conservatives who opposed the mediation scheme and were impressed by the scale of the upheaval in Vietnam showed little interest in moving away from the passive neutrality that had characterized American policy for months. "It is useless," the Francophile Bonbright asserted, "for the French to continually come to us for assistance in reestablishing ... authority." U.S. officials even hinted from time to time that American policy could still shift against French interests if Paris did not live up to its promises of liberal reform in Indochina. Dean Acheson, the undersecretary of state, asserted at the end of September that Washington had "no thought" of opposing the reestablishment of French control, but he hastened to add that "the willingness of the U.S. to see French control reestablished assumed that [the] French claim to have the support of the population is borne out by future events." Vincent also seemed to hold open the possibility of a shift in the U.S. attitude when he advised Lacoste in October that the French government should "handle the matter in a manner least calculated to arouse American public opinion" and to choose a "middle ground solution" that encompassed negotiations with Vietnamese nationalists.[81] French policymakers could hardly miss the implication of these words: the United States was nowhere close to providing the kinds of support that Paris so desperately wanted.

CHAPTER 3

Illusions of Autonomy

Officials in the French ministries responsible for Indochina looked optimistically to Great Britain for the help that Washington refused to provide as the Pacific war came to an end. Undeniably, London had sometimes held back from close cooperation. Observers in Paris noted that the British government had occasionally wavered on colonial questions, cultivating a distressing "reform liberalism" to mollify the United States. But French personnel were confident that the March 24 declaration and other promises of reform in Indochina had eased British reservations. Best of all, the arrival of British occupation forces seemed to herald the beginning of a concrete kind of assistance that, once begun, would take the issue away from politicians in distant capitals and place it in the hands of military men who would surely see sense in letting the French resume control as quickly as possible. French officials also drew confidence from the fact that the Truman administration had given its imprimatur to the British occupation. Washington could hardly complain, they reasoned, when the British began doing what every reasonable observer expected them to do: restore French power. "We can expect complete cooperation from the British command," the Foreign Ministry wrote, "because American agreement will be explicit."[1]

In the short term, French confidence proved well placed. During autumn 1945 the British government provided ships to transport French troops to the Far East. Meanwhile, British occupation forces under General Douglas D. Gracey moved boldly to suppress the Vietnamese revolution and actively supported the restoration of colonial rule. Even as British enthusiasm for these tasks disintegrated as the weeks passed, French authorities wielded sufficient power by early 1946 to control major population centers. The wobbly revolutionary apparatus collapsed before the advancing French. For all intents and purposes, colonial rule had returned to the south—a foothold that enabled French officials to negotiate with China for the recovery of the north in the first weeks of 1946. There, Ho's provisional government posed a much more serious obstacle to French plans. But French officials could breathe a sigh of relief that what had seemed almost impossible a year earlier—the restoration of a French military and administrative presence throughout Indochina—was rapidly coming into view.

French gains in early 1946 inaugurated a distinct, albeit brief, phase in the international history of Vietnam that stands apart from the rest of the story narrated in this book. At other points—prior to March 1946 and again after the outbreak of the Franco–Viet Minh war at the end of that year—the French government attached overriding importance to the need to change international perceptions and to secure foreign support. During those periods, officials worked above all to cast the Indochina situation in a way likely to attract British and especially American backing. In the intervening period, however, with new French forces and a revived administration operating on Indochinese soil, many policymakers insisted that their country did not depend on foreigners to achieve its objectives in Indochina. France, they assumed, could master the situation by itself—through negotiations with Ho Chi Minh or through a military campaign to crush the Viet Minh. While French officials differed sharply over which of those paths to take, they were unanimous in viewing the diplomatic challenge as far less urgent than it had been earlier. Rather than aggressively soliciting foreign backing, they now accepted international ambivalence as a fact of life that, while hardly ideal, did not threaten crucial French objectives. They found, in fact, that ambivalence could be managed in ways that would serve French interests.

Developments in 1947 would show that French confidence was built on illusion. With the outbreak of war against the Viet Minh, the need for international support would once again press urgently on French policymakers, as would the fact that France had failed in previous years to lay any solid foundation for international cooperation in Indochina. Indeed, even the British government, apparently so eager to restore French colonialism, quickly soured on the task and sought to distance itself as much as possible from French activities. The Americans, meanwhile, held to the neutral policy that had gelled at the end of the Pacific war. For a brief time during 1946, however, none of this seemed to matter much. French leaders believed that they were once again masters of Indochina's destiny.

OCCUPATION AND DISILLUSIONMENT

In the days before the occupation of southern Indochina began, few British officials devoted much attention to the political problems they might encounter in Indochina. Only M. Esler Dening, Mountbatten's political adviser and an astute observer of Southeast Asian affairs, pointed to the risk of British forces becoming embroiled in a fight with Vietnamese nationalists if they did not take care to avoid siding openly with France. "We should avoid at all costs laying ourselves open to the accusation that we are assisting the West to suppress the East," Dening pleaded on September 10, just before British troops began arriving in Saigon. "Such an accusation," he added, "will rise very readily to the lips of the Americans and Chinese and would be likely to create an unfavorable impression throughout Asia." But most British commentary discounted such dangers. A report on conditions within southern Indochina prepared for British occupation forces in late August asserted that the "clamour for independence" came from only a "small minority," and that pro-independence propaganda spread by the Japanese had produced little effect due to a "lack of interest" among the Vietnamese. Except for a few individuals who had collaborated with Japan, the report said, the local population "would undoubtedly welcome the return of the European."[2]

British activities during the first days of the occupation reflected this confidence. British troops—a division of battle-weary Indian soldiers under the command of General Gracey, plus assorted air force and naval units—began by establishing an elaborate Saigon base that would eventually feature a bagpipe band, cinemas, and a brothel with segregated facilities for Europeans and Indians.[3] Then Gracey launched his bid to restore French control. An ardent colonialist who had served his entire career as an officer in the Indian Army, he had little sympathy for Vietnamese nationalists and moved decisively to put down the political agitation and street violence that had erupted in Saigon at the beginning of September. On September 21 Gracey proclaimed martial law. Although he vowed Britain's "strict impartiality" in local politics, he banned demonstrations, public meetings, and unauthorized carrying of weapons, warning that "wrong-doers" would be summarily shot.[4] Meanwhile, Gracey's troops rearmed hundreds of French soldiers who had been imprisoned by the Japanese six months earlier. The Viet Minh's Committee of the South, which had loosely governed the region over the previous weeks, fled the city as French colons reclaimed authority. Following a grisly massacre of more than 150 Europeans by enraged Vietnamese, Gracey encouraged French authorities to complete the takeover on September 24. An assortment of French soldiers and police, supported by Gracey's men, seized control of post offices, telegraph installations, and other city services in a coup d'état that restored colonial administration in Saigon.[5]

Still more British assistance followed. During October and November Indian troops, frequently supported by Japanese forces pressed into service, drove Viet Minh fighters from the Saigon area, fighting in frequent skirmishes. Casualty statistics suggest the intensity of the fighting. By November 9 the Indian division had suffered nineteen killed and sixty-eight wounded, while Japanese forces fighting on the British side had lost fifty-four dead and seventy-nine wounded. Meanwhile, Gracey's troops provided support for reorganized French forces, which took over the main burden of the fighting outside the immediate Saigon area. The first full division of French regulars arrived in late October, giving the French commander, General Philippe Leclerc, sufficient strength to mount operations in the Cochinchinese hinterland. Important provincial towns in the Mekong Delta and Vietnam's Central Plateau gradually fell to the French in November. Although precise amounts are difficult to calculate, it is clear that Gracey supplied Leclerc with an array of British equipment, including six hundred vehicles by mid-January 1946, with another thirty-two hundred promised over the coming months. Risking U.S. censure, Gracey also handed over Japanese and American gear for French use.[6]

Such naked support for French colonialism against a surprisingly robust Vietnamese nationalist movement ignited a firestorm of criticism in Britain and abroad as news of Gracey's activities spread. Within weeks, the controversy seemed to threaten the British government's relationship with the United States, its political standing at home, and its ability to manage Britain's Far Eastern empire. Most predictable, British officials grew fearful that British activities in Southeast Asia might push the United States back toward outspoken opposition to European colonialism. Momentarily in early 1946 U.S. hostility to British actions even seemed to endanger the whole principle of Anglo-American cooperation. Sterndale Bennett reported that U.S. anger might imperil London's chances of obtaining a $3.8 billion loan then under negotiation with Washington—a key part of the British government's plan for postwar recovery. Americans believed "that the position in Indo-China was getting much worse and might cause some trouble" in winning approval of the loan, Sterndale Bennett wrote after a conversation with U.S. embassy personnel in London.[7] U.S. warnings might have been mere bluff, and in any case the loan was duly signed. But the mere fact that one of the British government's most cherished postwar objectives could be linked to events in faraway Indochina left little doubt that Gracey's actions had taken on enormous stakes.

The British cabinet found another cause for alarm closer to home—in fact, within the very political party from which it sprang. The Labour cabinet that came to power in the July 1945 election took a relatively conservative approach in international affairs, stressing protection of Britain's traditional global interests and readily practicing what its critics to the left castigated as "power politics."[8] Yet the party could not ignore its rhetorical commitment to encouraging development and self-determination in the colonial world. Party activists had elaborated this vision through the wartime publications of the Fabian Colonial Society, an organization set up in 1940 to consider new approaches to imperial problems. In an April 1945 pamphlet indicative of the group's views, the society expressed hope for "far-reaching progress" in the colonies and called for an attitude of "crucial vigilance" to assure that old-guard imperialists did not derail the process.[9]

While many Labour politicians moved away from such language once the party assumed power, a minority remained true to that vision and applied steady pressure on the cabinet to maintain a progressive line in Southeast Asia. From October 1945 to January 1946 left-wing members of Parliament repeatedly placed cabinet ministers on the defensive by forcing them to answer for British activities in Indochina and the Dutch East Indies, where British imperial troops were also working to restore colonial rule against the wishes of a powerful nationalist movement. On October 24, for example, Foreign Secretary Ernest Bevin attempted to fend off criticism by asserting that the cabinet had no desire to see British forces "unnecessarily involved in the administration or in the political affairs of non-British territories." Bevin also tried to calm anxieties about French intentions by pointing to the March 24 declaration—a useful tool for British as well as American officials who defended pro-French policies. The declaration was, Bevin claimed, a sign that Paris planned to offer a "wide measure of autonomy in Indo-China." Already, he added with scant regard for actual events in Southeast Asia, "this liberal attitude on the part of the French Government has been reflected in the very conciliatory manner in which the local French representatives have dealt with the Annamite leaders."[10] Under similar questioning in the House of Commons, Philip Noel-Baker, the secretary of state for foreign affairs, showed equal determination to present British behavior in the best possible light. British forces had been engaged in a "purely military task" that had "nothing to do with the political or constitutional problems of [Indochina]," Noel-Baker claimed.[11]

Such assurances did not, however, assuage the concerns on the Labour party's left, and intraparty sniping continued. Indeed, as historian Kenneth O. Morgan has argued, foreign affairs was the one policymaking area in which the party was seriously divided during its tenure in power between 1945 and 1951. Few matters exposed this tension more clearly than British activities in support of French and Dutch colonialism. In October 1945, 58 of the 393 Labour members of Parliament sent the prime minister a letter angrily accusing the government of helping to restore repressive colonial rule in Indochina and the East Indies.[12] That position found support at all levels of the Labour hierarchy. Several trade unions adopted resolutions during the fall condemning government policy in Southeast Asia. Meanwhile Harold Laski, chairman of the party's executive committee, denounced government actions. "It is a matter of regret and bitter shame," Laski complained in November, "that British and Indian troops should be sent to restore tyranny in the Pacific areas."[13]

Stresses in the government's relationship with nationalists in Britain's own Asian possessions compounded the pressure to avoid close association with French colonialism. Within days of the British arrival in Saigon, nationalist leaders in India and other British territories in the Far East registered strong opposition to the suppression of Vietnamese nationalism. Criticism by Asian leaders not only embarrassed the Labour government but also raised the alarming prospect of a rift between London and the cohort of nationalists likely to achieve power as Britain moved ahead with plans to grant greater autonomy to its Asian possessions in the wake of the Second World War. Britain's use of Indian troops contributed heavily to the problem. Viet Minh propagandists moved quickly to exploit the bizarre spectacle of Asian soldiers under white orders suppressing a fellow Asian people in order to restore European colonialism. "Indian Soldiers!" proclaimed one Viet Minh leaflet distributed in Saigon, "India and Vietnam are in the same situation. Their people," it added, "must help each other in their struggle against the oppressors, British and French." Jawaharlal Nehru, the dominant figure within the Indian National Congress, saw a similar logic. Comparing Britain's role in Indochina and the East Indies to "the war of intervention which Fascist Italy and Nazi Germany waged in Spain," Nehru declared that Indians had watched "with growing anger, shame and helplessness that Indian troops should thus be used for doing Britain's dirty work against our friends who are fighting the same fight as we." Indian opposition became so vocal by mid-September that the British commander in chief in India refused to allow the subcontinent to be used as a transfer point for French troops going to Indochina.[14]

The problem only worsened as the autumn advanced. In October dockworkers in Ceylon refused to service French and Dutch ships headed for Indochina and the East Indies, forcing rerouting and delays. Meanwhile, Indian opposition to Britain's Indochina policy grew so powerful by the beginning of 1946 that British military planners began to foresee an apocalyptic scenario. The India Office in London predicted "strong pressure to release Indian troops from most, if not all, of the overseas military commitments they are now fulfilling" if at least the most controversial of those commitments—a category that obviously included Indochina—were not phased out. The possibility of sudden Indian refusal to participate in Britain's global military duties raised the nightmarish prospect that London would lack the manpower to fulfill its obligations throughout the Commonwealth and empire. "If we are unable to employ Indian troops outside India it will be necessary to reconsider our plans for deployment not only in South East Asia Command but throughout the world," the Joint Planning Staff warned in February 1946.[15]

With opposition to British actions in Southeast Asia mounting at home and abroad, the cabinet, Foreign Ministry, Chiefs of Staff, and other bureaucracies moved urgently to reevaluate British policy. "We have been faced with these problems with unexpected suddenness and . . . we are dealing with them piecemeal and empirically," Foreign Secretary Bevin complained in calling for fresh ideas in November.[16] The resulting deliberations never touched on the possibility of abandoning the French cause. Despite deepening political problems, study after study concluded that Britain still had a fundamental interest in seeing French control reestablished in Indochina. As before, British officials fixated on Indochina's importance to a regional system that included Malaya, Singapore, Burma, and India, territories that remained critical to Britain's postwar plans. "The security of Malaya depends on the defense of Burma, Siam, French Indo-China, Borneo and part of the Netherlands East Indies," the cabinet's Joint Planning Staff concluded. Indochina was, in fact, the key to the entire area. "If a hostile Power established itself in French Indo-China, naval and air forces based there would be able to control the South China Sea and dominate the approaches to Singapore," the Foreign Office maintained.[17]

Economic planners were equally adamant about the necessity of keeping Indochina within a stable regional order. Interconnectedness of regional economies, they believed, meant that chaos in one area would beget chaos elsewhere. Since Southeast Asian territories had similar, interdependent economies, they "must to a large extent sink or swim together with the general trend of world supply and demand," Ministry of Production experts asserted.[18] If some British officials viewed this problem with their eyes on the long-term prosperity of Malaya and Burma, others concentrated on the near-term economic crisis that worried them most. British anxieties about rice shortages mounted dramatically in late 1945 as the full extent of the problem became clear. Before the war, the world's three leading rice-producing countries—Burma, Indochina, and Siam—had together exported nearly six million tons annually, primarily to other colonial areas in South and Southeast Asia. Because of dislocation and destruction under Japanese occupation, production in those three nations by early 1946 was barely capable of satisfying domestic needs. Indeed, transportation problems, Japanese requisitions, and climatic variations combined to cause catastrophic famine in northern Indochina throughout 1945 and early 1946. By British estimates rice production in southern Indochina fell from 922,000 tons in 1943 to a mere 61,000 tons over the first nine months of 1945.[19]

Most important, Indochina's rice crisis seemed directly connected to the stability of Britain's Asian territories. Malaya and especially India imported huge quantities of Southeast Asian rice, and any shortfall in Indochinese production, combined with other dislocations in the postwar period, raised the specter of popular unrest that could place new economic and military burdens on Britain—a horrible scenario from the vantage point of British officials already struggling to cope with massive obligations amid straightened circumstances. "Even before the war, food supplies in many rice-consuming countries were marginal," wrote British food minister Tom Williams. "The effect of a reduction in supplies is therefore all the more serious," he added. Under the best conceivable scenario, British specialists expected that Indochina would not resume exporting rice until 1946. To ease the crisis, British authorities sought close cooperation with French administrators to revive Indochinese rice production as quickly as possible and assigned a high priority to rice transports, supplying all available landing craft and posting guards on French barges and trucks.[20]

British policymakers never wavered from the view that the French colonial administration should be restored as quickly as possible in order to begin work at once on these critical strategic and economic problems. To be sure, many studies of postwar problems in Southeast Asia insisted that France must concede a degree of self-rule in Indochina to alleviate nationalist unrest over the long term. But all of them asserted explicitly or implicitly that only the colonial power, with its resources, sophistication, and experience, would be capable of resolving such crucial problems with the speed necessary to avert a regional catastrophe. Southeast Asian nationalists "do not yet offer alternative governments," stated one Foreign Ministry study. "We cannot, in the name of liberty, allow territories which we control to fall into chaos and general unrest, nor such weakness and instability to create danger spots."[21] The British government desired stability above all and continued to regard French colonialism, whatever its drawbacks, as the best bet to promote it.

None of this meant, however, that British officials were content to proceed with the brazenly pro-French policy that Gracey had pursued during his first weeks in Indochina. Surging domestic and international criticism of Gracey's actions dictated that London find ways to insulate itself from the hazards of close association with France. The most obvious method was to limit direct British involvement in the suppression of Vietnamese guerrilla activity. As tensions in Saigon reached the boiling point in late September, Mountbatten ordered Gracey to restrict his activities to the Saigon region. In other areas, Mountbatten instructed Gracey to rely on rearmed French soldiers and, if necessary, Japanese troops to carry out police functions. British forces would intervene only in extraordinary circumstances. "Problems connected with the independence of Indo-China must be dealt with by the French, in the same way as the British had to deal with such problems in Burma, Malaya, and the Dutch in the Netherlands East Indies," Mountbatten insisted.[22]

Within Gracey's increasingly circumscribed field of operation, Mountbattten insisted that British forces avoid provoking the Vietnamese. An exchange between Gracey and Mountbatten at the end of October illustrates the growing alarm among British authorities in Kandy about developments in the Saigon area. Gracey's troops distributed a leaflet advising ordinary Vietnamese that the great powers had "no sympathy for those who attempt to attain their ends at the expense of bloodshed." It warned the Vietnamese not to be "misled by the extremist and irresponsible elements who are trying to continue this useless fight against the terrible might of tanks, aircraft, guns, ships, soldiers, sailors, and airmen." "Do you want a life of destruction, of misery, of famine and of unhappiness for yourselves and for your families?" it asked. In Kandy Mountbatten chastised Gracey for his confrontational approach. It was "most indiscreet," Mountbatten complained, "for a British Commander to put on record that 'tanks, ships, aircraft and guns' are massed against virtually unarmed people, and that 'useless misery' might ensue." The supreme allied commander insisted that, at a minimum, French authorities should have signed the leaflet, "for we must not further embarrass H.M. Government by making it appear that we are strongly threatening the Independence Movement." In an unusual handwritten addendum, Mountbatten added that he was "most distressed" to learn that Gracey's troops had been burning down houses. "Cannot you give such unsavory jobs (if they really are military necessities) to the French in future?" he asked.[23]

While trying to shift responsibility onto the French, the British government also responded to the embarrassing situation in Indochina by taking greater account of nationalist grievances. For its part, the Foreign Office moved in September to heighten British sensitivity to local politics by appointing new advisers to help British commanders in Saigon, Batavia, and Bangkok understand the unrest. A month later, London appointed a high commissioner to manage British policy across the region as a whole. At the same time, Mountbatten and even Gracey, apparently impressed by the scope of the political problem he confronted, urged the French to make conciliatory gestures. Mountbatten, echoing concerns most often voiced by American liberals, pressed French officials to announce further reforms in Indochina. To promote harmony and to "demonstrate our impartiality," Gracey's new political adviser, Harry Brain, mediated a series of meetings between Viet Minh representatives and the French high commissioner for Cochinchina. These talks achieved little beyond short-lived truces, but the role of

British officials in arranging them suggests their growing aversion to a naked policy of suppression.[24]

British policymakers also sought to ease criticism by implicating the United States as much as possible in British behavior. By embedding Gracey's activities within a broader Allied framework that included the United States, officials hoped to encourage the illusion, for public relations purposes, that British repression in Indochina was geared not to restore a fellow colonial power to its prewar position but to carry out a global strategy for disarming defeated enemies and restoring stability in Southeast Asia. Under hostile questioning in the House of Commons, Bevin emphasized that Gracey's forces were working principally to carry out duties that benefited all of the victorious powers in Asia: the disarmament of Japanese troops and the evacuation of Allied prisoners of war. Unfortunately, Bevin asserted, "in fulfilling the primary task entrusted to him" by Allied governments, Gracey had come under attack by Vietnamese nationalists and had responded with steps "necessary to ensure the proper execution of his task."[25]

While attempting in all these ways to ease criticism of Britain's role in Indochina, British policymakers also worked eagerly from mid-September to bring about the definitive solution to their problems: the full restoration of French control. Once sufficient French forces were in place to take over from Gracey's troops, officials understood, British forces could be withdrawn. Political controversies swirling around the British government would then presumably come to an end. The Joint Planning Staff in London laid out the logic in a report dated September 21, even before Gracey's coup sharply increased criticism of British behavior. "From the political point of view," the report stated, "the sooner British forces can be withdrawn from Indo-China, the better." Immediately after the coup, Mountbatten urged the Chiefs of Staff in London to give "over-riding priority" to the shipment of French troops, especially the twenty-six-thousand-man 9th Colonial Infantry Division awaiting transport to the Far East. "Every day of delay in providing sufficient French troops to enable Leclerc to take over responsibility," Mountbatten wrote, "magnifies the danger that British/Indian troops may become involved in large scale fighting on French territory."[26]

With this horrendous possibility looming, British authorities concentrated scarce resources on Indochina and, by the end of November, had restored a robust French force capable of operating independently. British success depended partly on finding indirect ways of exploiting American resources. British negotiators succeeded in October in convincing the U.S.

War Department to allow Gracey to use U.S.-supplied Dakota transport aircraft in Indochina as long as operations were linked to the primary task of disarming the Japanese.[27] Far more important, London allocated eight Liberty ships leased from the United States to help transport the 9th Colonial Infantry Division to Indochina during October. Since the British government paid for the ships, it could use them as it saw fit without fear of American censure, although some American crew members would later complain bitterly about abetting European colonialism.[28] The growing French presence made it possible for French forces to replace British troops in suppressing Vietnamese nationalism outside the Saigon area. By the beginning of December, at least 21,500 French troops were available in Indochina, with another division due to arrive from Europe in mid-January. Moreover, the pipeline of British supplies gushed as never before. By mid-March Britain had handed over or sold to the French more than twenty-five hundred tons of weapons, twenty-seven hundred tons of ammunition, and almost four thousand vehicles.[29]

Through all these efforts the British accomplished their objective. The new British consul in Saigon, Ernest W. Meiklereid, reported in mid-February 1946 that the French reoccupation could be considered complete, having been accomplished "very much faster than might have been expected." Meanwhile, Gracey's troops made quick progress around the turn of the year with their formal mission in Indochina, the processing of Japanese troops. After careful preparation, they began disarming and concentrating the sixty thousand Japanese troops in southern Indochina at the beginning of December. By February all but a few thousand had been rounded up in the Cap Saint Jacques (Vung Tau) area, the seaside resort east of Saigon. Meanwhile, the War Office in London and South East Asia Command laid down a tight schedule for the withdrawal of British troops. Gracey and most of his Indian division departed Indochina at the end of January 1946, leaving behind a small "interservice mission" to carry out a limited set of duties. The Chiefs of Staff took no chances that remaining troops would be drawn back into political entanglements, ordering them to offer no "direct or indirect assistance to the French forces" without explicit approval from South East Asia Command and to refrain from any action "against local inhabitants except when defensively necessary."[30]

Once most British troops began withdrawing, policymakers hoped to go further by dissolving all remaining links between Britain and the French presence in Indochina. In late January Mountbatten attempted to set the process in motion by asking London for permission to announce that Indochina would no longer form part of SEAC the moment Gracey's command left Saigon. Only U.S. objections stood in the way of the British government's rush to shed its responsibilities. The U.S. Joint Chiefs of Staff, which still shared formal control over SEAC policymaking, worried that French forces, if left on their own, would not be capable of managing the complex business of processing and repatriating Japanese troops, a duty that had been assigned to Britain under agreements worked out at the highest levels during the Potsdam conference. In Saigon Brain suspected that American resistance was motivated, too, by a fear of being associated with the handover of Indochina to the French and the risk that the French would undertake a severe crackdown once Britain's restraining influence had been removed.[31]

The U.S. position, ironically now insistent that Britain keep its authority over Indochina, predictably angered the British Chiefs of Staff, who charged that the United States "wished to have it both ways" by ending its own day-to-day involvement in SEAC out of fear of angering Asian nationalists while denying Britain the same right. As the controversy dragged on, British commanders grew increasingly anxious about further implication in French repression. In February Meiklereid captured mounting British anxiety in a report complaining of "somewhat medieval" interrogation tactics and "gestapo methods" practiced by French Sûreté agents increasingly active alongside French troops. By the first of March, the situation seemed only to worsen. British observers watched anxiously as French-instigated rioting broke out in Saigon. Meanwhile, they became aware that the French military was preparing advances against the Viet Minh in the south and a seaborne landing in the north—moves that, far more than any to date, promised to cast French rule in an unflattering light. At the end of February, the British command, desperate for any formula to dissociate itself, accepted a compromise specifying that SEAC would retain jurisdiction over Indochina only "for the limited purpose of co-ordinating policy in respect of the disarmament and evacuation of the Japanese." In all other respects, the British were off the hook.[32]

To make sure that its critics noticed this fact, the British military launched a public relations campaign stressing that the Indochina mission had come to a successful conclusion without undue interference in Vietnamese politics. At the time of the first withdrawals in January, the Chiefs of Staff instructed Mountbatten to issue a declaration asserting Britain's limited role in Indochina, describing rapid French progress in assuming control over local administration, and announcing the start of the pullout of Indian troops—all themes that British leaders had stressed

Illusions of Autonomy

in Parliament over the fall and early winter as criticism of British behavior had mounted. The Chiefs of Staff also urged "due publicity" for the removal of British troops "to impress upon world opinion that having completed our tasks we were leaving the country." At a January 27 ceremony in Saigon marking his departure, Gracey assured his audience that his mission in Indochina had been a "great success." Meanwhile, Gracey refused to accept decorations from the French military—a gesture calculated to impress upon international opinion that the British occupation had never been intended to serve French interests. A month later the Chiefs of Staff ordered as much publicity as possible for the decision to turn over virtually all authority to the French.[33]

British leaders expressed cautious confidence that they had escaped from Indochina without incurring lasting damage from the political hazards they had encountered there. A buoyant Mountbatten even declared in mid-March that Britain had come out ahead because it had garnered the "good will of both the authorities and the civil population"—a statement that presumably referred to Vietnamese elites who collaborated with French colonialists. "Our own position has never been better," Mountbatten asserted, noting an "enormous possibility of cashing in" by exploiting new trade opportunities.[34] On the whole, however, British officials wanted nothing more to do with Indochina. Increasingly aware of Britain's economic difficulties, sensitive to political risks in the Far East, and attuned to growing Cold War dangers closer to home, policymakers in 1946 strongly emphasized the need to scale back Britain's commitments in the area and to rely on the United States to defend long-term British interests in the Far East. In the immediate aftermath of the Second World War, British policymakers had seen no alternative but to depart momentarily from that principle. They had recognized that they simply could not count on Washington to act as British leaders desired on critical issues like Indochina. But British involvement had come at an extravagant material and, unexpectedly, political cost, which made further endeavors of that sort extremely undesirable. In the future, British leaders saw little alternative to obtaining what had so far eluded them: U.S. support.

THE REORIENTATION OF FRENCH POLICYMAKING

London's determination to withdraw as quickly as possible from Indochina left the French military scrambling in late 1945 and early 1946 to extract maximum assistance before it was left on its own.

Leclerc, the new French commander in the Far East, and Massigli, the French ambassador in London, pressed British authorities to allocate additional shipping to the task of ferrying French troops to the Far East and demanded loans of scarce equipment that French forces lacked. Meanwhile, French officials attempted to delay the departure of British troops as long as possible. The command in Paris knew that British policymakers had begun planning in early November to withdraw as soon as the task of disarming the Japanese was complete. Alarmed, General Alphonse Juin, de Gaulle's senior military adviser in Paris, urged diplomatic intervention in London to make the case that a premature British departure could leave France alone in a "particularly critical situation"—shorthanded for the twin tasks of maintaining internal order and completing the repatriation of the Japanese. The French command worried not only about insufficient numbers but also about low morale among conscripts who would face difficult fighting conditions and would likely resent the job of suppressing a people fighting for its freedom. So desperate were French officers to keep the British in Indochina that Field Marshal Lord Alanbrooke, a member of the Chiefs of Staff who toured the Far East in November 1945, suspected the French might provoke an incident to force the British to "come to their rescue" if they moved too quickly toward withdrawal.[35]

The French command did not go that far, but Alanbrooke was correct in judging that d'Argenlieu and Leclerc would attempt to coerce British authorities into remaining active participants in the reimposition of French control. The best example concerns French behavior on the vexed question of where to draw the postwar border between Cambodia and Thailand (Siam), the independent kingdom to Indochina's west. With Japanese connivance the Thai government had seized the Cambodian provinces of Battambang and Seamreap in 1941, claiming that the region had formed an integral part of Thailand before the French colonial conquest in the late nineteenth century. Following the Second World War, the French government sought to reannex the territories and demanded that Britain, the most powerful diplomatic and military presence in Thailand, lend support. As on the broader question of French sovereignty in Indochina, London had little difficulty determining that its interests lay in supporting French claims. The British government wished to gratify a close ally while weakening an ambitious Thai regime that shared few British objectives in Southeast Asia. At the same time, however, British officials saw good reason to avoid conspicuous involvement in the Battambang–Seamreap question, a complicated affair that threatened to reopen old colonial wounds and cast Britain in an unfavorable light with Asian public opinion.

In mid-November 1945 d'Argenlieu decided that the moment was ripe to force a resolution to the matter while there was still a prospect of capitalizing on British support. Never averse to coercive tactics, d'Argenlieu sought to present Mountbatten with a fait accompli. Without asking for British approval, the high commissioner ordered a group of French officers to parachute into the area to begin reasserting French control. D'Argenlieu justified the move by insisting that the Thai government was using its control over the region to undermine French rule in Cambodia and Cochinchina, notably by providing Vietnamese insurgents with weapons. Mountbatten responded angrily, accusing the French of violating occupation agreements painstakingly negotiated in earlier months. But the French ploy worked. Desperate to avoid any new controversies in Indochina, Mountbatten decided to tolerate the French officers and to "regularize" their presence by placing them temporarily under the aegis of the British command in Bangkok, where South East Asia Command maintained a separate occupation authority analogous to Gracey's headquarters in Saigon. Fear of further unilateral French action, including even an all-out French invasion of Battambang and Seamreap, also contributed to the Foreign Office's decision around the same time to address the territorial question in ongoing Anglo-Thai negotiations covering a range of questions. To French delight a treaty signed on January 1, 1946, included a declaration of Britain's refusal to recognize the Cambodian annexation.[36]

French officials obtained a similar kind of unenthusiastic support in early 1946 for their efforts to recover a far more important piece of territory—the half of Indochina above the sixteenth parallel. They had watched helplessly since September as tens of thousands of Chinese troops under General Lu Han, ultimately totaling more than 180,000, flooded into the region and established an occupation characterized by pillage, looting, rape, and meddling in local politics. Chinese troops not only seemed determined to prop up puppet nationalist organizations (notably the Vietnamese Kuomintang, the Viet Nam Quoc Dan Dang) to rival the Viet Minh but also barred French administrators from resuming their duties. Moreover, Lu Han refused to allow French authorities any role in the surrender of Japanese forces and outlawed the French flag everywhere. Even after Lu Han indicated in early December that he was willing to negotiate a withdrawal, Chinese activities continued to cause deep anxiety. In January 1946 d'Argenlieu noted with alarm that Chinese troops were busily tearing down fortifications along the Yunnan-Tonkin border, an activity that seemed to imply Chinese determination to assure access to Indochinese territory in the years ahead. Meanwhile, Lu Han's unwillingness to permit the economic integration of northern and southern Indochina stunted economic recovery and prolonged the Tonkin famine by preventing shipments of Cochinchinese rice to the north. All in all, Leclerc judged the Chinese occupation "a true scandal," while Pechkoff, at his post in Chungking, likened Chinese depredations to "the passing of a cyclone."[37]

Though occasionally tempted to take military action against the Chinese occupiers, French officials recognized that their country was too weak to contemplate such a course. The only possible solution was, as Leclerc put it, "a very vigorous diplomatic action by France" to try "at all costs" to limit the damage from the Chinese occupation and to end it as soon as possible.[38] Negotiations with Lu Han and the Chungking government opened in December 1945 but stalled several times as Chinese negotiators demanded exorbitant concessions. They insisted not only that the French government pay a steep monthly sum for the upkeep of Chinese occupation forces but also that Paris grant China special economic privileges in Indochina on a permanent basis.

While discussing these terms, French representatives desperately sought British backing. Above all, they wanted assistance in pressing Chungking to permit the economic reintegration of Indochina, a key step, in the French view, toward ending the occupation and restoring French control. Determined for their own reasons to restore traditional trade patterns in the region, British authorities responded positively. Around the beginning of 1946, British mediators helped arrange deliveries of Cochinchinese rice to the north. They also helped to convince Chinese authorities to permit shipments of supplies for disarmed French troops in Tonkin and southeastern China and even to hand over weapons to enable the roughly twenty-five thousand French nationals in Hanoi to defend themselves. As on the Cambodia issue, however, British assistance was grudging at best. British commanders accepted French requests for assistance largely out of a sense that quick restoration of French control would lessen the chance of British troops becoming involved in chaos above the sixteenth parallel. "The easier we make the French task in Northern F.I.C.," Gracey wrote on the day of his departure from Saigon, "the quicker we will be able to leave the French entirely to it." Intelligence reports expressed contradictory views about the staying power of the Ho Chi Minh government, but British commanders had little doubt that France, as one study phrased it, would be required to conduct "extensive operations against strong guerrilla resistance" once its forces began operating in Tonkin.[39]

The Franco-British relationship with respect to the Cambodian territories and northern Indochina reveals much about the state of French policymaking by the first weeks of 1946. On the subject that mattered most to the provisional government—progress toward the recovery of French territory—it had achieved decisive results. By pressuring the British government, playing on its anxieties about the Far Eastern situation, and making maximum use of the concessions and assistance it offered, French officials had attained objectives that had seemed impossibly distant a year before. Below the sixteenth parallel, French administration and military power had returned behind a temporary shield provided by Britain. Elsewhere, the situation inspired at least cautious optimism. Not only was France on the road to recovering the Cambodian territories, but officials also considered the recovery of the north to be increasingly within their grasp. All this was testament to the determined yet flexible policy executed by the small group of policymakers who concerned themselves with Indochinese affairs—a striking display of diplomatic effectiveness in a period of overwhelming French weakness.

The Franco-British relationship also, though, reveals underlying failures of French policy that rendered the provisional government's accomplishments incomplete. Paris, it is critical to underscore, had obtained what it needed from Britain (active support) as well as from Washington (noninterference) more through manipulation, opportunism, and coincidence of policy priorities than by genuinely convincing either government of the soundness of its methods or aims in Indochina. Without doubt, both the London bureaucracy and conservative policymakers in Washington believed that their nations' interests would be served by a French recovery of Indochina. But the French government had failed to translate that overlap of interests into sustained support. Indeed, the British government, France's boldest supporter during 1945, had distanced itself from French policy by the start of 1946, while the Truman administration, unable to resolve conflicting interests in Southeast Asia, kept aloof from the entire problem. Both governments harbored serious doubts about French policy and feared guilt by association in the eyes of the Asian public and their domestic constituencies. Whatever their successes in attaining short-term goals, then, French leaders had failed to cast the Indochina problem in a way that would attract the political, economic, and military aid that, according to their calculations, France would ultimately require.

While British policymakers struggled to disengage from the area, Washington clung to neutrality. On the Battambang–Siam Reap issue, the State Department gratified Paris by repeatedly declaring its opposition to Thailand's wartime annexation, which U.S. officials regarded as an illegal act undertaken with Japanese connivance. But the Truman administration qualified this position by asserting hopes that the two sides would peacefully redraw the Thai-Cambodian border at a later date to take account of demographic realities. On the question of northern Indochina, the United States offered even less. The State Department refused to act as an intermediary between Paris and Chungking and, whenever French diplomats pressed the matter, suggested that they take up their grievances directly with Chinese authorities. French observers suspected the Truman administration of secretly urging Chiang to hold onto northern Indochina, at least temporarily, so that Washington and Chungking could achieve greater political and economic control in the area. In fact, U.S. motives were more mundane. Like their British counterparts, U.S. officials wished to avoid implication in the French repression at a time of heightened anticolonial agitation in the Far East. Reports from Charles S. Reed, the newly appointed U.S. consul in Saigon, fed Washington's anxieties by stressing the unpredictable, irresponsible, and even dangerous character of the French reconquest. On March 1, for example, Reed reported that the French army appeared to be responsible for persistent rioting and attacks against Vietnamese nationalists in Saigon. Such behavior, the consul cautioned, was likely "a preview of what may well happen when operations begin in [the] north."[40]

These failures to win sustained foreign assistance receded into the background, however, as French power grew in all parts of Indochina during the first weeks of 1946. In the south, the arrival of another French division and various smaller units emboldened Leclerc to press his pacification campaign in the Cochinchinese countryside. In the north, negotiators took a key step toward recovering French control on February 28, when they accepted Chungking's onerous terms—payment of China's occupation costs plus various economic concessions—in return for the withdrawal of Chinese forces by the end of March. French officials lamented the lopsidedness of the agreement but contented themselves with the bottom-line result. The deal, as one Foreign

Ministry study phrased it, "permits the reestablishment of French authority in northern Indochina, without which we will lose all influence in Asia."[41]

The agreement also carried the advantage of ending French dependence on foreign powers to settle Indochina's fate. With the Chinese preparing to depart, the French government had successfully restored the principle—if not yet the reality—of French sovereignty in all parts of Indochina and seemed capable for the first time since at least 1940 of determining Indochina's destiny independently, an important breaking point that ushered in a roughly ten-month phase distinct from the rest of the 1944–1950 period. From February 1946 to the outbreak of the Franco–Viet Minh war at the end of the year, policymakers turned inward, hopeful of mastering Indochina on their own without catering first and foremost to the opinions and interests of other governments. With the period of overriding dependence on foreigners apparently over, French officials ceased viewing Indochina as primarily a diplomatic problem.

The shift did not occur all at once. Colonial Minister Paul Giacobbi detected the pivotal moment as early as November 1945, when he judged that France had gained a sufficient foothold in the south to resist any U.S. effort to enforce mediation between Paris and Vietnamese nationalists. "We have demonstrated, through our display of force and through the acceptance, even support, of other powers, that we are not, as the Annamites believed, a defeated people," Giacobbi wrote as the first large military units shipped from France began to operate around Saigon. Another key moment of transition came at the end of January, by which time French forces were fighting successfully in the Mekong Delta and, perhaps more important, French commanders recognized that they could no longer count on unstinting British help. In Saigon British officials noticed the shift in French attitudes. "Official policy has been recently promulgated in French circles here that this country is French, not Anglo-French," Brigadier M.S.K. Maunsell, the British commander who remained in Saigon after Gracey's departure, reported on February 3. In place of earlier French eagerness to keep as many responsibilities as possible in British hands, French authorities now showed an "urgent desire," as Maunsell put it, to take over all military duties. The French command went as far as to cut the British out of the decision-making loop. As Leclerc prepared in late February to land French troops in Haiphong, he did his best to keep the impending operation secret from British officials, who, Leclerc knew, would be anxious about a Sino-French confrontation. When British officers learned of the landing, Leclerc dismissed British concerns, assuring Meiklereid that SEAC "would not be involved in any additional responsibility" because of French actions above the sixteenth parallel. French forces, he suggested, had the matter entirely in hand.[42]

The turn toward self-reliance rested above all on the French military's expanding mastery of Indochina. Certainly, there remained many causes for concern, not least the hostility of both Chinese occupation forces and Vietnamese nationalists above the sixteenth parallel. Chaos surrounding the French landings at Haiphong left no doubt that hazards persisted. Chinese troops occupying the city, lacking orders concerning the French arrival, shelled French ships attempting to put troops ashore, igniting an exchange that resulted in sixty French casualties and substantial destruction in the city. Still, the two sides quickly negotiated a cease-fire, and thirteen thousand French soldiers occupied the city within five days, giving Leclerc a sturdy toehold for the recovery of the Red River Delta. The symbolic high point of the French return ensued on March 18, when a column of twelve hundred French troops paraded into Hanoi, greeted by an overjoyed French population.[43]

Confidence in the military situation stemmed not only from such operational successes but also from the high command's calculations that France had sufficient resources to maintain control over the long run. On this matter, too, the French position remained delicate. As Mountbatten observed in March, morale and discipline among French troops remained low. French conscripts, he noted, had shipped out to Indochina expecting to participate, however belatedly, in a war against Japan. Instead, they found themselves doing battle against the "maquis of the Annamites," a noxious duty for troops who considered themselves the embodiment of France's own liberation struggle. Financial problems and troop shortages also weighed heavily in French calculations. Plans drafted in early 1946 called for a force of seventy-five thousand in Indochina over the near term, a number that General Juin considered unsustainable in view of the simultaneous necessities of controlling costs, meeting military obligations elsewhere in the world, and repatriating the ten thousand or so French troops who had been in Indochina for more than five years. Nevertheless, Juin was increasingly confident that these problems could be managed. The general reckoned that French resources permitted a force of at least forty-five thousand for the years to come—enough, he wrote, to "assure peace" in Indochina as long as the government encouraged development of new

Illusions of Autonomy 123

air-mobile capabilities that would allow smaller forces to act with greater effect.[44]

If military control permitted the French government to act more autonomously in Indochina, it did not provide much guidance about what precisely French policy should be with respect to the principal remaining challenge in Indochina. How should France cope with the demands of Indochinese revolutionaries, above all Ho Chi Minh's government in Hanoi? Clearly, Paris had to reckon seriously with the Democratic Republic of Vietnam, which exercised far more power and influence in the north than in the south. But how should this be done? Should France undertake ambitious reforms to accommodate nationalist demands for greater self-rule? Or should it drive a hard bargain, refusing to entertain meaningful concessions? Each view had its champions, and as time passed, the French political and policymaking elite became increasingly polarized into two distinct groups. Each group, it is important to underscore, shared the same goal: to take advantage of the government's newfound freedom of action to place French rule in Indochina on a permanent footing. But their preferred tactics—and, of course, the precise degree of control that France would retain in the end—differed substantially. The debate between the reformers and the hard-line colonialists came strongly to the fore as France recovered control over Indochina during 1946. At the end of the year, the hardliners would prevail, sparking the war of colonial reconquest that lasted until 1954. As the debate began in early 1946, however, the reformers carried the day, a temporary victory that further diminished the diplomatic and military dimensions that had dominated French policymaking until that point.

To understand the cleavage among French leaders over Indochina, it is necessary to return briefly to 1944 and 1945. At that time, as discussed earlier, Free French policymaking with respect to Indochina—as with foreign and colonial policy more generally—lay in the hands of a small circle of political leaders (especially Charles de Gaulle), colonial experts, military officers, and diplomats, all of whom agreed on the necessity of restoring French sovereignty as a matter of high national priority. Within this group individuals entertained differing visions of precisely how French rule should be reconstituted, just as Free French leaders held contrasting ideas about how to recast the French empire more generally following the war. The 1944 Brazzaville Conference had highlighted a significant divide between one set of colonial officials, notably Henri Laurentie and other bureaucrats in the Free French capital of Algiers, who favored a federalized empire and others, especially the colonial governors from around the empire, who envisaged perpetuation of the highly centralized structure that France, with its assimilationist colonial traditions and romantic notions of republican indivisibility, had long maintained. This division did not produce much in the way of sustained debate, however, and colonial reform remained a low-profile issue. In connection with Indochina it arose hardly at all. For several reasons Indochina's future relationship to France remained merely a latent source of discord.

In the first place, different points of view within the bureaucracy failed to resonate with public opinion or with the reemerging political parties. As a result, there was little pressure on the specialists to push the pace of debate over Indochina's long-term destiny. Left free to operate as they saw fit, Indochina policy makers unanimously emphasized the simple goal of recovering the territory and showed no inclination to open thorny political questions that could complicate an endeavor that was already enormously challenging. Even if they had wanted to address long-term reform plans, policymakers lacked up-to-date information about political conditions within the country and the demands of local nationalists. Advocates of reform thus saw just as many reasons to postpone debate as their opponents. Indecision about long-range plans also carried another advantage. In their diplomatic campaign aimed at winning Allied support, French officials sometimes found it helpful to stress their government's uncompromising determination to recover Indochina, while at other points, they found advantage in emphasizing their country's intentions to carry out sweeping liberal reforms after the war. A clear choice would have diminished this flexibility and thereby deprived Paris of a useful diplomatic tool.

The final reason for the paucity of debate about Indochina's future status before 1946 is the peculiar ability of Charles de Gaulle to bridge divisions over colonial policy and preserve a sense of unity. Renowned for his boldness and unbridled dedication to French *grandeur*, the general was curiously ambivalent on certain colonial questions. To be sure, he staunchly defended the principle of French sovereignty over the full extent of the pre-1940 empire and tolerated no challenge from Vichy, the Axis powers, or his ostensible allies in London and Washington. His rhetoric reverberated with the themes of restoration and continuity. On the subtler question of the empire's future configuration, however, he frequently spoke of the need for reform and paid vague lip service to federalist ideas. De Gaulle's sponsorship of the Brazzaville meeting, as well as his close association with the March 24 declaration on Indochina and other assertions of liberal intentions in the colonies, positioned him as a reformer, as did his close association with Laurentie, the chief advocate of federalization within the colonial bureaucracy.[45] Undoubtedly, de Gaulle's ambivalence, like the indecision of the bureaucracy more generally, was partly instrumental. By avoiding clear positions, the general preserved his ability to tailor his message for maximum effect—an indispensable asset at a time when Indochina policymaking was almost entirely a matter of influencing other governments. But de Gaulle's ambivalence also reflected his unique ability to appeal to conflicting currents in French political life. More than anything else, the general dominated Free French politics by harnessing simultaneous impulses for renewal and restoration—*la France renouvelé* and *la France éternelle*. Under de Gaulle it seemed that both could be accomplished at the same time.

The defeat of Japan produced the first cracks in French unity on Indochinese questions. Reform-minded administrators in the Colonial Ministry urged that the moment had arrived to give substance to the vague promises of liberalization made during the war. Led by Laurentie, the reformers proposed that the government issue a new statement elaborating on the March 24 declaration by spelling out specific liberalization plans. In meetings with journalists, Laurentie, now the Colonial Ministry's director of political affairs, advocated substantial concessions to Indochinese nationalists, including promises of Vietnamese unity and a high degree of autonomy. There was simply no alternative to dealing seriously with the nationalist tide sweeping Vietnam, he insisted. "However the Viet Minh may seem to us," Laurentie declared in September 1945, "there is no denying that the government's only possible policy today is to do business openly, not necessarily with them directly, but at least with the nationalist aspiration which they represent."[46]

As long as de Gaulle remained in power, however, Laurentie stood little chance of producing a breakthrough. The general reiterated the vague promises of March 24 but staunchly resisted any drift toward implementation of a concessionary policy. In fact, de Gaulle's actions during his final months in power suggest that he increasingly preferred a hard line in favor of defending French interests—that under pressure to choose, he would opt for restoration over renewal. De Gaulle scolded Laurentie for airing his liberal views in public and rejected calls for a new declaration of French plans. A new statement was, he wrote, "out of the question" since it would give the impression that France was "backing down." De Gaulle's decision in August to appoint the unyielding d'Argenlieu as high commissioner also revealed the general's determination to hold the line against reform. Colonial Ministry personnel had urged the appointment of a high commissioner known for "flexibility, patience, sincerity, political sense, moral probity, strength of purpose, [and] local knowledge"—qualities likely to promote fruitful negotiations with Indochinese nationalists. De Gaulle's choice of d'Argenlieu, the icy former Jesuit once described as "the most brilliant mind of the twelfth century," suggested a very different agenda.[47] Indeed, de Gaulle's written orders for d'Argenlieu made that agenda explicit: the high commissioner's "primary mission," de Gaulle instructed, "was to reestablish French sovereignty over the territories of the Indochinese Union."[48]

De Gaulle's abrupt resignation as president of the provisional government on January 20—a decision unrelated to Indochina—tipped the scales in favor of the reformers. Undeniably, hard-line defenders of French colonial prerogatives, backed by the deeply conservative French community in Indochina, occupied powerful positions and would exercise substantial influence over Indochina policy throughout 1946. More important, d'Argenlieu and his staff of devoted Gaullists, strongly backed by French nationals in Indochina, held the reins of power in Saigon, a position that gave them sweeping discretion over implementation of policies established in Paris. De Gaulle's departure may, in fact, have strengthened d'Argenlieu's determination to resist concessions in Indochina, persuaded as he was that he bore responsibility for defending the Gaullist line until *le général* returned to power.[49] On balance, however, the policymaking and political establishment stood ready in early 1946 to move ahead with a policy of reform and negotiation—a willingness symbolized by the decision around the same time to rename the Colonial Ministry the Ministry of Overseas France. Laurentie and much of the ministry bureaucracy, the focal point of Indochina decision making, backed the new approach. Even the military, despite its natural institutional interest in a policy of reconquest, indicated support for a negotiated solution. General Juin, the chief of staff, regarded talks as a key part of any realistic French strategy to stabilize Indochina and reduce French manpower needs to bearable levels.[50] Leclerc's growing support for negotiation rested on his firsthand knowledge of the impossible task that confronted France if it chose a military solution in Indochina. "France is no longer in a position to control by arms an entity of 24 million people, among whom xenophobia and perhaps even nationalism have taken root," Leclerc asserted in early February.[51]

The resurgence of political parties also contributed to the momentum toward reform and negotiation. To be sure, party leaders gave colonial matters scant attention in the period after the war, a reflection of what historian Martin Shipway has dubbed "benign public indifference" to the empire within French society more generally.[52] Still, all three major parties that dominated French politics following de Gaulle's departure paid at least lip service to the goal of allowing greater autonomy for the Indochinese territories within a restructured French empire. The Mouvement Républicain Populaire (MRP), the centrist Catholic party that emerged from the wartime resistance, showed little enthusiasm for genuine federalism but embraced the notion of a reformulated French Union that would permit a higher degree of self-rule for Indochina and other French possessions. The Socialist party (Section Française de l'Internationale Ouvrière, or SFIO) held a generally warmer view of federalism but split over the question of how quickly it should come about. Some members favored immediate implementation, while others contended that France should concede genuine autonomy gradually as colonized peoples gained experience. Predictably, the Communist Party (Parti Communiste Français, or PCF) demonstrated the greatest willingness to consider far-reaching reforms, although the party kept a low profile on colonial problems and assiduously cultivated an image of moderation. The Communists sought in this period, as they had since the Popular Front years of 1936–1937, to promote their standing with the French electorate as a legitimate party of government that would reliably defend French interests.[53]

Disburdened of de Gaulle's obstructionism and with broad administrative and political backing, the provisional government, now under the leadership of Socialist president Vincent Auriol, moved ahead with a conciliatory policy aimed at achieving a negotiated settlement with Ho Chi Minh. French administrators had been talking in some fashion with the Viet Minh since August 1945, when Jean Sainteny, who shared the new reformist spirit in Paris, arrived in Hanoi as the senior French administrator for Tonkin.[54] By early fall Sainteny and Ho had begun a series of conversations that, from the French point of view, paralleled Sino-French negotiations aimed at ending the Chinese occupation above the sixteenth parallel. French reoccupation of the north, it was clear, depended not only on a deal with Chungking to remove Chinese forces but also on an agreement with the leadership of the Democratic Republic of Vietnam to accept the return of French troops. In February conditions for a deal quickly ripened. On the Vietnamese side, Ho not only recognized his government's inability to prevent a French return but also calculated that a deal to restore French control in the north would help end an oppressive Chinese presence that, he apparently believed, posed far greater dangers to Vietnamese independence over the long term than the negotiated return of a destitute European empire whose days appeared to be numbered. "If the Chinese stay now, they will never go," Ho famously stated in defending his willingness to negotiate a deal with France. "As for me, I prefer to sniff French shit for five years than eat Chinese shit for the rest of my life."[55]

On the French side, the absence of d'Argenlieu, who had temporarily returned to Paris to report on his policies, gave Leclerc and other reformers room for maneuver. On February 14 Leclerc, named acting high commissioner, appealed to Paris to endorse new concessions, including use of the word *indépendence,* which d'Argenlieu opposed. Leclerc acknowledged that using the word might have implied weakness in earlier months. But with the restoration of substantial French military and administrative power in the south, he contended, "now we can talk to the Annamites and make concessions, as a sovereign power and on terms most favorable to us."[56] In response the minister for overseas France, Marius Moutet, gave his go-ahead, signifying a rare meeting of reformist minds in the metropole and the Far East. Moutet told Leclerc that negotiators could offer Ho Chi Minh "self-government" within the framework of the Indochinese Federation and the French Union. In return Moutet insisted that Ho accept the return of the French army and concede substantial economic and cultural privileges to France. Moutet also rebuffed a key Viet Minh demand by refusing to guarantee Vietnamese unity. The minister specified that the future status of Cochinchina, the richest Vietnamese province, where Viet Minh influence was weakest, would have to be decided later by referendum. Ho Chi Minh quickly agreed in principle to the French position.

Ho later complained that the final accord, signed on March 6, 1946, represented a victory for France—and with good reason. Not only did the agreement defer the matter of Vietnamese unity, but it also permitted France to station twenty-five thousand troops in the north for five years and dropped "self-government" in favor of an even vaguer formulation that assured little. France, the accord stated, recognized "the Republic of Vietnam" as a "Free State with its own government, parliament, army, and finances, forming part of the Indochinese Federation and the French Union"—inchoate entities that would most likely constrain Vietnamese autonomy in various ways once subsequent negotiations gave them concrete form. All this was hardly what Ho Chi Minh and his followers had envisioned in the heady days of the August Revolution. Ho appears to have calculated, however, that it was the best he could do under the circumstances. The Democratic Republic of Vietnam, after all, had failed to win recognition from any foreign nation, was struggling with internal divisions, and faced a war for which it was unprepared if it refused to accept some sort of compromise embedding Vietnam within the French colonial structure and allowing at least the temporary return of French military authority.[57]

MANAGING AMERICAN NEUTRALITY

The diplomatic dimension of French policy did not drop away entirely during the period of French autonomy. French officials in both Paris and Saigon remained sensitive to foreign attitudes. But the tenor and purpose of French diplomacy changed significantly. In earlier months French diplomatic policy had reflected deep anxiety about foreign hostility to French objectives in Indochina. Officials had struggled to change international, especially American, views in a way that would unlock international support for long-term French aims. With the mounting confidence that emerged from the revival of French power in early 1946, French authorities approached the international situation differently. The new status quo—the presence of French military forces throughout Vietnam, international tolerance (however lukewarm) for the reestablishment of French rule, and the initiation of negotiations premised on Vietnamese adherence to the French Union—represented a remarkable improvement over the situation that had prevailed a year earlier. The problem of coping with Vietnamese demands remained complicated, of course, and reformers would continue to vie with hardliners for control over policy for the rest of the year. But diplomatically, the task for French policymakers was now relatively simple. Instead of changing the international climate, they needed only to preserve a situation that seemed, with proper management, conducive to the achievement of the central French objective: Indochina's permanent integration into a political and economic order controlled from Paris.

U.S. attitudes could still stir alarm among French observers. Evidence collected by French intelligence in the first months of 1946 suggested that

Americans had lost none of their enthusiasm for making political and especially economic inroads in Indochina. One report from Washington, for example, alleged that several members of the U.S. Congress hoped to exploit ongoing talks between Secretary of State James Byrnes and the French elder statesman Léon Blum on a large U.S. loan in order to extract economic concessions in the French empire, especially Indochina. American activities in Southeast Asia also fueled French apprehensions. The High Commission in Saigon reported that James O'Sullivan, the newly appointed U.S. consul in Hanoi whom French observers rightly suspected of harboring anticolonial views, was busily establishing contact with Vietnamese nationalist leaders to facilitate deals for American firms, especially the oil companies Texaco and Standard Vacuum. "Faithful to the slogan 'business is business,' American visitors seem to be more interested in Indochina to measure the economic potential of a country newly launched on the international market than in [politics]," complained d'Argenlieu, who warned that the United States seemed to be plotting an "economic takeover" of Indochina. On the base issue, too, American ambitions seemed to remain alive. French anxieties flared in May amid sudden indications that the U.S. Army hoped to establish an airfield at Tan Son Nhut airport outside Saigon.[58]

French observers also fretted about persistent anticolonial currents in American society. P. E. Naggiar, a French diplomat posted to Washington, reported in February that ordinary Americans retained a "particular sensitivity" on colonial matters and showed attitudes "hardly favorable toward the colonial powers." With respect to Indochina specifically, he pointed out that Americans sympathetic to Vietnamese nationalism had recently formed an "American-Vietnam Friendship Committee" with the obvious goal of promoting Vietnamese independence. Nor did French observers take much solace from the U.S. reaction to the British government's announcement in March of its intention to grant independence to India in 1947. In Washington Ambassador Bonnet reported not only the overwhelmingly positive American reaction but also specific U.S. designs on the new nation. The State Department, reported Bonnet, viewed India as a potentially critical U.S. ally in a future global war because of its geographical position and economic potential. It required no leap of imagination to conclude that American officials thought in similar terms about the value of an independent Vietnam to U.S. national security.[59]

To resist American threats, French officials proved willing to confront the United States with unprecedented forcefulness. In earlier months calculated concessions—economic privileges for foreigners or tolerance of foreign bases on Indochinese soil—had formed part of the French strategy to bring about a shift in U.S. attitudes. Now, increasingly confident policymakers flatly rejected American overtures. The French Defense Ministry, for instance, refused even to consider the proposal for a U.S. base at Tan Son Nhut airport, arguing that any willingness to meet U.S. demands would create a dangerous precedent.[60] Meanwhile, Sûreté agents in Vietnam, wary of American efforts to open economic or political discussions with nationalist leaders, intensified surveillance of U.S. officials, especially the American consuls in Saigon and Hanoi. Strenuous efforts by the High Commission in mid-1946 to interfere with the establishment of a U.S. Information Service office in Saigon furnish the best example of French determination to prevent Vietnamese-American contacts. Regarding the USIS mainly as an outlet for anticolonial propaganda and a cover for U.S. economic ambitions, French operatives harassed the agency's work from its start in March 1946. Saigon authorities denied the USIS adequate space for its offices, library, and display room, forcing it to accept a cramped upstairs space adjoining the U.S. consulate. Meanwhile, customs agents routinely intercepted shipments of books, films, and other materials while raising petty objections to showings of American films, intimidating Vietnamese and French nationals who took jobs at the office, and harassing Vietnamese who visited the reading room. Reed repeatedly lashed out against such behavior, charging that the only other government in the world that had treated the Information Agency with such hostility was Tito's communist regime in Yugoslavia.[61]

While displaying this new willingness to antagonize Americans, French officials also persevered with old efforts to resist U.S. hostility by reshaping American perceptions of French colonialism. French intelligence proposed a possible new avenue for exerting such influence in early 1946—cooperation with American Catholic organizations to promote a positive vision of French rule. Catholics in the United States, suggested one study, shared an interest "in seeing Catholicism spread in Indochina, including through the activities of French missionaries." The Foreign Ministry judged, though, that the best chance of changing American attitudes lay not in cooperation with a conservative minority but in stressing the liberality of French policy in ways calculated to appeal to the supposedly anticolonial mainstream of U.S. society. Claims about the progressive nature of French intentions, though less insistent than before, naturally centered on the Franco-Vietnamese negotiations, which continued over much of 1946 on the basis of the preliminary agreement signed on March 6. In April French and Vietnamese negotiators sat down in the Annam hill town of Dalat to open detailed discussion of various points left uncertain in the earlier agreement. Although those talks resulted in little progress, they were quickly followed in June by another round of negotiations at Fontainebleau outside Paris—talks that involved Ho Chi Minh himself and initially raised expectations of a lasting agreement. Throughout these negotiations the French government and Vietnamese leaders remained divided over major issues, above all the status of Cochinchina.[62] But French officials consistently stressed their commitment to live up to the government's promises of reform.

D'Argenlieu's chief political adviser, Pierre Clarac, told foreign diplomats in Saigon that the March 6 accord had, in fact, gone well beyond what the provisional government had promised in 1945. Although the ultimate shape of the French Union remained undecided, he sought to appeal to American interlocutors by comparing their country's intentions with the model of colonial devolution followed by the United States in the Philippines. At Fontainebleau Foreign Ministry delegates even held out the possibility that Vietnam and the other states of the Indochinese Federation would be entitled to join the United Nations, a right that French diplomats believed to be the ultimate attribute of independence in American minds. Even after d'Argenlieu threw the negotiations into crisis on June 1 by unilaterally declaring Cochinchinese independence—a step that violated earlier assurances that the territory's future status would be decided by referendum—French commentary was relentlessly upbeat. A public declaration approved by the cabinet to put France back on the diplomatic "offensive" stated that Paris hoped to restart the talks as soon as possible and was determined to respect the "rights and freedoms" of the Indochinese people.[63]

These assurances were accompanied by continued efforts to vilify Ho Chi Minh's government. As before, French representatives awkwardly mingled different conceptions of the Vietnamese. Sometimes French commentary described the Democratic Republic of Vietnam as a weak government unrepresentative of the population. In meetings with U.S. counterparts during the summer, French diplomats routinely demonized the Vietnamese government as capable of rallying support in Cochinchina only through "terrorist methods." French condemnation of Vietnamese treachery and political ineffectiveness was so adamant, in fact, that Americans could hardly miss the excess of their claims. After meeting with French officials, Charles Reed, the U.S. consul in Saigon, reported their obvious determination "to depreciate the achievements of the Vietnam Government." French personnel were especially eager to claim that Ho's government was "becoming unpopular with the people," wrote Reed, adding: "This is promptly translated by the French into the proposition that if the Viet-Minh are increasingly disliked the French are increasingly welcomed." Reed scornfully concluded: "What the French miss, I believe, is that while the Viet-Minh may be disliked, the French are hated."[64]

At other times, French commentary stressed the Viet Minh's communist affiliation, although this remained a problematic line of argument for French diplomats, perhaps even more so after de Gaulle's departure from government. Not only did French intelligence still lack any clear evidence linking the Democratic Republic of Vietnam with Moscow, but the presence of the French Communist Party in the governing coalition in Paris also inhibited efforts to raise the communist bogey. Indeed, National Assembly elections in November 1946 affirmed the party's status as the most popular in France. Clarac told Reed in September 1946 that it remained impossible to use the word *communist* in connection with the Viet Minh since the "strength of [the] Communist party in France precludes any unfavorable mention." All in all, Reed noted a tendency to "soft pedal Communist trends in Vietnam for political reasons." Nevertheless, the Foreign Ministry, the Ministry of Overseas France, and the High Commission in Saigon—bureaucracies where Communist Party influence was negligible or nonexistent—took pains during 1946 to substantiate communist influence within the Viet Minh, compiling lengthy reports about Ho Chi Minh's communist training and loyalties. The studies all drove toward the same conclusion: Ho ranked "in the category of the great international revolutionaries," as one study insisted.[65]

Efforts to control foreign perceptions sometimes took more forceful form during 1946, notably the application of new censorship rules on international correspondents in Indochina. Foreign Ministry personnel believed it was especially important to discourage reporting on atrocities committed by French troops operating in Cochinchina. Although French commanders readily acknowledged in internal correspondence that their troops were guilty of excessive violence, diplomats worried that journalistic reports undercut French morale and fueled hostile propaganda abroad.[66] French anxiety focused on the Associated Press, the American news agency that regularly reported on French military operations in Indochina. Complaining that the AP was spreading "anti-French propaganda," the Foreign Ministry authorized Ambassador Bonnet in August to deliver a formal protest to the State Department about the agency's activities and to demand "sincere cooperation at the local level between American and [French] authorities" to resolve the problem. After the State Department rejected that overture, the Foreign Ministry opted for a subtler approach, suggesting that French officials in Vietnam make a concerted effort to explain French policy to American reporters. The embassy in Washington also made new efforts to meet with sympathetic journalists and to monitor media across the country. If such benign tactics failed, though, the Foreign Ministry suggested a more direct method—instructing diplomats to "let it be understood" that dispatches would be intercepted by French censors if "the least incidents are distorted or presented to world opinion in a way unfavorable to our interests."[67]

Such outbursts were, however, the exception rather than the rule during 1946, more carryovers from the period of high Franco-U.S. tensions during 1944 and 1945 than indicative of the overall state of the evolving relationship. Hostility to French colonialism remained high enough in the United States to rule out any shift away from neutrality. But French leaders grew increasingly comfortable with U.S. noninterference policy. This comfort rested in part on the simple calculation that they needed less from the United States. Mere American toleration had proved adequate for the accomplishment of basic French objectives and did not seem to threaten the attainment of French goals in the future. Officials also drew satisfaction from the arrival of new U.S. personnel who were less openly hostile to French policy. Wedemeyer, Patti, and other leading American figures in Indochina had caused deep anxiety during the last months of the Pacific war and the early postwar period. French officials therefore breathed a sign of relief when a new cast of Americans, open to a more generous interpretation of neutrality, took over. Especially gratifying was the departure of the controversial OSS mission, replaced in January 1946 by a new team with much narrower duties of investigating war criminals and locating American servicemen shot down over Southeast Asia. Even Reed and, to a lesser extent, O'Sullivan, despite their flirtations with Vietnamese nationalists, seemed acceptable by comparison with earlier personnel. The changes, wrote d'Argenlieu, showed the development of a "different relationship between French and Americans" in Indochina. The new Americans, he continued, "seem to have changed their manner of conduct and abandoned the policies pursued up until now." Mounting anticommunism among U.S. officials also seemed to be helping to encourage a friendlier policy toward France. "At a moment when points of contention with the USSR are numerous, the USA is trying to avoid creating new confrontations," asserted a study by Leclerc's Far Eastern headquarters.[68]

French observers were correct in judging that Washington was becoming increasingly comfortable with French rule. Part of the reason was the growing conviction among U.S. officials stationed in Indochina that the Democratic Republic of Vietnam lacked the capacity to govern effectively or to resist French power. This view seems to have rested as much on French assessments as on any independent efforts to appraise the situation. Whatever the source of American information, however, U.S. officials returning to Washington from Southeast Asia spoke with conviction, providing a drumbeat of pessimistic opinion. One military officer reported at the end of 1945 that as many as 30 percent of Vietnamese who had once supported the Viet Minh had already shifted their allegiance. In early 1946 Philip Gallagher, the U.S. general excoriated by French officials for encouraging Vietnamese nationalism in late 1945, painted a more favorable portrait of the Hanoi government, praising the "remarkably effective Annamese administration" that had lasted for some time. But even he offered a gloomy prognosis. The Vietnamese, he said, "were not yet ready for self-government and in full-fledged competition with other nations ... would 'lose their shirts.'" Gallagher predicted an even worse fate if the Vietnamese chose to resist by force. "They are strong on parades and reiterate their willingness to 'fight to the last man,' but they would be slaughtered," he said. By March Kenneth Landon, deputy head of the State Department's Southeast Asia division, noted the emergence of a pattern in southern Indochina that seemed to spell doom for the nationalists: although the Viet Minh remained dominant in much of the countryside, the French had regained control in all the most important economic and population centers.[69]

Evidence of French willingness to negotiate with the Viet Minh during 1946 also helped put an end to any lingering American interest in obstructing a full French recovery. With the French government apparently prepared to offer significant concessions to Vietnamese nationalism, after all, liberals lost one of their most important arguments in favor of maintaining pressure on Paris. U.S. observers in Paris understood that French leaders were divided between those who favored reform and those who advocated a more severe, perhaps even military, solution. They also perceived that the reformist position had gained the upper hand following de Gaulle's resignation. "All indications in Paris point to the fact that the French government at this time favors a conciliatory and moderate policy," Caffery happily noted on February 4, noting that "certain old-line military leaders" had been marginalized by de Gaulle's exit. By contrast, Caffery reported, the newly ascendant tripartite government, centered on the Socialist party and the new Socialist minister for Overseas France, Marius Moutet, seemed to favor "a liberal and progressive colonial policy" even though both party and minister ruled out independence.[70]

The conservative viewpoint was also strengthened, as French officials observed, by Washington's growing anxieties about the Soviet Union over the course of 1946. The ominous events of that year, well narrated by other historians, need only brief summary here.[71] Alarm over Soviet expansionism in Iran and Turkey in late 1945 had already led the Truman administration to reconsider the possibility of a U.S.-Soviet accommodation in Europe. Over the course of 1946, superpower relations continued to deteriorate, especially over the question of German reunification, and Washington moved decisively toward a policy that would come to be known as containment. From the Truman administration's point of view, as historian Marc Trachtenberg has written, "The Soviet Union was an expansionist power, and it was coming to be taken as axiomatic that only countervailing power could keep her in line."[72] As the division of Europe into Soviet- and U.S.-dominated spheres grew increasingly apparent, the status of France became a matter of ever greater urgency in Washington. Policymakers regarded a militarily robust, economically vital, and politically reliable France as a cornerstone of Western strength. Yet weaknesses abounded. Not only did the French economy remain in crisis, but the French Communist Party strengthened its standing during 1946 as the nation's largest political force. Under these circumstances the possibility of obstructing French policy in Southeast Asia in any way faded as a realistic possibility. No one could contemplate contributing to political turmoil or economic difficulties in France over a secondary issue such as Indochina.

Unwillingness to obstruct French aims did not, however, mean that Washington moved away from its fundamental policy of neutrality. Even as Cold War tensions mounted in Europe, liberal determination to protect U.S. interests in Southeast Asia ruled out any abandonment of the position adopted in 1945. Liberal policymakers continued to argue powerfully that Washington risked fueling a communist menace in the

Far East by associating itself with the French cause. Already, they asserted, the U.S. failure to disassociate itself fully from French and British behavior had done great damage. America's standing with the Vietnamese had been "very high" at the end of the Second World War but had declined rapidly thereafter, according to one study by the Southeast Asia division, because of the widening gulf between U.S. toleration of European colonialism and "the cardinal principles of the Declaration of Independence, of the Atlantic Charter, and of the United Nations Organization." If the Viet Minh showed signs of attraction to Soviet communism, the report added, the United States was partly to blame. "The Annamites," it complained,

> witness French troops being landed from ships flying the United States colors, and they can see the French fighting them with American-made equipment, often bearing American markings. Furthermore, they feel that the Allied mission in Indochina, of which the United States is a member, and which was set up for the purpose of disarming the Japanese garrisons in Indochina, has done little but establish a convenient beachhead for the French.

Liberals warned against the temptation, strongly encouraged by the French, to view the Viet Minh as an arm of international communism directed from Moscow rather than an expression of anticolonial nationalism.[73]

Even as U.S. diplomats scrutinized communist tendencies among the Viet Minh more closely in the second half of 1946, no firm evidence emerged to suggest a strong connection between Moscow and developments in Vietnam. In Paris Ambassador Caffery, one of the strongest supporters of French policy in Indochina, reported in June that the French Communist Party was taking a more active interest in Ho's fortunes, suggesting a closer link between the communist threat in Europe and developments in Southeast Asia. Three months later Undersecretary of State Will Clayton, a conservative fixated on European priorities, circulated a War Department intelligence study purporting to demonstrate that the Soviet government was now anxious to see Ho succeed in Vietnam and had instructed the French communists to adapt accordingly.[74] But in Vietnam itself, American observers found little cause for alarm. Even Reed, under orders from the State Department to report on links between Moscow and Hanoi, saw no immediate problem, dismissing murky evidence of growing Soviet interest as "a straw in the wind." Only the "multiplying" of such straws over time could present the West with a serious threat, he wrote. The Southeast Asia division, meanwhile, clung to its earlier analysis. Moffat acknowledged that Vietnam was "probably fairly susceptible" to communist influence, but he attributed that susceptibility to an increasingly hard-line French policy that took little account of the Vietnamese position or the existence of the Democratic Republic of Vietnam. "The crux of the present situation," Moffat argued as Franco-Vietnamese negotiations proceeded during the summer, "lies in the apparent intention of the French to settle . . . matters to their own advantage and without reference to Viet Nam."[75]

Mounting Cold War anxieties in the United States, then, did not lead to any easy set of conclusions about Indochina. Unquestionably, the growing Soviet menace in Europe constituted a powerful argument for removing any remaining impediments to French control. But in Southeast Asia concern about communist expansion drove liberals to argue against any form of active association with French objectives. There was no question which set of concerns trumped the other: the destiny of Western Europe ranked as the top American foreign policy preoccupation in the early postwar period and overwhelmed any qualms about a remote part of the world such as Indochina. Yet neutrality held as the basis of U.S. policy. This perseverance owed something to the fact that Franco-Vietnamese negotiations seemed for most of 1946 to go fairly well. Under these circumstances there seemed to be no urgent necessity for the United States to lend political, economic, or military aid for French policy. Indeed, French appeals for such help dropped off dramatically as Paris grew more determined to end reliance on foreigners. But the reaffirmation of neutrality also reflected the lingering persuasiveness of liberal thinking. No American policymaker made a serious effort during 1946 to rebut the liberal understanding of events in Southeast Asia or to reconsider neutrality as the basis of U.S. policy toward Indochina.

The passive brand of U.S. neutrality that prevailed during 1946 left space for French authorities to obtain valuable, if limited, American assistance that enhanced French power and boosted the confidence of French officials that they could complete the work of recovering full political and economic control. This assistance, it should be emphasized, did not represent any sharp break in U.S. policy. Rather, it resulted from assiduous French efforts to exploit an international situation that featured new opportunities as French needs declined and Americans moved toward a less overtly hostile attitude toward French aims. The most remarkable success in managing American neutrality concerned French efforts to obtain ships, planes, and other military equipment from the United States over the course of 1946. British occupation forces, in their eagerness to get free of Indochina, had already quietly turned over large amounts of U.S.-manufactured military equipment during the end of 1945 and the first weeks of 1946. That aid violated U.S.-British understandings on the retransfer of American-made goods provided under Lend-Lease, and British officials made efforts to assure that it received as little attention as possible.[76] Americans themselves became increasingly willing during 1946, however, to provide equipment directly from U.S. stocks, insisting only on two conditions that made the transfers permissible under the neutral policy. First, they demanded payment; under no circumstances could transfers of U.S. equipment be seen as gifts. Second, they stipulated that only nonlethal kinds of equipment, suitable for economic purposes, could be sold. In practice these conditions amounted to surmountable obstacles for French officials determined to exploit every possibility to solidify French power.

The French government had long sought access to the vast American military stocks in the Far East, but with little hope of success. If the end of the Pacific war promised help by triggering the reclassification of much of these supplies as surplus, the simultaneous surge of U.S. alarm about colonial repression seemed to make European access to American gear even less likely than before. François Lacoste, the senior counselor at the French embassy in Washington, noted with discouragement in November 1945 that U.S. media were beginning to complain about the use of American goods by French and Dutch forces in Southeast Asia. Such complaints, he charged, were "clearly inspired" by U.S. officials who opposed French colonial aims. While there is no evidence to sustain that theory, liberals within the State Department remained keenly aware of the risk that the United States would inadvertently become associated with European objectives if it failed to resist French, British, and Dutch efforts to tap into American power. The Far Eastern office proposed issuing formal diplomatic notes to U.S. allies along with a public declaration opposing use of American equipment. "Such a statement," asserted one State Department official, "would probably fail completely to undo the damage now being done to American prestige through the use or misuse of American arms in China, Indonesia and Indo-China, but it might go a long way toward accomplishing that result." As usual, the administration chose a middle course, rejecting such a direct challenge to European initiatives but insisting on its policy of refusing to provide war materials of any sort for use by the colonial powers in Southeast Asia. To cope with the amount of U.S.-made equipment already in use, Washington insisted in October that the French,

British, and Dutch militaries remove U.S. insignia from any equipment being used to restore colonial control.[77]

In practice U.S. policy suffered from numerous loopholes, which French officials were quick to exploit. While some American officials championed a strict interpretation of the guidelines established by the State and War departments, others, whether more sympathetic to the French cause or simply less sanguine about the possibility of enforcement at a time when so much U.S. equipment circulated around the globe, proved willing to make compromises. Truman himself, in one of his rare personal interventions in Indochinese affairs, demonstrated the latter view in January 1946 when Dean Acheson, the undersecretary of state, informed him that the British military wished to turn over eight hundred jeeps, originally supplied under Lend-Lease, to the French. Truman approved the transfer because removing the vehicles would be "impractical" and because no additional equipment was due to be introduced into the region.[78]

Another loophole in U.S. policy resulted from growing concern in Washington about the recovery of the Southeast Asian economy. Several months after the end of the war, Indochina's vital rubber and rice industries remained in deplorable condition, a fact that alarmed American policymakers as much as their British counterparts. No one, after all—neither the French government nor the people of Indochina—stood to gain from prolonged economic chaos. In fact, communism, whether of the Soviet-inspired or indigenously cultivated variety, seemed likely to be the principal beneficiary. In the near term, it was clear that the French administration stood the best chance of putting Indochina back on its feet economically. Americans thus faced a difficult decision when French authorities sought equipment that might be used for economic rehabilitation. The solution was to permit sales of equipment that seemed to have principally civilian economic purposes, while barring all transfers of explicitly military gear.

French officials profited from the fuzziness of the distinction between civilian and military uses in obtaining U.S. equipment. The Paris government dispatched purchasing missions to Calcutta and Manila, where Washington had established "Field Liquidation Commissions" to supervise sale of vast stocks of surplus U.S gear at low cost. Eager to obtain critical supplies before competition emerged from China, Thailand, or other governments likely to seek good deals on military supplies, the French government scraped together scarce dollars to pay for a wide range of urgently needed gear, above all planes and landing craft. "The need to save currency has not escaped me," wrote d'Argenlieu, a principal champion of the purchasing missions, "but the consequences of shortages of certain materials [for Indochina] would be too serious for me not to insist." In communications with U.S. counterparts, French agents stressed the nonmilitary value of the goods they sought to buy. Above all, they emphasized the supplies' usefulness in advancing the project they believed to hold greatest importance in Washington—revival of the Southeast Asia rubber industry. In secret, French officials admitted that their aims ran far beyond economic revival. Leclerc, for example, wrote at the outset of the purchasing effort in fall 1945 that American goods were a "crucial necessity in order for French forces to carry out the occupation of Indochina." D'Argenlieu agreed, but underscored the need to soothe American sensitivities. "I emphasize the necessity of presenting [French] demands in the form of civil needs . . . for materials, some of which is also required for military purposes," d'Argenlieu wrote. Elsewhere, he was more succinct. "Vis-à-vis the Americans," he asserted, "everything must be presented as 'civilian use.'"[79]

American officials were not blind to French objectives. The OSS warned in December 1945 that France obviously sought equipment for military uses.[80] But French insistence that U.S. equipment was essential to Indochina's economic revival placed Americans in a bind. The Rubber Development Corporation, a U.S. government agency set up to oversee procurement of natural rubber abroad, expressed keen interest in restoring Indochinese production as quickly as possible. Since that project urgently required a great deal of material that only the United States could provide, especially riverboats and landing craft, U.S. officials were disinclined to look closely at other possible uses of the goods they sold.[81] Not even staunch liberals could object too strenuously, since their hopes of integrating Southeast Asia into an open global trading system depended on Indochina's economic recovery. Their relatively high opinion of the Vietnamese and other Southeast Asian peoples stopped well short of any confidence that those indigenous populations might be able to manage economic recovery better than the French (although at least one report in August 1946, apparently ignored in Washington, suggested that recovery was proceeding better in areas controlled by the Viet Minh).[82] Under conflicting pressures to avoid military support but provide economic help, the State Department's legal office threw up its hands at the end of 1945, concluding that judgments about whether to proceed with sales of U.S. gear could be made only on a case-by-case basis.[83]

Total French purchases are impossible to calculate from the fragmentary documentary record, but it is clear that U.S. officials consistently approved sales at the end of 1945 and throughout 1946. The flow of American goods increased especially after the Franco-Vietnamese agreement of March 6, which strengthened the French case that such equipment would be put to purely civilian uses and seemed to take some of the political hazard out of the transactions. "The clarification of the political situation has had much to do with the success of the negotiations," wrote Ambassador Bonnet as prospects for a lasting Franco-Vietnamese accommodation seemed to brighten further during the summer.[84] U.S. authorities still scrupulously refused to sell lethal equipment such as ammunition. The State Department even blocked London's attempts to sell 150 British-manufactured Mosquito aircraft to the French for use in Indochina because the planes were equipped with U.S.-made propellers.[85] But in other categories of equipment, French purchasing missions in Calcutta and Manila managed in the first four months of 1946 alone to buy at least several million dollars' worth of cut-rate U.S. equipment, including Dakota transport aircraft, landing craft, trucks, and jeeps, along with spare motors, batteries, and tires. Still more U.S. equipment followed over the remainder of the year.[86]

As they purchased American equipment, French officials also found, to their satisfaction, that American neutrality did not rule out useful diplomatic assistance on the two international problems that vexed them most during 1946: getting Chinese occupation troops out of the north and securing the Thai border provinces. Under the Franco-Chinese agreement signed on February 28, Chinese troops were due to leave Indochina by the end of March, but the evacuation quickly fell behind schedule. The desire of Chinese commanders to extract as much booty as possible before leaving probably helped create the delay, but a logistical matter also contributed: the French administration lacked the ships necessary to ferry so many soldiers back to China. Chinese troops could have withdrawn overland, but French authorities opposed that solution out of fear that it would produce more looting and violence. The only solution was to obtain U.S. shipping. To do so, French officials relied on the fact that the leading American role in China Command conferred on Washington a degree of responsibility to enable the Chinese government to carry out its obligations. Convinced that such a legalistic approach by itself would not suffice, however, some French leaders sought to extract American assistance by playing on Washington's obvious desire to avoid turbulence in Southeast Asia that might force it to take bold positions. French officials understood that the American commitment to maintaining a low profile could be exploited to their profit. In May, as the Chinese occupation dragged on, Leclerc hinted to Reed that French forces in Hanoi were prepared to fight to keep the Chinese from reneging on withdrawal commitments—a threat probably calculated to stoke U.S. apprehension about the possibility of becoming involved in fighting between two allies. In more diplomatic language the French government sent the State Department a formal note on June 21 warning that a continued Chinese presence in Tonkin threatened to "complicate the political situation" and dangerously damage Franco-Chinese relations.[87]

The French tactic had some effect, demonstrating again that American neutrality could be managed to serve limited French purposes. In Chungking General George Marshall, the wartime U.S. chief of staff now attempting to broker peace between China's Nationalists and Communists, was especially susceptible to French overtures due to his determination to keep Chiang Kai-shek's besieged government from becoming embroiled abroad. Marshall promised to do "everything possible" to accelerate the repatriation of Chinese troops by sea. The State Department, too, alarmed by the prospect of Sino-French confrontation, accepted French claims that Chinese forces might have been planning a coup against both the French and Ho Chi Minh government. In its reply to the French note, the State Department asserted that the United States was "well aware of the desirability" of removing Chinese occupation troops. "Everything possible" must be done, Acheson insisted, to ease out the Chinese and to "avoid further incidents." Douglas MacArthur's command in Tokyo, while distinctly unenthusiastic, received orders to supply a number of U.S. ships for the task in June and July. Although persistent shipping shortages and delaying tactics by local Chinese commanders continued to retard the process, the last Chinese forces sailed home in September, carried by a combination of Chinese and U.S. ships.[88]

On the Thai border question, the French government similarly found American neutrality could be exploited for its purposes. The Franco-Thai dispute simmered through early 1946, with Paris conceding only that "technical readjustments" of the border might be possible following the restoration of French territories. Tensions erupted into violence in May, when French troops in eastern Cambodia, aware of Thai support for nationalist groups operating in Indochina, stepped up harassment of Thai troops and Cambodian guerrillas along the Mekong River. Finally, on May 24, about two hundred French troops launched a small but bloody invasion into the disputed areas. As in Tonkin, full-scale fighting threatened to break out between two countries whose good will Washington hoped to maintain. Eager to avoid that scenario, the State Department offered its "good offices" to mediate between the two sides. D'Argenlieu remained deeply suspicious of American motives, but the Foreign Ministry and even some of d'Argenlieu's staff saw no alternative to accepting. By the fall, they had become heavily reliant on U.S. mediation but also confident that they could achieve their objectives without making major concessions. French diplomats applied steady pressure on U.S. mediators to defend the French position. In Washington Ambassador Bonnet described the Thai regime as nothing other than "a former Axis ally" still technically at war with France, while in Saigon d'Argenlieu told Reed he had a dossier "a foot high" documenting Thai depredations on the eastern bank of the Mekong. French condemnation of Thai activities became so intense, in fact, that the interministerial committee that supervised Indochinese affairs in Paris warned the High Commission against overstating its case.[89]

Whether constant French vilification of the Thais had any effect on American efforts is impossible to establish, but there is no doubt that the U.S. effort produced a satisfactory result for the French government. Americans played a critical role in convincing the Thai government to agree in October to return the disputed provinces in exchange for a French commitment to set up a conciliation commission to draw a new border consistent with ethnic and economic realities. After the two sides signed the final accord on November 17, the Foreign Ministry sent a message of thanks to the State Department for its help during the lengthy negotiations.[90] French appreciation marked a notable shift from the hostility that greeted U.S. proposals for mediation between France and Vietnamese nationalists a year earlier. The contrast epitomizes the distance French policymakers had traveled in a year. French resentment against U.S. neutrality and fear of the consequences in fall 1945 had given way to acceptance of the U.S. position. To be sure, part of the reason for this shift was the subtle change that had taken place in the American attitude as men such as Patti and Wedemeyer left Southeast Asia. But the difference stemmed as well from growing confidence among French officials that their country could restore its sovereignty in Vietnam without active backing from the United States and could even exploit American sensitivities to French advantage. American neutrality, in short, ceased to be a threat, a policy to be overturned at all costs. By late 1946 France seemed, after all, to have the Indochina issue entirely in its own hands.

PART TWO

Constructing Vietnam

CHAPTER 4

Crisis Renewed

In the late fall of 1946, the effort to reach a negotiated settlement in Vietnam came to an abrupt and violent end. The talks had snagged over the summer on a variety of issues, especially the all-important question of Vietnamese unity. Only a "modus vivendi" reached on September 15—a halfhearted effort to patch up the dispute through vague compromises—kept the negotiations alive for a few more uninspired weeks. By mid-November both sides were readying for war. In Hanoi Ho Chi Minh gave in to mounting pressure from militants and accepted the need for military preparations. On the French side, a similar process unfolded. Advocates of negotiation steadily lost control over events, outmaneuvered by d'Argenlieu and others who leaned increasingly toward armed solutions. Tensions broke into the open on November 20, when French customs officers attempted to seize a shipment of fuel oil aboard a Vietnamese vessel in Haiphong harbor. The incident sparked a shootout that quickly escalated into a pitched battle resulting in 240 Vietnamese deaths. More death and destruction followed. Starting on November 23, the French military bombarded the city for two days, reducing some districts to rubble and killing roughly six thousand Vietnamese. Tensions then simmered for another three weeks before Vietnamese forces took the initiative on December 19, attacking French strongpoints in Hanoi and throughout the Red River Delta. Full-scale war had come to Vietnam.

To d'Argenlieu and other hawks the turn to force was a logical step in the evolution of French policy, a desirable shift from the conference table to the battlefield, where they were certain that French power would prevail. The high commissioner had always viewed negotiation principally as an expedient to buy time until France had amassed sufficient military power.[1] By the fall, the talks seemed to have served this purpose, and the army seemed ready to make war in the Democratic Republic of Vietnam's Tonkin heartland. Diplomatically, the choice for war appeared to pose few problems. French officials had grown increasingly confident over the course of 1946 that their country had insulated itself from the vicissitudes of foreign opinion. If the French government had failed to win British or U.S. support for its efforts, that failure seemed inconsequential. Indeed, for adamant colonialists the situation carried significant advantages. French officials had worried that international support in Indochina would come only at the stiff price of increased foreign meddling in Indochina's politics and economy—a development that might render meaningless the whole French struggle to maintain colonial rule. Now that danger seemed to be passing.

Ironically, the move to military solutions, championed by officials most concerned with preserving France's freedom of maneuver in colonial matters, had precisely the opposite effect of what the hawks intended. Instead of completing the process of colonial recovery begun in the last months of 1945, the Franco–Viet Minh war quickly exposed French weakness and generated a new sense of crisis among French policymakers about their ability to remaster Indochina. Most significant, the outbreak of war rendered the French government once again dependent on its allies. This new dependency brought Paris face to face with the underlying failure of French diplomacy during 1944 and 1945. Under altered circumstances, mere U.S. and British toleration of French policy would not suffice. Altogether more active forms of assistance were required—precisely the sorts of help that Washington had refused to provide and London, stung by the controversies of autumn 1945, had quickly abandoned in favor of a wary circumspection. The challenge confronting French officials, just as in 1944 and 1945, lay in finding a way to alter the policies of other governments and to tap into their material power. But the obstacles promised to be even higher than before. If the U.S. and British governments had shown caution in earlier months, they would presumably be still more reluctant to involve themselves once France was actually at war with Vietnamese nationalists.

Amid this gloomy situation French proponents of force and their sympathizers in the United States and Britain held one high card. The intensification of the Cold War lent increasing urgency and persuasiveness to calls for solidarity among the Western powers to resist communist expansion. The problem was to recast the situation in Indochina as an expression of Cold War rivalries that most Western policymakers still viewed overwhelmingly as European in origin and significance. Anticommunism had not so far worked especially well as a device for building international consensus behind French policy in Vietnam. To be sure, alarm over communist influence in France had helped to drive the Truman administration to abandon attempts to impose conditions on the restoration of French control in 1945. So far, however, fear of communist expansion in Southeast Asia was as likely to work against the further evolution of U.S. and British attitudes toward support for French policy as in favor of such a shift. In Washington and London many policymakers doubted Ho Chi Minh's connection to international communism and argued that French repression, by constantly frustrating legitimate nationalism, was as much responsible for creating a communist menace as holding it in check. During 1947 French policymakers who were determined to carry on with the war took the first steps toward redefining the conflict in a way that would put an end to international indecision and, they hoped, attract international support.

DOMESTIC SOURCES OF CRISIS

The French government's efforts to recast the Indochina war grew out of a sense of alarm that steadily intensified over the course of 1947 as French policymakers, once so confident, grew increasingly discouraged about the military situation. French anxiety stemmed largely from the country's persistent difficulties in winning international support for its policy choices—a subject discussed in the next section of this chapter. Mounting French alarm also had its roots in the complicated and turbulent world of French domestic politics. As discussed earlier, French policymakers concerned with Indochina, after years of consensus during the Second World War, began to delineate clashing positions on Vietnamese affairs during 1946, especially after Charles de Gaulle's departure from government in January. This process continued over the remainder of the year, with the result that two groupings of policymakers became increasingly distinct. In this respect the bifurcated policymaking community in France came to resemble the U.S. and British establishments, both of which had been beset by conflicting impulses over Vietnam for some time.

In the French case, liberal reformers who were concentrated in the Ministry of Overseas France, backed to some degree by the left of the political spectrum in the National Assembly and public opinion more generally, constituted one pole of opinion. On the other side were the ultranationalists and colonial enthusiasts who advocated sharp limits on reform and the firm defense of metropolitan interests in the empire. D'Argenlieu's High Commission increasingly became the focal point of this view, but it enjoyed the backing of bankers, planters, and other French colonials in Indochina as well as the right of the political spectrum in France and much of the military. The outbreak of war in December 1946 represented a clear victory for the latter group. When the war dragged into 1947 with no end in sight, however, the political situation changed dramatically, leading these "hawks" to despair of their ability to carry on the war.

To appreciate the shifting balance of power among French policymakers requires returning briefly to mid-1946, when the two schools of thought became more distinctly etched as policymakers struggled to answer the vital question that confronted the French government: how to proceed with the negotiating process started at the beginning of the year. The policy of resolving Indochina's future status through negotiation and liberalization rested on the dominance of reformers within French policymaking circles in the wake of General de Gaulle's retirement from the presidency. Following the March 6 agreement, d'Argenlieu and other conservatives, appalled by what they saw as excessive French concessions, moved to recapture the initiative. Although this group probably represented a minority among French officials concerned with Indochina affairs, it dominated the High Commission in Saigon, where officials skillfully exploited political uncertainty in Paris and a lack of determination among the liberals there to take charge of the policymaking agenda for Indochina. The result of d'Argenlieu's efforts was a new swing of the French policymaking pendulum—slow at first, gathering speed later on—away from conciliation back toward confrontation.

The hardening of the French position became especially clear on the vexing question of the future status of Cochinchina, Indochina's wealthiest province and the focal point of French investment in Southeast Asia. French officials of all stripes wished to keep Cochinchina separate from the Democratic Republic of Vietnam and to preserve it as a distinct unit of the Indochinese federation under a more direct form of French control. Liberals and hardliners split over the matter of how the French government should pursue this objective. Under the March 6 accord, Vietnamese and French negotiators agreed to hold a referendum to determine whether Cochinchina would join Ho Chi Minh's "free state" or remain a separate entity. D'Argenlieu distrusted this approach, however, and, in the first of many acts of defiance during 1946, acted unilaterally to settle the matter in France's favor. Without consulting Paris, the high commissioner declared the Autonomous Republic of Cochinchina on June 1, 1946.

New unilateral acts over the following weeks further poisoned the negotiating atmosphere. On June 21 the French army occupied the Moi Plateau in southern Annam, an aggressive gesture timed to demonstrate to the Vietnamese—and probably to liberals in Paris as well—that talks were not the only possible means to resolve Indochinese questions. Three days later French forces in Hanoi, again acting on the high commissioner's instructions, reoccupied the Government General, the prewar seat of French authority. By the time French and Vietnamese negotiators resumed talks at Fontainebleau on July 6, conditions were hardly ripe for progress toward a lasting settlement. Moutet, Laurentie, and others committed to the negotiating process continued to seek points of compromise. The talks, Moutet declared in August, must "not be purely and simply a point of departure for the restoration of French sovereignty by force." But d'Argenlieu and his close associates had come to view the negotiations in precisely that way. "Tomorrow's negotiations are a round in the battle we are fighting, in which we are trying to reinstate ourselves in Indochina and they are trying to see us off," Léon Pignon, a key member of the French delegation, wrote on the eve of the first session. In his view, further negotiations amounted to appeasement. "The question we should be asking ourselves at this moment," Pignon wrote, "is the following: Do we or do we not wish to keep Indochina?" D'Argenlieu similarly dismissed the possibility of good-faith negotiations with the Vietnamese, whom he described as "enemies at heart."[2]

D'Argenlieu moved quickly to ratchet up the pressure on the Hanoi government. On July 22, as the talks continued in Fontainebleau, the high commissioner announced that a separate set of talks on the shape of the Indochinese Federation would open in Dalat on August 1 with delegations from the Republic of Cochinchina as well as Cambodia and Laos. As historian Martin Shipway has pointed out, the new talks reflected a legitimate concern. The narrow focus to date on negotiations with Ho's government had diverted attention from a slate of pressing questions related to the structure of Indochina as a whole. Those issues gained urgency as Ho's government demonstrated its dynamism and ambition, raising worries that it would seek to dominate the entire federation.[3] In announcing the new conference, however, d'Argenlieu was more interested in undermining the Fontainebleau negotiations than in seeking a reasonable solution to these concerns. As with his earlier proclamation of the Cochinchinese republic, the high commissioner acted without approval from Paris. Indeed, Ho Chi Minh learned of the initiative and protested to Moutet before the Ministry of Overseas France had received confirmation of d'Argenlieu's gambit. The announcement had precisely the effect that the high commissioner seems to have intended. When the rival conference opened in Dalat on August 1, Pham Van Dong, head of the Vietnamese delegation at Fontainebleau, presented his French counterparts with an ultimatum: the French government must suspend the Dalat talks or the Vietnamese would walk out at Fontainebleau. The Dalat meeting continued, and Pham delivered on his threat. The Fontainebleau talks broke off for a month.

Liberals complained bitterly about this state of affairs. The French negotiating team was "riddled by deep internal divisions on essential subjects" and lacked "precise instructions," noted Pierre Messmer, a leading policymaker within the Ministry of Overseas France. In a thinly veiled reference to d'Argenlieu, Messmer excoriated sabotage of the conference "by those who want to see the negotiations fail."[4] There was no doubt, though, which faction held the upper hand as the summer advanced. In fact, only a last-ditch attempt at agreement by moderates on both sides, drawn together by a common fear of war, prevented a total collapse of the negotiating process. On the French side, Marius Moutet led the effort, clinging to the hope that the Cochinchina problem could ultimately be papered over through establishment of an autonomous state within a Vietnamese union. Under Moutet's guidance the French delegation offered a new proposal promising to hold the referendum after the cessation of violence and anti-French propaganda in Cochinchina. Such moderation pulled the Vietnamese back to the conference table in late August but failed to yield an agreement. Complaining that French proposals still failed to set a date or other details of the referendum, Pham Van Dong broke off the talks again. The Vietnamese delegation set sail for Haiphong on September 14. Only Ho Chi Minh remained behind, determined like Moutet not to let the whole endeavor come to naught. In the wee hours of September 15, the two men met in Moutet's Paris apartment to sign a "modus vivendi," a temporary arrangement designed to resolve immediate problems and lay the groundwork for further talks in 1947. The agreement left open the status of Cochinchina but called for a cease-fire in the province to take effect at the end of October.[5]

The modus vivendi marked an uninspiring end to Franco-Vietnamese talks that had seemed to hold real promise around the time of the March 6 accord. The Ho Chi Minh government and French negotiators would not sit down at a conference table again until 1954, following eight years of war. Fighting did not, of course, break out immediately. The modus vivendi went into effect as planned, and moderates on both sides continued to plan for the resumption of talks. But the situation increasingly favored military solutions. In Hanoi Vietnamese militants condemned the modus vivendi, and a new, more hawkish cabinet took office in November. General Vo Nguyen Giap, Hanoi's defense minister, ordered intensified preparations for war, including the augmentation of militia units, the construction of fortifications, and the relocation of essential industries to the countryside.[6] On the French side, General Jean Valluy, an outspoken hawk who had replaced Leclerc as head of French forces in July, also prepared for war. In mid-October Valluy formally proposed the strategic shift that would lead to war a few weeks later. Since late 1945 French forces had focused on suppressing guerrilla activity in Cochinchina. Now Valluy urged that the military turn its attention to a strike against the center of Viet Minh power above the sixteenth parallel. "Instead of contenting ourselves with controlling rebel attacks in the south," Valluy suggested, "we should put serious pressure on the rebels by taking large-scale initiatives in Hanoi and Annam." Intrigued by this proposal, d'Argenlieu asked Paris for a light armored division of ten thousand men to reinforce the existing expeditionary corps in Indochina. General Juin approved the request on October 23.[7]

Not all French commanders welcomed this drift toward confrontation. While d'Argenlieu and Valluy showed unbridled confidence in French military strength, Admiral Pierre Barjot, acting chief of staff during Juin's temporary absence, challenged Valluy's focus on the north, arguing that Cochinchina remained the key to retaining influence over all of Indochina and that French resources did not permit a bold approach. "We cannot maintain a general presence and occupy every point in strength," Barjot wrote in late November, following the Haiphong incident. Barjot doubted whether ten thousand or even fifteen thousand additional troops would suffice, guessing that the necessary number might run closer to twenty-five thousand—a figure that, if met, would undercut the French government's ability to respond to military crises elsewhere in the empire.[8] Already in September a cabinet study had indicated that military spending for Indochina was running about 50 percent above what the budget would bear.⁹ General Georges Humbert, the cabinet's chief military adviser, put the case bluntly on the eve of the war. If reinforcement of French forces was intended simply as a "limited" gesture in the wake of the Haiphong incident, that was one thing. "But if it is the prelude to a policy of force in Indochina, it seems especially dangerous," Humbert warned. "Indochina," he added, "would be a bottomless pit [*tonneau des Danaïdes*] for the French army since military operations in Indochina would exceed our resources."¹⁰ Leclerc, although no longer principally concerned with Indochinese affairs, chimed in with his own warning in December. "Since we do not have the means at our disposal to break the back of Vietnamese nationalism by force of arms," he wrote, "France must seek every means to reconcile French and Vietnamese interests."¹¹

Like Moutet's desperate bid in September to head off a resort to arms, these warnings did little to stop the drift to war. It was not that the cautious view lacked persuasiveness or influential supporters. Rather, voices of moderation were drowned out in the political cacophony that prevailed in Paris in the second half of 1946. In the battle for control over French policy, the High Commission enjoyed a decisive advantage: it operated in Saigon, far from the chaos that characterized French politics as the metropole passed through the final convulsions of controversy that finally, at the end of the year, brought the Fourth Republic into being. The High Commission and Valluy maintained a consistent approach and were not timid about forcing showdowns with Paris or presenting the ministries with faits accomplis. Policymakers in the Paris ministries, by contrast, were at the mercy of the Indochina-based officials and suffered from frequent cabinet reshuffles that often brought weak ministers to power, none of them having the confidence to take a strong stand on Indochina. Léon Blum's caretaker government at the end of 1946 offers the best example of the moderates' ineffectiveness against d'Argenlieu's determination. Two days before the Socialists' grand old man accepted the premiership, Blum published an earnest appeal for peace in the party's newspaper, *Le Populaire*. "There is one way, and only one way, to preserve the prestige of our civilization in Indochina, our political and spiritual influence, and our legitimate material interests," Blum wrote. "That is through sincere agreement on the basis of independence, through trust, through friendship." Blum then fired a broadside at the Saigon hawks who had hijacked French policy: "Decision-making power does not belong to military authorities or civilian settlers in Indochina, but to the government in Paris."¹²

Blum's appeal accomplished nothing. Small-scale skirmishes mounted through mid-December, and French officials on the scene showed no interest in heeding the new government twelve thousand miles away. "If these gooks want a fight, they'll get it," Valluy declared in Haiphong on December 17, one day after he met with other senior commanders in a session that, in one historian's estimation, "bore all the signs of a war council."[13] Pignon expressed similar determination to take up arms. "No meaningful agreement can ever be reached with the Viet Minh party," he contended.[14] To assure that the Paris ministries could not derail their efforts, authorities in Saigon indulged in their most sensational act of treachery. On December 15 Ho Chi Minh gave his old negotiating partner, Jean Sainteny, a message for Blum laying out various suggestions aimed at avoiding war. Sainteny dutifully sent the message to Saigon on the assumption that it would be forwarded to Paris without delay. In Saigon, however, Valluy, sensing that war was nearly at hand, withheld the message for four days. When it finally arrived in Paris, fighting had already broken out in Tonkin. The episode stands out not because it marked any real lost opportunity for peace. As numerous authors have made clear, Viet Minh military preparations were far advanced by mid-December, and in any case, it is not clear that Ho Chi Minh regarded the establishment of Blum's all-Socialist cabinet as a meaningful opportunity. In his memoir Giap contends that the Hanoi government saw no real hope of avoiding war by that time.[15] The episode's significance lies, rather, in illustrating the ability of officials in Saigon to commandeer the policymaking process. On the defensive only a few months earlier, the hawks had made a remarkable comeback and worked skillfully to bring about the war that they desired.

Immediately following the outbreak of sustained fighting on December 19, French officials of all persuasions rallied behind the French war effort—a predictable display of national unity at a moment of crisis. Blum clung to his general approach, telling the National Assembly on December 23 that his goal remained to establish a "free Vietnam" within the French Union. "You may rest assured," he affirmed, "that we will do everything possible to reach agreement with the government of Viet-Nam." But he insisted at the same time that law and order would have to be reestablished before any further discussions would be possible.[16] Moutet, whom Blum dispatched to Indochina to inspect the situation firsthand, made the same point and accused the Viet Minh of provoking the war. "There is nothing left but military action," Moutet stated on his return to France in early January. "I regret it," he added, "but they have systematically destroyed all hopes we had and the premeditation of their acts has been established beyond doubt."[17] Leaders of the other major political parties responded in similar fashion. For the Mouvement Républicain Populaire, little debate was necessary. The leadership had already declared its position in mid-December, condemning Viet Minh "terrorism" and demanding that Blum maintain a tough line "in defense of the rights of France."[18] Even the Communists, despite increasing sympathy for the Viet Minh, were prepared to back military operations. On December 24 L'Humanité, the party's main newspaper, declared it "perfectly reasonable" to put off new negotiations with the Hanoi regime "until peaceful law and order are re-established."[19]

As the initial shock of fighting began to wear off in the first months of 1947, however, the French policymaking and political establishments began to differentiate themselves again into the two rough groupings that had become clear the year before. In fact, controversy soon became more intense and public than it had ever been, as Indochina for the first time became a major issue of contention among the political parties. As discussed earlier, the major parties that emerged from the Second World War showed little interest in colonial affairs during 1945 and 1946, an understandable state of affairs given the enormity of the political and economic problems that confronted France after the liberation. On Indochina the parties, with slight variations in their policy preferences, generally backed the guardedly reformist program that prevailed among ministry experts in early 1946 and then put up little opposition as French policy drifted toward the confrontational stance that led to war by the end of the year. The whole affair simply did not command close attention. But in 1947 the situation changed markedly for various reasons. Naturally, the parties could no longer ignore Indochina once the issue commanded daily headlines and involved French casualties—more than a thousand in the first two weeks of fighting alone. In addition, the National Assembly unavoidably became the scene of debate as questions of funding for the war arose in late winter and spring 1947. At first after the outbreak of war, the cabinet, hoping to minimize controversy over external affairs at a delicate moment in international negotiations over Germany and other issues critical to European security, sought to avoid any Assembly debate over Indochina. In March, however, with French material and human losses mounting at alarming rates, the subject surfaced during a debate over military credits. For the first time, the parties were forced to clarify their positions on Indochina.

The polarization of French politics during 1947 ensured that the debate would be acrimonious. This trend stemmed partly from the growing conservatism of the Mouvement Républicain Populaire, the Christian Democratic party that sought to reconcile Catholic traditionalism with modernizing republicanism in a new centrist political force. The shift to the right reflected the party's increasingly conservative constituency as rightists discredited by their allegiance to Vichy gradually returned to French political life and found their home in the MRP. In part, too, the rightward shift resulted from increasing competition for conservative votes between the MRP and Charles de Gaulle's Rassemblement du Peuple Français, the ultranationalistic political movement founded by the self-exiled general in April 1947. Although intended as something larger and more profound than a traditional political party—the general's principal critique of the Fourth Republic was, after all, that France was already saddled with altogether too many of those—the RPF functioned essentially in that way, putting up candidates for office and sparring constantly with the others for the loyalty of French voters. The MRP felt the Gaullists' surge keenly since the two groups sought to appeal to the same conservative electorate. Increasingly the MRP found itself on the defensive. Large numbers of voters deserted the MRP for Gaullist candidates in municipal elections in 1947. In 1951, the first time RPF candidates ran for the National Assembly, about half of MRP voters in 1946 opted for the Gaullists. Under these circumstances, as historian R. E. M. Irving has pointed out, MRP leaders inevitably felt strong pressure to accede to Gaullist views, especially on colonial affairs, a subject where de Gaulle's powerful nationalist appeal was bound to resonate.[20]

At the other end of the spectrum, the French Communist Party moved dramatically toward a more confrontational position over the first half of 1947, one of the epic shifts in the life of the Fourth Republic. The Communists chose in the wake of the Second World War to seek power through constitutional means and assiduously cultivated the image of democratic legitimacy, soft-pedaling doctrinaire notions of class conflict. Whether the party chose this route on Moscow's instructions or on the basis of independent calculations, it largely succeeded through the first postwar year. The party won a plurality of seats in the November 1946 National Assembly elections, emerging just ahead of the MRP and Socialists. Communist ministers meanwhile sat in every postwar cabinet until late 1946, albeit often with portfolios of secondary importance. By 1947 this arrangement, always a source of discomfort to the parties further right, started to come unraveled.

The intensification of the Cold War clearly heightened tensions between the Communists and the other parties, but it was a dispute over domestic economic policy, rather than Cold War tensions or instructions from Moscow, that caused the rupture. The beginning of the end of tripartite cooperation came in December 1946, when Blum's all-Socialist cabinet, responding to perpetual economic crisis, froze wages and prices. The following April, when Renault factory workers called a strike to protest the wage freeze, the party was forced to choose between the strikers and the government line. The Communists opted for the strikers and voted against the cabinet in a National Assembly vote in May. The brief era of *tripartisme* was over. The Communists, now in opposition, were free to criticize the government without restraint.

The debate over Indochina clearly reflected the growing polarization of French politics. By spring 1947 the MRP had fully embraced a bellicose policy on Indochina, advocating bold steps to destroy the Viet Minh and ruling out any further negotiations with Ho Chi Minh's government. Party leader Maurice Schumann told the National Assembly in March that Hanoi had "stabbed France in the back." It would be an "insult," he insisted, "to suggest that France resume negotiations with the perpetrators of such an act."[21] The Communists took precisely the opposite position, assuming the stance they would hold through 1950 and beyond: France must end an unjust war and resume negotiations with Ho Chi Minh. Even as interparty tensions mounted in early 1947, the Communists took care to cast their protests against the war in terms that emphasized their dedication to the republic and the health of the French empire. In a resolution passed in mid-March, the party's central committee charged that the war was bound to diminish French prestige and influence throughout the empire. It also warned that a war would quickly render France dependent on "financial and military aid from abroad, which would mean the surrender of our national independence."[22] The only solution, asserted Communist leaders, was to resume negotiation with Ho. To deal with anyone else would mean, as *L'Humanité* put it, "treating with nobodies or with puppets."[23]

The Socialist party occupied the middle ground between these two views but failed to carve out a distinct position of its own. Instead, the party split into factions that sided with either the MRP to the right or the Communists to the left. For the most part, Socialist cabinet ministers took the former course and adopted a hawkish attitude on the war. During the March assembly debate, Premier Paul Ramadier declared that Paris was ready to negotiate with representatives chosen by the

Vietnamese people, but he heaped scorn on Ho Chi Minh and his associates as traitors and criminals.[24] Moutet, having abandoned his earlier liberal inclinations, made clear that the Hanoi government was no longer a contender to negotiate with France and carefully avoided Ho Chi Minh during his inspection tour of Vietnam in early January. In fact, Moutet attacked the Democratic Republic on multiple fronts, blaming it for the breakdown of negotiations and describing it as a radical cabal that represented only a small fraction of the Vietnamese people. "Vietnam is only part of Indochina," Moutet declared, "and the Viet Minh are only a tiny part of Vietnam."[25] Much of the Socialist party, however, took a different view. In the Assembly debate, the prominent Socialist deputy Daniel Mayer held the door open to new talks with Ho Chi Minh. "We must negotiate with those who hold authority with their people," declared Mayer, insisting that it made sense to reach agreements only with counterparts able to live up to them.[26] The Socialists' national council in March seems to have agreed with this view, calling for negotiations "with all those qualified to represent Vietnam, including the Viet Minh."[27]

The political underpinnings of the bold "politique de force" favored by d'Argenlieu, the military, and the metropolitan right were, then, shaky at best, a fact that caused mounting anxiety among the hawks as 1947 advanced. In the short term, it is true, the advocates of force had a good deal going for them. The Communists' growing dissatisfaction and eventual departure from the government had the effect of pushing the Socialists to the right since partnership with the MRP was the only way to maintain a modicum of political stability and perhaps even the republic's survival. The hawks also benefited from the simple fact that they exercised tight control over the institutions most responsible for implementing French policy in Indochina. Even after d'Argenlieu's recall in February 1947, the High Commission remained in the hands of officials who hoped to prosecute the war with vigor. The expeditionary force as well, under the command of the ever bellicose Valluy, boldly backed the policy of force. This determination among officials in Indochina meant that in the absence of specific and forceful insistence from Paris on a new policy—an unlikely prospect, at least in the short term—the hawks would continue to have their way.

At least as important to the hawks' ability to control policy was their domination of key ministries in Paris. Historians of the Fourth Republic have often described France as a hopeless political morass, guided by ineffective, revolving-door governments that managed to maintain little policymaking consistency. This view obscures the remarkable continuity that characterized the Ministry of Foreign Affairs and the Ministry of Overseas France during the first postwar years. While a dozen premiers came and went between September 1944 and May 1950, only two men—Georges Bidault and Robert Schuman, both of the MRP—presided over the Foreign Ministry. Meanwhile, the two most influential French ambassadors—Henri Bonnet in Washington and René Massigli in London—were both close to the MRP and held their posts through the entire period between the end of the Second World War and 1950. Conservatives also presided over the Ministry of Overseas France, although they represented different parties. Moutet, the conservative Socialist, was preceded by Paul Giacobbi, a staunch Gaullist, and followed in November 1947 by Paul Coste-Floret of the MRP. Even more notable consistency prevailed within the ministries' staffs. Since long before the Second World War, both institutions had become fiefdoms of a conservative policymaking elite dedicated to the grandeur of France. Both were virtually off-limits to Communists.[28]

During 1947, however, three trends worked against the hawks and raised doubts about whether, over the long term, they would be able to persevere with the war and hold off renewed negotiations with the Ho Chi Minh government. First, large chunks of public opinion leaned toward pacific solutions and blamed the French government for the war. One poll published in early February found that 42 percent of respondents favored negotiations with Hanoi and 8 percent believed that France should abandon Indochina entirely, while only 36 percent preferred settling the matter by force.[29] Another survey conducted around the same time offered more discouraging data. When asked to indicate where responsibility for the war lay, 18 percent named the Vietnamese, and another 10 percent blamed "communist propaganda." But 11 percent pinned responsibility on "French policy," 4 percent on French military leaders, and 5 percent on "international capitalism."[30] A third poll in May brought the worst news of all for supporters of the war. Of respondents who identified themselves as Socialist voters, 65 percent backed an immediate turn toward a peaceful solution, as did a remarkable 34 percent of MRP supporters.[31] Such numbers could lead to only one conclusion: Socialist and Christian Democratic leaders' support for a hard-line policy rested on a wobbly base that might disintegrate if the war went badly.

Indeed, the military effort lagged significantly behind French expectations—the second cause of the hawks' anxiety during 1947. In some respects French forces performed well in the opening stages of the war. During the first weeks, they seized most of the major population centers of Tonkin and Annam and reopened major transportation routes along the coast and in the Red River Delta. French forces captured the imperial capital of Hue in February after a destructive six-week siege and pushed Viet Minh forces out of Hanoi in the same month, a success possibly delayed by French reluctance, in the presence of so many foreign diplomats in the city, to use the same harsh methods employed elsewhere.[32] These advances came at a considerable cost, however, and French troops confronted an increasingly difficult situation as the year dragged on. For one thing, the war quickly assumed the pattern that would hold over the next eight years: although the French dominated the cities, the Viet Minh reigned supreme in the countryside, an almost limitless source of supplies and conscripts that would keep the war going despite vast technological inferiority. Under these conditions the French military quietly began to lose some of its initial enthusiasm for war. A Foreign Legion officer who refused to be identified gave voice to growing French anxieties in late January, telling a *New York Times* correspondent that the Viet Minh were better prepared than the French for this sort of war. "Except in armed convoy," he said, "no Frenchmen can venture off their posts." The officer predicted that France would require half a million troops to achieve victory—a number that, in the officer's view, would produce an economic catastrophe at home. Disease among poorly trained French conscripts also caused problems, with many French units losing as much as one-third of their manpower to illnesses.[33]

The third source of anxiety for supporters of the war was the nearly constant danger that moderates on both sides—peace-minded Socialists on the one side and Ho Chi Minh on the other—would force their hand by quietly opening new negotiating contacts. To date, the disorganization of French policymaking had worked almost entirely in favor of the hawks, who had repeatedly exploited the lack of clear policy at the highest level to create faits accomplis. Now it seemed possible that others might take a page from the same script. Certainly, Ho Chi Minh left little doubt of his desire to resume negotiations. In early January Ho proposed a cease-fire and new talks in Paris. In March and April he and his foreign minister, Hoang Minh Giam, offered more detailed proposals, accepting French economic and cultural influence in Vietnam and association with the French Union in exchange for Vietnamese unity and control over financial, military, and foreign policy. French hard-liners first attempted to discredit the Vietnamese messages as fraudulent.[34]

When that gambit failed, the cabinet engineered a new solution to keep the moderates at bay, ordering the French scholar and civil servant Paul Mus to meet with Ho Chi Minh at the Viet Minh's jungle headquarters outside Hanoi. Mus's appointment seemed to bode well for a harmonious exchange, but the conservatives had taken care to assure that there would be no agreement. Mus had orders to offer Ho negotiating terms that, in the Frenchman's own estimation, amounted to "a request for guarantees equivalent to surrender."[35] Ho readily dismissed the French offer of a cease-fire in return for the disarmament of Vietnamese forces, the handover of French deserters, and an agreement that French troops could circulate freely in Viet Minh–controlled areas.[36] In the end, then, this episode amounted to little more than a charade. But it also suggests that French hard-liners were waging an uphill battle to resist pressure for new talks with Ho. The next time Ho and French moderates tested the negotiating waters, after all, the hawks might not be so successful. There was little reason to believe that time was on their side.

INTERNATIONAL SOURCES OF CRISIS

International hostility to the war compounded the problems confronted by the war's French advocates in 1947. Only a few months earlier most French officials had come to believe that colonial control in Indochina no longer depended primarily on the attitudes of other governments. Events proved that confidence to be built on illusion. The interministerial committee foresaw the problem in November 1946 as war grew increasingly likely, noting that foreign opinion would not respond well to French provocations. "International public opinion would not allow us the freedom to do this, nor would we have the support of the French nation," the committee concluded.[37] The Communists anticipated still another problem: if the government opted for war, France would inevitably become dependent on foreign aid, especially that of the United States, and lose its freedom of action. Such warnings had little apparent bearing on governmental decisions. They were, however, prophetic. As the war dragged on through 1947, French policy increasingly encountered either ambivalence or outright hostility abroad. "International opinion is in an uproar over the situation in Indochina," noted the interministerial committee in mid-January.[38] Most distressing, it became clear that such hostility threatened the French government's ability to carry on the fighting.

The most immediate threat came not from the Western powers but from within Asia. Across the continent, nationalists seized on the Franco–Viet Minh conflict as a rallying point for anticolonial agitation. In Thailand anti-French fervor rose to new heights even as the conciliation commission that had assembled to adjudicate the border dispute began its work. In Colombo Ceylonese stevedores refused to service French ships, forcing the French navy to seek alternative refueling points. Labor unions in Malaya and Singapore took similar action, refusing to handle goods on French ships carrying war matériel or troops to Indochina. The war sparked an even more dramatic nationalist surge in India, where the interim government under Jawaharlal Nehru quickly proclaimed the Viet Minh's fight part of Asians' larger struggle against European colonialism. "All the countries of Asia and all Asians recoil before the spectacle of a powerful nation like France using planes, cannons and tanks against a small country fighting for its independence," Nehru told one French diplomat in mid-January. In the most overt display of anti-French sentiment, leftist students in India declared January 21 "Vietnam Day," an event marked by violence when Calcutta police enforcing a ban on public demonstrations killed one protester, wounded at least fifty, and arrested another two hundred. Under these circumstances French officials feared that the Indian government would provide diplomatic or even military support for Hanoi's war effort. In the spring and again in October 1947, Viet Minh diplomats based in India asked the New Delhi government to take up Hanoi's cause in the United Nations Security Council.[39]

Still more troubling to Paris, Indian and Burmese nationalists took steps to provide various types of military assistance for the Viet Minh. Shortly after the outbreak of war, Sarat Chandra Bose, a former member of India's interim cabinet, appealed to Indians to "rush in thousands and tens of thousands to help the brave Vietnamese" and declared his intention to raise volunteers, collect funds, and send a medical mission to Vietnam.[40] At nearly the same moment, Bo Yan Naing, a former colonel in the Burmese force that had collaborated with Japan during the Pacific war, proposed a joint Indian-Burmese expeditionary unit to fight alongside the Viet Minh. By early February the two men were collaborating on plans for an "Indo-Burma Volunteer Force," consisting of about 150 soldiers and an ambulance corps. None of these plans ever came to fruition, partly because of funding and transportation problems but largely due to Nehru's skepticism. Although a harsh critic of French behavior in Indochina (and simultaneous Dutch repression in

Indonesia), the Indian leader raised legal objections about intervening in another country's affairs. Nations must, he told Bose, observe certain "rules and decorum."[41] As historian S. R. SarDesai has speculated, Nehru's circumspection also surely stemmed from his suspicions about Hanoi's communist tendencies and his reluctance to alienate France, which continued to rule five small enclaves within India—vestiges of French ambitions in the subcontinent dating from the seventeenth century.[42] Initially, however, French officials could not predict Nehru's behavior and, although they had little fear that a volunteer force would alter the military balance in Vietnam, worried about the propaganda implications of pan-Asian solidarity against France.

A more immediate source of concern was the reluctance of the Indian and Burmese leaders to permit French ships and aircraft to pass through their territories on the way to Indochina. Their refusals raised not only propaganda problems but also serious doubts about whether the French military would be able to maintain its lifeline of reinforcements and supplies to Southeast Asia. The situation became so dire that it commanded the attention of the premier, Paul Ramadier, who ordered Foreign Minister Georges Bidault to take up the question immediately with Indian leaders. Ramadier declared that nothing less than "the continuation of our military action" might be at stake. French diplomats sought help from the British government, which retained a significant degree of authority in India and Burma even as those countries moved toward independence. London proved extremely reluctant to intervene on France's behalf, however, and did little more than lend its cautious support to agreements worked out among French, Indian, and Burmese authorities to permit limited numbers of flights. In Rangoon the Burmese interim government agreed to allow no more than two French planes per day to land on its soil. Indian officials, meanwhile, permitted only one French plane per week to land in India or to fly through Indian airspace. British officials warned the French military that any attempt to circumvent that limit might lead to India's refusal to allow any flights at all. Indeed, Indian authorities impounded twenty-nine Mosquito fighter planes purchased from Britain for nearly a month after they landed in India without clearance to pass through the country. The French navy encountered similar problems as Indian dockworkers in Bombay and other ports boycotted ships ferrying supplies and troops to Indochina, forcing costly diversions to Trincomalee, Singapore, and other destinations where French ships were scarcely more welcome.[43]

While South Asian nationalists posed such threats to military operations in Indochina, French officials also feared the response to the outbreak of war from a more familiar adversary, China. The fighting seemed to create new opportunities for both Communists and Nationalists to meddle across the border. French authorities in Saigon had suspected since at least mid-1946 that small numbers of Chinese Communist troops were cooperating with Viet Minh forces in Tonkin.[44] After the outbreak of war, intelligence agents watched for signs of heightened collaboration and infiltration across the border. It was not until early 1948, however, that the issue grew into a major preoccupation for French authorities, and in the first year of the Indochina war, they worried far more about Nationalist ambitions. The High Commission fretted in particular that Chiang Kai-shek's government might use the fighting along his southern border and the ostensible threat to the 1.2 million ethnic Chinese who lived in Indochina as a pretext for an attempt to squash the Ho Chi Minh government in favor of a Kuomintang puppet regime that would be at least as hostile to French rule. Rumors abounded among French diplomats in early 1947 about Chinese scheming to form a Vietnamese government-in-exile that could be implanted in Hanoi when the moment came—an echo of French anxieties during the Chinese occupation a year earlier. French personnel also worried that the Nationalist government might respond to surging communist military strength in Vietnam by seeking UN intervention or might itself attempt to mediate the conflict. Indeed, the Nationalist Foreign Ministry in Chungking proposed a joint Chinese-British-U.S. mediation effort in the final days of December 1946.[45] The Chiang government soon lost interest in the initiative but, in French minds, remained unpredictable.

Amid these perils French supporters of the war turned again toward Great Britain. This time, however, French officials were disappointed with London's response. The British government had soured markedly on French policy during the occupation of southern Indochina—a bad taste that lingered in British mouths in early 1947. Without question, British strategists in the Foreign Office and military never doubted that their nation still had a strong interest in propping up French rule in Southeast Asia. London did not, therefore, refuse all French requests for assistance. Instead, the cabinet embraced a new principle: it would approve military support as long as British officials were confident there would be no damaging publicity. When the French military mission in

Singapore requested large stocks of British equipment in late January, for example, the cabinet agreed, but only after finding a way to complete the deal with the least possible risk to Britain's standing in Asia. In Singapore Lord Killearn, the senior British official in the Far East, protested that any agreement to supply the munitions from British stocks in the region could land Britain "in extremely deep waters" if it became known to Asian nationalists. Foreign Secretary Bevin's solution, endorsed by the prime minister, was to send the munitions not from Singapore to Saigon but from Britain to metropolitan France. The French would then ship the matériel to the Far East and use it as they wished. Deliveries on that basis began immediately.[46]

New agitation among Asian leaders made clear that any overt or large-scale British backing for the French war was out of the question. The danger of damaging British prestige in Asia seemed to grow dramatically as nationalists rallied behind the Viet Minh in the opening days of the war. In Malaya British authorities squashed an attempt to organize a volunteer force to fight in Vietnam, while in India they worked to discourage the dispatch of the Indo-Burmese force. Otherwise, however, the British government assumed a low profile on the Indochina issue, even when the Royal Air Force raised the possibility that French authorities, angered by Britain's unwillingness to press the Indian government over landing rights, might retaliate by barring British planes and ships from using Indochinese territory. Behind such caution lay mounting conviction that protecting Britain's interests in the Far East over the long term would depend on the cultivation of constructive relations with India and Burma after their independence. Although Britain would retain a strong colonial position in Singapore and Malaya, its influence in the Far East seemed likely to depend far more heavily than before on the good will of independent peoples. "Our aim [should] be to contrive a general partnership between independent or about-to-be-independent Eastern peoples and the Western Powers," wrote Esler Dening, who now headed the Foreign Office's Southeast Asia division. Close association with France clearly threatened to undermine that objective.[47]

Resurgent political pressure within the Labour party also dictated caution. The party's left wing had continued during 1946 to snipe at the government's approach to foreign and colonial affairs, putting the cabinet on the defensive. The Fabian Colonial Bureau, the party organization devoted to study of imperial issues, took the government to task for a lack of imagination and leadership. "The Labour Government should, without equivocation, have made it clear by some deliberate act or gesture, that it stood for principles other than those of its Tory predecessors," insisted *Empire*, the colonial bureau's journal. Given this discontent, the cabinet and the civil service had good reason to fear a new groundswell of opposition to any hint of British support for French repression after the outbreak of war in Indochina. One Asia expert at the Foreign Office wrote at the end of January 1947 that he dreaded the moment when "awkward questions will be asked in Parliament" about the Attlee government's support for French colonial policy.[48]

The dreaded moment arrived two weeks later when a Labour member of Parliament, Ronald Chamberlain, objected to the cabinet's plan to sign a defense alliance (the Treaty of Dunkirk) with Paris at a time when, he charged, France was grossly violating socialist principles on colonialism. "Many of us are extremely concerned at this recrudescence of Imperialism on the part of France," Chamberlain told Bevin during a House of Commons debate. "Will he bear in mind," Chamberlain continued, addressing the Foreign Secretary, "that we are not only a Socialist Party, but an international Socialist Party?" In his reply Bevin's discomfort was plain. Avoiding any mention of the cabinet's calculations about French policy, he sought to distance Britain from the matter. "I think I must leave this particular dispute to France," he declared, while reaffirming the cabinet's intention to go ahead with the treaty. In a letter to another Labour backbencher, G. E. Hicks, Bevin admitted that the French government had "no doubt committed faults, both political and military" in Indochina but insisted that French operations were now aimed not at "reconquering" Indochina but at "restoring law and order and creating conditions in which her liberal programme can find its realisation." Such reassurances did not, however, put an end to the matter. On March 24 Labour MP Woodrow Lyle Wyatt placed the cabinet in a delicate position by demanding to know whether, as Agence France Presse had just reported, Britain had delivered "no less than £20 million worth of military equipment" for use in Vietnam. The senior Foreign Office representative present, Minister of State Hector McNeil, resorted to semantic games, telling the House of Commons, "No aid specifically designed for Indo-China has been given to the French armed forces." Under questioning, he refused to elaborate.[49]

Skittish of association with France, the Foreign and Colonial offices retreated from the keen interest they had shown in earlier months to involve Indochina in various international schemes to promote economic development in Southeast Asia. During 1946, as London had scaled down its military commitments, it had also moved boldly to establish a peacetime supervisory apparatus to promote British interests in the region. In February the government had sent Lord Killearn to Singapore as Britain's "special commissioner" to coordinate the activities of the innumerable agencies working on economic, defense, health, and food supply questions. Convinced as always that only coordinated planning across Southeast Asia would bring about real recovery and head off mass social unrest, Killearn's bureaucracy had organized cooperative schemes with French, Dutch, and sometimes Portuguese authorities concerned with similar questions and, by early 1947, had begun exploring the possibility of establishing a more formal international association to undertake this work. "We might be sure we are none of us going to repeat our prewar mistake of water tight compartments each acting on separate or at least uncoordinated lines," Killearn had written in August 1946.[50] After the outbreak of war in Vietnam, however, British enthusiasm waned. Cooperation on food distribution and other wholly technical matters unlikely to attract much public notice continued as planned. But when the French embassy in London took the initiative in February 1947 by pressing for a higher-profile partnership in Southeast Asia, the Foreign Office balked. Dening insisted that French proposals could be accepted only on technical matters, "leaving aside political matters for the time being." A Colonial Office specialist, G. T. Seel, insisted that if any agreements for regional cooperation were reached, they should be agreed "orally rather than in writing."[51]

Torn between a desire to assist the French war effort and the need to protect the government from criticism at home and abroad, British officials settled on a familiar solution: bringing U.S. power to bear in the region on behalf of French objectives. During the closing year of the Pacific war, British planners had repeatedly urged efforts to pull the United States into the region and to capitalize on American power so as to facilitate the restoration of European hegemony in the area. In the tumultuous fall of 1945, an additional reason for involving the United States became clear to those who backed French efforts to restore control over Indochina. A strong U.S. role in supporting European policies would enable London to lower its profile and conserve its resources without compromising the essential British interest in seeing French policy succeed. British officials in London and Singapore worked strenuously during 1946 to pull Washington into performing the active role in Southeast Asian affairs that they had scripted for it. "If we manage the transition [of U.S. policy toward a peacetime posture in the Far East] carefully and maintain the necessary prudence, it is not impossible that the United States will naturally assume the place that we have from the beginning reserved for it in the eventual grouping of the powers in Southeast Asia," Michael Wright, Lord Killearn's deputy in Singapore, told d'Argenlieu.[52]

The problem, as always, was to find a way to convince a persistently reluctant Washington to take such a step. By the middle of 1947, one issue—the danger of Soviet expansionism—had obviously led Washington to close ranks with the West European powers. The president's landmark "Truman Doctrine" speech in March, declaring that the United States would come to the aid of nations threatened by communist subversion, suggested that U.S. policy was evolving toward a willingness to assume heavy military and economic burdens in peripheral areas of the globe where the Europeans had generally predominated. It remained unclear, however, whether American fears of communist expansion would have a similar effect on Washington's policy toward Southeast Asia. British officials themselves doubted whether the situation in Vietnam could reasonably be described as part of the unfolding Cold War. To be sure, consul Ernest Meiklereid reported as early as November 1946 that the Viet Minh was gradually adopting communist characteristics. But even alarmist opinions were fuzzy at best. "It is not always easy to say where nationalism ends and communism begins, and if we are trying to back the one and not the other, we may sometimes find that we are backing a horse from the wrong stable," wrote Killearn. "The fact is," he continued, "that these are restless days, and with whatever labels one attaches to the various movements, they all spring from much the same soil and much the same seeds."[53]

British officials could find virtually no evidence of contact between Hanoi and Moscow, and meticulous examination of Soviet policymaking revealed a resounding lack of interest in Southeast Asia. A week after the start of the Franco–Viet Minh war, the British embassy in Moscow called the Soviet media's lack of focus on Indochina one of its "most conspicuous omissions." Nor did British officials attach much significance to contacts between the Viet Minh and the French Communist Party. Even as tensions mounted between the Communists and their coalition partners in December 1946, in fact, J. O. Ashley-Clarke, Britain's second-ranking representative in Paris, noted that Communist ministers had "behaved very correctly" by supporting the cabinet's policies on Indochina.[54] British observers were aware of the possibility that

Moscow and the French Communist Party were intentionally holding back on Indochina in the hope of capturing power in France, a much bigger prize than Vietnam. They were undoubtedly correct in this judgment. But the fact nevertheless remained that Communist commentary on Indochina, even following the outbreak of war, remained within a sphere of legitimate political discourse in France and, in fact, resembled the policy preferred by liberals in the United States, India, and other decidedly noncommunist areas. In any case, the preponderance of British official opinion doubted whether foreign communists could control the Viet Minh even if they wanted to. "The Annamite population as a whole, other than the extremists, is not a particularly favorable breeding-ground for communism," Meiklereid reported from Saigon.[55]

The start of the Franco–Viet Minh war, then, exacerbated the dilemma that had hampered British policymaking toward Indochina at least since the occupation began in 1945, leaving London in a state of limbo by the middle of 1947. On one hand, most policymakers believed that British interests lay in boldly supporting the French war in Southeast Asia. But opposition within the Labour party and among Asian nationalists made that course problematic. As a result, British policy settled into a pattern that lasted through the rest of the year: London quietly supported the French war with limited amounts of military hardware and worked strenuously to avoid acts that would alienate anticolonial opinion; meanwhile it sought U.S. participation in Southeast Asia as a way of overcoming the entire problem. Unfortunately for London, the Washington bureaucracy showed few signs of catering to British wishes. Indeed, the outbreak of the Franco–Viet Minh war revived old controversies over the future of French rule in Indochina and, by the end of 1947, left U.S. policy as much as ever in a state of stymied indecision.

French diplomats in Washington, distrustful as usual of U.S. attitudes toward Indochina, feared that the outbreak of hostilities would produce a decisive turn against France. Ambassador Bonnet detected a sense of "prudence" and "caution" among U.S. officials after the Haiphong incident, but he and other close observers of the Washington decision-making scene predicted multiple dangers in the weeks ahead. The War Department seemed determined to tighten restrictions on the French government's ability to transfer American-supplied military equipment to the Far East. Bonnet also worried that Washington, possibly in combination with Britain, might attempt to promote a settlement through the United Nations. In Bonnet's view, that course remained unlikely because Americans would not wish to risk either directly affronting Paris or inviting Soviet involvement in the region—a likely result of UN participation. But given the "Puritanism" and overbearing sense of "superior moral duty" that seemed to inspire American public opinion, Bonnet warned darkly that "circumstances can change." Indeed, a Foreign Ministry appraisal of American opinion in January 1947 suggested a hardening of anti-French attitudes and a growing preference for a UN solution. The possibility of a unilateral American effort at mediation also loomed as an uninviting possibility. After a meeting with Dean Acheson at the end of December, Bonnet warned Paris to expect such an initiative if peace were not quickly restored.[56]

In fact, the U.S. bureaucracy responded to the war with less coherence than Bonnet feared. Part of the reason was the persistent lack of detailed information about events in Tonkin, the result of the sheer complexity of events but also, perhaps, of successful French efforts over the previous year to manage the flow of information about Vietnamese affairs. Another reason for American indecision was the same one that had stymied U.S. policymaking for years: the inability to decide between competing interests in Indochina. The debate between liberals and conservatives, increasingly a clash between the State Department's Asian and West European offices, had subsided during 1946. Washington had gradually replaced several of the most outspoken liberals in the Far East, while the French government's apparent dedication to a negotiated solution with Ho Chi Minh seemed likely to relieve Washington of the need to choose between its conflicting impulses. The outbreak of war put an end to this comfortable situation and rekindled the old debate—a debate that, as it turned out, proved as resistant to solution in 1947 as it had in 1944 and 1945.

As before, the two groups found agreement in some areas. There was consensus, for example, about the undesirability of UN action. Both sides agreed that if another country raised the Indochina conflict in the Security Council, the U.S. government would have to go along with whatever collective action was proposed. "This government, having regard for the state of American public opinion, could only support such a motion," Kenneth Landon wrote after consultation with the West European office. But the two sides also agreed that Washington must do everything possible to avoid such a position. Even a liberal such as Landon had little doubt that Moscow would insist on membership on any investigative commission established by the United Nations and would use the opportunity to call into question the full range of Western policies in Asia.[57]

On other issues, however, the start of the war drove the two policy-making factions to reassert their differences. Conservatives, buttressed by the growing role of Dean Acheson, the undersecretary of state, viewed Indochina increasingly in the context of the deepening confrontation with the Soviet Union. Most important, conservatives returned to one of their most important points from 1945: the necessity of backing French policy as a means of maintaining a close Franco-American partnership in an uncertain postwar global environment. Indeed, as the Soviet clampdown in Eastern Europe continued in 1946 and early 1947, France assumed an increasingly pivotal role in U.S. planning for the military and economic security of the West.

In a wide-ranging memorandum for the secretary of state in January, Woodruff Wallner, the new chief of the State Department's West European office, made the case with new fervor, arguing that a robust French state under the control of Western-oriented moderates was so important that the United States could not afford to quibble over French policy in Indochina, a territory of peripheral importance at best. Asserting that a "friendly and militarily powerful France" remained a "cardinal tenet" of U.S. foreign policy, Wallner argued that American interests in France were under threat from a "powerful and disciplined Communist Party" controlled by the Soviet Union. If the Communists had so far refrained from seizing power, he continued, it was only because of Moscow's determination to avoid an international crisis while the future of Germany hung in the balance. Moscow had merely instructed the French party to "bide its time and concentrate all its efforts on extending its penetration of all phases of French national life, perfecting its illegal apparatus and gradually exercising a more direct influence on the foreign and colonial policy of the [French] Government," Wallner claimed. Under the circumstances, he insisted, Washington must "support those aspects of French foreign policy which are considered vital by the democratic majority in France and which do not run directly counter to our own interests and those of world peace"—a category that first and foremost included Indochina.[58]

Conservatives also insisted on the Viet Minh's connection to international communism. Significantly, they acknowledged the utter lack of evidence to support this view and even conceded that many supporters of the Hanoi government were motivated purely by nationalism. As international tensions worsened, however, conservatives attached less importance to the lack of specific evidence and grew more inclined to operate on worst-case assumptions about communist machinations.

Wallner speculated that the Soviet government was skillfully concealing its ties to Southeast Asian nationalist movements in order to preserve the illusion that they sprang entirely from the legitimate desires of the local population. "There, more than any other region," Wallner wrote, "[Soviet agents] will seek to extend their influence through indigenous movements while seeking to avoid any color of direct interference." Acheson took a different route to the same conclusion, pointing out that while the Viet Minh had never acknowledged any tie to Moscow, neither had it ever explicitly disavowed such a connection. Following similar logic, Acheson attached less significance to the lack of praise for Ho Chi Minh that Americans found in the French or Soviet press than the fact that those media had never actually criticized Ho. Cautious in the extreme, Acheson called for a policy based not necessarily on managing the current political realities in the Far East but on avoiding at all costs the "least desirable eventuality"—a "Communist-dominated, Moscow-oriented state [in] Indochina."[59]

The conservative approach gained strength during 1947 from a new set of calculations related to the postwar status of Japan. Since the end of the Pacific war, U.S. plans had emphasized the necessity of transforming Japan into a passive, deindustrialized state with diminished capacity to upset the international order in the Far East. By 1947, however, two considerations drove Washington to reconsider this approach and to lean toward permitting Japan's full revitalization. First, U.S. officials wished to put an end to Japan's reliance on the United States for a staggering $400 million per year in economic aid, the amount deemed necessary to prevent the country's economic collapse. Second, policymakers determined that a fully revived, industrially powerful Japan could be an important U.S. ally and bulwark against Soviet expansionism in the Far East. As historian Michael Schaller has demonstrated, this shift had profound implications for U.S. policy not just toward Japan but toward neighboring areas as well. If Japan were to become an economically robust nation, U.S. planners concluded, it would require access to raw materials and markets in quantities far exceeding what the home islands could provide.[60]

The obvious solution was to reestablish the old nexus between Japan and the Asian continent, ironically the very relationship that the United States and its allies had in some sense fought to destroy during the Second World War. In February 1947 the State Department's Division of Japanese and Korean Affairs laid out a comprehensive recovery scheme involving the removal of punitive controls on Japanese industry and efforts to place the country once again at the hub of an integrated Asian trading system in which Southeast Asia would serve as a "natural frontier" for Japanese economic expansion. As political chaos accelerated in China during 1947 and 1948, the importance of Southeast Asia only increased. To ensure Japan's economic revival and reliability as a U.S. ally, American officials focused increasingly on keeping Indochina in the hands of those most likely to ensure its stability and avoid the danger of communist takeover. Conservatives had no doubt that France was best suited to that task.

Despite these arguments for supporting the French war, the persistent influence of liberal ideas blocked any shift away from neutrality. As in earlier periods, liberals advocated U.S. activism to bring about a peaceful solution. For Abbott Low Moffat, Kenneth Landon, and their Far Eastern office associates in the State Department, the war seemed increasingly likely only to radicalize Vietnamese nationalists and destroy any possible basis for a compromise settlement that would promote lasting stability in the region. In Saigon on December 21, 1946, Moffat returned to an old liberal theme, expressing alarm that continued fighting in Tonkin might turn the Vietnamese against "all whites" and destroy any possibility of sustaining Western involvement in the area. The only answer, he concluded, was U.S. mediation, a solution Moffat repeatedly advocated during and after his tour of Southeast Asia in the last days of 1946 and the start of 1947. Without "prompt U.S. action," he warned in a cable to Washington, war would inevitably cost "countless lives" and shatter U.S. prestige in the region. Moffat protested that the "hands-off" policy practiced up to that point seemed to be based entirely on "European considerations" and the "temporary French political situation." To the Vietnamese, he warned, U.S. inaction was bound to suggest "U.S. approval [of the] French military reconquest." If the Hanoi government's record was imperfect, he added, it was "no worse than the French."[61]

Liberals argued with new fervor that French repression was largely responsible for generating a communist danger. They readily conceded that devoted communists were active within the Viet Minh's leadership. Liberals had never denied the communist risk and even, back during 1945, had been in front of the conservatives in calling attention to this danger. But they argued that unrest in Vietnam resulted mainly from popular radicalism that fed on colonial repression, war, and instability—conditions that enabled the Soviet Union to pose plausibly as the defender of peoples struggling for their independence. While French intelligence purported to discover new evidence of the Viet Minh's essential communist identity around the outbreak of the war, Moffat, Landon, and their colleagues expressed suspicion of what they considered facile French attempts to raise the specter of Moscow-directed communism. In Saigon consul Charles Reed complained that d'Argenlieu had "given undue emphasis" to the communist threat and asserted that many French claims could be "discounted." The French, Reed observed in March 1947, were increasingly inclined to brand the Viet Minh as communists even though, in his opinion, Vietnamese unrest was mainly attributable to "a desire for independence and a burning wish to strike back at the French for their high-handed exploitation."[62]

The first thorough State Department analysis of the communist role within the Viet Minh sustained this view. Although the movement's leadership contained "a strong Communist element," the report asserted that there was "little reason to believe that a large Communist mass movement exists at this time." Popular demands for land reform, democracy, and fair taxation "are not Communist in character," the report stated, pointing out that those objectives worked against communist ambitions by promoting private ownership. "Only in view of the failure of liberal elements to secure these long-overdue reforms peacefully is the Annamese population now pinning its hopes on Communist leaders and guerrilla warfare," the report added. Liberals had no doubt that the Soviet Union would attempt to exploit this situation. Like the conservatives, they attributed Moscow's silence on the issue largely to its desire to strengthen the Communists in France. But liberals pointed out that the Soviets might become more attentive to Indochina once political conditions changed in France. It was therefore essential, Landon wrote, that the United States attempt to mediate the dispute—both to undercut the appeal of radicalism within Vietnam and to deny the Soviets a propaganda advantage.[63]

Landon, Moffat, and other State Department officials were not the only ones who made such arguments. The outbreak of fighting brought the Indochina issue to the sustained attention of the American media for the first time, and the editorial responses of mainstream publications frequently echoed the liberal ideas of the Asia specialists. In an editorial that made no reference to communism, the *New York Times* described the fighting as "a violently inflamed symptom of the eagerness of all former colonial peoples of the Far East for national independence." The *Times* expressed ambivalence about the Vietnamese themselves, noting that they had not yet demonstrated their "capacity for self-government." But the paper pointed out that they were nevertheless "determined to have it" and that Paris was heading down a dangerous road by resisting. The editorial singled out France as "the only European nation attempting to retain her grip in the Far East by force" and warned ominously that the French government would have to "determine how long it can allow its shaky economy to be drained by a costly and unwanted overseas war." The *Washington Post* showed far more concern about the communist risk, even describing Ho Chi Minh as "a disciple of Moscow." But the *Post* also accused the French government of inflaming local resentments through its "dilatoriness" in fulfilling its promises of real autonomy.[64]

With old disagreements reasserting themselves powerfully, the State Department sought a compromise between the conservative and liberal viewpoints. With the consent of both John Carter Vincent of the Office of Far Eastern Affairs and H. Freeman Matthews of the West European office, Dean Acheson announced during his meeting with Ambassador Bonnet on December 24, 1946, that the U.S. government stood "ready and willing to do anything which [the French government] might consider helpful" to bring the fighting to an end, warning that prolongation of the war might invite UN (and therefore Soviet) involvement. Acheson's offer of "good offices" clearly did not go as far as Moffat had urged, especially because it ruled out "mediation" for the time being. In addition, the State Department chose not to make its offer public, most likely to avoid any possibility of embarrassing Paris if it rejected the bid. Still, even this meager proposal alarmed French officials who watched anxiously as Moffat continued to push for more assertive diplomatic intervention. Following instructions from Paris, François Lacoste, the senior counselor at the French embassy in Washington, flatly rejected the U.S. offer on January 8. The French government would address the issue "single-handedly," Lacoste told Vincent. Lacking any other ideas and prevented by policymaking paralysis from moving in any bold new direction, Washington could do little but meekly renew its offer over the following weeks.[65]

French rejection of the "good offices" proposal left Washington with no policy at all toward the deepening crisis in Indochina. As so often in previous months, U.S. indecision conceded the initiative to the French government and left policymakers across the American bureaucracy deeply dissatisfied with the flow of events. With a remarkable tone of frustration and despair, the new U.S. secretary of state, George Marshall, instructed Ambassador Caffery on February 3 to have yet another talk with French leaders about the dangerous situation unfolding in Indochina, even though Washington had nothing new to offer. Marshall squarely acknowledged the fundamental dilemma that had stymied American decision making on Indochina. On one hand, he wrote,

> we have only the very friendliest feelings toward France and we are anxious in every way we can to support France in her fight to regain her economic, political and military strength and to restore herself as in fact one of [the] major powers of [the] world. In spite [of] any misunderstanding which might have arisen in [the] minds [of the] French in regard to our position concerning Indochina they must appreciate that we have fully recognized France's sovereign position in that area and we do not wish to have it appear that we are in any way endeavoring [to] undermine that position.

On the other hand, Marshall, far more attuned to the complexity of colonial problems than his predecessor as secretary of state, did not shy away from criticizing French policy. "We cannot shut our eyes," he wrote Caffery,

> to [the] fact that there are two sides [to] this problem and that our reports indicate both a lack of French understanding of [the] other side (more in Saigon than Paris) and continued existence [of a] dangerously outmoded colonial outlook and methods in [the] area. Furthermore, there is no escape from [the] fact that [the] trend of [the] times is to [the] effect that colonial empires in [the] XIX century sense are rapidly become [a] thing of [the] past.[66]

On the key question of the Viet Minh's essential identity, the secretary of state was equally attentive to both sides of the argument. Marshall's recent experience as the Truman administration's mediator between the Chinese Nationalists and Communists left him with a keen awareness of the complexities of Asian politics, not least the risks of painting the Viet Minh as a simple tool of Soviet expansionism. "We do not lose sight [of the] fact that Ho Chi Minh has direct Communist connections," Marshall wrote, "and it should be obvious that we are not interested in seeing colonial empire administrations supplanted by [a] philosophy and political organizations emanating from and controlled by [the] Kremlin." But Marshall simultaneously acknowledged the liberal position that Vietnamese nationalists were animated above all by anticolonialism—and that Washington would therefore have no choice but to support a UN inquiry into the situation if another government took the initiative. All in all, Marshall threw up his hands in frustration. "Frankly," he confessed in a remarkable statement of impotence, "we have no solution [to the] problem to suggest."[67]

U.S. actions in the following days reflected the ambivalence of Marshall's cable. On the secretary's instructions, Ambassador Caffery handed French Foreign Minister Georges Bidault an aide-mémoire on February 6 asserting that Washington had only the "friendliest feelings for France" and wished to see the country restored to its prewar position. It asserted that it was not appropriate for the United States to propose a solution to the crisis in Indochina, which, it said, must be resolved through "direct negotiations between the French Government and Vietnam." But the aide-mémoire also insisted that Paris recognize that colonial empires were "a thing of the past" and urged the French government to move down the road of colonial devolution already traveled by the British and Dutch governments. The situation was becoming critical, the document said, and "no longer could be seen as strictly a local issue." For its part, the United States stood ready "to help in any useful way to find a solution to this difficult problem." Meanwhile, Marshall ordered O'Sullivan, the consul in Hanoi, to maintain contacts with Viet Minh representatives in order to keep information channels open and possibly to lend humanitarian assistance.[68]

Some aspects of the American position gratified French supporters of the *politique de force*. The "good offices" proposal, after all, stopped well short of mediation, and Americans repeatedly emphasized their dedication to the principle of French sovereignty in Indochina. Yet there was plenty in the American attitude to inspire anxiety. The State Department's assertions that the United States would have no choice but to cooperate with any UN initiative raised the prospect of French isolation against a group of powers including both the United States and the Soviet Union. Meanwhile, U.S. contacts with the Viet Minh, although carefully monitored by French intelligence, suggested that Washington might yet deal with the nationalists behind French backs. Most significant, American moves to tighten restrictions on the transfer of equipment compounded shortages faced by the French military. The start of fighting increased French dependence on U.S. supplies by creating new needs for spare parts as well as additional landing craft, planes, and other gear. Yet U.S. authorities rejected French requests, while also cracking down on resale of U.S.-manufactured equipment by other governments.[69]

Relaxation of the American equipment transfer policy during 1946 had stemmed partly from a sense that the political risks were declining in Indochina as the French and nationalists moved toward compromise. After the outbreak of war, old worries came back. U.S. officials showed unprecedented sensitivity to press reports and even letters from private citizens complaining about French use of U.S.-made gear. When a Manila newspaper pointed out that the French military was using equipment acquired from the U.S. Liquidation Commission there, State Department officials insisted that such equipment had been intended for purely nonmilitary functions and briefly contemplated confronting the French government over the issue. In reply to letters from private citizens a carefully crafted department response emphasized that Washington unfortunately lacked control over the use of large amounts of equipment provided to various combatant forces during the Second World War. "The arming of those forces saved thousands of American lives which otherwise would have been lost," the department pointed out.[70]

So critical was the problem of acquiring U.S. equipment that Premier Ramadier took the initiative. The obvious solution was to acquire U.S. equipment in Europe, where it was more freely available, and then transfer it to the Far East. But that solution threatened to overburden French shipping while also posing the risk that Washington might object, throwing into jeopardy American military aid programs considered vital to the defense of metropolitan France. Under the circumstances, Ramadier insisted that French officials must attempt to conceal the ultimate use of equipment acquired in Europe. France had a "major interest" to avoid conversations with U.S. military officials that included "any mention of the final destination of material with military uses that we are acquiring now in the United States," Ramadier wrote in instructions to the Finance Ministry. French officials appear to have acted accordingly. During negotiations on the purchase of fifty-five thousand tons of U.S. munitions, for example, the French military attaché in Washington informed his superiors in Paris that he had scrupulously omitted any reference to Indochina, even though the equipment was to be sent to the Far East.[71] The ruse made no difference, however, and equipment shortages pinched ever more tightly as 1947 advanced.

TOWARD THE BAO DAI SOLUTION

The lack of domestic and international support might not have become critical if the war had gone as well for the French military in 1947 as the hawks had expected the year before. But French forces suffered unexpectedly heavy casualties and lost tremendous amounts of equipment in the first months of the war. Estimates of the manpower necessary to cope with the situation grew alarmingly to half a million men or more. In moments of honesty, French officials marveled at the magnitude of the problems they faced. In June 1947 Philippe Baudet, head of the Foreign Ministry's Asia-Oceania department, told an Australian diplomat that the military situation was rapidly becoming "hopeless" and even that "there was nothing more which the French could do." French military authorities told Caffery as early as March that they had already "scraped the bottom of the barrel" for new recruits—a problem that would worsen as a nationalist rebellion in Madagascar, another French territory, exploded into an additional burden demanding at least fifteen thousand troops. Viet Minh destruction of rubber plantations and other French assets in Vietnam also complicated the manpower problem by forcing military planners to assign troops to guard exposed agricultural and mining areas even as they tried to maintain combat operations.[72]

As the journalist Bernard Fall later pointed out, even the high point of French military success during 1947—"Operation Lea," a major autumn offensive into the Tonkinese countryside aimed at capturing top Viet Minh leaders—was, in fact, no success at all. To be sure, French forces inflicted as many as ten thousand Viet Minh casualties, captured large parts of the Viet Minh–controlled "liberated zone" in the Tonkinese mountains, and reinforced a chain of forts along the Chinese border. But the entire operation amounted to a "gambler's last throw," in the words of one British observer, a desperate bid to achieve a decisive military victory before equipment shortages and parliamentary opposition forced a return to the bargaining table. In pursuing this goal the operation was an utter failure. French forces not only failed to seize Viet Minh leaders but also let thousands of Viet Minh fighters slip away from the battlefield to fight another day. Meanwhile, French costs reached unbearable levels. In the war's first year, France spent an unsustainable sixty billion francs and suffered five thousand casualties.[73]

French leaders who controlled Indochina policy making—the cabinet, the ministries of Foreign Affairs and Overseas France, and the military—responded to this mounting crisis in a way that echoed French behavior in 1944 and 1945: lacking adequate resources of its own and desperately in need of international legitimization, Paris looked outward for support. If they could garner British and especially U.S. backing, the hawks would be able to carry on their war. The challenge, of course, remained precisely what it had been in the earlier period—to recast French ambitions in order to overcome opposition within the British and American policymaking establishments. For a time during

1946, French leaders had turned away from this effort, confident that they could remaster Indochina without first considering the sensitivities of foreign nations. Now, with French weaknesses freshly exposed, diplomacy returned to the center of policymaking. "It appears that the Indochina affair must now be dealt with not so much on its actual merits but even more so by taking account of the likely international impacts and consequences," Jean Chauvel, the Foreign Ministry's secretary general, wrote in February 1947.[74] These words might just as easily have been written in 1944, but there was a crucial difference between French thinking then and French calculations during the first year of the war against the Viet Minh. During the closing stages of the Second World War, the diplomatic approach had rested on a consensus among Free French policymakers that their country could achieve its objectives in Indochina only with foreign backing. Diplomacy now stood out as the solution principally for one faction of French policymakers: those who wished to carry on the war. For this group foreign partnerships offered a means of compensating for domestic ambivalence and avoiding the necessity of compromise with those who favored renewed negotiations with Ho Chi Minh. It was, in short, the only way to preserve French colonialism in Southeast Asia.

During 1947 French diplomats followed many of the same strategies as in earlier years. Above all, they struggled to recast French policy as liberal and enlightened. To encourage this view, French hawks knew they had no choice but to replace d'Argenlieu as high commissioner. The anti-American firebrand, widely believed to have sparked the war through his defiance of policies made in Paris, had become a liability to any effort to persuade foreigners of the justice of the French cause. The high commissioner's bellicose avowals of French power and grotesque depictions of the Viet Minh as a bloodthirsty communist cabal caused increasing anxiety within the Foreign Ministry in the first weeks of 1947—and with good reason. By this point both American and British diplomats in Vietnam had lost all trust in d'Argenlieu. In Hanoi the U.S. consul, O'Sullivan, warned that d'Argenlieu's denunciations of the Viet Minh seemed intended to "divert attention" from French aggression. The equally skeptical British consul in Saigon, Ernest Meiklereid, similarly warned his superiors in London that "the sudden raising of the communist bogey" seemed part of d'Argenlieu's plan "to discredit the Viet Nam government and to obtain support, or at least non-interference, from the United States, China and ourselves in their dealings with the Annamites." Policymakers in Paris shared that goal, of course, but they had no confidence that d'Argenlieu's blunt methods could achieve it. The government recalled the admiral in February and replaced him a few weeks later with a figure ideally suited to the new image that French officials wished to cultivate abroad, Emile Bollaert.[75]

A civilian and a moderate (despite his membership in the misleadingly named Radical party), Bollaert exuded reasonableness and liberality as he took up his duties as high commissioner. Bollaert's orders from the cabinet instructed him to emphasize that France did not want "to reestablish the old kind of rule over its overseas territories" or "to interfere with or intervene against the wishes of the governments of the Indochinese states." Bollaert carried out those instructions faithfully, reassuring Caffery even before leaving for the Far East that "any attempt to return to previous colonial practices is inconceivable." Bollaert added that he was leaving with a "determined intention to carry out all promises hitherto made by the French Government in regard to the 'independence of various countries within the French Union.'" His foremost task, he added, was to "come to an agreement with whatever authorities really represent the people of Indochina." Implicit in that formulation lay the possibility that eventual negotiations would involve not Ho Chi Minh's government but a new Vietnamese authority. But for the time being, Bollaert's main concern, like that of French diplomats around the world, was to strike a conciliatory tone, not to lay out a specific policy. In his first major speech in Hanoi Bollaert took much the same approach. French participation in Indochinese affairs, he stated, should not be "a humiliating constraint on the legitimate patriotism of the Indochinese peoples, who ought to have their place in the sun." The contrast with d'Argenlieu could hardly have been sharper.[76]

The French campaign to influence international opinion also involved new efforts to control media reporting. The ministries and the High Commission worried especially about anti-French reporting in the U.S. press, including dispatches that noted (accurately) that as much as 28 percent of the French Foreign Legion in Indochina was comprised of German mercenaries who had served in the Nazi military. A Defense Ministry report expressed fear that Americans readily accepted such unflattering reports while also uncritically imbibing the Viet Minh's "simplistic propaganda." In the United States, the report asserted, press articles, no matter how biased, "found the complacent ear of a puerile readership." To remedy the problem, the High Commission and the military sharply tightened censorship rules for both local and foreign reporters—rules that Moffat complained had already been taken to "fantastic lengths" suggesting the practices of "a totalitarian regime at its worst." From the standpoint of the French military, however, such tactics were successful. As the *New York Times* ruefully observed, censorship forced the world press to depend "upon Paris for detailed news on the Indo-China conflict." Meanwhile, the Foreign Ministry instructed diplomats to be more aggressive in refuting unflattering reports, while officials in the Washington embassy suggested new efforts to supply sympathetic reporters with pro-French material. Most promising of all were Catholic publications, which seemed to offer "propitious terrain" for French influence. The French government also began establishing information offices in Asian capitals to counter Viet Minh propaganda.[77]

Efforts to monitor and restrain the ability of Vietnamese nationalists to influence foreign opinion also became a central part of the French campaign to control international perceptions of the war. In the United States and Western Europe, French intelligence stepped up surveillance of émigré groups such as the Vietnamese-American Friendship Association, which spread anti-French propaganda, organized demonstrations, and urged Western governments to take the Indochina matter to the Security Council. But French authorities reserved their closest scrutiny for the activities of Viet Minh diplomats as Ho Chi Minh's regime established a diplomatic network throughout Southeast Asia in mid-1947. Vietnamese representatives set up offices in India, Burma, Malaya, and Thailand, which one French intelligence report rated as the "principal center" for the conduct of Viet Minh foreign policy. Viet Minh officials in Thailand, the report asserted, not only obtained weapons and spread propaganda but were also "very well placed to spread freely throughout the world, and especially among the Americans." The possibility of an understanding between the United States and the Viet Minh remained the nightmare scenario for the French government. Viet Minh propaganda frequently appealed to the United States on the basis of a common opposition to colonialism. The Viet Minh–controlled Radio Vietnam flattered the United States in September 1947, for example, as "the first country to fight for independence and democracy, [the] first to free colonies."[78]

To prevent Americans from taking the lead in reaching any sort of rapprochement with the Viet Minh, French authorities exploited restrictive commerce rules to exclude U.S. businesspeople as far as possible, stepped up surveillance of American missionaries, and complained to the State Department when they suspected U.S. diplomats of meeting with proscribed nationalists. So thorough were French efforts to constrain American activities in Indochina that the High Commission lodged a formal complaint in March 1947 when the U.S. Information Service office in Saigon, still a focal point of controversy, showed Frank Capra's 1943 film *Divide and Conquer,* a harsh portrayal of France under the Nazi occupation.[79]

None of these efforts to manage international perceptions of the Indochina war achieved significant results. As usual, French observers discerned some encouraging signs. A High Commission study of American attitudes in October considered it "unlikely" that Washington, increasingly concerned about maintaining stability in peripheral areas of the globe as international tensions mounted, would return "to its past errors," meaning its presumed support for the Viet Minh during 1945. "For a while yet, order is synonymous with the French presence," the paper stated. But other appraisals revealed deep anxiety about U.S. views. In Washington, Lacoste wrote in September 1947 that any easing of American anticolonial attitudes might be only "temporary." If deepening U.S.-Soviet tensions seemed likely to push American policy in helpful directions, Lacoste noted that Washington's attitudes on colonial questions remained unpredictable. The Truman Doctrine, proclaimed in March 1947, could, after all, cut two ways. It could lead the United States to form partnerships with the European powers to defend peripheral areas from communist encroachment, or it could move the Americans, determined to leave nothing to chance, to replace the colonial powers as the dominant outside influence in threatened areas. If carried too far, then, anticommunism could bring about the least-desired outcome, the eclipse of French colonial power.[80]

Rumors of mounting U.S. ambitions circulated among the French community in Vietnam throughout the year, with one Saigon newspaper reporting in October that the United States would soon send troops to settle the war on terms favorable to it. U.S.–Vietnamese contacts around the same time suggested the less spectacular but equally troubling prospect that a deal would be reached at the expense of France. French authorities watched anxiously as U.S. officials in China seemed increasingly intent on opening new channels to the Viet Minh leadership. Even when American officials readily admitted to meetings with Vietnamese leaders—as when the U.S. consul in Hong Kong met with Ngo Dinh Diem, the anticommunist nationalist who would play a major role following the French defeat in 1954—American motives were a matter of debate among French observers. Ironically, French officials seem to have been less aware of more meaningful activities in Bangkok, where Pham Ngoc Thach, a deputy minister in Ho Chi Minh's government, met repeatedly with U.S. diplomats in late 1947 and early 1948 to seek U.S. assistance. In one meeting, Pham invited Washington to send an observer to visit Viet Minh–controlled areas in Tonkin. In another, he asked that the United States apply economic pressure on France to ease its Vietnam policy. U.S. officials appear to have treated such requests cautiously but, for the time being, saw value in keeping the discussion channel open.[81]

Even without detailed knowledge of these conversations, French officials saw plenty of evidence by the end of 1947 to know that Washington was nowhere near a decision to provide political or material support for French policy. In fact, Washington seemed to be moving in the opposite direction. In January 1948 the State Department formally excluded Indochina from the Marshall Plan, the massive U.S. aid program begun in mid-1947 with the aim of rehabilitating the West European economy. French officials had hoped that Washington would agree to channel some funds to French colonies, but the State Department adamantly refused. U.S. economic support for French colonialism not only seemed likely to tarnish American prestige in Asia but also, Landon warned, threatened to generate opposition to the entire European Recovery Program when implementing legislation came before Congress in early 1948.[82]

There remained, of course, the risk that the French government would simply divert Marshall Plan aid to support the war in Indochina. Indeed, one State Department study concluded that France might be able to reroute as much as $900 million over a four-year span. U.S. officials discussed various methods of coping with that problem but, in the end, found no answers, concluding that the only way out of this conundrum was to help bring about an early end to the war and a comprehensive settlement. If this arrangement offered the French hawks some hope, they were less encouraged by the American attitude on the transfer of military equipment. On that subject U.S. authorities only tightened their restrictions. Even Woodruff Wallner, who had recently argued for active American support of French policy, warned French interlocutors that Washington was now in no mood for flexibility on the matter. He admitted that U.S. officials had sometimes been willing to "close their eyes" to the French military's use of American hardware in 1946 but now insisted that the "goodwill of American authorities could go no further." Indeed, the State Department rejected French efforts to purchase landing craft and took steps to crack down on private American shipping companies alleged to have transported 110 tons of ammunition to Indochina earlier in the year in ships owned by the U.S. War Shipping Administration.[83]

British attitudes were hardly more encouraging. Foreign Office personnel never lost their conviction that French suppression of nationalist unrest offered the safest path to restoring the Indochinese economy. Chaos in the Vietnamese countryside continued to stunt rubber production and led to a new downturn in rice production, a matter of severe alarm for British food production experts in Singapore. Whatever the temptations to assist the French war effort, however, the British government moved further away from that course because of the risk of backlash in India and Burma. British authorities ruled out new French purchases of arms and other equipment in the second half of 1947 and, because of the risk of stirring opposition in India, refused to go ahead with a previously agreed sale of British vehicles stockpiled there. In a debate that paralleled the division in the United States, Duff Cooper, the British ambassador in London, insisted that the sale go ahead, because French goodwill was far more important than Indian. Specialists in colonial and Asian affairs, however, refused to risk such a direct affront to Indian sensitivities in the weeks before independence. As a solution, the Foreign Office suggested that Paris approach Indian authorities on its own.[84]

Under these worsening circumstances, French supporters of the war faced difficult decisions. They could accede to the liberals by agreeing to renew negotiations with Ho Chi Minh in hopes of reaching an accord that would preserve as much French authority as possible despite the failure to achieve military victory. Or they could move toward a new approach to the entire problem by calling for talks with a different, more compliant Vietnamese leadership to which Paris could more safely concede all the trappings of autonomy. The latter approach appealed as a possible way to resolve domestic and international problems confronted by advocates of the *politique de force*. At home, it promised to ease political opposition by enabling supporters of the war to refashion themselves as moderates and by pulling waverers toward a position that could be described as firm but reasonable. Internationally, it promised to garner support by recasting the war as a conflict between moderate nationalists willing to cooperate with the West and radicals who, once there was a new variant of nationalism in the mix, would appear increasingly to be the servants of international communism. In this way the French could claim more plausibly to be defending the Western position in the global Cold War.

From this blend of considerations emerged the "Bao Dai solution," a bold departure in French policy designed largely to shatter existing international perceptions of the Indochina conflict and, essentially, to start over with a new configuration that might attract a more favorable view. "The attitudes of Great Britain and the U.S.A. make it inconceivable to follow a policy of reestablishing our sovereignty on the old terms," explained a December 1947 memorandum by Jean Ramadier, a former colonial administrator in Indochina who enjoyed access to high-level policymaking through his father, the recently resigned French premier. The paper noted that among Southeast Asian territories only Indochina and Indonesia had not achieved formal progress toward self-rule. The previous few months had shown, it added, that it would be impossible to obtain any dramatic easing of foreign opinion toward French policy without comparable progress in Indochina. The Bao Dai option would enable the French government to claim it was moving toward colonial devolution and would appeal to Washington because of the parallels with American policy in Japan, the paper asserted. The United States, it noted, had decided to preserve the Japanese imperial system after 1945 believing that the emperor, who inspired absolute obedience, could help instill Western-style democracy in a people lacking democratic traditions. Ramadier and other supporters of the Bao Dai alternative hoped that the former emperor of Annam might play a similar role in Vietnam, or at least that the possibility would generate support for French policy in the United States and elsewhere.[85]

The MRP politicians who increasingly dominated foreign and colonial policy in the early Fourth Republic made clear shortly after the outbreak of war in Indochina that if France went back to the negotiating table, it might well do so with a Vietnamese leadership other than Ho Chi Minh's government. Officials quickly settled on Bao Dai as the best candidate for the position. French representatives in Hong Kong established contact with him in late fall 1946 as all-out warfare with the Viet Minh grew increasingly likely. But the French government proceeded cautiously and revealed few details to foreign diplomats, frequently downplaying the significance of the entire enterprise. Only in summer 1947 did hawks in the cabinet, frightened by new pressures for conciliation, move boldly toward the Bao Dai solution.[86] Bollaert, exceeding his mandate to moderate the implementation of French policy, responded to new peace feelers from Ho in mid-July by telling the press that if the fighting could be stopped, the French government would negotiate with "all parties and groups—except the irreconcilable enemies of reason—grouped together under the banner of patriotism"—a category that seemed to include Ho and other more "reasonable" elements within the Viet Minh. Bollaert later told an interviewer that he had hoped to mark Indian independence on August 15 with a major speech declaring conditional independence for Vietnam. Under his plan France would have withdrawn thirty thousand troops immediately and, as long as the Viet Minh agreed to turn over French prisoners, declared full independence on November 1. General Valluy caught wind of Bollaert's ideas, however, and rushed to Paris to inform the cabinet of the high commissioner's plan. On August 12 the cabinet, under the control of MRP and moderate Socialist ministers, recalled Bollaert for consultations. In Paris a few days later, the cabinet, with Bollaert and Valluy in attendance, reined in the high commissioner's ambitions and ordered him to chart a course that pointed directly toward the Bao Dai solution.[87]

Under a broiling Tonkin sun on September 10, Bollaert laid out the French government's new approach in a speech sharply different from the one he had planned a month earlier. The high commissioner offered two significant concessions. First, he indicated that the French government was prepared to accept unification of the three parts of Vietnam (Tonkin, Annam, and Cochinchina). Second, he offered Vietnam "independence" within the French Union (using the Vietnamese word *Doc Lap* rather than the French *indépendence*). In other respects, however, the terms outlined in the speech fell far short of anything that the French government could have expected Ho's government to accept. Above all, Bollaert indicated that membership in the French Union would bar Vietnam from setting its own military or diplomatic policy, aspects of sovereignty central to Viet Minh demands for many months. Bollaert also declared that his offer was nonnegotiable, explaining that bargaining over such matters "would be in truth unworthy of such a noble cause." He called on "all the political and cultural groups within Vietnam" to respond to his initiative by bringing forth a "qualified government" to lead the country into this promised place in the French Union.[88]

Although the speech did not explicitly rule out negotiations with Ho Chi Minh, it was clearly intended to eliminate that possibility. Bollaert's terms represented a long stride backward from French concessions contained in the March 6 accord. The atmosphere surrounding the speech made French intentions even clearer. A banner hung nearby proclaimed

"Vive l'ex-Empereur Bao Dai," and the Tonkinese delegation that shared the stage with Bollaert consisted of two obscure mandarins and two Catholics, one a former Sûreté agent. A listless crowd of one thousand hastily assembled by colonial authorities offered polite applause while wondering, as the British consul put it, "what was going to happen next to them." A unit of Senegalese troops stood nearby to make sure the event went according to script.[89]

The speech, punctuated by squeaks from a faulty microphone, hardly amounted to an inspired launch for the Bao Dai solution. Indeed, Bollaert never mentioned the former emperor by name. But the decisive turn in French policy was unmistakable. When Ho Chi Minh offered new negotiating terms in the early fall, the French government offered no reply.[90] Meanwhile, talks with Bao Dai intensified, especially after the failed October offensive demonstrated that France could not win a quick military victory. Momentum toward the Bao Dai solution increased again in November, when Robert Schuman, a prominent MRP politician, became premier, pushing French colonial and foreign policies further to the right. Schuman's appointment of his close party ally, Paul Coste-Floret, as minister of overseas France completed the MRP's control over the institutions with responsibility for Indochina. At the same time, Bollaert dissolved d'Argenlieu's separate "Republic of Cochinchina" to entice Bao Dai to go along with French plans. Under pressure from Vietnamese nationalists and apparently anxious to protect his own reputation for nationalism, Bao Dai demanded more, including even a firm pledge of independence like those given to India and Burma in earlier years, in return for his cooperation. But the French government prevailed. On December 7, 1947, aboard a French warship in Tonkin's Ha Long Bay, Bao Dai and Bollaert signed an agreement in which the former emperor agreed to negotiate on terms sharply restricting the "independence" that the document ambiguously promised. After further talks with Bao Dai in Geneva and consultations with the cabinet in Paris, Bollaert proclaimed in a speech on January 29, 1948, that henceforth France would negotiate only with Bao Dai. Whether the new approach would at last unlock international backing for France remained to be seen.

CHAPTER 5

Domestic Divides, Foreign Solutions

In Bao Dai the French government selected a man ill suited to the task of rallying his nation. Born in 1913, Bao Dai ("Keeper of Greatness"), became the thirteenth emperor of Vietnam's Nguyen dynasty in 1926. As so often over the course of his life, Bao Dai ruled in name only. The French administration appointed a regent to supervise court affairs while Bao Dai completed his education in France. After returning to Vietnam in 1932, the emperor, imbued with European ideas and tastes, worked to modernize the monarchy and to implement Westernizing reforms—evidence of a genuine desire to serve his nation. Much of the time, however, he devoted himself to gambling, hunting, womanizing, and spending the generous allowance paid by the French government, activities that earned him an unshakable reputation for hedonism. Legend had it that the emperor, known for his lengthy hunting trips, single-handedly killed off a significant part of Vietnam's population of wild tigers.

Whether preoccupied by such adventures or convinced that his country stood no chance of resisting foreign powers, Bao Dai repeatedly transferred his loyalties as political winds shifted during the turbulent 1940s. Following the German defeat of France, he threw his support behind Admiral Jean Decoux's Vichyite regime, only to tack again after the Japanese takeover on March 9, 1945. For nearly six months Bao Dai presided over the puppet regime that collaborated with Tokyo. On August 30, 1945, with the Vietnamese revolution sweeping over his country, Bao Dai shifted yet again, abdicating in exchange for a position in the latest regime to claim power, Ho Chi Minh's Democratic Republic of Vietnam. Bao Dai served as "supreme advisor" to the Hanoi regime for seven months before decamping to Hong Kong in early 1946. It was there that French agents found the former emperor and began the campaign to coax him into reentering Vietnamese politics on behalf of yet another sponsor, the new French republic.[1]

Given this record of fecklessness and toadyism, it is little surprise that Bao Dai failed to unite Vietnam behind his rule or to establish a viable Western-oriented state. The Bao Dai experiment whimpered to an end in the mid-1950s, crippled by the French defeat in 1954 and finally destroyed by a 1955 referendum that left Ngo Dinh Diem in control of a new South Vietnamese state under U.S. tutelage. Bao Dai relocated to the French Riviera and, until his death in 1997, pursued the pleasures for which he had become famous in earlier days. Surveying this dubious performance, most historians have had little difficulty judging the Bao Dai solution an abject failure.[2] Yet in at least one critical respect, the venture deserves to be rated a remarkable success. The manufacturing of an alternative nationalism within Vietnam in 1948 and 1949 served as the catalyst for the creation of an international coalition behind French policy in Vietnam, the objective that French leaders had hoped to achieve for several years. French efforts to attract international support had achieved only limited results before 1948. The critical shift came in that year and especially the first half of 1949, when the Bao Dai experiment recast the political situation in Vietnam in a way that facilitated international backing for French aims.

During this critical transitional period French policy in Vietnam assumed a sufficiently liberal veneer to enable French, British, and American advocates of suppressing the Viet Minh to hold their adversaries at bay and lay the groundwork for political and military partnership. In earlier years the policymaking community in each of these three countries had become sharply divided over Vietnam. In the United States, the division had long roots, running back to wartime debates over how to balance the need for cooperation with West European allies against the desire to align the country with the forces of sociopolitical change in Asia. In the British case, the cleavage had opened in 1945, when the Labour party's left wing and Asian nationalists crucial to Britain's long-term interests in the Far East challenged the previously unified foreign policy establishment in London over its vigorous support for French colonialism. In France policy differences emerged later, in 1946, after a lengthy period of consensus among the policymaking elite that had presided over the Free French movement and then the nascent Fourth Republic.

In each case, division had produced policymaking paralysis by the start of 1948. Stymied by competing impulses, neither Washington nor London had crafted a coherent, assertive policy toward the Franco–Viet Minh war. In France, meanwhile, the prowar faction and the group favoring new talks with Ho Chi Minh roughly balanced each other, precluding bold moves in either direction. For American and British officials, mounting Cold War anxieties offered little guidance. Fighting the Viet Minh promised to strengthen anticommunist elements in France while eliminating the explicitly procommunist Viet Minh leadership, but it also threatened to radicalize the situation in Vietnam, pushing greater numbers to embrace communism as the sole effective way to resist colonial repression. Repression also promised to alienate Asian opinion beyond Indochina. The first year of fighting only heightened those risks by exposing the brutality of French methods. The French doves stepped up pressure for a peaceful solution, while emboldened skeptics in Washington and London closed down the channels of military and political assistance that had briefly opened during the optimistic days of 1946.

The proclamation of the Bao Dai policy reversed this trend. The new, ostensibly nationalist regime provided a convenient fiction that the hawkish element in each government could exploit to redefine the war against the Viet Minh as part of the emerging global struggle against communism. In earlier months French, British, and U.S. opponents of the war had constantly returned to the same theme: Ho Chi Minh represented legitimate Vietnamese nationalism and resorted to force largely because French unreasonableness left no other choice. With Bao Dai in the offing, this view became more difficult to sustain. British and U.S. advocates of backing France could contend persuasively that Paris had demonstrated its willingness to make concessions to moderate nationalists who would cooperate with Western interests. They could also argue with greater conviction that Ho Chi Minh occupied the radical end of the political spectrum, a position that became more difficult to refute once Bao Dai claimed the middle. For the first time, French efforts to cast the Indochina conflict in a way likely to garner international support began to bear fruit.

SELLING BAO DAI

Initially, the Bao Dai policy did little to ease the crisis confronting French supporters of the war. Part of the problem was the sheer difficulty of persuading Bao Dai to play the role scripted for him in Paris, even after he agreed in December 1947 to open negotiations. Heavily criticized by many of the noncommunist nationalists he allegedly represented, the former emperor fled to Europe to dodge responsibility for agreements that fell short of full guarantees of Vietnamese independence and unity. Only after tracking him down in Geneva and Cannes did French officials convince Bao Dai to hold further talks. After months of dogged French pressure the situation grew momentarily more hopeful for advocates of the war on June 5, 1948, when Bollaert and Bao Dai sat down once again on a French warship in Ha Long Bay. Bollaert and Bao Dai's proxy, General Nguyen Van Xuan, signed an accord "solemnly" recognizing the "unity and independence" of Vietnam within the French Union and formally establishing a provisional government. While these developments represented an improvement over the previous agreement, the new deal was riddled with familiar ambiguities. To what extent would Vietnam control its own economic policies? Would Vietnam have its own army or foreign policy? On these crucial matters the meaning of *indépendence* remained vague at best. Newly disappointed, Bao Dai again fled Vietnam, pledging not to return until "true unity and real independence" had been offered. The Bao Dai policy was again in jeopardy.[3]

This uninspired start emboldened those on the French left who insisted that the government seek an end to the war through negotiations. Most significant, the Socialist party, the centrist linchpin of French politics in this period, threatened to destroy the war's political foundation. At a party meeting on July 5, 1948, Socialists voted by a narrow margin to seek an end to the war and to reopen negotiations with Ho Chi Minh. The vote, although opposed by Socialist members of the cabinet, threw into question the Socialist–Christian Democrat coalition that had supported the war since its outset and threatened to demolish the Bao Dai solution as its designers in the Ministry of Overseas France, the Foreign Ministry, and the High Commission envisioned it. Coste-Floret, Bidault, Bollaert, and the military, had, after all, planned that the installation of a noncommunist alternative to Ho would justify continuation of the war to eradicate the Viet Minh and its leader once and for all.

The new Socialist attitude deprived the Mouvement Républicain Populaire of a critical asset it had held thus far in pursuing the Bao Dai strategy: the majority, albeit embattled and slim, in favor of the war policy in the National Assembly. Although Socialist ministers continued to support the government's approach, the diminishing reliability of the rest of the French parliament left the cabinet with the choice of acceding to the Socialists or pushing ahead with its policy without firm political backing. The decision for the latter course was sealed by another development in French politics around the same time, a Gaullist surge so powerful that U.S. intelligence came to believe by fall 1948 that the general might return to power.[4] The Gaullist challenge for the allegiance of conservative and Catholic voters had already pushed the MRP to the right on a range of issues. As the possibility of negotiation in Vietnam reemerged in mid-1948, the MRP felt this pressure more keenly with respect to Indochina. Even more than MRP officials, Gaullists viewed Vietnam as a test of French determination to preserve the empire. If Paris showed insufficient will in Southeast Asia, the Gaullists warned, it would invite further challenges in the South Pacific, the Middle East, and especially North Africa. With the Gaullist Rassemblement du Peuple Français advocating relentless pursuit of the war, Bidault (Foreign Ministry), Coste-Floret (Ministry of Overseas France), and other MRP leaders could accept no softening of their Indochina policy.

Through shrewd parliamentary maneuvering, proponents of the war succeeded in buying time. In a mid-August Assembly debate over Indochina, the Radical premier, André Marie, a close ally of the MRP, reasserted the government's intention of continuing the war and then asked that the house defer debate on the entire matter. A vote in favor amounted to ratification, or at least toleration, of the Bao Dai policy, while a vote against amounted to a gesture of no-confidence in the cabinet. Marie banked on the Socialists' unwillingness to press their negotiations at the cost of bringing down the government. The ploy worked. Pulling back from the brink, the Socialists joined with the MRP and Radicals in outvoting the Communists and the right-wing fringe, 347–183, to put off debate. For the time being, the war policy survived. The hawks could hardly doubt, however, that the Bao Dai solution had done little to shore up domestic political support and that they might not be so lucky next time.

If early efforts to negotiate with Bao Dai did little to ease the domestic problem confronting the French government, they did even less to soften foreign skepticism about the war. U.S. officials expressed strong doubts about the Bao Dai solution from the moment they first heard rumors of French flirtation with the former emperor. At the end of 1947, CIA analysts concluded that any regime under Bao Dai would be hopelessly tainted by association with France and could never hope to challenge the "fanatical loyalty" inspired by Ho Chi Minh. "The prestige and native support of such a government," the CIA asserted, "will be vitiated by its collaboration with the French, by its inability to enforce its decrees except by French force, by determined reprisals against its leaders by agents of the Vietnam Republic, and by constant raids, sabotage and terrorism by guerrilla units within the area of its jurisdiction." Indeed, the paper doubted whether the French military, despite its obvious technological superiority, could ever defeat the Viet Minh, which had proved itself "capable of fanatically stubborn resistance for a sustained period of time." Following the June 5 Ha Long Bay Protocol, the new U.S. consul in Saigon, George M. Abbott, found a glimmer of hope in the French government's use of the word *indépendence* for the first time. But he concluded that any positive effect would "rapidly evaporate" unless Paris offered more concessions and cleared up the agreement's many ambiguities through quick follow-up negotiations.[5]

British doubts in the first months of the Bao Dai solution were even more severe. Bao Dai seemed to face an impossible task in seizing the mantle of nationalist leadership from Ho Chi Minh, a towering figure who had proved his dedication to the anticolonial struggle over a lifetime. When Ngyuen Van Xuan, now head of Bao Dai's provisional government, asserted at a May news conference that 75 percent of Viet Minh sympathizers could be lured away, the British consul in Hanoi mocked the idea. The Viet Minh, insisted A. G. Trevor-Wilson, was probably closer to the truth in contending that Bao Dai could avoid assassination only if he remained "constantly in a French tank" while he was in Vietnam. After attending a ceremony in Hanoi marking the Xuan government's formal establishment, Trevor-Wilson called the event a "farce" and noted that barely fifty Vietnamese (excluding the formidable police and military presence) had bothered to attend. "The general opinion here is that Bao Dai has committed political suicide by countersigning an agreement which does not mean independence and by so doing recognizing a Government which appears more and more to be a puppet set-up," he reported. Only if the French government quickly offered new concessions did Bao Dai seem to have any chance of success, but few British observers held out much hope. "Until now," asserted one military intelligence report, "French politicians seem to have regarded any attempt to deface their minds with the true facts about Indochina as nothing less than vandalism."[6]

Foreign skepticism was hardly lost on French diplomats, many of whom doubted Bao Dai's chances. Growing pessimism in early 1948 rekindled fears that the United States or another government would raise the Indochina issue in the United Nations. French intelligence even worried that Bao Dai himself was secretly betraying Paris by encouraging King Farouk of Egypt to demand UN action. Increasingly gripped with despair, the Foreign Ministry began planning in September for the possibility that the United Nations would take up the issue during the fall General Assembly meeting.[7] Underlying French anxiety about the diplomatic situation lay, as usual, keen awareness of French military shortcomings. The start of the Bao Dai solution did nothing to isolate the Viet Minh or to dry up its pool of recruits, while French military problems grew more desperate. General Valluy complained in February 1948 that his forces could attempt "nothing decisive" because of manpower and equipment shortages. Indeed, Valluy warned that he could maintain the status quo—occupation of major population centers and fortified locations—only if his forces retreated to a defensive posture. By the end of 1948, Valluy warned that he might not be able to do even that "if military resources are not increased to the necessary level."[8]

Competition for resources from metropolitan France, North Africa, and Madagascar assured, however, that the French command would have to make do with even less. The intensification of Cold War tensions in Europe and the signing of the Brussels Pact, the forerunner to the 1949 North Atlantic Treaty, created an urgent need to build up Europe-based defenses and left few resources to expand an expeditionary force for Indochina that already numbered approximately 140,000, including about 98,000 troops from the metropole. Under these circumstances and with no foreign help in sight, Valluy's staff began planning for extreme scenarios. One proposal called for the evacuation of northern Tonkin. French fortifications there were already badly exposed to Viet Minh attack, and the growing prospect of Chinese Communist activity along the border only heightened doubts that the area could be held. Another contingency—the outbreak of war in Europe—led French commanders to consider still more extreme possibilities. In the event French forces had to hurry back to Europe, planners contemplated a poison gas campaign to offset sudden French military weakness. Aware that such an idea would engender massive public condemnation, the commander of French ground troops in the Far East, General Marcel Alessandri, asserted that it could be safely adopted as long as "all necessary precautions are taken to keep it secret." The situation was too desperate, he contended, for the French army to stand on moral principle. "We cannot ignore anything that would allow the metropole to make its maximum effort in the theaters where the critical phase of the conflict would take place," Alessandri insisted.[9]

Through all these problems—tottering political support, foreign skepticism, and persistent military crisis—the French government clung to the Bao Dai experiment. If the odds of success were long, the potential payoff was massive. Officials calculated that foreign backing for Bao Dai, especially U.S. support, would discourage the Viet Minh and its sympathizers while casting the French presence in a new, more liberal light. One Foreign Ministry report asserted that the Vietnamese were strongly attracted to the American "way of life" and U.S. economic power. "If they believe that we are supported by the United States," the report concluded, "they will be more disposed to reach an accommodation with France."[10] More important, foreign support for Bao Dai promised to ease the worsening political predicament confronting proponents of the war as the coalition behind the *politique de force*, already riven with fracture lines, threatened to crumble altogether. By forging an alliance with foreign governments, the hawks could, in effect, bypass the skeptics on the center-left and carry on the effort to crush the Viet Minh. As the possibility of a solid domestic coalition behind the war faded, international coalition held increasing promise. It seemed that the latter could substitute for the former.

American material power remained the biggest prize. With the government alarmed that the next Assembly debate on Indochina might throw its entire policy open for debate, Coste-Floret, the minister for Overseas France, insisted on the "absolute priority" of obtaining new sources of supplies for Indochina. "The morale of our troops as well as the prestige and success of France in the Far East" hung in the balance, he asserted. With Washington still refusing to sell most types of gear and foreign exchange shortages limiting French purchasing power in any case, the Foreign Ministry intensified its efforts to convince the Truman administration to direct Marshall Plan funds to Indochina. Although that step would not directly ease the military problem, it would help indirectly by easing the war's overall budgetary burden. Indochina's admission to the Marshall program also promised to bring major political advantages, since it would tend to legitimize French policy in the eyes of the leftist opposition, other governments, and the Vietnamese themselves.[11]

In pressing for American aid, French diplomats emphasized the need for Western solidarity behind an infant state confronting a challenge that outstripped French capabilities. Central to this effort was an intensified bid to vilify the Viet Minh as the servant of international communism—an endeavor that seemed more likely to succeed now that Ho Chi Minh could be contrasted with an explicitly noncommunist alternative. In secret appraisals of the situation in Southeast Asia, the Foreign Ministry remained uncertain about the link between the Soviet Union and the Viet Minh. The French embassy in Moscow reported heightened Soviet criticism of French colonialism during 1948, a trend that, in view of the simultaneous surge of communist political activity in various parts of Southeast Asia, suggested Soviet direction and a degree of international coordination. Yet intelligence reports from Asia indicated that the Viet Minh had received no external support and that the relationship between the Viet Minh and the Chinese Communists was uneasy at best. In diplomatic encounters, however, French officials masked their doubts and accentuated evidence of the Viet Minh's communist allegiances. Above all, they emphasized information suggesting that Viet Minh propaganda had abandoned its earlier ambivalence about the United States and increasingly mimicked Soviet-style attacks portraying the United States as a reactionary defender of moribund colonial regimes.[12]

Advances by avowed communists in Burma, the Philippines, Malaya, and especially China also provided the French government with useful evidence of a parallel danger in Vietnam. French intelligence suspected that the Chinese Communists had decided to step up action in Southeast Asia at a September 1947 party congress and even that they had signed a mutual aid agreement with Ho Chi Minh's government in June 1948.[13] On the latter point, we now know that French suspicions were groundless. Historians Qiang Zhai and Chen Jian, relying on newly available sources, have made clear that Chinese Communist aid between 1946 and 1949 was limited to minor assistance with military training and intermittent provisions of funds. On the whole, Zhai has argued, Chinese–Viet Minh cooperation "remained limited" during these years, when the Chinese Communists concentrated on waging civil war in North China and Manchuria. The Viet Minh, Chen Jian has asserted, "had to fight a war against the French basically by themselves from 1946 to late 1949."[14] At the time, however, French officials sensed a growing menace from Chinese activity inside Vietnam and began cooperating with Nationalist forces to police the Tonkin border. By the end of 1948, mere policing seemed inadequate. The looming Communist victory in China meant that Mao's troops would arrive at the Tonkin border en masse, perhaps even within a few months. That development would not only provide the Viet Minh with a tremendous propaganda advantage but also enable the Chinese Communists to supply the Viet Minh with weapons and training.[15]

This effort to control the meaning of the evolving communist challenge formed part of the broader endeavor to manage foreign opinion about Vietnam. French authorities continued to enforce stringent censorship and withheld basic information about the war, especially French losses. Bonnet and other French representatives in the United States and Vietnam worried about the frequency with which Americans still managed to write critically. An appeal by *The Nation* for money to purchase medicines for the Viet Minh particularly angered Bonnet in July 1948. Bollaert, meanwhile, fixed his ire on the High Commission's usual bugbear, the Associated Press, and lodged a formal complaint with the U.S. embassy in Paris about unfavorable reporting. A few months later, when *Life*, the highest-circulation magazine in the United States, printed an article critical of France, the senior political adviser in Saigon again complained to U.S. authorities. Bemused State Department officials suggested that the High Commission write a letter to the editor. At other times French authorities had more leverage in the matter, as when they denied a visa to the American scholar Harold Isaacs, who had written critically of French colonialism and wished to visit Indochina in early 1949.[16]

As that case suggests, the Foreign Ministry and High Commission continued the effort to keep foreigners, especially Americans, out of contact with Vietnamese. In part, that objective remained critical in order to deny Americans access to Viet Minh representatives at a time when the Ho Chi Minh government's diplomatic efforts seemed to be achieving some results. While the Arab League showed sympathy, the Soviet government, taking modest steps toward support for Ho Chi Minh, indicated in November 1948 that it would sponsor membership for the Democratic Republic of Vietnam in the Economic Commission for Asia and the Far East (ECAFE), a UN agency designed to promote development in the region. The DRV government submitted an application a few days later. Revealingly, French officials showed as much concern about contacts between Americans and Vietnamese as about these indications of Viet Minh ties to anticolonial leaders abroad. The most horrible scenario for many French officials remained the possibility of private deals between U.S. and Vietnamese (whether Viet Minh or otherwise) officials, a fear fueled by persistent suspicions about the activities of American businessmen and diplomats in the Far East. The U.S. consul in Hanoi complained that "French intimidation" was causing local Vietnamese to stay away from the consulate, while Vietnamese employees were subjected to "constant surveillance." The Sûreté even managed to plant an agent on the premises as a low-level employee, the consul reported. The High Commission, meanwhile, carefully monitored American movements. The Sûreté reported in May 1948 that U.S. agents were busy cataloging Indochina's economic assets to gauge the area's ability to sustain U.S. troops in case of occupation during a global war. Another report suggested that an American arms manufacturer was channeling weapons to the Viet Minh through Bangkok.[17]

While limiting American contacts with Vietnamese, the French government sought to cooperate as closely as possible with Washington. French cultivation of American good will in this period sometimes emerged from the stark divisions that ran through the Paris bureaucracy. Policymakers vying for greater influence over Indochina policy looked to Washington for help in advancing specific agendas—small instances of the broader approach of exploiting foreign assistance in order to compensate for weaknesses at home. The Foreign Ministry, for example, appealed to U.S. diplomats in late summer 1948 to support its efforts to promote a ministry official as the next high commissioner and to gain a more powerful voice in Indochina affairs. The military similarly appealed to U.S. officials to back its candidate for the job, promising that he would "work very closely" with Washington. Wherever it came from, however, the message was fundamentally the same: the French government hoped for close cooperation with the United States in waging the war and promoting Bao Dai. American diplomats noted the distinct change in tone. By May 1948 Bollaert and other High Commission personnel had launched an effort to cultivate American friendship so obvious that the U.S. consul in Saigon, George Abbott, suspected that there had been a general order from Paris to cooperate wholeheartedly with U.S. officials and to suppress rampant anti-Americanism within Indochina's French community.[18]

The French government also launched its most ambitious proposals so far to involve the United States in regional cooperative schemes, including, for the first time, joint military planning for Southeast Asia. The aim was both to strengthen the French case for foreign assistance in Vietnam and to legitimize French policy in the international community by embedding it as deeply as possible in a broadly Western approach to the region. The Foreign Ministry's office for U.S. affairs reported that

Washington's mounting concern about communist advances would eventually drive it to the conclusion that Southeast Asia must be defended and that the United States could not do it alone. Washington would clearly require partnership with Britain and France, the nations with long military and administrative experience in the region. French optimism was also encouraged by the continued evolution of American policy in favor of regional economic arrangements centered on a revitalized Japan. Since the end of 1946, French officials had observed mounting U.S. interest in reviving Japanese trade and investment in Southeast Asia. That tendency inspired mixed feelings since French officials wished to encourage Americans to regard Indochina as a key Cold War battleground but not to invite economic penetration from abroad. As the French situation grew more desperate during 1948, however, some of the subtlety dropped out of the French position. If the drive to resuscitate Japan led Washington to think in regional terms, it was all to the good. "Indochina will be called upon to play an essential role in the economic rehabilitation of the Far East," wrote one satisfied Foreign Ministry official, noting the obvious implications for American willingness to enter into defense arrangements for Southeast Asia.[19]

THE REORIENTATION OF BRITISH POLICY

While U.S. aid remained the ultimate prize, French officials redoubled their efforts in 1948 to secure more active British assistance. French hopes were encouraged by the prospect that the outbreak of communist insurrection in Malaya in June would put an end to the caution that London had shown in connection with Indochina since 1945. The French consul in Singapore, for one, could hardly contain his pleasure over London's misfortune, noting that the British government now faced the same problems as France and the Netherlands and could no longer avoid a more active partnership. "The fire ended up spreading to their house," the consul exclaimed. Newly optimistic Foreign Ministry officials in Paris believed that proposals to extend Franco-British cooperation into the political and military arenas held new promise of success—a prospect that would bring much-needed British assistance and render U.S. participation more likely. "To the extent that a Franco-British accord brought about effective action," the Asia division asserted, "the United States would aid it politically and materially." A brief for Premier Henri Queuille expressed a similar hope, asserting that if France, Britain, and the Netherlands established effective military cooperation in Southeast Asia, "the United States will rally to this entente."[20]

French calculations about British thinking were essentially correct. The new challenge to British interests in Southeast Asia during 1948 produced a shift in British attitudes toward the Indochina problem and led London to step up pressure on Washington to support the fight against the Viet Minh. The reorientation of British policy began in summer 1948 when a communist-led rebellion erupted in Malaya, the resource-rich peninsula that ranked as one of Britain's most important overseas economic resources. The Malayan Communist Party traced its origins to the prewar period but surged powerfully during the conflict with Japan, when it forged a temporary alliance with the Western powers. Following the war, the party lost much of its prominence and, outside of trade unions, wielded little influence. But in June 1948 the party launched armed attacks, the opening shots in a conflict that would last for more than a decade. Malcolm MacDonald, Killearn's successor as British commissioner general for the Far East, declared a state of emergency as the rebels began targeting British economic assets, especially rubber plantations and tin mines. MacDonald mobilized a twenty-thousand-man police force, while London dispatched military reinforcements. Amid mounting economic crisis caused principally by Britain's acute dollar shortage, Malayan rubber and tin stood out as two of the most important dollar-earning commodities in the entire empire. As historian Andrew Rotter has observed, London could brook no threat to continued production.[21]

Alarm about the Malayan situation was reinforced by new turmoil in other parts of Southeast Asia. Most worrying for British policymakers, Burma descended into civil war within two months of gaining its independence on January 4, 1948. The Burmese government faced insurrection not only by communists but also by the Karens, a minority group that demanded greater autonomy. In London the crisis raised alarm because of the importance of British investment in Burma, as well as the country's status as a showcase of Britain's purportedly liberal colonial practices. Fighting in Burma also threatened to exacerbate problems across the region as a whole. As usual, the food supply lay near the heart of British concerns. Conflict seemed likely to compound the difficulties in Malaya because of the latter's dependence on rice imports from Burma, the world's leading rice exporter before 1940. Statistical predictions suggested good reason for alarm. In September 1948 British experts revised their estimate of Burmese rice exports over the last quarter of the year from 400,000 tons to a mere 80,000 tons.[22] Almost as worrisome, Burma's geographical position and the long-standing ties between Burmese and Indian communists raised the specter of instability spreading to India, where independence in August 1947 and the subsequent partition of the country had already produced massive turmoil and bloodshed.

Inclined as always to view Southeast Asia as an integrated whole, British policymakers focused new scrutiny on Indochina, where instability seemed to be farthest advanced. Foreign Office specialists believed that the fighting in Vietnam contributed to unrest across Southeast Asia, largely because of its disruptive impact on regional economic recovery. The British consulate in Saigon noted in early 1949 that Indochinese rice exports in the previous year had totaled only 170,000 tons, down from 1.5 million tons in 1938. British officials also worried about the political impact of the Indochina war as new points of turmoil appeared across the region. The Viet Minh, they feared, might prove to be a dangerous source of inspiration and possibly even material support for radical elements elsewhere in Southeast Asia. Indeed, British intelligence detected ominous signs that the Burmese communists had embraced Ho Chi Minh as one of their heroes and watched carefully for connections between the Viet Minh and the Malayan insurgency. Although analysts lacked specific evidence of Viet Minh encouragement for insurgencies elsewhere, they had little doubt that the Democratic Republic of Vietnam had ambitions in this regard, noting that by the end of 1948, the DRV had established a diplomatic network with offices in Rangoon, Singapore, Bangkok, and Hong Kong.[23]

The prospect of an outright Viet Minh victory conjured up the ultimate nightmare for British policymakers—the gradual toppling of other Western-oriented regimes in the region. "French evacuation of Indochina would undoubtedly have a grave effect on the rest of South East Asia," asserted one Foreign Office study, adding:

> Burma, already beset with a major Communist problem, and Siam, would find a Communist-controlled country on their border. Chiang Kai-shek would find himself sandwiched between two Communist-controlled territories and his position would be even worse. It would also give fresh impetus to the extremist and Communist elements in Indonesia who wish to see the Dutch clear out lock, stock and barrel. Nor would the situation in Malaya be in any way improved.

Recalling events of 1940 and 1941, another Foreign Office paper noted that Indochina had been "the springboard for the Japanese attack against South East Asia" before and might serve the same function for a new aggressor, international communism. Protecting British interests west of Indochina therefore seemed to require holding the line in Vietnam. The British ambassador in Bangkok, G. H. Thompson, put it succinctly: "The frontiers of Malaya are on the Mekong."[24]

British defense planning for Europe also pointed to the need for dramatically increased assistance for the French war effort. The drain on French manpower and resources in Indochina threatened to weaken the French contribution to European defense at a time when the Attlee government urgently hoped to demonstrate to the United States the vigor of military cooperation among West European states. Washington had already given its blessing to the March 1948 Brussels Treaty, a mutual-defense pact among Britain, France, Holland, Belgium, and Luxembourg, and promised to provide it with military assistance. But Foreign Secretary Bevin hoped for much more—nothing less than a North Atlantic Treaty carrying a guarantee from the United States to come to the defense of its West European allies in case of aggression against any of them. While the Truman administration generally backed that idea, reservations lingered through 1948 within the State Department and, more importantly, in Congress, where many wished to keep the United States free from such commitments. For London the key to allaying American concerns was to demonstrate a significant degree of European power and self-reliance—a task complicated by the French preoccupation with a draining war on the other side of the globe. Even after the signing of the North Atlantic Treaty in April 1949, British officials worried that the French commitment in Asia would prevent Paris from fulfilling its assigned role at the heart of the emerging Western security system. "Everything that France sends out to Indochina is, in a sense, at the expense of the Western Union," R. H. Scott, chief of the Foreign Office's Southeast Asia department, complained in July.[25]

Motivated in all of these ways, the British government grew markedly more willing in the second half of 1948 to assist the French war effort. Since 1945, the British government, beset by conflicting impulses, had generally stood aloof from the Indochina situation. Many British policymakers grew restless with this temporization, however, as equipment and manpower shortages increasingly bedeviled the French command and the specter of Chinese–Viet Minh cooperation loomed closer. By early 1949, in fact, a French collapse seemed possible. British military planners estimated that overextended French forces would soon have no choice but to withdraw from exposed positions along the

Tonkin border.²⁶ Under these conditions priorities shifted. When the French military asked for twenty thousand rounds of a type of ammunition that had previously been denied, J. O. Lloyd, a Foreign Office specialist on Southeast Asia, enthusiastically endorsed the request. "We feel that, in view of the present situation in French Indo-China, anything that can be done to assist the French is of value," Lloyd wrote to the War Office. British officials also showed less sensitivity about publicity surrounding British assistance and sometimes even invited it. When the French air force purchased several state-of-the-art Vampire aircraft from Britain, British authorities enthusiastically arranged a demonstration of the plane's capabilities in the skies over Cochinchina.²⁷

London also shifted gears by agreeing to hold talks with Paris on joint defense planning for Southeast Asia—a matter previously excluded from Anglo-French discussions because of political sensitivities. To be sure, limits remained. The Foreign Office adamantly opposed French proposals to extend the Brussels Pact to the Far East. British officials had no patience for a step that seemed likely only to weaken the budding system of collective defense in Europe, to discourage the United States from participating, and to send the message to Asian governments that their defense was merely an offshoot of European concerns. But less sweeping proposals for military cooperation found a suddenly warmer reception in London, where French aspirations now meshed with mounting British interest in establishing a multinational security system for Asia. Preliminary British ideas were vague but ambitious, aiming at nothing less than an arrangement encompassing Britain, Australia, and New Zealand as well as the other European colonial powers, the United States, and independent Asian nations, ideally including India, Burma, and Thailand. Anglo-French partnership appealed, then, as both a helpful response to the immediate crisis in Indochina and as a stepping stone to a multilateral system.

The Foreign Office, Malcolm MacDonald's bureaucracy in Singapore, and the British Chiefs of Staff for the first time welcomed French proposals for bilateral consultations, even when it became clear that French authorities would lose no opportunity to publicize them. Amid fanfare unthinkable a few months earlier, the commander of British land forces in the Far East, General Sir Neil Ritchie, visited Saigon in December 1948 for talks with his French counterpart, General Roger Blaizot, to discuss intelligence sharing, joint action against arms trafficking, and other fields of potential cooperation. Undeterred by heavy media reporting, Ritchie invited Blaizot to visit Singapore. Within three months the two commands had established rudimentary mechanisms for sharing various types of information.[28]

These developments did not mean that British anxieties about close association with the French war had evaporated. All of the old doubts about French policy remained even as new fears tipped the scales toward closer cooperation in 1948. Officials most attentive to developments within Asia warned that mounting British military support would only chain Britain to French policies that had little prospect of success—above all the Bao Dai policy, the centerpiece of the entire French approach. As usual, those closest to the fighting discerned the problems most clearly. In Saigon consul Frank Gibbs detected little improvement in the situation by March 1949, warning that the French government was negotiating in bad faith and had no intention of conceding meaningful autonomy. "Everyone agrees," he wrote, "that this is France's last card, [and] many suspect that she is playing it in the hope of getting American aid," Gibbs wrote to Bevin. The Foreign Office's Southeast Asia department took an equally dim view around the same time. One study concluded that Paris was seeking a formula under which it could get away with granting "token rather than real independence," hardly an approach likely to establish real stability over the long term.[29]

Meanwhile, many British observers kept alive the idea that the French themselves were responsible for creating whatever communist menace existed in Indochina. Evidence of Soviet interest in Indochina remained "remarkably small" throughout Southeast Asia, Paul Grey, head of the Foreign Office's Southeast Asia office, noted in September 1948. A separate Foreign Office report asserted that it was "especially important" not to overestimate communist strength or the extent to which Southeast Asian communist movements were creatures of the Kremlin. "French opposition to legitimate nationalist aims," the report contended, still provided a "particularly favorable field for Communist penetration of the whole nationalist movement." Grey advised Bevin to resist the growing temptation "to see a Communist behind every Nationalist bush." "It is important," he wrote,

> to distinguish at the start between two distinct forms of opposition to Western colonial rule in the territories of S.E. Asia. The one is the legitimate and natural desire of the colonial peoples to rule themselves and to achieve this aim by peaceful and orderly transition to self-government. The other is the Communist conspiracy, which follows the world pattern of class struggle, to overthrow colonial rule by violence and force instead of by democratic processes, for the usual spurious and intolerant ends.

The trick for Western powers was, in Grey's view, to encourage the former through sincere devolution of power—something, he argued, that the British had generally succeeded in doing but the French (and Dutch) had not accomplished. In Vietnam, he complained, the French government had granted autonomy "hedged around with numerous qualifications which seem virtually to emasculate the new Government's real powers and reduce its independence to a shadow of the real thing."[30]

Moderate nationalist leaders in Asia, so crucial to London's plans for the postwar order in the Far East, judged French behavior even more harshly. Most alarming to British authorities, Jawaharlal Nehru lost few opportunities to criticize the war and showed no change of view following the outbreak of new instability across Southeast Asia during 1948. It is critical to note that Nehru, a vigorous anticommunist, generally aligned himself with Western governments in crafting policy toward the new communist-tinged insurgencies in Southeast Asia. The Indian leader condemned the Malayan insurgents and supplied besieged moderates in Burma with weaponry and funds. In his own country, too, Nehru denounced the Indian Communist party in early 1949 for its agenda of "murders, arson, and looting, as well as acts of sabotage" and banned the party in several states. On Vietnam, however, he took a starkly different approach, a reflection of his infinitely greater respect for the Viet Minh as a genuine embodiment of Vietnamese nationalism, whatever the communist sympathies of some of its leaders.[31] Certainly, New Delhi avoided any sort of material support for Ho Chi Minh's cause. Nehru was sufficiently concerned about Ho's communist proclivities and sufficiently determined not to alienate the French government to avoid that path. But he and his government remained adamant about the injustice of French repression and the cynicism behind the Bao Dai solution. In late summer 1948, in fact, the Indian government moved again to tighten restrictions on the use of Indian airfields by French military aircraft.[32]

Hostility within the Labour party also remained a concern for the British government. Unsurprisingly, intraparty rifts over foreign policy narrowed as Cold War tensions mounted during 1948, the year when the Berlin blockade began and, still more threatening, communists seized power in Czechoslovakia. Tory pressure no doubt encouraged this trend. During a House of Commons debate about the cabinet's policies in September 1948, Conservatives repeatedly demanded that the government take a harder line against Moscow, implying frequently that divisions within the Labour ranks undermined British efforts to craft an effective policy.[33] But the Labour party hardly required badgering from the right to embrace a more uniformly anti-Soviet approach. Staunch anticommunists such as Attlee and Bevin left no doubt of their opinions about Moscow, and backbench dissenters, under the pressure of ominous events, lost much of their enthusiasm for outright criticism that might be construed as pro-Soviet. Still, the cabinet remained sensitive to the possibility of renewed criticism over Indochina and Indonesia. When one Parliament member suggested in May 1948 that Britain, in view of its role in reinstalling French colonialism in 1945, had a duty to stop the bloodshed in Vietnam, Foreign Office aide Gerard Mackworth-Young conceded in internal ministry correspondence that there was undeniably "some truth" in that position. It would be politically "difficult," he wrote, to dodge pressure to criticize the brutality of French policy if the issue came up for debate.[34]

The problem confronting the British government was clear: how could it reconcile the apparent urgency of assisting the French military with the necessity of avoiding deep involvement in the Indochina morass? The question was hardly a new one. Indeed, it had nagged at British officials for the better part of five years. By late 1947 and early 1948, the dilemma was more acute than ever. As fears of communist expansionism mounted, major British interests in both the Far East and Europe seemed to hang in the balance. British leaders saw no alternative to increased military cooperation in these months. But how could London do this without generating political opposition, outstripping British resources, or compromising Britain's good name in Asia? Old answers quickly came to the fore. Grey proposed that intensified Anglo-French cooperation be arranged "behind the scenes" in the hope that London could have it both ways—more effective collaboration without the political consequences.[35] Others fell back on another old expedient, insisting that London shield itself from political dangers by drawing sharp distinctions between various types of assistance.

The leading idea was to permit strictly military support for the French war against "communism" while guarding against other kinds of cooperation that would suggest British approval of the French political strategy in Indochina. "We cannot afford to give the French the impression that we endorse their general policy in Indochina," asserted a Foreign Office briefing paper for Bevin's talks with French foreign minister Robert Schuman in January 1949. Dening, head of the Southeast Asia division, elaborated this view in a separate paper that embraced military cooperation as the necessary price of defending British interests in Southeast Asia but rejected other steps that would imply a unified policy among the European colonial powers. In particular, Dening rejected French proposals for a Franco-British-Dutch "colonial charter" spelling out common policies and objectives. "The United Kingdom cannot offer to underwrite the colonial policies of either the French or the Dutch in South East Asia," wrote Dening, who justified his position mainly in terms of domestic politics. "Though it is no doubt true to say that France and the Netherlands are also aiming at some form of autonomy in their colonial territories in South East Asia," he asserted, "we here cannot ignore the fact that their methods have from time to time met with a good deal of criticism from Government benches in Parliament, where there is considerable sympathy for the nationalist aspirations of these territories." Military resistance against communist expansion would presumably find approval in Parliament; any hint of support for the broader French agenda might land the government in hot water.[36]

Attempts to hide British activities or to justify them through semantic distinctions held little promise, however. The line between military and political backing, just like that between anticommunism and antinationalism, would obviously be exceedingly difficult to establish, much less to maintain. In addition, the British military's eagerness to publicize its new determination to contribute to the French war effort ran directly counter to the subtle approach favored by Grey and Dening. While political considerations dictated caution and obfuscation, the increasingly urgent priority of helping the French military stabilize Indochina would be served by demonstrations of Anglo-French solidarity. There seemed to be only one way to escape these problems: the establishment of a multilateral coalition behind French policy. By positioning its own support of the French war within a much larger effort aimed at fighting communism in Indochina, the British government might be able to achieve all its vital objectives at once. It could ensure robust support for the French war while dampening criticism of Britain's role and easing its material and financial burdens. It could, in other words, escape its internal dilemmas through international solutions. There was, of course, nothing novel about this approach. British planners had insisted since at least 1944 that the key to protecting their nation's interests in Indochina lay in pulling other governments, especially that of the United States, behind French objectives. In 1948 and 1949 British officials saw far more urgency in the matter than at any time since the end of the Second World War.

They also saw significantly improved prospects for achieving their goal. By late 1948 growing anticommunism in the United States seemed to create new possibilities of overcoming resistance within the Washington bureaucracy and attracting active American involvement in the region. Capitalizing on this opportunity depended on successfully casting the Vietnam conflict as a battle between communism and moderate Asian nationalism, rather than between colonialism and nationalism. In this endeavor Bao Dai was as critical to British objectives as to French. Much as British officials scorned the erstwhile emperor and doubted French dedication to making him an effective ruler, they readily understood that Bao Dai represented their best chance of forging the U.S.-French-British combination in Indochina that they so desired. In this way British policymakers became at least as concerned as their French counterparts to sell Bao Dai internationally. Just like French advocates of the war, they viewed him as a means of recasting the Viet Minh as simple communists and the war as a whole as a Cold War struggle.

Increasingly convinced of Bao Dai's importance as the linchpin of an international coalition, British officials began in late 1948 to pressure the French government to offer further concessions to the former emperor and to submit the entire program to the National Assembly as soon as possible for ratification. Only by taking such steps, London officials believed, could the French government strengthen Bao Dai's chances and thereby attract U.S. support. British policymakers anxious to see Bao Dai succeed also began offering more hopeful appraisals of the entire project, a trend that reflected the sheer lack of alternatives as much as any genuine conviction that the experiment could work. Nothing significant, after all, had changed since the June 1948 agreement—a deal greeted by British officials with universal skepticism—to give them more confidence in Bao Dai's long-term prospects. But the tone of British commentary softened appreciably by the first months of 1949 as officials concluded that Bao Dai might serve a vital diplomatic purpose amid increasingly urgent circumstances, whatever his actual popularity in Vietnam itself.

A suddenly upbeat Frank Gibbs, the British consul in Saigon, wrote to the Foreign Office in November 1948 that Bao Dai stood a reasonable chance of attracting a following if he returned to Vietnam to lead a "representative Nationalist government to which a real measure of independence had been granted." A "large majority" of Vietnamese "detest communism" and would therefore be open to a genuine option to Ho Chi Minh, Gibbs insisted. In March 1949 J. O. Ashley-Clarke, the second-ranking official at the British embassy in Paris, echoed Gibbs's view, asserting that there were now "modest grounds of hope" for Bao Dai. "The French have at long last not only chosen a figure round whom genuine Vietnamese nationalists can group themselves, but they have also conceded him powers and a measure of prestige which should enable him to build up something substantial and coherent if he has the skill to do so," Ashley-Clarke wrote. Unlike Ashley-Clarke, most British officials placed the onus on the French government, rather than Bao Dai, to make the new policy work. New French concessions were essential, they argued, in order to capitalize on Bao Dai's potential before the situation deteriorated beyond repair. In a flurry of meetings with French representatives in Paris, London, Saigon, and Singapore, Foreign Office personnel emphasized the need for further progress toward establishing a genuine government under Bao Dai.[37]

In part, British pressure for concessions was aimed at appeasing Asian opinion. Winning support, or at least tolerance, of Asian nationalists for the French war promised to remove a key political constraint on more active British support for the French war and to ease material shortages by increasing the possibility that resource-rich Asian nations such as India or Thailand would contribute to a multilateral war effort. A changed Asian attitude also promised to encourage Washington to take a more supportive role by helping to legitimize the French war as a struggle against communism rather than a bid to restore colonialism. To bring about such a shift in Asian views, British diplomats pressured government leaders in New Delhi, Bangkok, Manila, and other Asian capitals to reconsider the French war in light of communist assertiveness across the region. The payoff of bringing Asian states into a Western-oriented system promised to be enormous. "If a common front can be built up from Afghanistan to Indo-China inclusive," asserted Dening, "then it should be possible to contain the Russian advance southwards, to rehabilitate and stabilize the area, and to preserve our communications across the middle of the world." Failure, on the other hand, threatened dire consequences. It would, Dening asserted, be "fatal" to British objectives—not only that of checking the spread of communism in the short term but also that of pulling the United States into the region over the long term—if Asian countries took no initiative. They must not get the impression, he added, that they could "sit still and do nothing and leave it to us and the United States to defend them."[38]

British pressure in Asia brought few results. Only the new military regime in Thailand indicated interest in aligning Western and Asian states against communist expansion. The Thais were now prepared, as the British ambassador in Bangkok phrased it, "to shoot in the right direction." But this success, as the ambassador's comment suggests, brought little satisfaction among British officials, who remained deeply disappointed with Asian attitudes. Convincing local governments to take the communist threat seriously and to contribute to a multilateral solution was going to be "a major task" and a "long-term project," Dening concluded. "It is not going to be easy for Asiatic countries to set their houses in order, and for various reasons it is equally not going to be easy to induce them to adopt a common front," he added. As it was, he wrote, even those countries most favorably disposed to international action seemed inclined to use the communist threat mainly as a pretext for extracting Western aid for themselves. "The habit of oriental countries of asking what we or the United States will do for them without making any serious effort to do anything for themselves is by now so familiar to both of us that we should not take it too seriously," Dening opined. Still, it was another category of governments—those that took no apparent interest whatever in an anticommunist coalition—that most worried British officials. Most important, the Indian government remained implacably hostile to the French war, insistent that the Viet Minh, communist-tainted or not, represented genuine nationalist aspirations.[39]

Unavoidably, then, British policymakers concentrated on the United States as the only hope for establishing international cooperation of the type that they believed necessary to defend British interests in Southeast Asia. By the first weeks of 1949, British attention was fixed as never before on Washington in connection with Southeast Asian matters. "The U.S.A. is the focus of the whole, and without the U.S.A. the whole conception would break down," asserted one Foreign Office study in March 1949. In Singapore, Malcolm MacDonald thought in increasingly grandiose terms about the U.S. role. "We need the Asian equivalents of the Marshall Plan and the Atlantic Pact," he wrote in March. "We appreciate," he added, "that in many respects they would have to be very different from the arrangements in Europe, but in general they should offer Asian governments and peoples economic, political and, if necessary, military aid in their resistance to Communism." British officials were wary of giving Washington the impression that they were interested only in U.S. resources, and the embassy in Washington had instructions to "disabuse" the State Department of any notion that "we are thinking of an anti-communist front in South East Asia in terms of

U.S. dollars." In fact, however, that is precisely what many British policymakers had in mind. Sir William Strang, the Foreign Office's powerful permanent undersecretary, made this much clear in a March 1949 memorandum to the cabinet. "We have a part to play in this area which can best be played by no other power," wrote Strang. "It can best be played," he added, "by a combination of British experience and United States resources."[40]

The problem, of course, remained precisely what it had been for years: to convince American leaders to play the role written for them in London. Even as the Southeast Asian crisis mounted in late 1948 and early 1949, Foreign Office policymakers saw few signs that the United States was moving in the right direction. In February 1949 the embassy in Washington reported to London that the State Department, to the extent it was interested in a more assertive policy in Asia, seemed determined to focus on "perimeter problems"—Japan, Korea, Formosa, and Indonesia—and to "steer clear of the continental countries." The cataclysmic U.S. failure in China seemed to sour Washington on any ventures on the mainland. In April the new secretary of state, Dean Acheson, disappointed British observers by flatly ruling out a "Pacific Pact" modeled on the North Atlantic Treaty. British officials found some reason for optimism in President Truman's promise in his January 1949 inaugural address to provide technical assistance to underdeveloped countries. The so-called "Point IV" program suggested a growing interest in Washington in providing aid to combat dangerous instabilities in the Asian periphery. London also welcomed indications that Washington was prepared to grant export licenses to allow sale of weapons for use in Malaya and was considering the possibility of approving aid, including even military assistance, for the Thai government. But these gestures seemed to promise modest amounts of help at best and to herald no dramatic change of course. Certainly, wrote Hubert Graves, a counselor at the embassy in Washington, no American "grand plan" for Southeast Asia was taking shape. Following talks between Bevin and Acheson in April 1949, Dening reported "no indication" that the United States would provide material support of any kind in the region.[41]

The U.S. attitude deeply frustrated British officials. One Foreign Office official wondered when the Americans would "wake up to the fact that they, as well as ourselves, ought to do something about South East Asia?" It was "high time" that Washington "realized that our influence . . . throughout the Far East is beneficial to them and that they agreed to work with, and not against, us," wrote G. H. Thompson, the

British ambassador in Bangkok. Much like the French Foreign Ministry, the Foreign Office saw its challenge in helping lead Washington to that conclusion. In the last months of 1948 and especially the first half of 1949, the British government intensified its effort to achieve this result with respect to Indochina more than any other Southeast Asian territory. British diplomats opened a new campaign to change American attitudes—both public and official opinion—toward Southeast Asia.[42]

In public, British leaders sought to cultivate a vision of global Anglo-American solidarity against the growing communist peril. The founding of the NATO alliance in April 1949 gave concrete expression to that cooperative spirit with respect to European security. But Southeast Asia was an entirely different matter, as London officials well knew. More than any other part of the world, the region had engendered Anglo-American rivalry and distrust, and the imbroglio in China clearly meant that the Truman administration would not easily make new commitments on the Asian mainland. Fully aware of the challenge at hand, Bevin resorted to bombastic Churchillian rhetoric during an April 1949 visit to Washington. Speaking at the National Press Club in Washington, the foreign secretary called on Americans to recognize that, thanks to British influence, there were "millions of Asians who knew a good deal of our language" and a growing number of independent Asian states embracing parliamentary democracy. "The maintenance of Britain and Europe in this great combination," he added, "will mean an adhesion and a comradeship that will keep us free of totalitarianism, and will succeed in maintaining the greatest proportion of the population of the world based on liberty and freedom of the individual."[43]

Behind closed doors, the message was much the same: the United States and Europe must band together to resist a communist threat that imperiled Southeast Asia's transition from colonialism to independence. In January 1949 embassy officials in Washington submitted two memorandums to the State Department insisting that the challenge in Southeast Asia was communist in nature and urging material aid to help legitimate nationalists defend themselves. "It has been frequently suggested," acknowledged one memo, "that the Chinese Communists are Communists only in name, and this view has been justified by the fact that up to the present the Soviet Union has not taken an overt part in the civil war and that the Chinese Communists have not found it necessary to make any appeal to their compatriots [outside the country]." The story, the document insisted, was much more complicated. "Careful study of official [Chinese] pronouncements," it said, show that the Chinese Communist leader, General Mao Tse-tung, pays at any rate whole-hearted lip-service to the Marxist-Leninist philosophy, and it is considered that it would be highly dangerous to assume, should the Communist administration initially pursue a policy of development and exploitation of Chinese resources on traditional lines, that this initial policy would be likely to develop into something more enduring.

In Southeast Asia, the memo continued, Communist successes in China would surely "stimulate Communist movements throughout the area." Communists were sure to gain the upper hand in areas like Indochina where communism and nationalism existed side by side. "If the Chinese Communists succeed in over-running the whole of China," it asserted, "the possibilities of contacts with the Communists in Siam and adjacent territories will be greatly facilitated, and it may be expected that Communist agitation in various forms will be increased to a marked degree."[44]

BREAKING THE AMERICAN STALEMATE

As British observers noted, the Truman administration showed few signs by the start of 1949 that it would close ranks with the Europeans. On the issue that mattered most to French hawks—access to U.S. material power—they met with no more success in 1948 than they had previously. Purchasing missions, it is true, continued to buy small amounts of surplus gear in Manila, but this source did not come close to meeting French needs. Meanwhile, U.S. authorities continued to insist that equipment could not be used in Indochina and rejected French efforts to obtain aircraft engines, landing craft, and coastal patrol boats. The French military encountered no American resistance to its practice of transferring U.S.-manufactured equipment from Europe to the Far East, but that scheme posed serious transport problems and cut into resources desperately needed in Europe. Even more discouraging was the possibility that the practice might lead to a damaging diplomatic confrontation with the United States. Certainly, Americans were not pleased by the situation. Charles Reed, head of the State Department's Southeast Asia division, complained in early 1949 that the Truman administration, "at great effort and with special presidential sanction," had provided equipment for three French divisions stationed in Germany while 100,000 French troops armed with U.S. equipment were "being squandered in Indochina on a mission which can be justified only in terms of Gallic mystique."[45]

The French government found even less satisfaction in its bid to obtain Marshall Plan funds for Indochina. Although Ambassador Bonnet noted that the State Department was increasingly sensitive to the war's financial burden on France, he detected no change in Washington's refusal to entertain the possibility of incorporating Indochina within the program. As on the matter of military equipment, French authorities found it possible to rechannel American resources from the metropole for use in Indochina. Still, this solution was hardly ideal from the French standpoint. The Foreign Ministry considered the U.S. refusal to include Indochina in its own right not only a major financial setback but also a "failure of French diplomacy" that would tend to "encourage the hopes of hostile factions and deliver a serious blow to the confidence of elements favorable to us" in Vietnam.[46]

Such persistent hostility to French requests masked subtle movement beneath the surface of American policymaking during 1948, however, as the Bao Dai experiment and the deteriorating situation across Southeast Asia began to affect U.S. calculations. Like their British counterparts, American officials greeted the initiation of the Bao Dai project with skepticism and even scorn. But as crisis spread across the region in the middle months of 1948, they began to see Bao Dai in a different light—no longer as a hopeless case but now as an expedient that might succeed with proper nurturance. This new attitude began to take shape in June at an emergency meeting of U.S. diplomats and State Department personnel in Bangkok. The session, coming just after the outbreak of insurrection in Malaya, generated unprecedented assertions of alarm about communist expansion in Southeast Asia.

State Department liberals now registered little dissent against the view that Asian insurrections served Moscow's interests and were somehow directed by the Kremlin. Soviet behavior in Europe, coupled with the obvious links between the Malayan insurgency and Chinese communism, weakened the liberal thesis that Asian instability, while providing fertile soil for Soviet influence, was not directly instigated by Moscow. Vincent, Stanton, and other liberals now fell back on a different line of argument. Bold Western moves to build anticommunist resistance in Southeast Asia, they contended, would only exacerbate the problem by fueling a perception among Asians that the West was once again, on a new pretext, seeking to control their destiny. It was therefore vital that Asian nations themselves, exercising genuine independence willingly granted by the Western colonial powers, take the lead in resisting communism. With respect to Vietnam this line of thinking meant that the French government must be pressured to make thoroughgoing concessions to Bao Dai. Only if his government could capture the genuine mantle of nationalism in Vietnam, the liberals contended, could Ho Chi Minh be defeated.[47]

Conservatives within the U.S. bureaucracy could hardly object to the idea that Washington must press France to implement the Bao Dai solution more fully. There was no question during the second half of 1948, after all, that French authorities were failing to give substance to the Bao Dai solution. Bao Dai himself refused to return to Vietnam, and the French government took no formal steps to abolish Cochinchina's separate status, making a sham of French assurances of Vietnamese unity. Meanwhile the government failed to submit the Ha Long Bay agreement to the National Assembly for ratification. The entire experiment, then, remained in limbo, with little to recommend it for any sort of international endorsement. U.S. officials noted that not even the Vatican, the foreign entity most strongly inclined to favor French policy in Indochina, had yet taken a stand on the Bao Dai policy. Even for a strongly Francophile conservative such as Woodruff Wallner, head of the State Department's West European office, further action to solidify Bao Dai's standing could only serve U.S. objectives and generally improve the international situation. It promised to help check the appeal of anti-Western radicalism in Asia by demonstrating liberal Western intentions. More significant to Wallner and others who focused on European issues, by draining support from Ho Chi Minh it promised to ease the military and budgetary burden on France, permitting Paris to devote a greater share of its resources to European defense priorities that stood uppermost in American planning in this period of intensifying concern about Soviet expansionism in Europe. In a paper laying out the West European office's views, Wallner wrote that France must "at the very least" grant Bao Dai's state "real political and economic autonomy" and "an international status ultimately if not initially that of a dominion of the British Commonwealth."[48]

In mid-1948, then, a compromise position began to take shape within the U.S. bureaucracy. Liberals, impressed by the surge in communist activity across Southeast Asia, would accept the Bao Dai solution. To be sure, they remained deeply uncertain that it could succeed. But under increasingly desperate circumstances they believed "it should be given every chance to do so," as Walton Butterworth, the new head of the State Department's Far Eastern office, put it.[49] Meanwhile, the West European office agreed to liberals' insistence that Washington apply pressure on the French government to go further toward granting real independence before the United States would consider political or material support for the French war. The two offices did not, it is critical to note, specify precisely how far Paris needed to go in order to satisfy the United States or what Washington might be willing to offer as support for Bao Dai if the French government met U.S. demands. These ambiguities constituted a weakness in the U.S. position that would help the French hawks and those who sympathized with them in Washington to have their way during 1949. But in 1948 these problems received little attention. The sheer pressure of events, and perhaps a modicum of relief on both sides over the discovery at last of a basis for breaking the long-standing policy stalemate, left neither side with much incentive to inspect the U.S. position too closely.

Following minimal deliberation in Washington, Secretary of State Marshall ordered Ambassador Caffery in July 1948 to communicate the new position to the French government. Marshall instructed the ambassador to use "persuasion and/or pressure" to make clear Washington's insistence that the French government move ahead with implementation of the Bao Dai solution as soon as possible. Marshall, seeking to use the carrot as well as the stick, even permitted Caffery to assert that the State Department would be "disposed [to] consider" making a public statement of support for the French policy once Paris had taken the necessary steps—the first indication that Washington might throw its support behind France. This initiative brought no results, however, leading to a new barrage of gloomy assessments from George Abbott, the U.S. consul in Saigon. At the end of August, Abbott reported that the failure to win Assembly ratification had emboldened Vietnamese opponents of the Ha Long Bay agreement and "discouraged and weakened" its supporters. "I feel the situation has reached the critical point," asserted Abbott, "and only prompt and decisive action by [the] French can save what chance remains of success of French plans." Without ratification of the agreement, any unilateral American move to support Bao Dai would only confirm communist propaganda alleging that the former emperor was a Western puppet and thus weaken him further. Alarmed by Abbott's report, Marshall ordered Caffery to turn up the heat in Paris, insisting that although the Truman administration could understand the political "difficulties" facing the cabinet, the State Department believed the situation would deteriorate irrevocably unless Paris committed itself to ratification of its agreement with Bao Dai, to a change in Cochinchina's status, and to quick resumption of negotiations with Bao Dai regarding

Vietnam's status within the French Union. "Nothing should be left undone which will strengthen [the] truly nationalist group [in] Indochina and induce [the] present supporters [of the] Viet Minh [to] come to [the] side [of] that group," Marshall stated.[50]

The consensus among U.S. policymakers to accept the Bao Dai solution while applying pressure for its elaboration solidified over the second half of 1948, culminating in a new State Department policy paper on Indochina at the end of September—the first formal clarification of U.S. policy since the beginning of the Franco–Viet Minh war. The secret document asserted that the United States must attempt to "strike a balance between the aspirations of the peoples of Indochina and the interests of the French." Much of the paper's analysis reflected persistent skepticism about the French role in Indochina. "Postwar French governments have never understood, or have chosen to underestimate, the strength of the nationalist movement with which they must deal in Indochina," it said. All in all, the paper wrote off French policy since 1945 as "a failure" that had only encouraged the growth of communist tendencies within the nationalist movement. The document held out hope, however, that the Bao Dai policy might turn the situation around. Although Ho Chi Minh had the support of "a considerable majority" of the Vietnamese population, the nationalist movement might yet be lured away from communist control. The key, of course, lay in convincing the French government to grant adequate concessions to Bao Dai. To that end the statement advocated steps to "press the French to accommodate the basic aspirations of the Vietnamese" by granting to Bao Dai at least the concessions that had been offered to Ho in 1946. It insisted that Paris formally approve Vietnamese unity and even proposed that the French government must grant Vietnamese people "the right to choose freely regarding participation in the French Union"—a new idea apparently inserted at the suggestion of liberals who still insisted on far-reaching French concessions.[51]

The statement hastened to add, however, that the United States could not go too far in pressuring the French government. Two considerations underpinned this view. First, officials calculated that unless the United States was willing to take an active role in Indochina, it could not reasonably insist that Paris make sweeping concessions. "We are naturally hesitant to press the French too strongly or to become deeply involved so long as we are not in a position to suggest a solution or until we are prepared to accept the onus of intervention," the statement declared. Second, the paper's authors returned to the old idea that the United

States required French cooperation in pursuing its highest global priorities and could not afford to alienate a valuable ally. As the Cold War intensified in 1948, Washington officials grew increasingly willing to state baldly that Europe simply mattered more than Southeast Asia. The United States, the statement asserted, had an "immediate interest in maintaining in power a friendly French government, to assist in the furtherance of our aims in Europe. This immediate and vital interest," it added, "has in consequence taken precedence over active steps looking toward the realization of our objectives in Indochina."[52]

The paper ranks among the most revealing U.S. documents from the 1945–1950 period because, while laying out a position that was nuanced and balanced in its policy prescriptions, it shied away from any stiff demands on Paris. The paper paid lip service to liberal concern for the establishment of a genuinely independent and nationalist government, but it also provided a rationale that would enable conservatives to steer U.S. policy squarely behind French policy once Paris had made gestures, even token ones, to confer legitimacy on Bao Dai. Indeed, this pattern played out over the last weeks of 1948 and the first half of 1949. Initially, American officials, notably new secretary of state Dean Acheson, expressed skepticism about French policy to date and maintained pressure on the French government for fuller implementation of the Bao Dai solution. American demands for progress only intensified, in fact, as French negotiators resumed talks with Bao Dai in Cannes, the Mediterranean resort town where the former emperor resided during his self-imposed exile. Shortly after assuming his new post in January 1949, Acheson wrote to Ambassador Caffery that he doubted Paris was really prepared to offer concessions that would induce Bao Dai to return to Vietnam or that would enable him to siphon support from Ho Chi Minh even if he did return to his native land. Despite constant reassurances of liberal intentions, insisted Acheson, the French government had shown "no impressively sincere intention or desire [to] make concessions which seem necessary [to] solve [the] Indochina question." Acheson instructed the embassy to "make clear" once again that the State Department was not prepared to offer any support for France until it had given Bao Dai what the secretary vaguely called "the means to succeed." Caffery reported ten days later that he had "made broad hints" to the Foreign Ministry and the Ministry of Overseas France, suggesting that "the sooner we received [the] text [of a] Bao Dai agreement [the] sooner [the] U.S. Government could make [the] decision as to what, if any, degree of support it would give."[53]

American pressure frustrated French hawks, who understood the magnitude of the problem their government faced in winning Assembly approval of the Bao Dai policy. They had conceived the whole experiment, after all, largely in an effort to sidestep the domestic political problem that they faced in sustaining the *politique de force*. Now the Truman administration was demanding that they force the matter domestically before any U.S. assistance would be possible. Washington officials were essentially doing what like-minded policymakers in Paris and London did around the same time: in order to escape an internal decision-making dilemma, they looked to a foreign government to alter its approach in Vietnam. Predictably, French officials disliked U.S. pressure. Bonnet worried that it would take so long to achieve full implementation of the Bao Dai solution that the United States would give up on French policy altogether.[54] But this gloomy situation had a silver lining. French officials could hardly miss the shift taking place beneath the surface of American policy. Most important, they noted that the State Department had abandoned any belief that France would be best served by dealing with Ho. Even in its rudimentary and incomplete form, therefore, the Bao Dai policy had yielded important results. Whatever the lingering U.S. concerns about implementation, Washington had clearly embraced Bao Dai as the only viable option. Critical to the shifting American attitude, French observers understood, was growing U.S. acceptance that Indochina was linked to the broader struggle against communism in both Europe and Asia, a point that French diplomats had insisted on for months. At last, through the instrument of Bao Dai, French policy had capitalized on the shifting international situation so as to recast the Vietnam war in a way likely to attract sympathetic Americans.

Most encouraging were repeated indications by American diplomats in the second half of 1948 that the United States was reconsidering its long-held neutrality with respect to Indochina. At a minimum, as Bonnet put it in July, Washington was "looking for ways to give us moral support." More encouraging were hints starting in the early fall of 1948 that Washington might alter its position on the matter of economic aid for Indochina. Caffery told Foreign Ministry interlocutors in September that the Truman administration might change its view if Paris met U.S. demands for full implementation of the Bao Dai policy. The ambassador cautioned that Washington could not "imagine changing its current policy in this respect as long as real progress has not been made toward a non-communist solution of the Indochina problem relying on the cooperation of real nationalists in the country"—meaning that fuller implementation of the Bao Dai solution remained the price of U.S. assistance. There also remained the possibility that Washington, seemingly beholden to a population that remained anticolonial in outlook, might not deliver on its vague promises even if the French government met its conditions. The U.S. decision at the end of 1948 to cut off economic aid for the Netherlands because of the Dutch repression in Indonesia seemed to demonstrate the danger.[55]

Still, French officials began to prepare detailed proposals for U.S. assistance that could be submitted as soon as it became possible to meet American conditions in any way. As early as January 1949 the Foreign Ministry's Asia office concluded that U.S. policy seemed to be evolving to the point where Paris could reasonably request part of the $75 million fund that the Truman administration had indicated might become available for fighting communism in Southeast Asia. Time, French officials believed, was on their side, and U.S. officials would be less and less inclined to drive a hard bargain. American eagerness to resist communist expansion in Southeast Asia, in other words, would eventually surpass Washington's determination to see the Bao Dai solution implemented in a far-reaching way. "All other concerns are becoming secondary," one Foreign Ministry report asserted about Washington's anticommunist preoccupation. "The United States can no longer ignore Indochina as a critical element for their security in the Pacific." Best of all, the State Department's new assistant secretary for European affairs, George W. Perkins, explicitly assured Bonnet in January that the United States would provide aid following Assembly ratification of the Bao Dai solution and invited the French government to make clear what it needed most. Perkins even stated that Washington would consider granting de facto recognition for Bao Dai's government. Perkins said his promises should be seen "as proof of the understanding that the United States had decided to show for French efforts in the Far East and the heavy sacrifice it is making for the common cause."[56]

The signing of a new agreement with Bao Dai on March 8, 1949, and its partial acceptance by the National Assembly four days later greatly strengthened the French position. The new accord, enshrined in an exchange of letters between Bao Dai and President Vincent Auriol at the Elysée Palace in Paris, affirmed the principle of Vietnamese independence within the French Union and laid out procedures for the incorporation of Cochinchina. It also contained provisions making clear that, in practice, the new state's autonomy and sovereignty would be tightly constrained, with France retaining control over Vietnam's defense, diplomatic, and financial policies. But for Americans searching for justifications to shift U.S. policy toward France, the agreement's most salient feature was the speed and decisiveness with which it won a degree of legislative approval. On March 12 the National Assembly approved creation of a Cochinchinese territorial assembly that would provide democratic cover for the new French policy of Vietnamese unity. The new body, elected by a farcical turnout of about seven hundred Vietnamese and nearly five hundred French, reflected the same cynicism with which French authorities had always manipulated the concept of Cochinchinese independence. But it served its purpose. On April 23, by a vote of 55–8, the territorial assembly put an end to the separatist experiment that d'Argenlieu had undertaken less than three years before. The French National Assembly ratified the result by a vote of 352–208, and unification became official on June 4.[57] Inspired by this burst of progress, Bao Dai returned at last to Vietnam, to the immense relief of his French, American, and British champions.

Neither the former emperor's arrival on Vietnamese soil nor the ceremonies marking the establishment of the new Vietnamese state inspired much optimism among observers in Vietnam. Western reporters ridiculed the elaborately choreographed reception that Bao Dai received in his homeland. A Reuters report on June 1 painted an absurd picture of three hundred elephants kneeling before the former emperor at the provincial capital of Ban Me Thuot while leaders of the Moi ethnic group—"a tiger hunting tribe"—presented Bao Dai and his ever present chaperon, High Commissioner Léon Pignon, with a plate of rice and a raw egg, symbols of protection.[58] The ceremony marking the implementation of the Elysée accords on June 14 had an equally grotesque aspect. Because the French administration refused to hand over the Norodom Palace, the traditional seat of authority in Saigon, to the new head of state, the event took place at the less imposing city hall. Authority and awe were wholly lacking from the occasion, despite the twenty-one-gun salute and the unfurling of the new red and gold flag. The British consul could not help remarking in his dispatch to London that Bao Dai's Vietnamese guards, dressed in white with their peculiar berets, "strangely resembled a detachment of cooks." More seriously he noted that "in spite of some hardworking cheerleaders among the crowd, little enthusiasm was shown." A French journalist, Lucien Bodard, later described the scene in even more pathetic terms. "A dreary ceremony took place at the inevitable town hall, with the inevitable Vietnamese and French notables," Bodard wrote. There was, he added, "not a scrap of color in the streets, in spite of the order to hang our flags. Not a moving creature either, nothing but an emptiness and a silence that meant contempt."[59]

The obvious lack of enthusiasm for Bao Dai left some of the most senior State Department officials wary of any quick rush to the French side. Despite the Elysée agreements, Acheson instructed Abbott in early May to "guard carefully against any action which might be seized upon as premature endorsement or de facto recognition" of Bao Dai. The State Department, Acheson wrote, wished to "retain as much freedom of action . . . as possible" in Vietnam. A week later, the secretary sent a similar cable to Saigon asserting that the administration would consider economic and military aid for Bao Dai's regime only "at [the] proper time and under proper circumstances." Unsurprisingly, the Far Eastern office was even more insistent that the United States avoid surrendering its leverage over French behavior through overhasty endorsement of Bao Dai. Charlton Ogburn, an outspoken critic of the drift of U.S. policy toward Southeast Asia, argued in an impassioned memorandum on April 20 that Bao Dai resembled Chiang Kai-shek too closely for comfort. "Unless . . . the French show themselves willing to make the required concessions and Bao Dai proves able to attract the mass of nationalists away from the Communist dominated Viet Minh League," Ogburn wrote, "we should not accede to these [French] requests since we do not wish to involve this government in the support of what may prove a little Kuomintang."[60]

For other U.S. officials, however, the Elysée accords in March and the installation ceremony in June signaled that the time had come to throw American support behind French policy. If Paris still dragged its feet in certain respects, it had, in this view, done enough to warrant international help. "The Bao Dai solution represents at this time the only apparent alternative to Communist domination in Indochina," asserted one paper. In Saigon Abbott cabled that the only other options were unappealing: "continued costly colonial warfare or French withdrawal leaving a Communist-controlled government in a strategic area of Southeast Asia." Caffery concurred, insisting that Washington should "take the risk" of backing Bao Dai since the only alternative seemed to be Ho Chi Minh.[61] Undeniably, U.S. intelligence still lacked evidence that Ho took his orders from the Soviet Union. "If there is a Moscow-directed conspiracy in Southeast Asia, Indochina is an anomaly so far," asserted one State Department report in October 1948. In fact, the report continued, Viet Minh media had not adopted an anti-American position, in sharp contrast to a French colonial press that "freely accused the U.S. of imperialism in Indochina to the point of approximating the official Moscow position." But U.S. advocates of Bao Dai highlighted circumstantial evidence suggesting Ho's loyalty to the Soviet Union. They noted especially that Moscow was in the process of establishing an elaborate diplomatic and intelligence network in Bangkok. "There can be little doubt," asserted one State Department paper, "that the Kremlin seeks ultimate control over [Southeast Asia] as a pawn in the struggle between the Soviet world and the Free World." Acheson, meanwhile, despite an intermittently nuanced approach on Indochina for much of 1949, branded Asian communists as "Stalinists" and, in the first such statement by a cabinet-level official, labeled Ho Chi Minh an "outright Commie."[62]

For Europe-oriented officials in Washington, the precarious political situation in France also seemed to demand new assurances of U.S. support. By early 1949 the centrist ("third force") governments comprised of the MRP, Socialist, and Radical parties faced ever more assertive challenges from Communists on the left and Gaullists on the right. With the North Atlantic Treaty close to signing and U.S. defense planning for Europe increasingly focused on France and French North Africa, U.S. officials were loath to create any difficulties for the politicians and parties most open to the idea of close cooperation with the United States—precisely the politicians and parties most heavily invested in the Vietnam war and the Bao Dai experiment. The fragility of the situation became abundantly clear in March 1949, when the Gaullists tried to exploit the Indochina issue to create political havoc on the eve of cantonal elections. The Gaullist objective, according to British observers, was to provoke the Socialists into breaking with the MRP over Indochina and thereby to bring down the government. The ploy failed, and the government's Indochina policy won a vote of confidence in the National Assembly by a count of 350–228 when the Socialists, desperate to preserve the third force, voted with the government. The episode nevertheless confirmed the sense among many Americans that Washington could not afford to apply additional pressure over Indochina. To do so, warned Charles Reed, would result in either a stiffening of French recalcitrance or an internal political crisis with "repercussions adversely affecting the cohesion of the Atlantic Community." Insistence that further concessions to Bao Dai would ease French problems in Vietnam would, Reed added, carry little weight with the Paris government, which he described as beset by "irrational" fears of any new departures in Indochina. "We are not dealing in the realm of pure reason," Reed asserted. "Paranoia is no less substantial a factor in international relations than in individual associations."[63]

Economic and strategic considerations also led American conservatives to warn against further pressure on France. Economically, it remained primarily the interests of American allies, rather than of the United States itself, that drove American calculations. Insurgencies throughout Southeast Asia seemed to threaten not only Britain's crucial dollar-earning capacity in Malaya but also the prospect of finding the markets and raw materials to sustain a reindustrialized Japan as the bulwark of Western security in the Far East.[64] Strategically, U.S. planners increasingly focused on the possibility that communist expansionism in Southeast Asia would deprive the West of valuable military bases and sources of raw materials essential to the successful prosecution of a global war against the Soviet Union, an increasingly likely prospect in the crisis-filled year 1949. In May the National Security Council pointed to an "immediate and continuing" U.S. interest in keeping the region out of the Soviet orbit. The possibility that the loss of Vietnam would lead to communist gains across Southeast Asia—a notion prevalent in British strategic thinking since 1945—now captured American attention as well. "The security of the three major non-communist base areas in this quarter of the world—Japan, India and Australia—depends in large measure on the denial of [Southeast Asia] to the Kremlin," asserted one State Department memorandum. "If [Southeast Asia], particularly the Philippines and Indonesia, is lost, these three base areas will tend to be isolated from one another," it added.[65]

French leaders, desperate to end American pressure for further reforms, had little compunction about playing on emerging American fears about the possible loss of Indochina. On May 10 Jean Daridan, counselor at the French embassy in Washington, warned State Department counterparts that any attempt by Washington to stop the French government from shipping U.S.-supplied military gear from the metropole to Southeast Asia might lead France to withdraw entirely from Vietnam. French officials usually took a less combative tack, however, reassuring Americans repeatedly of their determination to work closely with Washington to find a solution to the Indochina problem. Immediately following the exchange of letters between Bao Dai and President Auriol on March 8, the Ministry of Overseas France demonstrated the central purpose of the accords when it shared the texts with U.S.

diplomats before Premier Henri Queuille had made them available to the National Assembly. While Assembly members complained that the government was keeping them in the dark, ministry officials assured Caffery that they stood ready to provide details of any aspect of the treaty of concern to U.S. embassy personnel. Over the following weeks, as steps were taken to implement the Bao Dai solution more fully, French diplomats pressed American officials for firm commitments of support, stressing not only the liberality of French policy but also the idea that Bao Dai was the only hope of averting a communist takeover. Bonnet urged Walton Butterworth, head of the State Department's Far East office, to recognize that France had made significant concessions to Bao Dai and that the burden was now on the United States and other Western powers to help ensure his success. In May the Foreign Ministry notified the U.S. embassy in Paris that it intended in the near future to ask friendly powers including the United States to accredit diplomatic missions to the Bao Dai government, a preliminary form of diplomatic recognition with heavy symbolic value.[66]

French officials regarded such political support as a stepping stone to material assistance—the key that finally, after years of frustration, seemed to be within reach. The urgency of obtaining foreign assistance only mounted as the war dragged into a third year. Military shortages and setbacks had become so severe, noted the High Commission in Saigon, that the French command could consider no bold new operations "without the effective and immediate cooperation of the United States and Great Britain." As on the broader approach to Washington for assistance, it was the Bao Dai contrivance that enabled French authorities to make a pitch more likely to succeed than earlier efforts to obtain American backing. Diplomats could now claim that Vietnam was rapidly achieving its independence and would require its own military forces. American aid, therefore, could be sought on behalf of Bao Dai's state rather than for the direct benefit of the French army. Paul Devinat, a National Assembly deputy and a top adviser to Premier Queuille on Indochinese affairs, promised Caffery on March 18 that France would gradually withdraw its troops to supporting roles as a planned fifty-thousand-man Vietnamese army took over the main defense burden. Devinat asserted that fighting communism was "an international job" and that France had done its part by signing a "liberal agreement which it would loyally implement." Vietnam, he added, desperately required "support from outside in the next few months." Following two months of consultations between the foreign and defense ministries to determine desirable types and quantities of American equipment, the French government lodged its first formal request for U.S. arms in May.[67]

In applying pressure for American assistance, French officials tailored their message in order to head off two problems that threatened to kill their chances just when victory seemed to be at hand. First, they were careful to avoid painting so bleak a picture of the military situation in Vietnam that the Truman administration, stung by the imminent Communist victory in China, would concede the entire area and draw the line of containment either further to the west (perhaps on the Thai border) or at the chain of offshore islands stretching from the Aleutians through Japan to the East Indies. Even as the prospect of American aid in Vietnam seemed to brighten in spring 1949, High Commissioner Pignon, for one, worried that the United States would ultimately opt for the "offshore" strategy in Asia, a choice that would not only doom French chances of obtaining U.S. help but also cripple French policy in the eyes of the Vietnamese. "We have always promoted the belief that solidarity among the Western powers should be extended to Indochina," Pignon wrote in May. "For the success of our policy," he added, "I dread the discouragement this will bring at the very moment when we need everything working in our favor." In conversations with American counterparts, French representatives drew a careful distinction between the Viet Minh, which they insisted French forces were capable of defeating, and the threat posed by international communism, which they depicted as part of a much larger trend that France could not confront alone. Schuman told Acheson in mid-April that France was still "master of the situation" in Vietnam but could not withstand a "real offensive" from the 100,000 or so Chinese Communist troops expected to arrive at the Tonkin border by the fall.[68]

Another risk was that the United States would accept the burden of providing military aid but would insist on channeling it directly to the Bao Dai government, bypassing French authorities. French anxiety on this score represented a new twist on the old fear that the United States, instead of forming a partnership with France, would push France aside as the principle foreign influence in Indochina and pursue self-serving deals with local nationalists. There was some basis for French concerns in the spring of 1949. French intelligence was probably aware that Nguyen Van Xuan, premier in the provisional Bao Dai government, approached U.S. representatives in March for help in persuading the French to make concessions and even asked that Washington sponsor the new state for membership in the United Nations. Similarly, French officials knew that Bao Dai himself met with Caffery in Paris just after the Elysée agreements and asked for some form of American endorsement or recognition for the new state. In June, moreover, Bao Dai's representatives in Paris bypassed French authorities in making specific requests for U.S. arms to equip the embryonic Vietnamese army. The French government was, of course, pursuing precisely the same goals. But French architects of the Bao Dai solution insisted that it must be French, not Vietnamese, officials who dealt with the Americans. To minimize U.S.-Vietnamese contacts in the future, the French Foreign Ministry rejected a proposal by one of Bao Dai's chief advisers for permission to send Vietnamese "goodwill missions" to the United States and Britain. The Bao Dai state, it was increasingly clear, could have formal contact only with other Asian nations.[69]

Mounting French attention to the modalities of U.S. aid reflected growing confidence that the question of whether the Truman administration would provide help was settled. Indeed, the most strongly pro-French officials, above all Caffery and his successor, David Bruce, gave repeated assurances that they backed French requests for material and political support. Encouraging signs came even from the U.S. consulate in Hanoi, long a bastion of skepticism about French behavior and one of the main points of contact between Viet Minh and U.S. representatives. In April the new consul, William M. Gibson, assured French officials that he would recommend to the State Department that the United States provide equipment for two divisions, even if it had to do so discreetly by sending the material first to France and then encouraging French authorities to ship it to Indochina. By the first week of June, General Georges Revers, chief of the French general staff, felt confident enough of U.S. sympathy to request that Washington send a military liaison officer to Saigon. Such conversations inevitably leaked out to the French, Vietnamese, and American media, leading to numerous erroneous reports stating that Washington had decided to send military assistance. Rumors to this effect circulated so convincingly within Vietnam that the U.S. consul in Hanoi had to cable the State Department to ask whether they were true.[70]

The obvious momentum toward American aid for the French war effort led skeptics, clinging to old liberal ideas, to launch an impassioned plea for calm deliberation in the days following Bao Dai's installation in Saigon. These views found eloquent expression in a memorandum of June 6 intended to inform the French Foreign Ministry that the United States would require more indications of French liberality before it would back the Bao Dai policy. The memo insisted that certain unspecified provisions of the Elysée accords were "incompatible with Vietnamese national pride" and therefore were likely to engender only resentment and resistance. "Should such feelings determine the reaction of a majority of Vietnamese to a Government formed under the March 8 agreement," the paper argued,

> then it must be supposed that the Communist-dominated "Democratic Republic of Vietnam" will continue to receive the support of these Vietnamese. Certainly as long as the Vietnamese are persuaded that the two-and-a-half-year-old war with France must be prosecuted to a conclusion if the goals for which they have fought are to be won, they will continue to regard the dominant Communist element of the Viet Minh League in the light of its effective leadership of the nationalist movement, and not of its inevitable intention to subvert the nationalist cause in the end to the requirements of international Communism, with which they have had little acquaintance as yet.

To succeed, the paper continued, the new state must "exercise control of its destinies," but the new agreement permitted no such thing. The implication was clear: unless more were done to strengthen Bao Dai's appeal, he would fail in his principle mission of pulling apart the communists and genuine nationalists who had become jumbled together through their common opposition to French oppression.[71]

Conservatives exploded with anger on reading the document, destroying the fragile consensus that had formed behind the Bao Dai policy and setting off the worst internecine battle over Indochina in three years. The new U.S. ambassador in Paris, David Bruce, no less fervent in his support of French policy than his predecessor, shot an impassioned cable to Washington contending that it would be a "serious mistake" to hand over the document. The shaky government of Premier Henri Queuille had risked its life for the Elysée agreements, Bruce wrote, and had emerged "battered and bruised by the long struggle against prejudice, self-interest and political opportunism" with a deal that, while hardly perfect, represented a "partial triumph" that deserved a chance to succeed. To demand further concessions at a time when the cabinet had already pushed its luck to the breaking point would be extremely counterproductive, insisted Bruce. In the eyes of French officials, he argued, the paper would be "discouraging" by seeming to prejudge "the outcome of an experiment which has not yet got off to a fair start" and implying that the United States would support the Bao Dai experiment only in the "unlikely event that it succeeds." The ambassador proposed that, instead of handing over the document, he merely convey orally the State Department's desire for liberal interpretation of the Bao Dai agreements. Bruce and his allies in Washington had their way. The French Foreign Ministry never glimpsed the memo.[72]

Conservatives made strenuous efforts to place a positive spin on Bao Dai's installation in the days leading up to the Saigon ceremonies. On June 2 Ambassador Bruce asserted in a report to the State Department that implementation of the Elysée accords marked a "milestone" and amounted to a "major step" by France to recognize Vietnamese nationalism. If the agreements fell short of American aspirations for self-rule, he wrote in a separate dispatch, it was only because the French understood Vietnamese limitations. Reflecting the skeptical view of the Vietnamese people that had colored conservative commentary since 1944, Bruce insisted that the agreements gave as much latitude for self-rule as the Vietnamese themselves "are now able to cope with." In any case, he eagerly passed along any hints of optimism about Bao Dai's chances of success. Queuille was expressing "restrained confidence" about Bao Dai, while Coste-Floret, the minister for overseas France, showed "considerable enthusiasm." Bruce reported as well that Catholic groups seemed to be rallying to Bao Dai's side. In Saigon Abbott showed less confidence in Bao Dai's chances but urged on June 10 that Washington do everything it could to help him. Above all, the U.S. consul urged the State Department to issue a statement of support for Bao Dai immediately after his inauguration on June 14, warning that any delay might cripple him among other nations and in the eyes of his own people.[73]

The conservatives had their way, assuring that Bao Dai's installation as head of state, rather than some more meaningful indication of his political viability or any new concessions by the French government, would suffice to bring about a decisive shift in U.S. policy. After Bruce quashed the State Department paper calling for additional French concessions, James Webb, the acting secretary of state during Acheson's momentary absence from Washington, approved Abbott's proposal that the administration issue issue a declaration of support for French policy. The statement, issued publicly on June 21, proclaimed the formation of the Bao Dai government and promises of a new Vietnamese constitution to be "welcome developments" that would allow the "reestablishment of peace" and "the attainment of Vietnam's rightful place in the family of nations." The statement hinted at the necessity for further progress toward true Vietnamese independence, expressing hope that the Elysée accords would "form the basis for the liberal realization of the legitimate aspirations of the Vietnamese people." Indeed, as historian Andrew Rotter has pointed out, the statement was hardly profuse in its praise for the Elysée agreements. Nor did it say anything about the possibility of U.S. aid. Yet it offered a hearty endorsement of the process that the French government and Bao Dai had begun. The Truman administration expressed confidence that "continuing statesmanship such as that already displayed by both parties" would bring positive results. For the first time since Indochina had become a significant policy issue during the Second World War, Washington weighed in publicly on the French side.[74]

Liberals who demanded American pressure for further concessions immediately lashed out in horror. While the statement was still under consideration, Edwin Stanton, the U.S. ambassador in Thailand, insisted that it was "strongly inadvisable" to pledge U.S. support for Bao Dai before he had demonstrated any capacity to attract support or prove that he was not "merely [a] puppet government of [the] French." If a statement must be issued, the ambassador wrote, it should be amended to insist that the Elysée accords be "fully and expeditiously implemented."[75] After the declaration was issued, Charlton Ogburn of the Far Eastern office expressed similar anxieties and accused the West European department of once again running roughshod over policymakers more sensitive to the situation in Southeast Asia. Ogburn noted that Bruce and his allies in Washington had first carried out a "complete reversal" of the nuanced approach embodied in the June 6 State Department paper calling for further French concessions, then had exploited Acheson's absence from Washington and "forced us to issue a statement welcoming the Bao Dai Government." The result, Ogburn contended, "is that [the Southeast Asia division's] policy has been junked, nothing effective is being done to promote a non-Communist solution in Indochina, and [the Far Eastern office] is being put in an extremely vulnerable position." All in all, he asserted, "I think we are heading into a very bad mess in the policy we are now following toward Indochina."[76]

CHAPTER 6

Closing the Circle

The months between mid-1948 and mid-1949 brought a dramatic transformation in the geopolitical situation in Southeast Asia. The eruption of insurgencies in Malaya and Burma, as well as the advance of Mao Zedong's armies in China, posed a major challenge to Western governments, which inevitably viewed these events through the lens of worsening tensions in Europe. Under the circumstances, Indochina was bound to attract greater U.S. and British attention. Policymakers in Washington, London, and Paris increasingly accepted the need for a coordinated, multilateral approach to the Vietnam problem. But a major question remained: how could the three powers overcome their differences over colonialism and settle on a common approach that would permit formation of a real international partnership? During the critical stretch between the start of the Malayan emergency and the inauguration of Bao Dai's government, the three Western governments moved toward a common answer to these questions—a development that makes the 1948–1949 period one of the most important spans in the history of Vietnam's wars after 1945.

A grand compromise among the three Western powers began to take shape. Britain and the United States fell in line behind the French war effort in return for the establishment of an ostensibly independent Vietnamese state within the French Union. It was a bargain that promised to facilitate formation of a trilateral partnership built around Cold War objectives and aimed at eradicating the Viet Minh. The compromise functioned principally by enabling advocates of closer cooperation to overcome internal constraints on their capacity to close ranks. In France the Bao Dai solution weakened support for new talks with Ho Chi Minh and, more importantly, gave advocates of the *politique de force* reason to believe they could attract international support as a substitute for firm political backing at home. In Britain the Bao Dai solution eased the government's long-standing concerns about close association with French colonialism. The new French approach, despite its obvious shortcomings, enabled London to cast its support for France as part of the liberal, devolutionary policy it championed in the Far East. Similarly, in the United States, the Bao Dai solution weakened liberal demands for thoroughgoing French reforms by purporting to go some way toward satisfying them. Advocates of strong trans-Atlantic cooperation could reasonably argue that the French were doing what they could and that, even if there remained space for improvement, Paris had gone far enough to merit U.S. backing.

The U.S. statement of support for Bao Dai in June 1949 marked a significant moment in this evolution, a sign that the balance in Washington was tipping in favor of French policy in Vietnam. It did not, however, complete the process. The grand compromise was as yet more probability than accomplished fact. Many British and U.S. officials remained wary of French determination to constrain the autonomy of Bao Dai's government. Some continued to question whether the former emperor could realistically challenge Ho Chi Minh for the loyalty of genuine Vietnamese nationalists. Some continued to doubt, too, whether French policy was more likely to defeat communists than to create them. On the strength of partial French implementation of the Bao Dai solution, Washington proved willing in mid-1949 to make its cautious declaration of support. But its willingness to lend military or economic backing remained uncertain.

Would the three powers be able to close the deal on a multilateral partnership? The worsening geopolitical situation clearly militated in favor of a positive answer. Mao's Chinese Communists achieved their final victory and declared the People's Republic of China in October. Four months later Moscow and Beijing announced a treaty of alliance, an ominous development that implied unity among world communist movements. There could now be little doubt in the minds of U.S. or British policymakers that a Viet Minh victory would mean the further extension of the Sino-Soviet bloc. Longstanding connections between the Viet Minh leadership and international communism ruled out any other way of understanding the situation among officials disinclined to take risks and under increasing pressure to treat the communist menace with deadly seriousness. If this situation dictated Western partnership, it did not, however, determine the terms on which it would be formed. That required another year of negotiation—a period of continued diplomatic activism, acrimony, and anxiety as all three governments sought to promote their objectives in Southeast Asia. Only in May 1950 did the three countries fully and formally strike the bargain that would bring Paris the prize it had sought for so many years. At last, U.S. economic and military aid began flowing to support French policy in Indochina. The Vietnam conflict had become a Cold War battleground, with horrific consequences for all concerned.

PRESSURE AND COUNTERPRESSURE

Washington's cautious embrace of Bao Dai in June 1949 reflected the Truman administration's growing conviction that Southeast Asia represented a new front in the struggle against communist expansion. A lengthy State Department study prepared for the National Security Council in July directly linked the Kremlin to the surge of unrest in Southeast Asia. "It is now clear," the report stated, "that SEA as a region has become the target of a coordinated offensive plainly directed by the Kremlin." There could be "little doubt," it added, "that the Kremlin seeks ultimate control over SEA as a pawn in the struggle between the Soviet World and the Free World." The paper asserted that Soviet leadership was willing to rely largely on the Chinese Communist Party to promote its agenda in Southeast Asia. Geographical proximity meant that it was simply more feasible for the Chinese to take the lead, while the presence of eight million ethnic Chinese in Southeast Asia and greater Chinese experience with the two most salient issues underlying Southeast Asian unrest—nationalism and agrarian revolt—seemed to give them more influence in the area. The report insisted, however, that the Soviet government was determined to increase its own role in the region, not least because Moscow feared Chinese "hegemony" there.[1]

While specific evidence of Soviet ambitions remained scarce, the paper left no doubt that communist takeover of the region would be disastrous. It acknowledged that Southeast Asian nations had little "power potential" of their own and were unlikely to be a significant battleground in any U.S.-Soviet war. But economically, the report argued, Southeast Asia had a key role to play in sustaining successful worldwide resistance against communist expansion. "SEA is important to the free world as a source of raw materials, including rubber, tin and petroleum and as a crossroads in east-west and north-south global communications," the paper asserted. "It is therefore in our interest," it added, "to prevent these resources and passageways from falling under a control hostile to us." It was not that the United States itself depended heavily on Southeast Asian materials or shipping lanes. Rather, it was the destiny of three other parts of the world—Western Europe, Japan, and India—that seemed to hang in the balance. At the moment, the paper pointed out, military commitments in Southeast Asia made the region a net drain on the French and Dutch economies. The study left open the possibility, however, that a stable Southeast Asia could be an important economic advantage for Europe. Similarly, it asserted that a stable, Western-oriented Southeast Asia would help ease worries about looming food shortages in India and, most important of all, provide the markets and resources necessary to Japan's economic revival.[2]

Political and strategic considerations also pointed toward resisting communist takeovers in Southeast Asia. Mao's nearly completed victory in China represented a "grievous defeat" for the United States, asserted the State Department study. "If SEA also is swept by communism," it said, "we shall have suffered a major political rout the repercussions of which will be felt throughout the rest of the world, especially in the Middle East and in a then critically exposed Australia." The West therefore needed to stand its ground along China's southern periphery. "With China being overwhelmed by communism," the paper stated, "SEA represents a vital segment on the line of containment, stretching from Japan southward around to the Indian peninsula." The study predicted utter catastrophe if the line were not held, arguing:

> The security of the three major non-communist base areas in this quarter of the world—Japan, India, and Australia—depends in a large measure on the denial of SEA to the Kremlin. If SEA, particularly the Philippines and Indonesia, is lost, these three base areas will tend to be isolated from one another. If SEA is held, the links will exist for the development of an interdependent and integrated counter-force to Stalinism in this quarter of the world.[3]

All of these considerations led to the conclusion that the Viet Minh, with its avowedly communist leadership, represented a threat to U.S. interests. They did not, however, point to the conclusion that the United States should immediately throw its economic and military power behind the French war in Indochina. Indeed, the State Department report roundly condemned French decision making and expressed caution about deeper U.S. involvement on the French side. Old liberal concerns continued to weigh heavily in U.S. policymaking, especially the notion that French colonialism was responsible for generating the very threat of radicalism that Washington wished to oppose. Deploying the medical metaphor common in the early days of the Cold War, the paper argued that suppression of nationalist grievances was "no antidote to communism." On the contrary, a policy of force, by stirring up old anticolonial hatreds, was "an ideal culture for the breeding of the communist virus." Satisfying "militant nationalism," rather than quashing it, was "the first essential requirement for resistance to Stalinism," the State Department paper insisted. So far, it argued, the French government had failed to follow this path. After an "initial show of conciliation" in 1946, Paris had opted for a policy of naked force. When that failed, the paper continued, the French government opted for a political solution. But to date the French had shown more interest in establishing a "puppet regime" that would "allow France to retain its paramountcy" than in a solution that would realistically siphon support from the communists. "A constructive solution of the Indochina impasse depends on the French yielding their claims of sovereignty to a native regime," the study asserted.[4]

The report's expression of discouragement about French policy extended even to the suggestion that a French withdrawal in favor of Viet Minh rule might be preferable to the current state of affairs. Gratification of nationalist demands might, after all, lead to a future in many ways preferable to the "Stalinist blind alley down which French policy is now blundering." Clearly, however, the paper's authors preferred to see the Bao Dai solution succeed. To achieve this result, they proposed renewed U.S. pressure on the French government to implement the Bao Dai solution more fully and to offer additional concessions aimed at giving the former emperor a realistic chance of rivaling Ho Chi Minh for the mantle of leadership. The United States must, as the paper put it, "induce" the French "to adapt their policies to the realities of the current situation in Southeast Asia." Only with a truly independent nationalist government in power could a genuine commitment to resist communism sink "deep and extensive roots in the Indochinese scene," the report contended. Conditions would then be ripe for the United States to throw its weight behind the Vietnamese state. "It would then be necessary for us, working through a screen of anti-communist Asiatics, to ensure, however long it takes, the triumph of Indochinese nationalism over Red imperialism." At the same time, the paper urged that the

United States carefully embed its policy in the region within a multilateral framework involving the British Commonwealth as well as independent Asian states, notably India and the Philippines. Washington, in other words, should avoid taking the lead in a way that might give rise to charges of U.S. imperialism or U.S. support for European domination.[5]

The State Department thus specified two conditions that had to be met before the United States would go further toward supporting French policy in Vietnam. The French government had to give further indications of its dedication to meaningful Vietnamese independence, and other Asian states had to pledge their support for the Bao Dai state. Without these prerequisites American officials doubted that U.S. material backing would help. "The overriding preoccupation of Vietnamese intellectuals and common people alike is the issue of independence," as another State Department study put it in September 1949. In the absence of propitious political circumstances, no amount of material aid, it seemed, would do much good. American insistence on further elaboration of the Bao Dai solution centered on the need for the National Assembly to approve the Elysée agreements. The legislature had approved Vietnamese unity—an important precondition for implementation of the Bao Dai policy—in May, but the fate of the Bao Dai agreements themselves remained uncertain. Sometimes U.S. ambitions ranged further, with officials expressing hope that the Elysée accords would be merely a starting point for further negotiations leading to full independence. Indeed, Secretary of State Acheson instructed George Abbott, the U.S. consul in Saigon, to make that view clear to the French high commissioner at the end of June. As an opening bid, the State Department pressed the French government to transfer responsibility for Indochina from the Ministry of Overseas France to the Foreign Ministry—a step that would highlight the Bao Dai regime's status as a sovereign government.[6]

For the most part, however, U.S. pressure focused on the more limited goal of Assembly ratification of the existing agreements—a move that became a litmus test of the sincerity of French intentions in Vietnam. U.S. officials acknowledged that they could not press Paris too hard. Given the fragility of the French political scene, Washington had to avoid "riding rough-shod" over French "sensibilities" by demanding too much, as State Department officials put it. Antagonizing the French government, they warned, would risk hardening its attitude, provoking an internal political crisis damaging to the parties most cooperative with the United States, and even disrupting the cohesion of the nascent "Atlantic community." Still, Americans repeatedly hammered away on the need for Assembly ratification. Ambassador Bruce insisted to Foreign Minister Robert Schuman at the end of June, for example, that the cabinet seek an early vote on the agreements and then dedicate itself to a "liberal and enlightened" interpretation of its provisions. In Saigon Abbott made a similar appeal, complaining to Pignon's senior political adviser that on their face the Elysée agreements did not seem to contain "a single right accorded to the Vietnamese which was not limited in some way to [the] requirement for approval or consultation with [the] French." If Paris continued to drag its heels or refused to embrace a liberal interpretation of the agreements, Abbott and other Americans insisted, Vietnamese nationalists would never rally to Bao Dai.[7]

The second U.S. demand—that Asian nations must indicate their backing for Bao Dai—was still more ambitious. The Truman administration hoped to achieve this goal, partly through its own diplomatic pressure. It worked throughout 1949 and early 1950 not only to persuade the Indian, Philippine, Thai, and other governments to endorse the Vietnamese regime as a genuinely nationalist government but also to head off any actions that would call attention to its dependence on the Western powers. For example, the State Department worked strenuously in June to prevent the Dutch government from publicly endorsing Bao Dai, a move that Acting Secretary of State James Webb believed would fuel Soviet propaganda portraying Bao Dai as the "puppet of imperialists." U.S. officials believed, however, that they could do only so much to enhance Bao Dai's standing in Asia. For the most part, as Bruce insisted to Schuman, his success or failure in the eyes of Asian nationalists depended on French willingness to concede meaningful autonomy.[8]

The British government backed Washington in its two conditions. As usual, the Foreign Office was torn between conflicting objectives. With persistent disorder throughout Southeast Asia and the Chinese threat pressing against Tonkin, British policymakers believed more than ever that the French presence in Vietnam was critical to their country's economic and strategic interests in the Far East. Anxious to see the French military restore stability in Vietnam, some British officials were inclined to accept the Elysée accords as sufficiently liberal and to call for diplomatic recognition of the new state. In the view of Esler Dening, head of the Foreign Office's Southeast Asia division, the establishment of the new regime represented "a genuine effort on the part of the French to meet the nationalist aspirations of the Vietnamese" and, as such, deserved British support. In Saigon consul Gibbs was especially anxious to extend British backing for French policy by officially recognizing Bao Dai, proposing as early as April 1949 that the Foreign Office begin exploring the possibility. When Bao Dai formally requested recognition by several Western and Asian nations in late August, Gibbs and several other British diplomats in the Far East advocated "de facto" recognition pending ratification of the Elysée accords by the National Assembly. After that, they urged, British recognition should become "de jure."[9]

Familiar considerations deterred the British government from taking any bold, unilateral step. For one thing, British policymakers feared that overzealous support for French policy would damage British relations with Commonwealth governments that remained skeptical of Bao Dai. Indian and Burmese objections to the Bao Dai solution were longstanding, while the Australian and New Zealand governments remained to be convinced that the policy would help to resolve, rather than to inflame, a Southeast Asian situation that seemed increasingly to menace their security. But it was the attitude of the United States that weighed most heavily in British calculations with regard to Bao Dai. Foreign Office policymakers believed that Britain's best hope of achieving its long-held aim of gaining U.S. support for British objectives in Indochina and elsewhere in the region depended on satisfying Washington's insistence that Paris quickly advance the Bao Dai policy and that Asian nations take the lead in forming an anticommunist coalition. The second condition seemed especially important in view of the possibility that Britain might use its considerable influence in Asia to promote the American objective. "Only if we show our willingness and ability to bring about greater Asian solidarity," a Foreign Office memorandum asserted in August 1949, "will the Americans be prepared to assist or come into any regional arrangements."[10]

In the second half of 1949, British officials saw mixed prospects of success in their bid to attract U.S. involvement. On the positive side, they recognized the rapid evolution of American attitudes toward Southeast Asia. Both public and official opinion in the United States seemed to be moving steadily in the direction of accepting a commitment to fight communism in Asia. Eventual American membership in a "Pacific Pact" or some other kind of organization involving both Asian and Western nations seemed to be possible. Above all, the Washington embassy reported, the Chinese Communists' looming victory was generating a strong sense within the Truman administration that the United States needed to "do something" about the spread of communism in Asia. Most promising of all, the Republican-controlled U.S. Congress was beginning to press the administration to spend $75 million previously allocated for the Chinese Nationalists on assistance for other Asian nations threatened by communism. In September the State Department issued a public declaration supporting the principle of Asian independence while warning against the dangers of communism and promising American aid for countries attempting to resist outside aggression. At last, a consensus seemed to be forming behind U.S. aid for Southeast Asia.[11]

The impact of Mao's victory on U.S. policy was not altogether clear, however, and some British officials, like their French colleagues, worried that it would render Washington more reluctant, rather than more eager, to take an active role elsewhere on the Asian continent. One Foreign Office report noted in August that the State Department, stung by the China debacle, was "holding aloof" from Southeast Asia because of reluctance to make any new commitments in a part of the world where the political tide seemed to be running against the West. The apparent American preference for a "perimeter defense" of island bases only encouraged British fears that the United States would choose to leave Southeast Asia as a problem for the Europeans to solve on their own.[12] Even if Washington did come forward with aid, Dening worried that it would be too little, too late. "We must not run away with the idea," Dening wrote,

> that because the Americans are now taking an increased interest in the state of South East Asia they are in a position to furnish large quantities of dollars to meet the needs of that area. Our studies show that the bill is virtually unlimited, but even when we have narrowed it down to those projects which really merit support, it is doubtful whether United States aid will be forthcoming in sufficient volume to meet what is required.

Chances of gaining American support in Vietnam seemed especially slim. The new British ambassador in Washington, Oliver Franks, reported in November 1949 that the State Department, anxious to avoid another China imbroglio and uncertain how to balance its conflicting interests, had "thrown up its hands in despair over Indochina." Under the circumstances, mounting evidence of French military inadequacies seemed more likely to dissuade Washington from deeper involvement than to encourage it. R. H. Scott, chief of the Foreign Office's Southeast Asia division, anxiously reported in November that

American diplomats were convinced that French forces in Vietnam would soon be forced to withdraw into the main cities.[13]

British officials complained bitterly about the slow evolution of U.S. policy. Commissioner-General MacDonald, perhaps the British official most eager for a major U.S. commitment in Southeast Asia, charged at the end of 1949 that Washington showed "inadequate appreciation" of the urgency of the situation in Indochina. U.S. policy, he complained, was "developing much too slowly."[14] Most, however, held out hope that Washington, even if a major disappointment so far, would soon provide what was needed. Skillful diplomacy, they believed, might bring results. "The present is probably a favorable opportunity for influencing the State Department in the way in which the United Kingdom would like them to go," wrote J. F. Ford, a senior adviser at the embassy in Washington. In London the government considered its ultimate goal—a combination of British ideas and U.S. resources—to be within reach. "It should not be impractical to maintain the political influence of the United Kingdom in South East Asia while arranging for the United States to provide much of the capital investment that was required," the cabinet concluded at a late October meeting.[15]

The key to winning active American support for Bao Dai clearly lay in convincing Washington that its final conditions for doing so were being met. For that reason British diplomats supported American efforts to apply pressure on the French government to ratify the Elysée accords and to implement them liberally. British officials left no doubt of their fundamental support for France. The Foreign Office readily approved MacDonald's proposal in September that he visit Saigon later in the year as a sign of British support for French policy.[16] In private, too, British policymakers expressed sympathetic understanding for the political constraints on the French government and worried that granting too much autonomy to Bao Dai would only compound Paris's problems. Yet British diplomats also recognized the need to do whatever it took to win American involvement and repeatedly stressed to French counterparts the necessity of submitting the accords for speedy ratification and interpreting the agreements liberally. In talks with Foreign Minister Schuman and Secretary of State Acheson in November 1949, Bevin asserted that the "immediate obstacle" to British recognition of Bao Dai was the French failure to ratify the Elysée agreements. Once the Assembly had acted, Bevin asserted, London would "take the necessary steps."[17]

British officials were even more fully committed to satisfying American insistence that Asians, rather than Westerners, be the first to throw their support behind Bao Dai—a stipulation that meshed neatly with London's long-standing determination to cater to Asian nationalist opinion. "If the countries of South East Asia, such as India, Siam or the Philippines, could be persuaded to take the initiative, we and the United States could follow suit without fear of giving the impression of too much ganging up of the Western powers in this part of the world," wrote Donald Hopson, an aide in the British consulate in Saigon. Efforts to generate regional collaboration moved ahead on two tracks. First, the Foreign Office sought to use Commonwealth mechanisms to create embryonic forms of international cooperation that non-Commonwealth nations could join later. At a conference in Singapore in November 1949, British colonial administrators and diplomats agreed that the Commonwealth should move urgently to build economic cooperation as a near-term method of countering communist expansion. Over the longer term, the meeting concluded, Britain should aim to form a "regional pact" grouping Commonwealth nations, especially Australia and New Zealand, with the North Atlantic powers and independent Asian governments such as Thailand, the Philippines, and Vietnam.[18]

The second strand of Britain's regional policy consisted of diplomatic efforts to persuade Asian governments to take a positive view of Bao Dai. Unsurprisingly, the Foreign Office focused its efforts on New Delhi, the biggest potential prize among Asian regimes. British observers expected that, if Nehru embraced Bao Dai as a genuine nationalist alternative in Vietnam, other Asian regimes would follow suit. Following Bao Dai's return to Vietnam and his inauguration on June 14, the British high commissioner in India detected some softening of Nehru's attitude toward French policy. The U.S. statement of support for Bao Dai rekindled Indian hostility, however, and Nehru lodged new complaints about Western interference in Indochina. Nehru persisted in his view that the Viet Minh was essentially a nationalist movement. "One of the main difficulties" in Anglo-Indian relations, reported one British diplomat passing through Delhi at the beginning of August, "was the reluctance of the Indians in high places, and particularly of Pandit Nehru himself, to believe that Ho Chi Minh was really a Communist." Stymied by Indian firmness, British diplomats resigned themselves to a long campaign to change Nehru's mind.[19]

By fall 1949 U.S. diplomats were working along the same lines. Just like Foreign Office personnel, U.S. representatives pressured Nehru to throw his support behind Bao Dai, repeatedly pointing to Moscow's pro–Viet Minh statements as evidence of Ho Chi Minh's affinity for

Stalin. When Nehru insisted that the Vietnamese people must be allowed to choose Ho's leadership if they liked, Dean Acheson contended that no free people had ever chosen communism; all communist regimes, he asserted, were imposed by conspiratorial cliques. Such blandishments brought no results. Indian foreign secretary Sir Girja Bajpai told a British diplomat in December that New Delhi had no intention of using its influence on Bao Dai's behalf. So far, Bajpai complained, the French government's only objective in Vietnam seemed to be "to hold onto the imperialist position they had before the war."[20] Elsewhere in Asia, things went little better. By the end of the year, only Ceylon had responded favorably, sending Bao Dai a message of "good wishes." Elsewhere the boldest step toward regional cooperation against communism was hardly what London and Washington had in mind. In July Chiang Kai-shek, newly established in Taiwan, South Korean strongman Syngman Rhee, and Philippine president Elpidio Quirino proposed formation of a "Pacific Pact" centered on their triumvirate. Washington immediately dismissed the idea, not only because Chiang's role would alienate other Asian nations but also because the proposal was an obvious scheme to extract aid from the United States. Not even the Thai government, despite its eagerness for U.S. aid, showed signs of interest in backing Bao Dai. The former emperor was proving to be merely a "French puppet," the Thai ambassador in Washington told State Department officials in December.[21]

French supporters of the war grew increasingly anxious as these time-consuming diplomatic initiatives unfolded. To be sure, the French government was gratified by small alterations in U.S. policy. Despite persistent reservations, the State Department acquiesced to French pressure in the late summer by permitting Paris to transfer U.S.-manufactured equipment to Southeast Asia without explicit permission.[22] From the vantage point of French generals in Indochina, however, far more was required. The French command insisted that the arrival of some twenty thousand Chinese Communist troops at the Tonkin border during the fall made it vital to achieve a diplomatic breakthrough before long. In fact, the command in Saigon calculated that without significant international help, French forces would be unable to hold their positions in Tonkin. French hawks also worried about plummeting morale among French troops, a trend they attributed to low pay and lack of equipment. As usual, the situation promised only to worsen. In November the minister of Overseas France, Jean Letourneau, ordered Pignon to cut French spending in Indochina, asserting that "all economies [and] all reorganizations must be studied." Faced with these circumstances, the military and the High Commission urged the ministries in Paris to do all they could to close ranks with the United States and Britain. Hoping for the best, the French command continued drafting lists of equipment that it hoped to obtain from the United States. Around the same time, it handed British officers in Singapore a similar wish list, including ammunition of various kinds, several varieties of vehicles, landing craft, and radios.[23]

Rigid limits remained, however, on how far the French government could go to satisfy U.S. and British demands. The cabinet clearly wanted the Assembly to ratify the Elysée accords as much as Washington or London. The Bao Dai solution was, after all, the linchpin of the whole effort by the French hawks to keep the war going. But the political situation in Paris remained extraordinarily fragile in 1949, and Assembly endorsement remained problematic. The Socialists once again demonstrated their unreliability during a party conference in July, when the rank and file endorsed a proposal calling for a UN-brokered armistice and, in a clear bid to reopen the possibility of dealing with Ho Chi Minh, for negotiations with "all elements of Viet Nam, without excluding anyone."[24] With the Gaullists and Communists stridently opposed to government policy, the cabinet remained cautious about bringing the matter to a vote. But there were deeper reasons for the government's resistance to U.S. and British demands. Those who supported Bao Dai and wished to see the Elysée accords approved did not, after all, share the American view that those agreements should be liberally implemented, much less that they should be the starting point for further concessions to Bao Dai. The MRP-dominated ministries that presided over the Bao Dai solution accepted the long-standing assumptions underpinning French exertions in the Far East: their country's standing as a global power depended on its position in Southeast Asia, and any climbdown there would inevitably call into question French rule in North Africa and other parts of the French empire. Full independence for the Indochinese states was simply incompatible with fundamental French geostrategic objectives.

Accordingly, French concessions to U.S. and British pressure during 1949 were modest at best. Most were targeted at easing criticism alleging that France was denying the Bao Dai state the right to conduct an independent foreign policy. In August French authorities arranged for Bao Dai to send letters notifying other Asian governments of the formation of the new Vietnamese state and its readiness to "participate in international life." Similar letters were sent to Washington and several European capitals shortly thereafter. The new government followed this gesture by dispatching "goodwill missions" to India and Thailand. In October the Bao Dai government, thanks to strong French support, won associate membership in ECAFE, the UN economic development organization for the Far East. Even if French advisers retained a prominent place in any future Vietnamese delegation to the organization, Vietnamese membership suggested at least a semblance of independence.[25] Beyond that, though, French leaders would not go. They dismissed the possibility of supporting Vietnamese membership in the United Nations. The French government refused in August even to allow Bao Dai to send a note to the United Nations secretariat notifying the organization of his government's establishment. Similarly, the French cabinet barred Vietnamese representatives from taking part as an independent delegation in regional conferences of international bodies such as the International Monetary Fund, the World Bank, the International Labor Organization, and the World Health Organization. In internal correspondence, French authorities left no doubt of their fear that Bao Dai would use any autonomy he was given to escape French control. When the new government sought to take advantage of its new latitude in the fall by sending an unofficial delegation to meet with State Department officials in Washington, French officials in Saigon insisted that the mission be carefully monitored in case it sought to obtain U.S. political support against France or to arrange U.S. aid in a way that bypassed the French government.[26]

The challenge for French officials lay in convincing Washington and London that Paris had gone far enough to merit substantial foreign backing. As so often in the past, French diplomats strongly accentuated the positive in hopes of tipping the balance in foreign capitals. In Saigon Pignon urged new efforts around the world to highlight the degree of independence enjoyed by the Bao Dai regime. "It seems to me," he urged, "that we should underscore that the [autonomy] offered by the French government on the diplomatic matter will always be very significant." If France had denied Vietnam certain privileges, Pignon suggested, it was only to "avoid wide divergences" between French policy and the policy of a small state with limited international experience. For his own part, Pignon announced to the Foreign Ministry his intention, "in order to deprive our adversaries in America and India of easy arguments to use against us, to give as much publicity as possible to the transfer of authority that has been or will soon be carried out by the High Commission." French officials also sought to downplay restrictive aspects of the Elysée accords by suggesting that some of them were necessary in order to win political support for the agreements in Paris and were not intended to be permanent. In response to U.S. pressure for ratification, meanwhile, Foreign Minister Schuman promised in summer 1949 to submit the accords to the Assembly before its term ended in October. When that date passed without action, Schuman promised ratification no later than mid-January 1950. Meanwhile, he gave favorable, if vague, responses in late 1949 to U.S. insistence on expanding Bao Dai's diplomatic powers and shifting responsibility for Indochinese affairs to the Foreign Ministry.[27]

At a ministerial meeting in Paris in November 1949, Schuman deployed these and other arguments in an effort to meet U.S. and British pressure with some counterpressure of his own. France had acted "with determination" to defend against communist expansion but was now, Schuman told Acheson and Bevin, running into "great administrative, military and financial difficulties" because of the enormity of the task at hand. At present, the military situation was "relatively good," but he could not predict, Schuman added ominously, "what would happen if two to three hundred thousand Communist troops were just across the frontier and if they were co-operating with Ho Chi Minh in his subversive activities." The foreign minister added that Bao Dai was prepared to "proceed on his own initiative" to build a state capable of resisting communist expansion. But, Schuman asserted, Bao Dai was "given over to much reflexion and required a lot of assurances." The former emperor also "worried about whether French policy with respect to himself was supported and approved by the Governments of Great Britain and the United States." These circumstances, said Schuman, led him to pose a question: would the U.S. and British governments inform Bao Dai that they "approved of him and French policy toward him?" Schuman said he understood that Washington and London would not extend diplomatic recognition until after the assembly had approved the Elysée accords. But Schuman, according to Bevin's record of the meeting, "urged once more upon us the importance which he attached to an expression of good will from our governments."[28]

RECOGNITION

In the final weeks of 1949, then, the French government and its key Western partners reached a new deadlock over Vietnam. Paris demanded that Washington and London offer a gesture of support for Bao Dai and insisted that he could not succeed without it. In the French view, American insistence on additional concessions was meaningless since without some sort of immediate Western endorsement, the Bao Dai experiment would not survive long enough to make the ultimate degree of self-government enjoyed by the new state a relevant topic. U.S. officials, generally backed by their British counterparts, viewed matters differently. Only if the French government clearly laid out a plan for full Vietnamese autonomy could Bao Dai succeed in winning the support of his people. And only when he had succeeded in doing that would other nations embrace him as a legitimate ruler deserving international support. In this view any quick move by Washington or London to endorse Bao Dai would inevitably seem to be merely part of a Western bid to establish a puppet regime and to deny the Vietnamese, once again, control over their own destiny. Indisputably, the three Western governments had greatly narrowed their differences over the previous two years. All three spoke of the need for recognition of Bao Dai and the need for an international partnership in Southeast Asia that would bring material assistance for political movements fighting communism. But the conditions under which these steps would be taken remained a source of sharp disagreement.

To French disappointment, the diplomatic letters that Bao Dai sent to various Asian and Western capitals in August yielded meager results. In Asia the governments in New Delhi, Colombo, Bangkok, and Manila continued to express grave reservations about Bao Dai's prospects and resentment against French methods, both military and diplomatic. Even in Thailand, the nation most amenable to the idea of endorsing Bao Dai, French efforts failed. Indeed, they were counterproductive, producing a minor diplomatic clash. Following receipt of Bao Dai's letter, the Thai foreign ministry accused the French embassy in Bangkok of attempting to trick the government into publicly endorsing Bao Dai by claiming that other Southeast Asian nations had already done so.[29] In Europe and North America the situation was hardly more promising. By the end of the fall, only the Vatican had responded favorably to Bao Dai's initiative by replying with its own letter vowing support for the new Vietnamese state. Meanwhile, the British government, apparently determined to avoid moving ahead of the Americans, decided against replying to Bao Dai's letter on the grounds that it did not yet recognize the Vietnamese regime and therefore should not correspond directly. Instead, the London government offered informal assurances through the British embassy in Paris of general backing for

French policy. The Truman administration similarly decided against replying to the letter, reasoning that Bao Dai's Vietnam was not yet an independent state.

For French advocates of the *politique de force,* such a feeble response came as a grave disappointment. "The reestablishment of confidence [in French policy] in the West is the basis of success for our entire policy," Pignon wrote in late December. With Chinese Communist forces now ensconced across the Tonkin border, U.S. and British material support was more critical than ever to French plans to keep the war going. Although the Chinese showed no signs of overt intervention in Vietnam, the prospect of Chinese–Viet Minh cooperation nevertheless loomed. With military problems mounting, the French government focused above all on Western recognition for Bao Dai's government—a step that French officials saw as a stepping stone to the broader objective of military partnership. Still more important, Western recognition seemed certain to bolster the French government's chances of winning Assembly ratification of the Elysée agreements. Support from French allies thus remained the key to avoiding political defeat domestically—a situation that was hardly lost on astute observers of the French policymaking scene. In London Foreign Secretary Bevin concluded that the French government hoped to use Western recognition of Bao Dai as a "lever" in the Assembly. The French, Bevin suggested, wanted U.S. and British recognition "so they could present a 'fait accompli' to the Assembly and the Assembly would have to ratify the Elysée agreements."[30]

To accomplish these objectives, French diplomats insisted to U.S. and British counterparts that the best way to strengthen Bao Dai in the eyes of other Asian governments was to lend him their recognition first—a reversal of the timetable preferred by many U.S. officials who insisted that any indications of U.S. support must follow gestures of support by Asians. Asian governments, insisted French officials, would regard Bao Dai as capable of surviving in power, and therefore worthy of their support, only if he had Western backing. At the moment, as Pignon put it, the whole matter was caught in a "vicious cycle." Western governments demanded evidence that Bao Dai would be accepted as a legitimate nationalist leader by Asian opinion before they would embrace him, but Asian nations as well as ordinary Vietnamese nationalists would regard him as a good bet only if he had Western support. French officials appealed to U.S. and British counterparts to break the cycle. "Genuine nationalists would be encouraged to join in with Bao Dai and the Western powers in opposition to Chinese communism if they had the impression that the Western powers were really serious about it all," Pignon's senior political adviser told British embassy aides in Paris.[31]

French officials accompanied this line of argument with assurances that any constraints on Bao Dai's autonomy were probably temporary and would be reconsidered once the military crisis had subsided. The indefinite postponement of further concessions enabled the French government to avoid specific commitments while offering foreign opinion some hope that demands for further reforms would be accommodated. In this way, French officials sought to turn the severe problems confronting the French military to their advantage. Premature concessions, they insisted, would harm the Western cause in Vietnam by weakening the military effort at precisely the moment when strength and cohesion were most urgent. Pignon suggested to Paris that the government inform U.S. representatives that "we would be ready, *once the crisis is passed,* to give the Vietnamese a more complete political, diplomatic and administrative independence than they now have."[32] Through the fall, diplomats stressed that greater autonomy could not be transferred quickly because of the danger of contributing to the chaos in Vietnam. During a trip to Paris, for example, Pignon told U.S. ambassador Bruce that Asian leaders had "neither the strength of character, nor the necessary cohesion," to resist communism "without a minimum of Western guidance." The terms of the Elysée accords could not therefore "be considered a subject for revision as long as the current international crisis in the Far East persists," Pignon argued. His political adviser, Robert du Gardier, struck much the same theme in Saigon, telling British diplomats that the Elysée accords were "only a temporary measure while the civil war continued."[33]

If France seemed stingy, diplomats emphasized, it was only in order to serve the broader Western interest in putting up effective resistance against communist encroachment. "The situation has gone well beyond the defense of French interests," Foreign Minister Schuman told Acheson during a meeting in September. "We are blamed and even penalized instead of supported," he complained. Two months later Shuman returned to the same theme, telling Acheson and Foreign Secretary Bevin that France was "erecting a barrier against the advance of Communism" and required the assistance of its allies. Indeed, the French government began in November to press Washington and London for public declarations stating that they not only backed Bao Dai but would also come to the aid of France in the event of a Chinese attack on Indochina. Pignon turned up the rhetorical heat further in January

1950. In a meeting with U.S. special ambassador Philip Jessup, the high commissioner insisted that while France was actively working to counter the "constant dynamism of the Soviet bloc," the "great democratic states" were conspicuously failing to show the same will by coming to the aid of a loyal ally.[34]

Under the circumstances, French diplomats insisted that the Western powers must not demand perfection. There had been plenty of occasions in the past, Pignon noted in internal correspondence, when Washington and London had recognized new quasi-independent governments "for reasons of opportunity." In the Vietnam case, they must be led to do so again. The High Commission in Saigon and the French embassy in London were especially hopeful that the British government might recognize Bao Dai without its conditions being met in advance. Du Gardier appealed to Ashley-Clarke in late October "not to be too legalistic in the matter of recognition," arguing that Britain had often experimented with in-between forms of independence in its own empire. "At its inception," du Gardier argued, "the British Commonwealth was full of features which were not easily capable of logical explanation." France, he continued, was "trying to work out something analogous and there were bound to be anomalies and imperfections, especially since the experiment was being made in an area which was in a state amounting to civil war."[35] To accentuate progress to date, French authorities in Saigon planned an elaborate ceremony to mark the formal handover of administrative authority to Bao Dai on December 31. The occasion carried little real significance, but it bore the trappings of a landmark event. More than fifty thousand people gathered in front of the Saigon city hall to hear self-congratulatory speeches by Bao Dai and Léon Pignon. As usual, of course, the most important audiences sat thousands of miles away in London and Washington.

By the turn of the year, French officials sometimes sprinkled their efforts at persuasion with threats. If the United States failed to act in Vietnam, they made clear, Paris might be left with no choice but to pull out of the country altogether—an eventuality that, it went without saying, would result in either an immediate communist victory or the transfer of the entire mess into American hands. Such threats reflected awareness among French officials that their military effort in Vietnam, no matter how fraught with problems, gave them leverage over Washington. By December 1949 they were willing to use it. In talks with U.S. consul Abbott in Saigon, Pignon warned of mounting "lassitude" among French public opinion as losses mounted in Vietnam—a warning that

France would not be willing to shoulder the burden in Vietnam for much longer by itself. The high commissioner's aide was more explicit. "Du Gardier claims to be much worried over [the] growing number of influential French whose reaction to this situation is 'to hell with it, let's pull out of Indochina, lock, stock and barrel,'" Abbott reported. Ambassador Bruce warned in January that French officials were "occasionally" raising this specter in Paris as well, while in London French embassy personnel asserted ominously that 1950 would be the "last chance" for the Western powers to bolster the French war effort.[36]

It is difficult to establish whether French decision makers seriously contemplated withdrawal. Unquestionably, though, U.S. and British policymakers saw good reason to take seriously the risk of a French pullout. The possibility of French withdrawal from Tonkin had long ago come to the attention of foreign officials. In addition, U.S. and British officials perceived in 1950 that the Indochina war, now three years old, was beginning to generate fierce opposition within France. In 1947 and 1948 the French left, consumed with economic and political crises closer to home, remained relatively inattentive to Vietnam policy. In the second half of 1949, however, surging antiwar dissent inside France began to attract attention internationally. British and American wire services reported a steady diet of stories about acts of defiance against government policy. In August Dunkerque dockworkers voted to stop work for two hours each day on a French cargo ship bound for Indochina and called on their colleagues elsewhere to do the same. At the end of October, Marseilles longshoremen belonging to the Communist-led Confédération Générale du Travail declared that they would no longer load arms and munitions on ships bound for Indochina. The following weeks produced new reports of unrest in Marseilles as well as evidence of growing dissent among French intellectuals. On December 27 the *New York Times* reported that a group of prominent leftists, including the writer André Gide, had written a letter to President Auriol protesting French policy and urging a UN-supervised plebiscite to resolve outstanding problems.[37]

By the turn of the year, key British policymakers concluded that the time had come for London to make a final push to overcome remaining obstacles to an Anglo-French-U.S. partnership in Indochina. While most still insisted on ratification of the Elysée accords—an event that seemed probable once a new French legislative session opened in January—the British government backed away from its support of Washington's other demands, including insistence that Asian recognition of Bao Dai had to precede any such step by Western nations. French insistence, along with the consolidation of Communist control in southeastern China, emboldened British officials to take this step. London was also motivated by its new determination to grant full diplomatic recognition for the new Communist regime in China. Concerned about protecting British rights in Hong Kong and keeping channels of communication open with Mao's regime, the Attlee government decided to set aside its distaste for the new Chinese leadership and take that step as soon as possible. The issue quickly became intertwined with the Vietnam problem. The Foreign Office calculated that Western recognition of Mao's regime without recognition for Bao Dai might amount to a stinging affront to the French government while undercutting the new Vietnamese state in the eyes of both the Vietnamese people and Asian opinion more broadly. The cabinet concluded that the best course was to grant recognition to both governments at the same time.

Another factor also contributed to changing British calculations at the end of 1949: a burst of enthusiasm for Bao Dai from Malcolm MacDonald, the British commissioner-general in Singapore. Previously skeptical of Bao Dai, MacDonald came away from a visit to Saigon in late November proclaiming to both London and foreign diplomats that Bao Dai was no mere puppet. It is impossible to know whether MacDonald, a fierce anticommunist, was sincerely impressed or simply believed that Britain must adopt a more active policy in Vietnam. In any case, he claimed in a cable to the Foreign Office that Bao Dai had a better than 50 percent chance of success in his bid to draw support away from Ho Chi Minh and create a viable Vietnamese state. MacDonald wrote that Bao Dai was not the "dull dog" that he was commonly believed to be. Rather, he was, as MacDonald put it, a "talkative, intelligent and charming" man, full of "physical courage and patriotism." The Foreign Office, in turn, passed along MacDonald's appraisal to the U.S. embassy. R. H. Scott, chief of the Foreign Office's Southeast Asia department, told an American diplomat that MacDonald had been "very much impressed with Bao Dai whom he considers a person of integrity and charm and altogether worthy of the support of the British government." Although Bao Dai was "not brilliant," Scott continued, "he was nobody's fool."[38] MacDonald's appraisal hardly amounted to a ringing endorsement, but with London teetering on the brink of moving ahead with a more assertive policy in Indochina, it helped create a more upbeat atmosphere.

For all these reasons, the British government took bold steps toward supporting Bao Dai in the closing days of 1949. First, Bevin promised

Paris that Britain would grant "de facto" recognition for the new government immediately after a meeting of Commonwealth prime ministers at the end of January. To announce the British decision ahead of that meeting, Foreign Office officials agreed, would diminish the chance of convincing other Commonwealth nations to follow suit. Although French officials worried that British recognition of Mao Zedong's government would distract attention from Vietnam, they nevertheless expressed satisfaction that at last they had achieved one of their major diplomatic objectives.[39] They may have taken particular pleasure in the fact that the British government made its intentions public. Western media reported during December 1949 that London would move toward recognition of Bao Dai on roughly the same schedule as it proceeded toward recognition of Mao Zedong.[40]

Those promises raised the prospect of other types of British assistance. In the second half of December, the British government showed new willingness to begin close military cooperation with France in Southeast Asia. Although the cabinet ruled out sending British troops to Vietnam, commanders in Singapore agreed to hold staff talks with French counterparts in Saigon with a view to coordinating French and British defense policy and even establishing a combined staff to plan for the possibility of Chinese aggression.[41] Old reservations about close Anglo-French cooperation lingered in the background. The British Far Eastern Command stipulated that the staff talks must focus on determining what assistance the French would need to resist external aggression and insisted that Britain would not involve itself in maintaining internal security. Moreover, the Foreign Office insisted that the talks not commit Britain beyond what its resources would allow or sacrifice the principle objective it had sought for more than five years—partnership with the United States. On the latter point, Scott insisted that the staff talks must under no circumstances alienate Washington by, for example, committing British and French forces, without American knowledge, to a potentially major undertaking that would inevitably rely on U.S. equipment. Furthermore, Scott insisted that London and Paris must do everything they could to involve the United States in the talks. "Without American participation," he wrote, "the defense of Indochina cannot be guaranteed."[42]

Despite these reservations, the British government had taken a dramatic step away from its earlier support for the conditions imposed by the United States for backing Bao Dai. London was rapidly closing ranks with the French government. Instead of insisting that Asian governments take the lead in recognizing the new state, the Attlee government was now ready to act unconditionally. "In view of the urgency of the situation Western nations cannot afford to await prior sponsorship of Bao Dai by the Asiatic nations" before taking action themselves, British diplomats agreed at a meeting in Singapore in mid-November.[43] In conversations with French counterparts, British officials sometimes pressed for additional concessions such as a declaration of future French intentions in Vietnam. But internally, the assumption increasingly took hold that, once the French National Assembly had acted, Britain would move quickly toward recognition. That shift, effectively abandoning insistence that France offer additional concessions, left the Truman administration alone in requiring conditions.

In Washington, however, the tide was also changing. To be sure, American officials continued to express anxiety about the inadequacy of French policy. Secretary of State Acheson insisted publicly throughout the fall that Bao Dai could succeed only if he were assured genuine autonomy.[44] As late as November the State Department's Southeast Asia division still weighed the possibility of involving the United Nations. Distrustful of French intentions, division head Charles Reed suggested that a UN commission might be appointed to oversee the transfer of powers to the Bao Dai government according to a timetable established through new negotiations between the French government and the former emperor.[45] Such schemes became increasingly fanciful, however, as French and British pressure mounted for a firm American commitment of support for the Bao Dai experiment as currently conceived.

French and British arguments in favor of Western partnership in Vietnam increasingly found favor among U.S. decision makers desperate by December to do something about worsening conditions in Southeast Asia. From Paris Ambassador Bruce insisted that the tumultuous state of French politics meant certain doom for any French government that promised full independence for Vietnam. At the moment, the Bao Dai solution was the best a moderate, Western-oriented government would be able to offer, Bruce asserted. Contributing to U.S. worries about moves that might inadvertently strengthen the French Communist Party, American diplomats in France reported at the end of the year that party propaganda was increasingly concentrated on exploiting popular discontent over the war in Vietnam. Meanwhile, the mounting threat from Communist China lent credibility to the French position that it was impossible to concede more autonomy to Bao Dai as long as a grave state of emergency persisted in Vietnam. Limitations on Vietnamese sovereignty established in the Elysée agreements could be "gradually removed when peaceful conditions [are] restored," asserted Bruce. Under wartime conditions, he added, there was no chance that the French government could accede to U.S. pressure for a timetable leading to full independence.[46]

At the same time, American officials eager to reorient U.S. policy followed McDonald in offering unprecedentedly upbeat appraisals of Bao Dai. Despite the lack of evidence that Bao Dai was in fact gaining ground, Walton Butterworth, chief of the State Department's Far East office, asserted in late November that "under certain circumstances," Bao Dai might be successful and that he deserved American support. "Because the odds are heavily against a horse entered in a given race," Butterworth added, "is no reason to withdraw that horse from the race, although I agree that there is likewise no reason in these circumstances to back that horse heavily." Here Butterworth came close to validating the logic so strenuously advanced by French officials: Bao Dai would have some chance with immediate international assistance but no chance without it. Acheson wrote a month later that Bao Dai, although "far from being a success at the present moment," was nonetheless "stronger today than was anticipated six months ago."[47]

Reappraising Bao Dai was only half the battle as U.S. officials searched for ways to justify decisions to throw U.S. support behind him. They also needed to overcome the nagging sense that ordinary Vietnamese would never back a leader who had been installed by a foreign power. Americans thus accompanied their reappraisal of Bao Dai with a reappraisal of the Vietnamese people. The innate qualities and capabilities of the Vietnamese had been discussed for years in American debates over Southeast Asia. During the Pacific war and in its aftermath, liberal policymakers had, as part of their push for an American policy that would back self-determination, described the Vietnamese as capable, energetic people. Other officials who supported restoration of French colonial power in Southeast Asia had generally written them off as badly unprepared for self-rule. As U.S. policy shifted gradually in favor of France, the question lingered: what was the appropriate solution for the people of Vietnam? By the start of 1950, Washington tottered on the edge of decisions that seemed to serve U.S. interests. But what about the Vietnamese? For American officials, who perceived their country as the purveyor of progress and democracy, it was a question that demanded an answer. A handful of diplomats eager for decisions in favor of supporting the French war provided one: the Vietnamese had few real political convictions and would willingly throw their support behind Bao Dai if they were confident that he would win.

In the last weeks of 1949 and the first part of 1950, U.S. officials, in an abrupt flurry of commentary aimed at clearing away old reservations about adopting a pro-French policy, recast the Vietnamese as inherently apolitical and ignorant of political ideologies except insofar as they affected their ability to subsist on the land. Some of this Orientalist commentary followed French opinion in suggesting that the Elysée accords should be accepted as the basis of Western policy in Vietnam because the Vietnamese were incapable of handling any greater degree of self-rule. But U.S. appraisals went far beyond French reporting, indulging in virulent depictions of the Vietnamese as wholly lacking in political sophistication—a kind of rhetorical overkill that suggests the difficulty American policymakers faced in embracing a political arrangement that ran roughshod over democratic principles. After touring Tonkin in fall 1949, William M. Gibson, the U.S. consul in Hanoi, reported to Washington that the typical Vietnamese peasant was "more interested in being able to tend his rice patch and pursue his village's trade in peace than in the relative merits of the Viet Minh and the Bao Dai government. If he must make a choice," Gibson added, "he will choose that which disturbs his own personal life least with little concern for political theories." The State Department's Policy Planning Staff warned U.S. officials in mid-1950 against taking "a folksy approach to foreign peoples," apparently alluding to the earlier tendency among liberal policymakers to describe Southeast Asians as well prepared for democratic government. "We sometimes tend to forget," the report continued, "that the majority of Asians is a peasant steeped in medieval ignorance, poverty and localism. Preoccupied with extracting a meager livelihood his horizon barely extends beyond the next village."[48]

This supposed lack of sophistication carried clear advantages: it would not take much to convince the Vietnamese that they should throw their support to Bao Dai, and once they did, other countries would follow. Consul Abbott wrote in January 1950 that Bao Dai might be the beneficiary of "the normal Oriental tendency to climb on the bandwagon of the winning side." But the same characteristics could also lead to disastrous consequences. If the West failed to back Bao Dai, the Vietnamese might just as easily fall prey to communist manipulation. This view reflected an increasingly prevalent belief among the American political elite by 1950 that communism found most support within inferior social groups. George Kennan, head of the Policy Planning Staff and one of the most influential architects of U.S. foreign policy in the early Cold War, expressed this view succinctly in 1949 when he wrote that communism appealed most to "maladjusted groups in our country—Jews, Negroes, immigrants—all those who feel handicapped in the framework of national society." The same generalization seemed to apply in Southeast Asia. Robert S. Folsom, the new U.S. consul in Hanoi, worried in late 1949 that the communists might succeed in Vietnam because the local people were "generally apathetic to all politics" and might be duped by communist promises of independence and prosperity. Communism, Folsom wrote, had succeeded elsewhere by appealing to "malcontents, opportunists, those in political disfavor, misguided idealists and reformers, and ignorant lower class elements" and was doing so again in Vietnam, where such people existed in abundance.[49]

Americans who backed the French government also asserted familiar concerns about security and stability in Europe as they sought to win their case in early 1950. The economic and military drain in Vietnam constituted "a major obstacle in the path of French financial stabilization and economic progress, with all that implies for the European Recovery Program as a whole," wrote Ambassador Bruce. Heavy French spending on Vietnam in 1949 imposed "such a burden on the French public finances as to constitute an important obstacle to the success of the whole French recovery and stabilization effort," Bruce argued. He acknowledged that France faced many other intractable problems, but, he asserted, the "Indochinese problem is one the United States can do something about." In the meantime, Bruce embraced French claims that the United States was unfairly letting down its ally. It was "small wonder," he contended, that the French government would consider withdrawing entirely from Indochina, since it was expending "so much money and blood" and receiving so little support.[50]

This view received powerful reinforcement from a series of high-level studies completed around the turn of the year assessing U.S. policy in light of Mao's victory in China. The most important of these studies, NSC-48/1, approved by the president on December 30, concluded that Washington must lend its support to regional anticommunist groupings and generally must meet communist threats in Asia "by providing political, economic and military assistance and advice where clearly needed to supplement the resistance of other governments in and out of the area which are more directly concerned." In places the paper stressed old themes about the dangers of seeming to prop up European colonialism. In Indochina, it stated, "action should be taken to bring home to the French the urgency of removing the barriers to the obtaining by Bao Dai or other non-Communist nationalist leaders of the support of a substantial proportion of the Vietnamese." Yet this compunction would no longer stand in the way of a more active U.S. role in the region. "The United States," insisted NSC-48/1, "should exploit every opportunity to increase the present Western orientation of the area and to assist, within our capabilities, its governments in their efforts to meet the minimum aspirations of their people and to maintain internal security." As a starting point, the paper committed the Truman administration to distribute "as a matter of urgency" the $75 million set aside by Congress in 1949 for military aid to Southeast Asia.[51]

In public, Truman administration officials held back from any bold statement of the new drift of American policy. In a widely reported speech at the National Press Club in Washington on January 12, Secretary of State Acheson stressed that American interests were concentrated on the periphery of Asia, the offshore island chain that included Japan, Taiwan, and the Philippines. On the Southeast Asian mainland, he insisted, the United States was only "one of many nations" interested in checking communist encroachment and would help only when U.S. aid was the "missing component" for success. In conversations with French officials, too, American officials made no promises and sometimes even renewed their demands for further liberalization of French policy. Internal correspondence makes clear, however, that officials had little doubt that the United States was nearing a decision to support Bao Dai. In Saigon Abbott, closely attentive to developments in Washington, wrote on December 27, 1949, that he "assume[d]" that the administration would extend diplomatic recognition to Bao Dai following ratification of the Elysée accords, now expected in January. No longer, it was clear, would Washington insist on Asian acceptance of Bao Dai as a condition for U.S. action. Like the Attlee government, the Truman administration, despite continued lip service to the principle that Asians would lead and Western nations merely support, effectively dropped any insistence on the point.[52]

This shift became abundantly clear when the French National Assembly at last voted on January 29, 1950, to ratify the Elysée agreements. In the end, the Socialists supported the government's policy, making possible a lopsided, 401–193 vote. During the frequently heated debate, Socialist deputies repeatedly voiced their unease about the Bao Dai policy, insisting that France keep its promises to establish a truly democratic state. But such subtleties dropped away as the government proclaimed its triumph to the world. Empowered by the Assembly's vote, the minister of Overseas France, Letourneau, declared Bao Dai's Vietnam, along with Laos and Cambodia, to be "Associated States" of the French Union, enjoying "unity, independence and sovereignty." There was "no incompatibility," he added, "between independence and membership in the French Union."[53]

To demonstrate the point, the Foreign Ministry quietly prevailed on the Ministry of Overseas France to permit Washington and London to exchange diplomatic missions with Vietnam—a provision that exceeded the letter of the Elysée accords but, in the words of one Foreign Ministry report, would show "the liberality of our intentions and would have a very favorable effect for our policy." With the long-awaited Assembly vote finally in hand, however, the French government made clear that it would offer little more. Schuman told U.S. ambassador Bruce on January 25 that it would be politically impossible for the government to gratify Washington and London by making a declaration of intentions to permit further liberalization in Vietnam. Similarly, Schuman refused any commitment to transfer authority over Indochinese affairs to the Foreign Ministry.[54]

French leaders correctly judged that they could now forthrightly resist U.S. and British pressure. Washington and London had, after all, gotten what they had demanded most adamantly—Assembly ratification. The road was open to diplomatic recognition and material support. Foreign Ministry officials understood that the State Department had already been studying the modalities of extending recognition since mid-January. And then on January 27, two days before the Assembly's ratification of the Elysée accords, Philip Jessup, the U.S. special ambassador touring Southeast Asia, handed Bao Dai a note informing the former emperor of the secretary of state's "best wishes for the future of the State of Vietnam" and promising "a closer relationship." U.S. recognition was clearly, as British consul Frank Gibbs put it, "only a matter of time."[55]

The Soviet decision to recognize Ho Chi Minh's Democratic Republic of Vietnam on January 30 provided the final impetus for Western decisions to open relations with Bao Dai. Mao's People's Republic of China had already become the first nation to recognize Ho's government on January 18—a move that had been under consideration among the Beijing leadership for nearly a month.[56] From the Western standpoint, Chinese recognition of the Democratic Republic of Vietnam had become inevitable following Mao's victory in the fall of 1949. Soviet recognition on January 30 marked the far more significant moment for Washington and London—an unambiguous indication of Moscow's links to Ho Chi Minh's movement. We now know that Stalin delayed the move because of his desire to avoid provoking the French government at a moment when Paris was steadfastly opposing U.S. plans to rearm Germany. But Western officials detected little subtlety in Stalin's approach. The Foreign Office quickly scrapped the idea of granting Bao Dai merely "de facto" recognition and embraced the full "de jure" variety. Britain became the first nation to recognize Bao Dai's government on February 7, followed quickly by Australia and New Zealand. In the United States, meanwhile, Acheson told the press on February 1 that Moscow's new relationship with Ho Chi Minh should remove any doubts about the latter's communist affiliation and the need for a strong U.S. stand. Two days later Truman and his cabinet approved Acheson's recommendation to recognize Bao Dai. Washington extended formal recognition on February 7, a few hours after London.[57]

THE BEGINNINGS OF PARTNERSHIP

Western recognition marked a major victory for the Bao Dai policy and for the entire French effort to recast the war. The Communist victory in China had dramatically increased Western anxiety about Indochina in the second half of 1949, but the gradual implementation of the Bao Dai solution provided the rationale that enabled the U.S. and British governments, determined as they were to protect their own self-images as champions of liberal progress in the colonial world, to act. It permitted, in short, the establishment of a partnership among the three key Western governments to wage the Cold War together in that part of the world. Predictably, Indochina assumed an ever more complete Cold War cast in the weeks that followed the Sino-Soviet recognition of Ho Chi Minh and Anglo-American recognition of Bao Dai. East European nations quickly followed Moscow's lead in opening relations with the Democratic Republic of Vietnam. On the other side, Bao Dai's Vietnam and the other two "Associated States" of Cambodia and Laos won recognition from Belgium, Luxembourg, Greece, Bolivia, Italy, Honduras, Brazil, Costa Rica, Jordan, South Korea, Spain, and the Vatican by March 10. Others followed close behind. Asian governments including India refused to go along, but French policy received an important boost on February 28, when the Thai regime, eager for U.S. aid of its own, became the first state in the region to open relations with Bao Dai. As this process went forward, French personnel delighted in their achievement. "The situation has had the effect of internationalizing a problem which up until now was a French problem," the Foreign Ministry's Asia desk exulted in a cable to the Washington embassy.[58]

French officials moved quickly to assure that recognition would result in further political assistance as well as military and economic backing. On February 16 Ambassador Bonnet handed Acheson a formal request for all three categories of help. In the political realm, the French government requested U.S. agreement to a tripartite declaration asserting Western determination to defend the Tonkin border, a statement, Paris believed, that would help discourage Chinese cooperation with the Viet Minh. With respect to military aid, French requests for the remainder of 1950 and all of 1951 totaled $70 million, with more than one-third of that sum categorized as "emergency" needs. As for economic aid, the French Foreign Ministry hoped that Washington would at last allow the Indochinese states to receive Marshall Plan aid or offer another mechanism for channeling large amounts of economic and technical aid. French officials did not come forward immediately with a precise request, but they revealed the scope of their ambitions at the end of February, when the Foreign Ministry balked at an initial American proposal of $5 million to cover the rest of fiscal 1950 and $15 million for fiscal 1951. The ministry's office for American affairs considered those sums "very low," estimating Indochina's minimum requirements at $13 million in immediate emergency assistance, to be followed by a much higher figure in 1951.[59]

Even as the tripartite partnership came into view, then, French officials worried that foreign aid would be too little, too late. U.S. diplomats left little doubt of their willingness to provide assistance of various types. American embassy staff in Paris informed the French Foreign Ministry and Defense Ministry in the days following the Assembly's ratification of the Elysée accords that the Truman administration was prepared to receive specific requests for military and economic aid. Charles Bohlen, a State Department counselor with close ties to the White House, even went as far as to tell French officials that Truman was anxious to distribute the $75 million in military aid at his disposal for Asia and that a French request for part of that sum would receive a "warm welcome." Nevertheless, French officials fretted that it would be months before U.S. aid would produce any real results on the battlefield or ease the strain on the French budget. The French commander in

Vietnam, General Marcel Carpentier, insisted that U.S. matériel must arrive "within an extremely short time, a month if possible" in order to bolster the French position. French anxiety was reinforced by lingering suspicions that Washington would insist on new political conditions. Indeed, American officials gave them reason to feel this way. Even as Acheson received French requests on February 16, he insisted to Ambassador Bonnet that Paris declare its intention to grant further autonomy to the Associated States. American officials also asked that the French government appease Asian opinion by turning over the governor's palace in Saigon, the seat of the French High Commission, to Bao Dai as a symbolic gesture.[60]

French officials had little but contempt for what they viewed as senseless American quibbling in the face of crisis. On March 22 Bonnet launched a stinging attack against Washington in a report to Paris that seethed with frustration. In his extraordinary twelve-page harangue, the ambassador surveyed the past five years of U.S. policymaking. In late 1945, he charged, the United States had "never ceased" to oppose the French return to Indochina and refused to help get rid of Chinese occupation forces. After the outbreak of war in 1946, Washington remained overwhelmingly "hostile" to French objectives, Bonnet continued. "Even after the United States was forced to discover the real Ho Chi Minh," he wrote, it "remained suspicious of our intentions, susceptible to the propaganda of our enemies, impressed by Ho Chi Minh's large following, and, with respect to Bao Dai, persuaded that we had nothing to gain from betting on such a bad horse." Only with the collapse of China did the United States reconsider its position, "obliged," Bonnet contended, "to act in Indochina if [it] wanted to prevent Moscow from extending its influence over the whole Asian continent." But even now, after recognizing Bao Dai's government, old American sentimentality for colonial peoples seemed to be bubbling once again to the surface. "Washington," Bonnet asserted,

> is hesitating on the brink of action. On the verge of an indispensable move, it persists in questing after the impossible. In order to satisfy a public opinion poorly informed of our precise problems, it wants to tie the arms of France even while arming her, condemning its partner to the loss of a nearly century-old position, while at the same demanding increased military action.[61]

From the French point of view, then, Washington's continued pressure was vexing and nonsensical: How could the United States, they asked, expect France to make massive sacrifices in Indochina if the goal was to grant the Associated States full independence? In coping with this dilemma, French officials recognized that they held high cards. They could argue that France must hold onto significant privileges in Indochina in order to keep the French public behind the war and to maintain solid support on the center-right in the Assembly. The United States, fearful of a French withdrawal from Indochina, would likely accept the French position. But the danger lingered that Washington, instead of taking the final step into an extraordinarily difficult situation, might opt out of the entire mess. French officials continued to fear that if conditions worsened in Indochina, the Truman administration would retreat to its line of offshore defenses. Foreign Ministry personnel even sometimes speculated that Washington and Moscow might cut a deal over Southeast Asia and other trouble spots around the world without consulting smaller powers like France.[62]

Although far less prone to fear such far-fetched scenarios, British officials shared many French worries about American sluggishness in following up on diplomatic recognition with tangible assistance. The absence of any firm U.S. commitment through early spring 1950 caused Dening to wonder whether Washington had backed away from the urgency with which it had regarded Southeast Asian affairs immediately after Mao's triumph. "The fact of the matter is that the United States have neglected and are neglecting the Far East, and unless and until they can be moved from their inertia, the rest of us will all be in very acute danger," Dening wrote on May 3. In Washington Hubert Ashton Graves, counselor at the British embassy, reported that there was "considerable confusion" within the State Department over the whole matter of aid for Indochina. "A month ago," Graves wrote, "it seemed possible to discern a determination to give aid fairly promptly but now they seem to have gone back to the formula 'in principle some aid will be given.'"[63]

Under the circumstances, British leaders calculated that they could not yet ease their own commitment to Indochina on the assumption that Americans would take up the slack. In fact, the British government offered new support for the French war effort in the weeks following its recognition of Bao Dai. Prime Minister Attlee agreed with his Commonwealth colleagues at Colombo to establish an economic assistance program for Southeast Asia including Indochina. The British government also approved new bilateral military cooperation, most significantly the opening of staff talks that had previously been accepted only in principle. Bevin insisted that the British delegation proceed cautiously, forbidding any hint that London would send ground troops to Vietnam and insisting that the talks be labeled "informal." But the Foreign Office, concurring with the chiefs of staff that the talks were necessary to stiffen French morale, agreed to a series of visits by British officers to Saigon in March, April, and May. Despite persistent shortages of military equipment for British purposes in the Far East, the War Office agreed to study a French request for new military aid and promised to "supply what we can."[64]

For increasingly desperate French officials, such assurances hardly inspired confidence. There was no alternative, then, to new efforts to lead Washington over the threshold. Mounting pressure from the right ruled out new concessions to Bao Dai as a way to impress Washington. The best that the French government could offer during the late winter and early spring of 1950 was a vague assurance that it would set up a new ministry to handle relations with the Associated States—a compromise between Anglo-American demands to place Indochinese affairs under the Foreign Ministry and insistence among French hard-liners that the Ministry of Overseas France maintain its control. In addition, the Ministry of Overseas France, under pressure from the Foreign Ministry, agreed to allow Bao Dai to open full diplomatic relations with the United States and Britain, a concession beyond the terms of the Elysée accords. In other respects, however, French authorities resisted U.S. pressure. The ministries refused to consider allowing the Associated States to join international bodies such as the World Health Organization or the International Labor Organization, while also barring them from making any moves toward membership in the United Nations. Meanwhile, French officials refused to hand over the governor's palace in Saigon to Bao Dai or to agree to issue a declaration of future French intentions in Indochina.[65]

The best French diplomats could do was to emphasize Indochina's importance as a major front in the Cold War—a line of argument that had clearly succeeded in drawing the United States a long way toward making a stand on the side of France. It promised now to provide the final nudge to elicit military and economic commitments. "It is only to the extent that we succeed in persuading them that the 'hot war' we are waging in Indochina is part of the cold war that the United States is fighting against Communism that we will be able to depend on their aid in Indochina," Bonnet wrote to Schuman on April 11. In London Foreign Office officials advanced the same point of view. In meetings with

U.S. officials and in statements to the international media, French officials went to new rhetorical lengths to stress their country's sacrifices on behalf of its allies. Premier Bidault told U.S. diplomats in March, for example, that the conflict in Vietnam had become "a full-scale war between two ways of life, the results of which would have serious repercussions for all the civilized world." In Saigon, meanwhile, General Carpentier warned U.S. diplomats that although he did not anticipate a Chinese invasion within the next six months, it was impossible to predict communist intentions—a clear warning that French forces might be unable to hold the line by themselves. Defense Minister René Pleven sought to exploit the Truman administration's main foreign policy sensitivity, asserting in early May that the burden France was bearing alone in Asia prevented it from making a greater commitment in Europe.[66]

At the same time, French officials grew more explicit in threatening that their country would withdraw entirely from Indochina if the United States did not provide material aid. That tactic carried obvious risks. Ambassador Bruce pointed out to Alexandre Parodi, the secretary general of the French Foreign Ministry, that the U.S. Congress might regard the threat as an attempt at blackmail and therefore balk at approving aid. For his part, Foreign Minister Schuman acknowledged that any consideration of withdrawal might provide a boost for the French Communist Party, which increasingly advocated precisely that step, and for nationalists in other parts of the French empire. In London, meanwhile, Ambassador Massigli warned that the tactic might also have a damaging effect on the British government by suggesting French willingness to engage in diplomatic blackmail.[67] Nevertheless, French officials made several "blunt suggestions" during February that abandonment was possible, as Ambassador Bruce reported to Washington. On March 18 High Commissioner Pignon explicitly called for even more pointed use of the withdrawal threat. If Washington continued to press for French concessions as a condition for material aid, Pignon proposed that the French government reply by insisting that "there could be no question of continuing to expose French troops for the defense of interests which had become foreign to France, and that we could be forced under these circumstances to recall the expeditionary corps." A few weeks later, French president Vincent Auriol made one of the boldest threats yet in an interview with a Reuters correspondent whom he had summoned to his office, apparently for that purpose. "The French were incapable of standing up to full-scale Communist attack and needed very substantial help if they were to hold out," Auriol stated, according to a British summary of the conversation. "If [France] were to clear out," Auriol added, "Indochina would fall straight into Communist hands." That, Auriol insisted, would be just the beginning of turmoil that would produce instability—and thereby threaten Western Cold War interests—around the world. "It would be not only French Indo-China but Madagascar, North Africa and indeed the whole French Union that would be at stake," Auriol contended.[68]

French threats hit their mark. Ambassador Bruce confessed to being "shaken" by talk of withdrawal. Edmund Gullion, the new U.S. consul in Saigon, noted that the French "would like to get out of [the war]" and that there was a "degree of truth" in French insistence that they were defending Western interests. With the French military effort in a state of crisis, Gullion urged that U.S. aid "should be of the most rapid character possible." Anxiety about a French pullout merely gave a final push to a process that had already gathered powerful momentum. Regardless of French threats, Americans had little doubt that the French campaign was faltering badly. The State Department concluded in the first week of April that the French military could hold out for only one more year without assistance, while another report concluded that Mao had stepped up his supply of weapons to the Viet Minh and had placed as many as half a million troops within a few days' march of the Tonkin border. Out of the view of French officials, the Joint Chiefs of Staff approved a plan in February to allocate $15 million in military aid for Indochina, and Truman approved the package in principle on March 10. Meanwhile, the administration offered assurances about economic assistance and in February dispatched a mission headed by R. Allen Griffin, head of the U.S. Economic Cooperation Administration, to the region to evaluate the needs of the Associated States and other Asian countries.[69]

By no means did U.S. officials abandon their belief that the Western position in Indochina would be immeasurably strengthened by further French concessions to Bao Dai. Acheson made this position clear in a March 7 cable to Paris instructing Ambassador Bruce to maintain pressure. "The U.S. [administration] believes that . . . it behooves the [French government] to do what it can to 'sell' Bao Dai to the SEA world and destroy by every means possible the legend that he is a [French] puppet," Acheson wrote. By that point, however, Acheson and most senior U.S. officials, recognizing the unlikelihood of further French concessions, had accepted the French thesis that foreign support, especially military aid, would give Bao Dai a jolt of power and legitimacy.

American military and economic power, in other words, might substitute for new steps toward autonomy. Following their visit to Vietnam in mid-March, Griffin and his advisers expressed hope that the spectacle of foreign powers lining up behind Bao Dai would be so impressive to ordinary Vietnamese that they would abandon their communist flirtation. The "application of American aid," Griffin wrote on March 16, could be the determining factor "psychologically" as well as "materially."[70]

Only one question remained: to whom precisely should American aid be given? On this matter U.S. authorities were almost unanimous in the view that it should go directly to the Vietnamese regime, with smaller chunks for the Cambodian and Laotian governments. American leaders still hoped, after all, to cast U.S. aid as assistance for an independent Asian nation struggling against communist aggression. Acheson acknowledged that French authorities would have to bear the "lion's share" of duties connected with actual distribution of aid simply because of their technical expertise and their overall command of the war. But formally, U.S. officials insisted, American aid must be negotiated and delivered on a bilateral basis with each of the three Associated States. In other respects, too, Americans hoped to minimize the chance of being accused of abetting French colonialism. Acheson ordered diplomats in Vietnam to report as quickly as possible any shreds of evidence that Bao Dai was succeeding in drawing support away from Ho Chi Minh, so the State Department could use them in its campaign to justify U.S. policy domestically. Similarly, the secretary asked the embassy in Paris for intelligence information on Ho Chi Minh to help with preparation of a brochure depicting Ho Chi Minh as a full-fledged servant of Moscow. Americans also showed their sensitivities when the U.S. Joint Chiefs of Staff flatly rejected the possibility of joining Franco-British staff talks in the Far East and when U.S. consulate staff in Saigon insisted that an upcoming visit by two U.S. destroyers must be described as a gesture of support for Vietnam, not for the French navy.[71]

French officials vehemently resisted arrangements that marginalized their role. To French minds, any American move to provide aid directly to the Associated States threatened not only to weaken the war effort but also to embolden Bao Dai, to undercut French prestige in Asia, and to create a dangerous precedent for American meddling elsewhere in the French empire. As early as June 1949 General Carpentier had foreseen trouble over the modalities of American aid and insisted that French forces must never lose their "military preponderance" over indigenous forces, even as France committed itself to establishing a nominally independent Vietnamese army. At about the same time, the Foreign Ministry had concluded that the French government must insist that U.S. economic aid be channeled through French authorities. By early 1950 officials at the Ministry of Overseas France conceded that the government might have to agree to certain superficial concessions on the matter "in order to appease American opinion." But U.S. insistence on direct delivery to the Vietnamese, Cambodian, and Laotian governments far exceeded what French officials were willing to allow.[72]

Beneath the French position lay concern about excessive autonomy for the Associated States as well as fear that bilateral arrangements would lead to establishment of a dangerously large U.S. administrative apparatus in Indochina. For several years the French government had struggled to minimize American involvement in Indochina even as it had sought U.S. aid for French aims. Fears that the United States and Vietnamese nationalists would cut a deal over the head of France had weighed heavily on Paris and dictated strenuous efforts to keep Americans out of Vietnam altogether. In negotiations leading to the Elysée accords, Paris had insisted on provisions guaranteeing that France would provide all foreign technical expertise required by the new Vietnamese state. But the growing likelihood of U.S. aid in early 1950 threatened this comfortable arrangement. In March the Foreign Ministry predicted that American aid might involve establishment of a large U.S. military mission in Saigon, a prospect that raised "certain dangers" for France.[73]

French fears of contacts between Vietnamese and American officials seemed to be borne out in February and March when members of Bao Dai's government attempted to convince the U.S. consulate to circumvent French authorities and provide aid directly. Prime Minister Nguyen Phan Long told Griffin that "his people [were] perfectly able to decide what they needed and it was impossible in Paris twelve thousand kilometers away to do as well," according to the American record of the conversation. By April High Commission personnel had become so alarmed that they arranged the ouster of Nguyen Phan Long, whom they rightly suspected of dealing with the Americans behind French backs. Meanwhile, Carpentier warned Paris against any move toward withdrawing French troops from Indochina as indigenous militaries were formed. Carpentier suspected that the Vietnamese regime, if it came to believe that French will was faltering, might invite the United States to make up the difference.[74]

The Franco-American clash over the details of U.S. aid contributed to mounting frustration and ill will on both sides. Acheson lashed out against the French position in March, charging that French preferences were "totally unacceptable." While denying that the State Department wished to interfere in internal French Union matters, the secretary insisted that Washington had the right to negotiate aid agreements directly with recipient countries. Acheson noted that the United States had reached bilateral aid deals with Belgium and Luxembourg despite their economic union and with the Federal Republic of Germany despite Allied controls dating from the Second World War. But this logic was unpersuasive to French officials, who refused to accept American preferences during meetings with Griffin in March. In place of the direct delivery proposed by the Americans, French participants in the talks insisted on creating a quadripartite body grouping French authorities and the governments of the three Associated States to negotiate and distribute the aid.[75]

French officials defended their position in a number of ways. For one thing, they argued that the Vietnamese, Cambodian, and Laotian governments were too inexperienced and weak to manage large-scale aid programs on their own. With respect to American military support, diplomats contended that it was the French army, not the Vietnamese, that was standing in the way of communist advances in Vietnam. "We are working hard to organize Vietnamese troops, but it will be a long time before they can play an important part in the common fight," asserted Ambassador Bonnet in Washington. On economic aid, French officials defended the quadripartite arrangement as more efficient than the alternatives and more in keeping with global trends toward economic interdependence. French authorities also insisted that an integrated administration would help preserve long-standing regional economic patterns, noting that Laos and Cambodia had historically provided raw materials for Vietnam and purchased manufactured goods in return. Most insistently of all, French officials contended that direct U.S. aid could impair implementation of the Elysée accords by undermining the internal bonds of the French Union.[76]

In London Foreign Office personnel were loath to become involved in this dispute. While sympathetic to the French position, they did not wish to cross the United States on a matter of secondary importance. R. H. Scott, chief of the Southeast Asia department, took a philosophical approach. "French policy has not been successful in Indo-China," Scott wrote, "and if we want the United States to help clear up the mess we must accept the possibility of some friction." The French government did not, however, require British support in order to prevail in the dispute with Washington. Military aid proved the easier case. With Carpentier, the senior French commander, threatening to resign if military assistance went directly to the Vietnamese government, most State Department and Pentagon officials recognized that it would be a severe blow to the French war effort—both materially and psychologically—to insist on U.S. preferences. William Lacy, assistant chief of the State Department's Southeast Asia division, told Bonnet in April that the State Department had decided to accept the French position, agreeing that the French high command was the only body capable of making decisions about the distribution of military assistance. "It would be a serious error to imagine another solution that would help advance military operations in Indochina," conceded Lacy. Although French officials continued to fret that Washington would insist on sending a large military mission to Saigon to manage the process, they were by and large satisfied that the Truman administration had accepted the principle of French supervision.[77]

The French government also prevailed with its proposal to distribute economic aid through a quadripartite mechanism. In April High Commissioner Pignon went as far as to threaten to suspend Franco-Vietnamese talks aimed at implementing and building on the terms of the Elysée agreements unless proposals to channel U.S. aid directly to the Associated States were dropped. The precise impact of the French threat on U.S. calculations is impossible to determine, but the timing of American acquiescence to the French position suggests that it may have had some bearing. U.S agreement followed almost immediately after Pignon's warning. The high commissioner still hoped to circumvent that arrangement by obtaining some American aid on an "emergency" basis and channeling it directly to the French military to distribute as it saw fit. But even Pignon was satisfied with the quadripartite arrangement, which he and other French officials viewed more as a concession to congressional and public opinion in the United States than as a serious impediment to French control over U.S. resources.[78]

By late April French officials had good reason, then, to believe they had made significant headway not only toward obtaining U.S. aid but also toward having it on their terms. Washington, it is true, had not yet made any formal, definitive offer. But upcoming ministerial meetings in Paris and then London during the first days of May seemed likely to yield results. French officials agreed that they must not let the opportunity pass, partly because Asian opinion was beginning to doubt whether the West, despite all its talk, would really act against communist encroachment. "In my opinion," wrote the French ambassador in Singapore, "if the meeting of the three ministers does not result in some concrete decisions, presented in some slightly spectacular way, the failure will have the most profound consequences for the future of Southeast Asia." The Foreign Ministry's Asia desk noted that nothing less than the continuation of the war against the Viet Minh hung in the balance. "The matériel available to the French expeditionary corps," concluded a ministry report on the eve of Foreign Minister Schuman's meetings with Acheson in Paris,

> has been stretched to the extreme limit. . . . If one considers that this matériel, which has been used to the maximum degree on especially difficult terrain and before that had passed the test of the German and Italian campaigns, one can easily understand that today we have reached our dying breath. The situation is such today that if massive American aid does not arrive in the shortest possible time, the war-making potential of the expeditionary corps will suffer total collapse at the end of this year or the beginning of 1951. The evacuation of Indochina will be the only option open to us.[79]

Schuman hoped to obtain military aid to equip sufficient Vietnamese forces to enable cuts in French manpower from the current level of about 150,000 men to about 130,000 by the end of 1951, with other reductions to follow. The French delegation did not place an exact price tag on such assistance, although the Foreign Ministry noted just before the London conference that various military-aid requests prepared since March totaled about $225 million—a figure clearly far beyond what Washington would be willing to provide in the near term. Beyond tangible assistance, Schuman and his advisers sought assurances of various types. First, they hoped to convince Secretary of State Acheson to pledge American assistance "throughout the whole period necessary"—an open-ended commitment that would cease only when the French government declared the state of emergency in Indochina to be over. In addition, the French delegation hoped to obtain U.S. and British agreement to issue a joint communiqué declaring the three governments' commitment to work together to resist communist expansion in Asia. In the days leading up to the Paris meetings, the French Foreign Ministry drafted a proposal pledging that the signatories would give the three Indochinese states "all the assistance in their power" and would take "all appropriate measures" to end the threat in the region.[80]

The French delegation was optimistic of success as the meetings between Schuman and Acheson opened in Paris. Although Jean Chauvel, the Foreign Ministry's secretary general, complained that Acheson was "dogmatic by temperament" and might be inclined to press for more French concessions in Indochina, he believed that the secretary of state could be persuaded, at last, to make a commitment. "Our chances of success will be tied to the way in which we conceive and present our arguments," asserted a Foreign Ministry study. Apparently taking no chances, the Foreign Ministry decided that, if necessary, it would offer the United States new inducements, including an agreement to toe Washington's line by declaring its refusal to recognize the Chinese Communist government. There was little doubt, however, about the centerpiece of the French claim for aid. In preparatory talks among diplomats from the three countries, French personnel dwelled on a single theme, pointing to the drain on the French economy caused by the war and the consequent problems of contributing successfully to European defense. The deputy French representative to NATO, Hervé Alphand, put the matter starkly in a conversation with senior State Department officials on April 29, telling the Americans that the war was costing more than one-third of the entire French military budget.[81]

Foreign Minister Schuman repeated the French position in his first meeting with Acheson on May 8. While stressing the liberality of French intentions in Indochina, he dwelled on his nation's inability to bear the costs of the war much longer. "The French government," Schuman said, "had deliberated and concluded that France cannot for long carry a double burden—in Indochina on the one hand, in Western Europe on the other." In requesting aid, Schuman continued, the French government was "thinking not only of its interests, but also of those of the general European defense." Schuman denied that his government had any thought of abandoning Indochina but made a threat likely to have an even greater impact on his American interlocutors. France, he asserted, might "be forced to change its military policy in Europe" if the United States did not help in Vietnam. In trilateral talks that opened the next day in London, Bevin followed a similar line of argument. "Britain was making a big contribution to the common cause," Bevin said, "and it would be fatal if this contribution were lessened by the loss of colonies by the Western European powers, since they were an essential part of the foundation of European economic existence." He therefore urged that Washington give "sympathetic consideration" to European requests for assistance.[82]

By this point Acheson needed no persuading. To French and British delight, the secretary of state gave a definitive statement of American willingness to provide aid. In his session with Schuman on May 8, Acheson promised that the Truman administration would make available $15 million in military and economic aid during the remaining weeks of the 1950 fiscal year. Further aid, he said, would depend on congressional approval, but there could be little doubt that an American commitment, once made, would be hard to reverse. Following the meeting, Acheson released a statement asserting that assisting the Associated States was "primarily the responsibility of France and the governments and peoples of Indochina." But, the declaration continued, "neither national independence nor democratic evolution [can] exist in any area dominated by Soviet imperialism." U.S. economic aid and military equipment would help Vietnam, Cambodia, and Laos "in restoring stability and permitting these states to pursue their peaceful and democratic development." Acheson thus embraced the French thesis that foreign support would create the conditions for democratization and full independence, rather than the other way around. Upon returning to Paris on May 15, an exultant Schuman told a news conference that the United States had given France "full satisfaction" and, perhaps of greatest importance, that there was "every reason to believe that this aid will be continued as long as it is necessary."[83]

Schuman failed, however, to accomplish all that he hoped for at the London ministerial meetings, which ended without agreement on a tripartite declaration concerning Southeast Asia. The principal objection came not from Washington but from the British government, which, even in its moment of victory, showed its accustomed sensitivity to Asian opinion. Any statement of Western solidarity, Bevin warned, might give the impression that Paris, London, and Washington were ganging up and failing to consult the Asian nations concerned. British officials had no objections to Western cooperation when it could be implemented out of the public eye. Indeed, just before Bevin raised his objections to a public statement, British and French commanders in Southeast Asia began drafting an agenda for the first sessions of their staff conversations. In public, however, Bevin would agree only to a mild statement pledging the three Western powers to support efforts by the Asians themselves to fight communism. For its part, the U.S. delegation had milder reservations, objecting only to the language proposed by the French government. A U.S. draft emphasized a point dear to the Americans. Although the United States was willing to supply military aid "within its capabilities," the draft said, France and Britain "have direct responsibilities in the area which make its security of even greater concern to them." That phrase irritated the French delegation, which recognized, in Ambassador Massigli's words, that the American position ran "exactly contrary" to French insistence that Indochina must engage all of the Western powers equally. Schuman lamented that Acheson and Bevin "were not sufficiently taking account of the fact that France is defending a common cause." But with Bevin opposed to any declaration at all, the French delegation saw no choice but to drop the whole matter, at least until the next three-power meeting. No statement at all was preferable to any backsliding. It had taken a long time, after all, to get to this point.[84]

Conclusion

On the last day of June 1950, eight American C-47 transport aircraft carrying a cargo of spare parts and maintenance equipment lumbered to a halt at Saigon's Tan Son Nhut airfield. U.S. aid had at last arrived. French officials, still fearful that U.S. help would amount to too little, too late, complained throughout the summer about the slow pace of U.S. deliveries and maintained steady pressure on Washington for greater and faster assistance. But there was little reason for worry. The decision to support the French war effort marked a major turn in U.S. policy. By early summer the U.S. military had begun channeling not only planes but also naval vessels, vehicles, weapons, ammunition, spare parts, and communications equipment to Indochina, while plans went ahead to establish an elaborate aid disbursement and military training bureaucracy in Saigon, the U.S. Military Assistance Advisory Group.[1] Meanwhile, U.S. specialists initiated public health, agricultural development, and other civilian programs.

The outbreak of the Korean War on June 25 produced a sharp intensification of American aid as U.S. officials sought to bolster Western defenses against the possibility of Chinese aggression in Southeast Asia. By the end of the year, the Truman administration had increased its near-term commitments to Indochina to about $133 million.[2] The National Security Council approved a paper insisting that the United States must back the French war effort "by all means practicable short of the actual employment of United States military forces."[3] Deliveries increased steadily. Washington sent about 11,000 tons of military equipment in 1950, 90,000 tons in 1951, 100,000 tons in 1952, and more than 170,000 tons in 1953.[4] As fighting climaxed in Vietnam in the spring of 1954, the United States bore more than 80 percent of the war's material cost. In all, the United States paid nearly $3 billion over four years.

In the end, of course, French and American exertions failed to achieve their objective. Part of the problem was the Viet Minh's growing military prowess. The infusion of American aid provoked the Chinese government to dispatch substantial assistance to Ho Chi Minh's forces for the first time. Between April and September 1950 China sent the Viet Minh fourteen thousand rifles and pistols, seventeen hundred machine guns, and 150 mortars, as well as munitions, medicine, communications equipment, and a seventy-nine-man advisory team. New archival evidence from China suggests that such assistance played a significant role in the Viet Minh's battlefield successes over the following four years.[5] In most ways, however, the war after 1950 resembled its course before that year, suggesting that the problems confronting the Western partners ran much deeper than mounting Chinese support for the Democratic Republic of Vietnam. As before, Viet Minh guerrillas controlled the Vietnamese countryside, partly through military proficiency and partly through greater appeal to the peasantry, while French forces could rarely extend their reach outside the cities and certain well-fortified locations.[6] Vietnamese troops successfully avoided major engagements, while inflicting heavy losses on French units. Despite occasional bright spots, American aid did little to change the overall pattern.

Nor did greater American involvement do much to alter the political situation that underpinned conflict in Vietnam. U.S. officials continued to apply pressure for new French concessions to the Bao Dai government, but American demands resulted in little more than French resentment and foot-dragging. Despite continued negotiations between Saigon and Paris between 1950 and 1954, the French government refused to concede self-rule in various key areas. Paris insisted on Indochinese membership in the French Union, an institution that left the metropole with authority over foreign, defense, trade, and other policies of member states. The French government also maintained its insistence on controlling the Vietnamese currency and preserving special economic and legal privileges for French citizens. Equally significant, French authorities failed to develop an independent Vietnamese National Army, as promised under the Elysée agreements. Although the VNA counted more than 200,000 Vietnamese soldiers by the end of 1953, French policy permitted these forces little autonomy and therefore little sense of nationalist purpose.[7] Americans found, to their discouragement, that the 1950 decision to extend aid left them little leverage over such French behavior. Once Washington had conceded that the French government had gone far enough down the reformist road to merit U.S. aid, it could do little to reopen the matter. Nor, given its deep anxieties about the implications of a possible defeat in Vietnam, could it back out of Vietnam and leave the French on their own once again.

In spring 1954 the entire arrangement, almost exactly four years after its establishment, came to a crashing end. At the remote mountain village of Dien Bien Phu in northwestern Vietnam, General Vo Nguyen Giap dealt the French army a crushing defeat. With support for the war disintegrating in France, the Viet Minh victory clearly meant an end to the conflict. Only one development might have prolonged the fight—full-scale military intervention by U.S. and British forces. The Eisenhower and Churchill governments weighed that possibility as the battle unfolded in March and April, with Washington even considering an atomic air strike to rescue twelve thousand French troops besieged at Dien Bien Phu. But they opted against any such action, unwilling to raise the stakes in a war that seemed to offer little prospect of success. With that decision, essentially a move to abandon the partnership established in 1950, the French could no longer stave off the outcome that they had managed to defer for a decade through shrewd efforts to obtain and exploit foreign assistance. On May 7, after weeks of bloody fighting, General Christian de Castries surrendered at Dien Bien Phu. A few weeks later the French government and other major powers signed the Geneva Accords, transforming Vietnam, Cambodia, and Laos into independent states. The era of French rule in Southeast Asia had come to an end.[8]

What was a decisive moment in the history of Southeast Asia produced only a limited change, however, in the minds of U.S. policymakers. To be sure, the impending French departure transformed the precise nature of the problem Washington faced in Southeast Asia. If it wished to exert influence in postwar Vietnam, it would have to do so directly, no longer as a member of a partnership that left primary responsibility to another power. The Geneva Conference's decision to divide Vietnam at the seventeenth parallel also sharply altered the situation. Although the accords specified that the division had merely the short-term purpose of enabling former combatants to regroup and demobilize in separate zones, the existence of a noncommunist administrative entity in the south clearly suggested a chance to keep half the country—and the wealthier half, at that—out of the communist orbit. But if the end of the French era transformed the modalities of exerting influence and the region's political geography, it did not alter basic perceptions of American interests in Vietnam. On that level U.S. thinking held steady after the spring of 1950. Policymakers saw the Vietnamese revolution as an extension of international communism. They believed that a communist victory in Vietnam risked toppling the rest of Southeast Asia. And they believed that the United States had the wherewithal to create a new political alignment in Vietnam that would reconcile the Western political and economic interests in Vietnam with those of Vietnamese nationalists.

The events of 1950–1954 had the effect not of altering these key American assumptions but of confirming them and leading Washington to act more boldly on these ideas than before. The peak years of the French war forced the Viet Minh into an ever closer alignment with Mao's China and the Soviet Union, giving substance, like a self-fulfilling prophesy, to American fears. By 1954 no American officials had any doubt—nor should they have—that Ho Chi Minh's movement served the interests of international communism. The link was real and obvious, even if Western policy was largely responsible for generating the outcome that Western policymakers most dreaded. Meanwhile, the wobbly French war effort encouraged American worries about the fate of the region as a whole in the event Vietnam fell under communist control. In 1954 President Eisenhower gave American fears their classic formulation, asserting that if Vietnam fell to communism, the rest of Southeast Asia would collapse like a row of dominos. Once the communists had their way in Indochina, he said, "you could have the beginning of a disintegration that would have the most profound influence."[9] Unsurprisingly, as the final French defeat neared, the U.S. administration moved boldly to form an alliance of Asian and Western states, the Southeast Asian Treaty Organization, to resist communist expansion beyond Vietnam's northern half.

The French defeat also immeasurably strengthened Americans' conviction that they could reshape Vietnamese politics in a way that would accommodate both Western and Vietnamese interests. The French and British had, of course, promoted precisely such a vision in the period leading up to the formation of the Western partnership in 1950. Unenthusiastically yet with determination, Americans accepted the possibility of such an outcome within the structure of the French empire. The dissolution of France's Southeast Asian empire in 1954 opened new possibilities, while not altering the basic American approach. Now U.S. authorities had the opportunity to apply American solutions directly, no longer encumbered by association with partners tainted by colonialism and the whiff of dishonesty in their endless assurances of reform.

Between 1954 and 1965 the Eisenhower, Kennedy, and Johnson administrations took up this challenge, drawing the United States ever more deeply into Vietnam as they sought to create a viable South Vietnamese state that would satisfy local nationalism while serving Western interests. This long and complex story has been well told elsewhere.[10] For the purposes of this study, it is important to point out merely that the set of assumptions that drove American policy forward departed little from the ideas laid in place in 1950. In recent years historians writing about the American war have emphasized contingency; that is, they have stressed variations over time as different administrations with different needs, perceptions, and personalities reckoned with the Vietnam problem in their own ways. Thanks to this scholarship, we can now see that there was nothing wholly inevitable about the U.S. decisions for full-scale war in 1965. Above all, it seems, the Kennedy administration entertained grave doubts about America's Vietnam commitment and might have acted to scale back U.S. involvement if JFK had survived for a second term as president.[11] Yet there is a danger in excessive attention to contingency. We can easily lose sight of the continuities that run through the entire American experience in Vietnam and of the possibility that these continuities may be the most important way to understand how the United States came to fight a war in Vietnam. The simple fact of the matter is that successive presidential administrations, however much latitude they enjoyed to change course in Vietnam, did not do so. In the end, patterns of thought laid in place in 1950 drove American policy uninterruptedly to 1965 and beyond. To understand the American war, then, it is vitally necessary to understand what transpired in the years leading up to 1950.

Vietnamese commentators have perhaps phrased the importance of these years most succinctly—no surprise given the fact that Vietnamese, much more than Americans, are likely to see the years around the end of the Second World War as the crucial ones in their nation's history. In a 1997 roundtable held in Hanoi to bring former American and North Vietnamese policymakers and academics together to discuss the war, Americans consistently focused on the importance of decisions taken during the early 1960s. For the Vietnamese, the important turning points came in the half decade after 1945—a time when a certain flexibility prevailed in international politics and when both sides in Vietnam's wars might have made different choices and gone down different roads. "The process of U.S. involvement in Vietnam began—seriously began—with the Truman administration and continued more or less uninterrupted through five presidents," argued Tran Quang Co, a long-time Vietnamese diplomat. The Kennedy and Johnson administrations, he added, merely followed the path of their predecessors "with readjustments made in accordance with the international context and the realities of the war at that time." Luu Doan Huynh, an eminent Vietnamese historian as well as veteran of the Vietnam People's Army, made the point even more boldly, asserting that the United States committed its "original sin" in Vietnam in 1950. In that year, Luu asserted, Americans abandoned their prudent neutrality and acted on the faulty belief that the Vietnamese revolution was simply the servant of international communism. "In 1950, not before, not after, is when you began your downfall," Luu insisted.[12]

What, then, happened in the years before 1950 that brought the United States to that point? This book argues that U.S. calculations about Vietnam must be seen as part of a complicated set of international interactions that gave shape and meaning to the Indochina problem in the years after the Second World War. Without doubt, the intensification of Cold War tensions around that time ensured that American policymakers would focus their attention on a country where unrest was partly communist-inspired and would look with some sympathy on the efforts of France, an important U.S. ally, to protect its interests there. But the perceived importance of France to U.S. global objectives and the reddish tint of the Vietnamese revolution do not, by themselves, explain the U.S. decision to support the French war effort in Vietnam and the Bao Dai policy more generally. Substantial parts of the policymaking bureaucracies in France, Britain, and the United States were deeply skeptical of the *politique de force* embraced by French hawks at the end of 1946—a skepticism that seems fully justified in retrospect. For at least some of these critics, the war against the Viet Minh promised only to undercut Western interests by driving the revolution into the embrace of Soviet and Chinese communism and by alienating the very parts of the Vietnamese population whose support would be required for any moderate solution to succeed. Outside of the French Communists, these skeptics generally backed Western efforts to resist Soviet expansionism; they were no starry-eyed idealists out of touch with the necessity of defending against communist advances. But they preferred to move forward in a way they considered likely to lessen communism's appeal to ordinary Vietnamese, rather than increase it. They wished, in short, to wage the Cold War with sophistication, nuance, and close attention to the social grievances that underpinned political instability in Indochina.

The persistence of these dissenters—liberal policymakers in the United States, the Labour left and Asian nationalist leaders in the British case, and the political left in France—reflected the inchoate, flexible nature of international politics in the years from the end of the Second World War through roughly 1948. In that period of flux—what political scientist Robert Latham has aptly dubbed the "liberal moment"—the international order had no clear shape.[13] Above all, the fate of European colonies remained uncertain. By weakening European states and eliciting promises of a new era of self-determination, the Second World War had loosed anticolonial passions around the globe. The creation of new international institutions, meanwhile, raised expectations that multilateralism and human development would displace force and exploitation as the underpinning of relations between the industrial West and the resource-producing periphery. And the emergence of the United States, with its powerful rhetorical tradition of anticolonialism, suggested that nationalist movements around the world had a powerful champion at last. Whether this swirl of possibility would translate into lasting change was, of course, an open question. For a time, Western officials who opposed the application of simplistic Cold War thinking in complicated colonial settings held sway or at least held their adversaries at bay. That they did so even as Cold War tensions took hold in Europe suggests the considerable appeal of this set of views—an appeal that has rarely found its rightful place in Cold War scholarship. On the whole, historians have emphasized the quick closing down of alternatives to the Cold War order in the aftermath of the Second World War and the rapid marginalization of policymakers and politicians who bucked the trend toward vigorous application of policies rooted in a Manichean vision of the global order.[14]

This period of possibility came to an end only in 1949 and 1950, a tragic moment when Western governments moved decisively toward forceful solutions that reduced complex social conflicts in many parts of the world to mere expressions of the confrontation between Western liberal capitalism and Soviet-led communism. This book offers a case study into how that process unfolded. Regarding Vietnam, this study shows, hawkish policymaking factions in France, Britain, and the

Conclusion

United States succeeded by 1950 in recasting the Vietnamese political situation in a way that helped overcome objections, most crucially in the United States, to an international partnership behind the French war. Only when the hawks found a way to dampen misgivings about supporting colonialism and to reclassify Vietnam as a Cold War battleground could they have their way. Only, that is, when they redefined Vietnam as a Cold War conflict, stemming from the same causes and requiring the same solutions as anticommunist fights elsewhere, could the three governments close ranks around a common policy. Dissenters still bridled against the drift of Western policy in 1949 and 1950. After the Communist victory in China, however, it became increasingly difficult to resist the notion that French policy served Western interests.

The Bao Dai solution was the key innovation. By fabricating a new Vietnamese nationalism unambiguously aligned with Western interests, it simplified matters for Western policymakers perplexed by Ho Chi Minh's complicated blend of nationalism and communism and by the difficulty of crafting policy in response to it. Few officials, even in France, were enthusiastic about Bao Dai or his chances of success. However, the former emperor's return decisively facilitated the shift of U.S. policy toward partnership with the European powers. Bao Dai represented a compromise between prolonged French rule and American insistence on thoroughgoing colonial reform in Indochina, a compromise that fully satisfied no one but provided a sound basis for the creation of an international partnership in Vietnam. The French could hold onto a significant degree of colonial control, while the Americans could be satisfied that the country had obtained at least a modicum of self-rule. All sides could then proceed on the assumption that in waging war against Ho Chi Minh, they were combating a movement that served the interests of international communism.

The European governments played the leading roles in redefining the nature of the war in Vietnam and bringing the United States into the region. Most important, the MRP-dominated French ministries crafted the Bao Dai solution in 1947 with the explicit intent of attracting American backing and thereby strengthening shaky support for the war within France. There is little question that American policymakers would have accepted—even welcomed—a deal between France and Ho Chi Minh at any point before 1950. But French officials rejected that course and worked strenuously to sell Bao Dai to their American counterparts. After the success of 1950, the French government continued to prove adept at manipulating American anxieties to preserve the partnership and to keep aid flowing. For one thing, Paris could wield the threat of withdrawing its forces from Indochina if Washington did not seem sufficiently forthcoming. Although French officials only occasionally dropped such hints, Americans had no trouble picking up the message. Secretary of State Acheson recognized that the United States might well "lose out" if it was seen as supporting "old-fashioned colonial attitudes," but he also saw that Washington could not press Paris to the point where French leaders would say, "Alright, take over the damn country. We don't want it."[15] By 1952 the French government had found another way to keep American aid on track. That year, West European states took steps toward establishing the European Defense Community, an organization strongly championed by the United States as a way to bring a rearmed Federal Republic of Germany into the Western fold through a multilateral mechanism that would threaten other West European states as little as possible.

The fact that the EDC required French ratification meant that Paris wielded enormous leverage over the United States—leverage that the French government skillfully exploited to its advantage in Indochina. French leaders repeatedly made clear that the scheme stood no chance of passage unless French military expenditures connected to Vietnam could be cut. The stated aim was to enable the French military to devote an appropriate share of its strength to Europe and thereby to counterbalance a rearmed Germany, a critical objective in view of long-standing French fears of the German military. Although French assertions about the danger of parliamentary rejection on these grounds were genuine—indeed, the EDC was rejected in August 1954—the government's insistence on the weakness of its forces in Europe was also motivated by the desire to extract more help from the United States in Indochina. The ploy worked by appealing directly to U.S. sensitivities, not only Washington's desire for robust defenses in Europe but also its interest in thrift. The Eisenhower administration reckoned in July 1953 that it should agree to French demands for a doubling of U.S. aid over the following months because the amount of American money that could be saved through successful creation of the EDC dwarfed what the French were demanding for Indochina.[16] The administration approved the funds but, of course, got no EDC in return.

Great Britain, too, adhered to the course it had charted between 1944 and 1950 over the years that followed. With the United States taking up the burden of backing France in Indochina, London could at last settle into the position to which it had aspired, that of benevolent but low-profile support for its close ally. Without doubt, the Labour cabinet, and the Conservative government that came into office in 1951, continued to hold staff conversations with French commanders in the Far East. In addition, Britain continued to make available modest, though not insignificant, amounts of military gear in a bid to be of some practical assistance as well as to maintain a degree of involvement and political influence in Indochina. For 1953, for example, British grants of military equipment for France amounted to about £7.4 million; sales of additional supplies pushed total aid figures higher.[17] The British government refused to go further, however, and rejected out of hand French requests for British troops.[18] Behind that caution lay the usual combination of concerns that had underlain policy debates since at least 1944—an awareness of political risks at home, worry about alienating Asian opinion, and resource shortages. The leading role was to be left to the United States. Indeed, the Churchill government took exactly that approach during the Dien Bien Phu crisis in 1954, adamantly refusing to join Washington in any sort of international intervention. If there were to be an international response, it would come from the United States alone.

Although the military results were disastrous, European diplomacy connected to Vietnam must be rated a remarkable success. French enthusiasts for maintaining their country's Southeast Asian empire in the post–Second World War period fully accomplished the goal they set out for themselves as early as 1944—to harness foreign, especially U.S., power on behalf of French objectives. By 1954 the United States had sent as much aid to Indochina as it had to France itself under the Marshall Plan. Even more remarkable, the French government largely set the terms on which the aid was provided; Paris successfully resisted pressures for meaningful concessions to Vietnamese nationalism and never had to concede more than the superficial sort of autonomy spelled out in the Elysée agreements. That was enough to break the policymaking deadlock in Washington and pull U.S. policy in the pro-French direction. Meanwhile British proponents of a strong French campaign in Indochina achieved their principal objective of involving the United States in the region in order to lessen the burden on Britain itself. Most impressive of all, the British government achieved that aim while preserving a significant degree of political leadership in Southeast Asia. The Foreign Office retained an important role in interpreting events in the area and continued to collaborate closely with Washington after 1950.

In France and Britain, constructing Vietnam as a Cold War battlefield enabled hawkish policymakers to attract U.S. support and thereby to overcome internal dilemmas that threatened to forestall an assertive policy in Southeast Asia. They would not have succeeded, of course, without strong allies in the United States—without, that is, Americans who embraced European objectives and sought to recraft U.S. policy in directions that favored them. Conservative American policymakers found European ideas and initiatives enormously useful in trying to bring about this shift. To prevail in the bureaucratic struggle in Washington, they had to demonstrate that support for the French war effort did not amount to naked support for colonialism. They needed to show not only that Vietnam was ill prepared for quick self-rule—that a degree of European tutelage remained essential—but also that communist influences were hopelessly corrupting Vietnamese nationalism and posed a threat to the region as a whole. French and British diplomacy reinforced such contentions by offering an interpretive framework for understanding the situation.

The tragedy of American policymaking in the 1944–1950 period lies in the fact that the Truman administration squandered the considerable leverage it held over France to force a better outcome to the Indochina problem. That leverage was jettisoned by officials who accepted the overriding need to protect French prestige and influence at all costs. There were, of course, good reasons to err on the side of caution in helping moderate French governments protect themselves from internal and external threats. The stakes in Europe were high. Progressive voices within the State Department did not discount such concerns, however. Other than Franklin Roosevelt's interest in taking Indochina away from France, a plan that was never more than an abstract possibility, liberals advocated merely that the United States demand a quid pro quo from the French government—that Paris must offer major concessions to Vietnamese nationalism, including (in most formulations) the prospect of eventual independence, in return for international recognition of its rights in Indochina. Conservatives, working in informal partnership with like-minded Europeans, rejected that balanced approach. Instead, they helped craft a new vision of Vietnam that justified sending substantial material aid to bolster French policy.

That vision, as Americans would discover in later years, was riddled with problems. The notion of the Viet Minh as a wholly communist organization that directly served the interests of Moscow and Beijing obscured the far more complex blend of motives that fueled the Vietnamese revolution and accounted for its remarkable resilience. As historians have come to understand, the Viet Minh's successes rested not only on the backing of the communist powers but also on its ability to respond effectively to the needs and desires of ordinary Vietnamese. Although some American policymakers understood the complexities of the Vietnamese revolution at the time the critical decisions were made, this more sophisticated view never dictated policy at the highest levels. Instead, the simplistic notions laid into place in 1950 continued to predominate. Still more damaging over the long term, American support for the Bao Dai solution established a precedent for the attempt to implant a new nationalism in Vietnam—a compliant nationalism that would, Americans hoped, draw support away from the revolutionary tradition embodied by Ho Chi Minh and the Viet Minh. Americans would learn at very high cost that such an attempt had little prospect of success.

But such solutions held profound attractions to American decision makers, not just in Vietnam but in many other areas of the decolonizing world where the United States would wage the Cold War after 1950. In Vietnam and elsewhere, American policymakers repeatedly crafted solutions that bore the outward trappings of liberality. In this way American officials satisfied themselves that they were holding true to their country's anticolonial traditions, bolstered their self-perception as advocates of progress, and perhaps most important, insulated themselves from challenges from those who demanded fundamental reform. Often, though, assertions of liberality masked an underlying agenda that sought to impose strict limits on the pace and scope of change. In Vietnam the conservatives' ambition to form a partnership among the Western powers in Indochina became feasible only after the Europeans offered them an apparently liberal political solution that enabled them to nullify or sidestep the hostility of their bureaucratic adversaries. Having mastered the rhetoric of liberalism, the conservatives achieved a total victory. One by one, progressive advocates of genuine change left government service or were forced out by Joseph McCarthy and his minions, who successfully silenced those Americans who viewed the decolonizing world with subtlety and sought to promote genuine change. The intimidation and incivility faded over time, but the effect was lasting. Leaders with scant regard for anticolonial nationalism maintained their grip on U.S. decision making, all the while proclaiming their country—and themselves—the champion of liberalism. It is a peculiarly American formulation, and one that led to great agony in much of the world.

Notes

ABBREVIATIONS USED IN THE NOTES

AN	Archives Nationales
AOM	Dépôt des Archive de l'Outre Mer
CAB	Cabinet Office
CAE	Comité des Affaires Etrangères
CFLN	Comité Français de Libération Nationale
CIA	Central Intelligence Agency
CV	Chateau de Vincennes
ESMSA	Economic Survey Mission to Southeast Asia
FO	Foreign Office
FRUS	*Foreign Relations of the United States*
HSTL	Harry S. Truman Library
LC	Library of Congress
LHCMA	Liddell Hart Centre for Military Archives
MAE	Ministère des Affaires Etrangères
memcon	Memorandum of conversation
NA	National Archives and Records Administration
NSC	National Security Council
OH	Oral history
OIOC	Oriental and India Office Collections
OIR	Office of Intelligence Research

ORE	Office of Research Evaluation
OSS	Office of Strategic Services
PP (DoD)	Pentagon Papers, Department of Defense edition
PREM	Prime Minister's Office
PRO	Public Records Office
PSA	Philippine and Southeast Asian Division
PSF	President's Secretary's File
RG	Record Group
SAC	Supreme Allied Commander
SACSEA	Supreme Allied Commander, South East Asia
SEAC	South East Asia Command
SHAT	Service Historique de l'Armée de Terre
STI	Strom Thurmond Institute
SWNCC	State-War-Navy Coordinating Committee
WO	War Office

INTRODUCTION

1. Dean Acheson, *Present at the Creation: My Years in the State Department* (New York: Norton, 1987), 382.

2. James Reston, "Big Three Face Vast Assortment of Problems," *New York Times*, 7 May 1950.

3. For trade statistics, see Gary R. Hess, *The United States' Emergence as a Southeast Asian Power, 1940–1950* (New York: Columbia University Press, 1987), 11–13.

4. Virginia Thompson, *French Indo-China* (New York: Macmillan, 1937), 9.

5. Foster Hailey, "Indo-China Has Become Vital Cold War Front," *New York Times*, 12 Feb. 1950.

6. CIA report, "Consequences to the US of Communist Domination of Mainland Southeast Asia," 13 Oct. 1950, RG263, Estimates of the Office of Research Evaluation, 1946–1950, box 4, NA.

7. See especially Fredrik Logevall, *Choosing War: The Lost Chance for Peace and the Escalation of War in Vietnam* (Berkeley and Los Angeles: University of California Press, 1999), but also Robert Dallek, *An Unfinished Life: John F. Kennedy, 1917–1963* (Boston: Little, Brown, 2003); Howard Jones, *Death of a Generation: How the Assassinations of Diem and JFK Prolonged the Vietnam War* (New York: Oxford University Press, 2003); and David Kaiser, *American Tragedy: Kennedy, Johnson, and the Origins of the Vietnam War* (Cambridge, Mass.: Harvard University Press, Belknap, 2000).

8. Most standard surveys of the American war in Vietnam pass over the early postwar years quickly. See, for example, Robert D. Schulzinger, *A Time for War: The United States and Vietnam, 1941–1975* (New York: Oxford

University Press, 1997); James S. Olson and Randy Roberts, *Where the Domino Fell: America and Vietnam, 1945–1995*, 3d ed. (St. James, N.Y.: Brandywine, 1999). The most authoritative survey of the U.S. war begins its story in 1950, with only brief discussion of earlier events. See George C. Herring, *America's Longest War: The United States and Vietnam, 1950–1975*, 4th ed. (New York: McGraw-Hill, 2002).

9. See especially Herring, *America's Longest War*, xiii. A variant of this geostrategic explanation of U.S. behavior stresses that the Truman administration took a sympathetic view of French aims not so much because of its determination to hold the line against communist expansion in Asia as because of its fear of communist influence in France. Central to this argument is the idea that U.S. policymakers calculated around the end of the Second World War that the United States would require French cooperation with its plans to refashion the international order in the postwar period. Washington therefore resolved to help the French overcome humiliations and divisions they had suffered during the Second World War and to reemerge as a robust and confident nation. Historians argue that the Truman administration calculated that any obstruction of French efforts to reestablish colonial control in Indochina would work directly against this goal by undermining traditional sources of authority in France, diminishing national morale and weakening the very political forces in Paris that were most sympathetic to postwar cooperation with the United States. In the worst case, American officials feared that any resistance to French ambitions in Indochina would promote political instability and embolden the French Communist Party, which had emerged from the Second World War as the country's most formidable political force. See George McT. Kahin, *Intervention: How America Became Involved in Vietnam* (New York: Anchor, 1986), 5, and Hess, *The United States' Emergence as a Southeast Asian Power*, 213.

10. CIA report, "Consequences to the US of Communist Domination of Mainland Southeast Asia."

11. For one articulation of this systemic argument, see Gabriel Kolko, *The Roots of American Foreign Policy: An Analysis of Power and Purpose* (Boston: Beacon, 1969), 85. See also Thomas J. McCormick, *America's Half-Century: United States Foreign Policy in the Cold War*, 2d ed. (Baltimore: Johns Hopkins University Press, 1995), esp. chap. 3. In studies emphasizing the British economy, scholars contend that U.S. policy toward Vietnam was driven by the Truman administration's belief that Britain's postwar recovery hinged on undiminished access to the economic assets of Southeast Asia, especially Malayan rubber and tin. British territory lies, of course, a good distance southwest of Indochina. But U.S. officials were in no mood to take chances, according to this argument. So important were Malayan commodities to Britain's postwar economic prospects that Americans saw no choice by 1950 but to help defeat the communist challenge throughout the region, especially in Vietnam, where the threat was most severe. See Andrew J. Rotter, *The Path to Vietnam: The Origins of the American Commitment to Southeast Asia* (Ithaca: Cornell University Press, 1989); Rotter, "The Triangular Route to Vietnam: The United States, Great Britain, and Southeast Asia, 1945–1950," *International History Review* 6, no. 3 (Aug. 1984): 404–423; Ritchie Ovendale, "Britain, the United States,

and the Cold War in South-East Asia," *International Affairs* 58 (summer 1982): 447–464. Other scholars have focused on American perceptions of Indochina's economic significance to Japan. By mid-1947, they argue, the Truman administration had become deeply worried about the tattered state of the Japanese economy, a situation that seemed to portend economic collapse and even, in the nightmare scenario, a communist takeover. With the civil war in China going poorly, the argument continues, Washington decided to take bold steps to rebuild the island nation into an industrial powerhouse capable not only of resisting communism but also of serving as a bulwark of U.S. power in the Far East. To accomplish this economic turnaround, American planners determined that Japan would require reliable access to markets and resources on the Asian mainland. China, beset by mounting chaos, obviously could not serve Japanese needs. American eyes therefore settled on Southeast Asia. The Truman administration sought to squelch political turmoil there and to cement the region into new regional economic arrangements. Vietnam became a natural focus of U.S. concern both because it could aid Japanese recovery and because it could block communist encroachment on areas that might prove even more valuable to Japan, notably the resource-rich East Indies. See Michael Schaller, *The American Occupation of Japan: The Origins of the Cold War in Asia* (New York: Oxford University Press, 1985); Schaller, "Securing the Great Crescent: Occupied Japan and the Origins of Containment in Southeast Asia," *Journal of American History* 69, no. 2 (Sept. 1982): 392–414; William S. Borden, *The Pacific Alliance: United States Foreign Policy and Japanese Trade Recovery, 1947–1955* (Madison: University of Wisconsin Press, 1984); Lloyd C. Gardner, *Approaching Vietnam: From World War II through Dienbienphu* (New York: Norton, 1988).

12. See especially Robert M. Blum, *Drawing the Line: The Origins of the American Containment Policy in East Asia* (New York: Norton, 1982), 5.

13. The notable exception is Mark Bradley's recent study of U.S. and Vietnamese cultural perceptions, which uses an array of Western sources. See Bradley, *Imagining Vietnam and America: The Making of Postcolonial Vietnam* (Chapel Hill: University of North Carolina Press, 2000). For other works that draw on British sources, see Gardner, *Approaching Vietnam;* Walter LaFeber, "Roosevelt, Churchill, and Indochina, 1942," *American Historical Review* 80, no. 5 (Dec. 1975): 1277–1295; Christopher Thorne, "Indochina and Anglo-American Relations, 1942–1945," *Pacific Historical Review* 45, no. 1 (Feb. 1976): 73–96; Christopher Thorne, *Allies of a Kind: The United States, Britain, and the War against Japan, 1941–1945* (Oxford: Oxford University Press, 1978); Rotter, *The Path to Vietnam;* and Rotter, "The Triangular Route to Vietnam." No study in English has made much use of French-language sources. French-language studies have used French sources but only a trickle of U.S. and British material. See Lucien Bodard, *La guerre d'Indochine: l'Enlisement* (Paris: Gallimard, 1963); Jacques Dalloz, *La guerre d'Indochine, 1945–1954* (Paris: Editions du Seuil, 1987); Georges Fleury, *La guerre en Indochine, 1945–1954* (Paris: Plon, 1994); Jacques de Folin, *Indochine, 1940–1955: La fin d'un rêve* (Paris: Perrin, 1993); Philippe Franchini, *Les Guerres d'Indochine* (Paris: Pygmalion, 1988); Alfred Georges, *Charles de Gaulle et la guerre d'Indochine*

(Paris: Nouvelles Editions Latines, 1974); Olivier de Maison Rouge, *La guerre d'Indochine, 1945–1954* (Paris: La Bruyère, 1989); Alain Ruscio, *La guerre française d'Indochine* (Paris: Editions Complexes, 1992); Jacques Valette, *La guerre d'Indochine* (Paris: Armand Colin, 1994).

14. For general discussion of "international history" and the ways in which it complicates "national history," see Robert J. McMahon, "The Study of American Foreign Relations: National History or International History?" in Michael J. Hogan and Thomas G. Paterson, eds., *Explaining the History of American Foreign Relations* (New York: Cambridge University Press, 1991), 11–23. See also John Lewis Gaddis, "New Conceptual Approaches to the Study of American Foreign Relations: Interdisciplinary Perspectives," *Diplomatic History* 14 (summer 1990): 403–425.

15. My concern here is with Western perceptions of the Vietnamese revolution, rather than the Vietnamese revolution itself. This study attempts, however, to provide sufficient background on Vietnamese society and politics to demonstrate the divergence between foreign perceptions and local reality. In its discussions of Vietnamese history, the book relies on an extraordinary outpouring of new scholarship. See William J. Duiker, *The Communist Road to Power in Vietnam*, 2d ed. (Boulder: Westview Press, 1996); Duiker, *Ho Chi Minh: A Life* (New York: Hyperion, 2000); and David G. Marr, *Vietnam, 1945: The Quest for Power* (Berkeley and Los Angeles: University of California Press, 1995).

16. Alexander Wendt, "Constructing International Politics," in Michael E. Brown, ed., *Theories of War and Peace: An International Security Reader* (Cambridge: MIT Press, 1998), 419, 421. See also Wendt, *Social Theory of International Politics* (Cambridge, UK: Cambridge University Press, 1999), and Charles E. Nathanson, "The Social Construction of the Soviet Threat: A Study in the Politics of Representation," *Alternatives* 13 (1988): 443–483.

17. This definition of "construction" comes close to Marc Trachtenberg's use of the term in *A Constructed Peace*. Trachtenberg traces the process by which the United States, the Soviet Union, France, Britain, and West Germany engineered a solution to the German problem in the years between 1945 and 1963. His central point is that this solution represented the culmination of a long process of debate, disagreement, and experimentation among the governments concerned. See Trachtenberg, *A Constructed Peace: The Making of the European Settlement, 1945–1963* (Princeton: Princeton University Press, 1999).

18. The argument offers a refinement of William Appleman Williams's thesis in his classic treatise, *The Tragedy of American Diplomacy*. This study borrows Williams's notion of the tragic nature of U.S. foreign relations but departs from the "revisionist" approach in a crucial respect. Whereas Williams and his students viewed international politics in the wake of the Second World War as characterized by the U.S. attempt to impose self-serving economic arrangements on the globe, this book argues that Washington was neither alone nor always preeminent in the establishment of the postwar order. Rather, certain interests in the United States worked together with like-minded interests abroad to set up the Cold War world. For the revisionist approach to understanding the beginnings of the Cold War in the Third World, see especially Williams, *The Tragedy of American Diplomacy*, new ed. (New York: Norton, 1988); but also Gabriel

Kolko, *Confronting the Third World: United States Foreign Policy, 1945–1980* (New York: Pantheon, 1988); Joyce Kolko and Gabriel Kolko, *The Limits of Power: The World and United States Foreign Policy, 1945–1954* (New York: Harper and Row, 1972); and McCormick, *America's Half-Century*.

19. For the classic expression of this view, see Geir Lundestad, "Empire by Invitation? The United States and Western Europe, 1945–1952," in Charles S. Maier, ed., *The Cold War in Europe: Era of a Divided Continent* (New York: Markus Wiener, 1991), 143–168. For a more recent elaboration of this argument, see John Lewis Gaddis, *We Now Know: Rethinking Cold War History* (Oxford: Oxford University Press, 1997). Other studies that make this point include William I. Hitchcock, *France Restored: Cold War Diplomacy and the Quest for Leadership in Europe, 1944–1954* (Chapel Hill: University of North Carolina Press, 1998); Thomas Risse-Kappen, *Cooperation among Democracies: European Influence on U.S. Foreign Policy* (Princeton: Princeton University Press, 1997); Tony Smith, "New Wine for New Bottles: A 'Pericentric Paradigm' for the Study of the Cold War," *Diplomatic History* 24 (fall 2000): 567–592; and various essays in David Reynolds, ed., *The Origins of the Cold War in Europe: International Perspectives* (New Haven: Yale University Press, 1994).

20. For elaboration, see Mark Atwood Lawrence, "Transnational Coalition-Building and the Making of the Cold War in Indochina, 1947–1949," *Diplomatic History* 26 (summer 2002): 453–480.

21. William Hitchcock's *France Restored* also argues for a new view of postwar French diplomacy. For the view that the United States dictated postwar economic and political arrangements, see especially Irwin M. Wall, *The United States and the Making of Postwar France, 1945–1954* (Cambridge, UK: Cambridge University Press, 1991). Revealingly, the individuals best known for crediting the French government with significant influence over U.S. behavior in Vietnam are former policymakers. In a later interview, Dean Acheson, the secretary of state who presided over the decision to extend U.S. aid to the French, insisted that Paris had "blackmailed" Washington by threatening to withdraw from Vietnam if the Truman administration did not give help. Quoted in David S. McClellan, *Dean Acheson: The State Department Years* (New York: Dodd, Mead, 1976), 383. In his memoir, Acheson does not use the word *blackmail,* but he expresses clear frustration over Washington's inability to exert leverage over French behavior. See Acheson, *Present at the Creation,* chap. 70. Acheson's successor, John Foster Dulles, made the point more explicitly in 1954, as he watched Western policy crumble at Dien Bien Phu. Trying to explain how the United States had become involved in the first place, Dulles asserted that "our Government allowed itself to be persuaded in this matter by the French and the British." Quoted in Gardner, *Approaching Vietnam,* 53. Historians have been understandably quick to dismiss these bald efforts at self-exculpation. This book shows that there was at least a grain of truth in Acheson's and Dulles's claims, although I attempt to do so without implying any sympathy for American behavior.

22. See Lawrence, "Transnational Coalition-Building and the Making of the Cold War in Indochina," and Risse-Kappen, *Cooperation among Democracies,* esp. 38–39. I am especially indebted to Risse-Kappen's discussion of transnational and transgovernmental coalitions.

1. VISIONS OF INDOCHINA AND THE WORLD

1. Several studies have explored French colonialism and Vietnamese nationalism before 1941. See Duiker, *The Communist Road to Power in Vietnam;* Huynh Kim Khanh, *Vietnamese Communism, 1925–1945* (Ithaca: Cornell University Press, 1982); Ngo Vinh Long, *Before the Revolution: Vietnamese Peasants under the French* (New York: Columbia University Press, 1991); and David G. Marr, *Vietnamese Tradition on Trial, 1920–1945* (Berkeley and Los Angeles: University of California Press, 1981).

2. For Franco-Japanese relations before 9 March 1945, see John E. Dreifort, "Japan's Advance into Indochina, 1940: The French Response," *Journal of Southeast Asian Studies* 13, no. 2 (Sept. 1982), 279–295; Eric T. Jennings, *Vichy in the Tropics: Pétain's National Revolution in Madagascar, Guadeloupe, and Indochina, 1940–1944* (Stanford: Stanford University Press, 2001); Marr, *Vietnam 1945*, 13–69; and James W. Morley, ed., *The Fateful Choice: Japan's Advance into Southeast Asia, 1939–1941* (New York: Columbia University Press, 1980).

3. *Ho Chi Minh: Selected Articles and Speeches, 1920–1967*, ed. and trans. Jack Woddis (New York: International Publishers, 1969), 31. For the founding of the Viet Minh, see Duiker, *The Communist Road to Power*, 69–76, and Duiker, *Ho Chi Minh*, 248–257.

4. De Langlade to Comité d'Action sur l'Indochine, 30 Jan. 1945, Asie/Indochine, file 42, MAE.

5. "Discours prononcé à la radio de Londres," 29 Aug. 1940, in Charles de Gaulle, *Discours et messages: Pendant la guerre, 1940–1946* (Paris: Plon, 1970), 32. For Vichy views, see Charles-Robert Ageron, *France coloniale ou parti colonial?* (Paris: Presses Universitaires de France, 1978), 270–274.

6. "France's Economic Relations with Her Empire," 25 Feb. 1943, RG59, Notter Files, box 62, NA; memo by Moffat, "Indochina: Proposed United States Policy," 29 July 1944, RG59, PSA, reel 8, NA.

7. "The Record of French Administration in Indo-China," 8 Jan. 1944, FO 371, file 41723, PRO. On Indochina's economic value, see Laurent Cesari, "The Declining Value of Indochina: France and the Economics of Empire, 1950–1955," in Mark Atwood Lawrence and Fredrik Logevall, eds., *The First Vietnam War* (Cambridge, Mass.: Harvard University Press, forthcoming).

8. For analysis of the Brazzaville Conference, see Andrew Shennan, *Rethinking France: Plans for Renewal, 1940–1946* (New York: Oxford University Press, 1989), 141–151, and Martin Shipway, *The Road to War: France and Vietnam, 1944–1947* (Providence: Berghahn, 1996), 21–63.

9. Quoted in Shennan, *Rethinking France*, 147.

10. Shipway, *The Road to War*, 30–36.

11. CFLN declaration, 8 Dec. 1943, in Philippe Devillers, ed., *Paris, Saigon, Hanoi: Les archives de la guerre, 1944–1947* (Paris: Editions Gallimard/Julliard, 1988), 23.

12. Meeting minutes, 24 Aug. 1944, Fonds du Secrétaire Général, file 7, MAE.

13. Pechkoff to Chauvel, 28 Nov. 1944, Asie/Indochine, file 47, MAE. Emphasis in original.

14. Foreign Ministry report, "La France devant les problèmes du pacifique," 1 May 1944, Asie/Pacifique, file 1, MAE.

15. Langdon to State Department, 24 Feb. 1945, RG59, Central Decimal File, 851G.00/2-2445, NA; memcon, Clarac and Acheson, 26 July 1944, RG 59, Central Decimal File, box 4002, NA; Pechkoff to CAE, 25 Aug. 1944, Asie/Indochine, file 29, MAE; Pechkoff to Foreign Ministry, 11 Oct. 1945, Asie/Indochine, file 29, MAE; "La sécurité dans le Pacifique," Feb. 1945, Asie/Pacifique, file 2, MAE.

16. William Roger Louis, *Imperialism at Bay: The United States and the Decolonization of the British Empire, 1941–1945* (New York: Oxford University Press, 1978), 20–21.

17. Foreign Ministry report, "L'Amérique et les colonies," 12 March 1945, Y-International, file 655, MAE. For persistent French images of Americans, see Richard Kuisel, *Seducing the French: The Dilemma of Americanization* (Berkeley and Los Angeles: University of California Press, 1993), 1–14.

18. Foreign Ministry report, "L'Amérique et les colonies."

19. "Situation en Extrême-Orient," 15 Oct. 1944, Y-International (Affaires Politiques, Asie et Extrême Orient), file 26, MAE; Bidault to Bonnet, 14 Jan. 1945, Asie/Indochine, file 49, MAE; "Etude sur les activités américaines en Indochine," 11 Sept. 1945, Amérique, file 128, MAE.

20. Report by Bureau des Etudes d'Après Guerre, 26 June 1944, Nations Unies et Organizations Internationales, file 6, MAE.

21. Pechkoff to CAE, 25 Aug. 1944, Asie/Indochine, file 29, MAE; "Collaboration franco-britannique en Extrême-Orient," 9 Nov. 1944, ibid.

22. "Collaboration franco-britannique en Extrême-Orient," 9 Nov. 1944, ibid.

23. "Renseignements recuillis sur les idées américaines relatives aux colonies et bases militaires," 1 April 1945, Y-International, file 655, MAE; "Note pour le ministre," 12 March 1945, ibid.

24. "Situation en Extrême-Orient," 15 Oct. 1944, Y-International (Affaires Politiques, Asie et Extrême Orient), file 26, MAE.

25. *The War Memoirs of Charles de Gaulle: Salvation, 1944–1946*, trans. Richard Howard (New York: Simon and Schuster, 1960), 187.

26. Blaizot to Juin, 21 Dec. 1944, Asie/Indochine, file 29, MAE; CAE to Hoppenot, 12 Sept. 1944, ibid.; "Situation politique et militaire de la France en Indochine," 1 Nov. 1944, FO 371, file 41724, PRO. For detailed discussion of these issues, see Peter M. Dunn, *The First Vietnam War* (New York: St. Martin's, 1985), 24–38, and Martin Thomas, *The French Empire at War 1940–1945* (Manchester, UK: University of Manchester Press, 1998), 205–214.

27. Foreign Ministry report, "Situation en Extrême-Orient," 15 Oct. 1944, Asie/Indochine, file 29, MAE; Caffery to Secretary of State, 4 Nov. 1944, *FRUS 1944*, 3:780–781; "Memorandum pour le Comité d'Action sur l'Indochine," 29 Aug. 1944, Asie/Indochine, file 42, MAE. For details of French efforts to join the fighting, see Dunn, *The First Vietnam War*, esp. chap. 4.

28. "La securité dans le Pacifique," Feb. 1945, Asie/Pacifique, file 2, MAE; "Le mouvement communiste en Chine," 1 March 1945, Etats-Associés, file 143, MAE; "Politique de l'URSS en Extrême-Orient," 20 Nov. 1944, Bidault papers, file 132, AN.

29. CAE to Hoppenot, 12 Dec. 1944, Asie/Indochine, file 29, MAE; Pechkoff to CAE, 25 Aug. 1944, ibid.
30. Massigli to Bidault, 9 Jan. 1945, Massigli papers, file 53, MAE.
31. "Collaboration franco-britannique en Extrême-Orient," 9 Nov. 1944, Asie/Indochine, file 29, MAE; Pechkoff to Bidault, 6 Oct. 1944, Asie/Indochine, file 47, MAE; Massigli to Bidault, 9 Jan. 1945, Massigli papers, file 53, MAE; Massigli to Bidault, 3 March 1945, Asie/Indochine, file 49, MAE.
32. Shipway, *The Road to War,* 35; CFLN declaration, 8 Dec. 1943, in Devillers, ed., *Paris, Saigon, Hanoi,* 22–23; French embassy in Chungking to U.S. embassy in Chungking, 20 Jan. 1945, *FRUS 1945,* 6:295–296.
33. Foreign Ministry report, "L'Action de la France en Indochine au point de vue économique," Nov. 1944, Asie/Indochine, file 322, MAE; *La France Libre* clipping, "Le ministre des colonies expose notre programme colonial à la presse alliée et française," 13 Oct. 1944, FO 371, file 41935, PRO. On Orientalism, see Edward W. Said, *Orientalism* (New York: Vintage, 1979), and for elaboration within the Vietnamese context, see Bradley, *Imagining Vietnam and America,* 55–57.
34. CFLN declaration, 8 Dec. 1943, in Devillers, ed., *Paris, Saigon, Hanoi,* 22–23; French embassy in China to U.S. embassy in China, 20 Jan. 1945, *FRUS 1945,* 6:295–296; "Au sujet de l'Indochine," 24 Aug. 1944, Fonds du Secrétaire Général, file 7, MAE; "Entretien entre le Général de Gaulle et Mr. Winston Churchill," 11 Nov. 1944, Massigli papers, file 53, MAE.
35. "Procès-verbal de la séance du 22 janvier 1945, Comité d'Action sur l'Indochine," 22 Jan. 1945, Asie/Indochine, file 42, MAE; Dunn, *The First Vietnam War,* 31–32; Massigli to Bidault, 27 Feb. 1945, Asie/Indochine, file 29, MAE.
36. For the importance of Southeast Asia to the British economy, see Thorne, *Allies of a Kind,* 17–19, and Thorne, *The Limits of Foreign Policy* (New York: Putnam's Sons, 1972), 49–50.
37. Briefing memo for Québec conference, Sept. 1944, FO 371, file 41720, PRO; minute by Cadogan, 2 Feb. 1944, FO 371, file 41723, PRO; Cadogan to Churchill, 13 March 1944, FO 371, file 41719, PRO.
38. Foreign Office report for Dominions Prime Ministers' Conference, 5 April 1944, FO 371, file 41931, PRO.
39. War Cabinet memo, 16 Feb. 1944, CAB 66, vol. 47, PRO; memo by Post-Hostilities Planning Subcommittee, 22 Jan. 1944, ibid.; Eden to Churchill, 27 Jan. 1945, FO 371, file 46336, PRO; Dening to Sterndale Bennett, 17 Jan. 1945, FO 371, file 46325, PRO; report by Joint Planning Staff, 1 Jan. 1945, FO 371, file 46336, PRO.
40. "The Record of French Administration in Indo-China," 8 Jan. 1944, M/4, file 2802, OIOC. For Thompson's views, see her book, *French Indo-China,* 43.
41. Churchill speech, 28 Sept. 1944, Europe/Grande Bretagne, file 35, MAE; Foreign Office report for Dominions Prime Ministers' Conference, 5 April 1944, FO 371, file 41931, PRO.
42. "The Record of French Administration in Indo-China," 8 Jan. 1944, FO 371, file 41723, PRO; "French Possessions in the Pacific," 22 Jan. 1944, ibid.

43. Minute by Foulds, 5 March 1945, FO 371, file 46304, PRO; SACSEA to Foreign Office, 30 Sept. 1944, FO 371, file 41720, PRO; Mountbatten to Eden, 16 Aug. 1944, FO 371, file 41719, PRO.

44. Mountbatten to Chiefs of Staff, 1 June 1944, FO 371, file 41719, PRO; Dening to Sterndale Bennett, 2 Feb. 1945, FO 371, file 46304, PRO; War Cabinet memo, "The Future of Indo-China and Other French Possessions," 16 Feb. 1944, CAB 66, vol. 47, PRO; report for War Cabinet's Far Eastern Economic Subcommittee, 1 March 1945, FO 371, file 46328, PRO; memo by War Cabinet's Far Eastern Economic Subcommittee, 9 Jan. 1945, FO 371, file 46327, PRO.

45. Force 136 report, "Future Plans," 28 Dec. 1944, WO 203, file 5559, PRO; aide-mémoire, 25 Aug. 1944, FO 371, file 41719, PRO; aide-mémoire, 22 Nov. 1944, FO 371, file 41721, PRO. For details of U.S.-British conversations in this period, see Walter LaFeber, "Roosevelt, Churchill, and Indochina"; John Sbrega, *Anglo-American Relations and Colonialism in East Asia, 1941–1945* (New York: Garland, 1983), esp. chap. 5; Sbrega, "'First Catch Your Hare': Anglo-American Perspectives on Indochina during the Second World War," *Journal of Southeast Asian Studies* 14 (1983): 63–78; Christopher Thorne, *Allies of a Kind,* chap. 20; Thorne, "Indochina and Anglo-American Relations, 1942–1945," *Pacific Historical Review* 45 (Feb. 1976): 73–96.

46. Franco-British scheming to send Blaizot to SEAC headquarters is traceable in a mass of documents in both Paris and London. See especially Massigli to Foreign Ministry, 2 Oct. 1944, Asie/Indochine, file 45, MAE; "Extract from SACSEA's 18th Meeting," 25 Oct. 1944, WO 203, file 5068, PRO; SEAC to Foreign Office, 27 Oct. 1944, FO 371, file 41720, PRO.

47. Force 136 report, "Future Plans," 28 Dec. 1944, WO 203, file 5559, PRO; Massigli to Bidault, 29 Nov. 1944, Asie/Indochine, file 45, MAE; J. Gorborg to P.N. Loxley, 5 Jan. 1945, FO 371, file 46304, PRO.

48. Thorne, *Allies of a Kind,* 110, 138; Thorne, *The Issue of War: States, Societies, and the Far Eastern Conflict of 1941–1945* (New York: Oxford University Press, 1985), 211–212. For Britain's problems with balancing European and Far Eastern obligations before and during the Second World War, see Correlli Barnett, *The Collapse of British Power* (London: Eyre Methuen, 1972), 440–448.

49. "Entretien entre le Général de Gaulle et Mr. Winston Churchill," 11 Nov. 1944, Massigli papers, file 53, MAE.

50. Quoted in Thorne, *Allies of Kind,* 450.

51. Minute by Butler, 22 July 1944, FO 371, file 41724, PRO; report by Joint Planning Staff, "Strategic Interests in the Far East," 1 Jan. 1945, FO 371, file 46336, PRO; Foreign Ministry report, "Conférence des Nations du Commonwealth Britannique," 3 March 1945, Europe/Grande Bretagne, file 28, MAE; War Cabinet memo, "The Future of Indo-China and Other French Possessions," 16 Feb. 1944, CAB 66, vol. 47, PRO.

52. Memo by Post-Hostilities Planning Sub-Committee of the War Cabinet, "French Possessions in the Pacific," 22 Jan. 1944, FO 371, file 41723, PRO; cabinet memo, "The Future of Indo-China and Other French Possessions," 16 Feb. 1944, CAB 66, vol. 47, PRO.

53. For overviews of Anglo-American tensions during the war against Japan, see Louis, *Imperialism at Bay;* Gabriel Kolko, *The Politics of War: The World and United States Foreign Policy, 1943–1945* (New York: Pantheon, 1968); and especially Thorne, *Allies of a Kind.*

54. Minute by Cadogan, 2 Feb. 1944, FO 371, file 41723, PRO; LaFeber, "Roosevelt, Churchill, and Indochina," 1285.

55. Report by Foreign Office Research Department, "Thoughts on Colonies," 13 Nov. 1944, FO 371, file 38524, PRO; Halifax to Eden, 13 May 1944, FO 371, file 41746, PRO.

56. Brief for Foreign Secretary, 9 Nov. 1944, FO 371, file 41721, PRO; memcon, Massigli with Eden, 24 Aug. 1944, FO 371, file 41719, PRO; report by Foreign Office Research Department, "Thoughts on Colonies," 13 Nov. 1944, FO 371, file 38524, PRO; Halifax to Foreign Office, 19 Jan. 1944, FO 371, file 41723, PRO. Churchill is quoted in Schulzinger, *A Time for War,* 14.

57. Seymour to Eden, 4 Aug. 1944, FO 371, file 41746, PRO; Halifax to Eden, 13 May 1944, ibid.; memcon, Stettinius with Halifax, 26 Dec. 1946, RG59, PSA, reel 9, NA. The connection between U.S. views of China and Indochina is especially well covered in LaFeber, "Roosevelt, Churchill, and Indochina."

58. Foreign Office report for Dominion Prime Ministers' Conference, "The Future of the French Colonial Empire," 5 April 1944, FO 371, file 41931, PRO.

59. Dening to Foreign Office, 19 Jan. 1945, WO 203, file 5561B, PRO.

60. War Cabinet memo, "International Aspects of Colonial Policy," 16 Dec. 1944, CAB 66, vol. 59, PRO; Foreign Ministry memo, "Projets britanniques et américains de réorganisation coloniale," 13 Nov. 1944, Asie/Indochine, file 52, MAE.

61. Dening to Foreign Office, 6 March 1945, FO 371, file 46325, PRO; British embassy to State Department, 23 Nov. 1944, *FRUS 1944,* 3:781–782; minute by Ashley Clarke, 25 May 1944, FO 371, file 41719, PRO.

62. Memo by H. Freeman Matthews, 2 Nov. 1944, *FRUS 1944,* 3:777–778.

63. Halifax to Eden, 13 May 1944, FO 371, file 41746, PRO; report by Joint Planning Staff, "Strategic Interests in the Far East," 1 Jan. 1945, FO 371, file 46336, PRO; Dening to Foreign Office, 19 Jan. 1945, WO 203, file 5561B, PRO; minute by Henderson, 7 March 1945, FO 371, file 46325, PRO.

64. Foreign Office report, "American Relations with the British Empire," 1 May 1944, FO 371, file 38523, PRO; minute by Henderson, 25 Aug. 1944, FO 371, file 41746, PRO. For British suspicions about U.S. economic ambitions in Southeast Asia, see Thorne, *Allies of a Kind,* 220, 342, 458.

65. Dening to Foreign Office, 9 Dec. 1944, FO 371, file 41746, PRO; Stanley to Colonial Governors, 27 Jan. 1944, FO 371, file 38552, PRO; Colonial Office to Ministry of Information, 29 Feb. 1944, FO 371, file 38552, PRO; report of Committee on American Opinion and the British Empire, 5 Sept. 1944, FO 371, file 38524, PRO.

66. For detailed discussion of Roosevelt's attitude toward Indochina and European colonialism more generally, see Robert Dallek, *Franklin D. Roosevelt and American Foreign Policy, 1932–1945* (New York: Oxford University Press, 1979), esp. chap. 14; Gary R. Hess, "Franklin Roosevelt and Indochina,"

Journal of American History 59 (Sept. 1972): 353–368; LaFeber, "Roosevelt, Churchill, and Indochina"; Sbrega, *Anglo-American Relations and Colonialism in East Asia*; and Thorne, "Indo-China and Anglo-American Relations."

67. Roosevelt is quoted in Bradley, *Imagining Vietnam and America*, 76–80, and Thorne, *Allies of a Kind*, 276, 463. See also Roosevelt to Hull, 24 Jan. 1944, *FRUS 1944*, 3:773.

68. Scholars have sometimes reduced U.S. policymaking toward Indochina to FDR's personal grudge against French colonialism. This tendency has obscured the extent to which the president's attitudes coincided with opinions of others within the U.S. bureaucracy. It has also created the misleading impression that once Roosevelt began changing his mind about trusteeship in early 1945—or at last once he had died in April—the bureaucracy readily shifted U.S. policy behind France and abandoned any meaningful concern with promoting self-determination in Indochina. For examples of this tendency, see Peter M. Dunn's *The First Vietnam War*; Hess, "Franklin Roosevelt and Indochina"; and LaFeber, "Roosevelt, Churchill, and Indochina."

69. Memo for president, "Indochina and Southeast Asia," 8 Sept. 1944, Clayton-Thorpe papers/China-General, box 1, HSTL.

70. OSS report, "American National Interests in Southeast Asia," 14 March 1945, RG59, PSA, reel 6, NA.

71. Foreign Economic Administration report, "Economic Program with Reference to Indo-China," RG169, box 17, NA.

72. Memo by Moffat, "Indochina: Proposed United States Policy," 29 July 1944, RG59, PSA, reel 8, NA.

73. Ibid. Moffat's office, a new branch of the Office of Far Eastern Affairs, was briefly called the Division of Southwest Pacific Affairs.

74. State Department memo, "The Dependent Territories in Southeast Asia," RG59, PSA, reel 6, NA; OSS Divisional Report no. 42, "Social Conditions, Attitudes and Propaganda in Indo-China with Suggestions for American Orientation toward the Indo-Chinese," 30 March 1942, RG59, OSS Research and Analysis reports, NA.

75. Memo for the president, "Indochina," 13 Jan. 1945, RG59, PSA, reel 7, NA; memo by Liberated Areas Division, 28 Jan. 1944, RG59, PSA, reel 6, NA.

76. Memo by Moffat, "Indochina: Proposed United States Policy," 29 July 1944, RG59, PSA, reel 8, NA; memo by Oakes, 6 Jan. 1945, RG59, PSA, reel 6, NA.

77. See Bradley, *Imagining Vietnam and America*, chap. 2. This book departs from Bradley, however, by attributing significance to the range of opinion about Vietnam and the Vietnamese among U.S. policymakers. Bradley argues that differences were superficial and masked an essential consistency of derogatory views throughout the U.S. bureaucracy.

78. Memo by Liberated Areas Division, 28 Jan. 1944, RG59, PSA, reel 6, NA; OSS Intelligence Report 86713, "Conditions in Indo-China," 8 July 1944, RG226, box 1003, NA.

79. Memo by Landon, 13 June 1944, RG59, PSA, reel 8, NA; T Minutes 56, 11 Nov. 1943, RG59, Notter Files, box 59, NA.

80. Landon to Moffat, 23 Nov. 1944, RG59, PSA, reel 9, NA; Harriman to State Department, 13 Jan. 1945, RG59, PSA, reel 6, NA; Colombo (Bishop) to State Department, 6 Nov. 1944, RG59, PSA, reel 7, NA.

81. For discussion of different currents within U.S. policymaking, see Michael H. Hunt, *Ideology and U.S. Foreign Policy* (New Haven: Yale University Press, 1987), and Walter A. McDougal, *Promised Land, Crusader State: The American Encounter with the World since 1776* (New York: Houghton Mifflin, 1997).

82. State Department memo, "American Policy with Regard to Indochina," 30 June 1944, RG59, lot file 1, box 9, NA.

83. Ibid.

84. For Stalin's statements, see report of Division of Historical Policy Research, "Treatment of Political Questions Relating to the Far East at Multilateral Meetings of Foreign Ministers and Heads of Government, 1943–1949," PSF, Subject File, box 177, HSTL.

85. State Department memo, "American Policy with Regard to Indochina," 30 June 1944, RG59, lot file 1, box 9, NA.

86. William Conrad Gibbons, *The U.S. Government and the Vietnam War: Executive and Legislative Roles and Relationships, Part I: 1945–1960* (Princeton: Princeton University Press, 1986), 5–10; Sbrega, *Anglo-American Relations and Colonialism in East Asia,* chap. 7; Thorne, *Allies of a Kind,* 371–372, 489–490, 597–598.

87. State Department memo, "American Policy with Regard to Indochina," 30 June 1944, RG59, lot file 1, box 9, NA.

88. See especially the records of the State Department's Subcommittee on Territorial Problems, which held a series of meetings on Indochina in fall 1943. T Minutes 55, 5 Nov. 1943, RG59, Notter Files, box 59, NA, and T Minutes 56, 11 Nov. 1943, ibid.

89. For the well-explored shift in U.S. attitudes toward China, see, for example, Warren I. Cohen, *America's Response to China: A History of Sino-American Relations,* 4th ed. (New York: Columbia University Press, 2000), chaps. 5–6; Dallek, *Franklin D. Roosevelt and American Foreign Policy,* 386–392, 535–536; Thorne, *Allies of a Kind,* 173–183, 322–326, 422–437, 563–573.

90. Quoted in LaFeber, "Roosevelt, Churchill, and Indochina," 1289.

91. For scholarship that identifies the period around Yalta as the watershed moment when the United States abandoned its anticolonial impulses and accepted a French return in Indochina, see especially LaFeber, "Roosevelt, Churchill, and Indochina." This view has taken hold especially on the political left, which prefers to emphasize the early foundations of America's counterrevolutionary policy. See, for example, Howard Zinn, *A People's History of the United States, 1492–Present,* revised and updated ed. (New York: Harper, 1995), 403.

92. Memcon, Taussig with Roosevelt, 15 March 1945, *FRUS 1945,* 1:121–124.

93. Marshall to Sultan, 7 Feb 1945, RG218, box 31, NA; Moffat to Ballantine, 5 Jan. 1945, RG59, PSA, reel 7, NA; Ballantine to Dunn, 23 Jan. 1945, RG59,

PSA, reel 7, NA; Bidault to Massigli, 24 March 1945, Asie/Indochine, file 30, MAE. For background on the dispute over theater boundaries, see especially Thorne, *Allies of a Kind*, 300–301, 454.

2. U.S. ASSISTANCE AND ITS LIMITS

1. Marr, *Vietnam, 1945*, 37–54. For other accounts of the coup's background, see Kiyoko Kurushu Nitz, "Japanese Military Policy towards French Indochina during the Second World War: The Road to *Meigo Sakusen* (9 March 1945)," *Journal of Southeast Asian Studies* 14, no. 2 (Sept. 1983): 328–353, and Ralph B. Smith, "The Japanese Period in Indochina and the Coup of 9 March 1945," *Journal of Southeast Asian Studies* 9, no. 2 (Sept. 1978): 268–301.
2. Quoted in Huynh, *Vietnamese Communism*, 292.
3. For the best account, see Marr, *Vietnam, 1945*, 54–69.
4. For developments within Indochina in the crucial five months from March to August, see Duiker, *The Communist Road to Power in Vietnam*, 85–93; Huynh, *Vietnamese Communism*, 290–322; Marr, *Vietnam, 1945*, 201–240. For an English translation of the "Historic Directive," see Gareth Porter, ed., *Vietnam: A History in Documents* (New York: New American Library, 1979), 9–11.
5. Aide-mémoire (U.S. translation), Bonnet to Stettinius, 12 March 1945, *FRUS 1945*, 6:279–299.
6. State Department memo, "French and British Activities Relating to Military Operations in Indochina, January to May 15, 1945," 15 May 1945, RG59, PSA, reel 9, NA; Caffery to Stettinius, 13 March 1945, *FRUS 1945*, 6:300.
7. Memo by Sterndale Bennett, "Brief for Secretary of State's Interview with Massigli," 12 March 1945, FO 371, file 46305, PRO. On Britain's inability to provide more help, see Mountbatten's gloomy assessment in Mountbatten to Chiefs of Staff, 21 March 1945, ibid.
8. Chiefs of Staff to Wilson, 19 March 1945, FO 371, file 46305, PRO; "Prime Minister's Personal Minute," 19 March 1945, ibid.
9. Washington to Foreign Office, 18 March 1945, FO 371, file 46305, PRO; memo for de Gaulle, "Compte-Rendu Analytique des Messages Parvenus les 14 &15 Mars 1945," 16 March 1945, Asie/Indochine, file 45, MAE; Pechkoff to Bidault, 16 March 1945, Asie/Indochine, file 50, MAE; Dunn to McCloy, 19 March 1945, RG59, 851G.00/3-1245, NA; McCloy to Dunn, 12 March 1945, RG59, 851G.00/3-1245, NA.
10. Stettinius to Roosevelt, "Memorandum for the President," 16 March 1945, PP (DoD), 1:A16–A17.
11. Bishop to State Department, 6 Nov. 1944, RG59, PSA, reel 7, NA; memo by Moffat, "Indochina: Proposed United States Policy," 29 July 1944, RG59, PSA, reel 8, NA.
12. Memcon, Dunn with Bonnet, 19 March 1945, *FRUS 1945*, 6:301–302.
13. Fenard to Defense Ministry, 3 April 1945, Asie/Indochine, file 50, MAE.
14. Stettinius to Bonnet, 4 April 1945, *FRUS 1945*, 6:303; Stettinius to Bonnet, 20 April 1945, *FRUS 1945*, 6:306–307; MacLeish to Office of War Information, 28 March 1945, RG59, 851G.00/3-2145, NA.

15. Fenard to Leahy, 20 March 1945, RG59, PSA, reel 9, NA.
16. Bonnet to Foreign Ministry, 22 March 1945, Etats-Associés/135, MAE; "Note sur les entretiens de M. Bidault avec M. van Kleffens," 22 March 1945, Asie/Pacifique Sud, file 2, MAE.
17. Massigli to Bidault, 19 March 1945, Asie/Indochine, file 53, MAE.
18. "La declaration du 24 mars," in Devillers, *Paris, Saigon, Hanoi*, 53–54.
19. Ibid.
20. MacKenzie to Chiefs of Staff, 9 April 1945, FO 371, file 46306, PRO; Mountbatten to War Office, 7 April 1945, FO 371, file 46321, PRO; memo by French Far Eastern Command, "Appui aux Troupes Françaises Repliées sur la Frontière de Chine," 14 April 1945, Etats-Associés, file 139, MAE.
21. Minute by Adams, 3 April 1945, FO 371, file 46306, PRO; minute by Sterndale Bennett, 4 April 1945, FO 371, file 46305, PRO.
22. Foreign Ministry to Massigli, 30 March 1945, Asie/Indochine, file 50, MAE; French Naval Mission to Combined Chiefs of Staff, 7 April 1945, FO 371, file 46321, PRO; Chiefs of Staff Mission to Chiefs of Staff (London), 22 April 1945, WO 203, file 2132, PRO.
23. Memcon, Roosevelt with Taussig, 15 March 1945, *FRUS 1945*, 1:121–124; memo by G. H. Blakeslee, April 1945, in Porter, ed., *Vietnam: A History in Documents*, 12–16.
24. Arnold A. Offner, *Another Such Victory: President Truman and the Cold War, 1945–1953* (Stanford: Stanford University Press, 2002), 23. For sketches of Truman and Byrnes as they took power, see Offner, 22–25, and Melvyn Leffler: *A Preponderance of Power: National Security, the Truman Administration, and the Cold War* (Stanford: Stanford University Press, 1992), esp. 26–30.
25. Minutes of SWNCC meeting of 13 April 1945, 23 May 1945, PP (DoD), 8:1.
26. Draft memo to the president by Office of European Affairs, "Suggested Reexamination of American Policy with Respect to Indo-China," PP (DoD), 8:6–8.
27. Draft memo to the president by Office of Far Eastern Affairs, "American Policy with Respect to Indochina," 21 April 1945, PP (DoD), 8:9–17.
28. Dunn to Grew, "Memorandum on Indochina," 23 April 1945, PP (DoD), 9:18; Moffat interview by Harry Maurer, in Maurer, *Strange Ground: Americans in Vietnam, 1945–1975: An Oral History* (New York: Henry Holt and Company, 1989), 44.
29. Memo for the president, "American Policy with Respect to Indochina," undated, PP (DoD), 8:19–21; State Department to Caffery, 9 May 1945, PP (DoD), 8:22–25.
30. Matthews to SWNCC, 23 May 1945, *FRUS 1945*, 6:309–311.
31. The precise fate of these documents is difficult to trace, but various clues seem to substantiate the account offered here. See PP (DoD), 8:4, and Moffat's reminiscences in Maurer, *Strange Ground*, 44.
32. George C. Herring, "The Truman Administration and the Restoration of French Sovereignty in Indochina," *Diplomatic History* 1, no. 2 (spring 1977): 104. See also Grew to Caffery, 9 May 1945, *FRUS 1945*, 6:307, for a sketchier account.

33. Pleven (Washington) to de Gaulle, 10 May 1945, Amérique, file 119, MAE; Washington to Foreign Office, 19 May 1945, FO 371, file 49088, PRO; report by Direction d'Amérique, 28 July 1945, Amérique, file 119, MAE; Pechkoff to Foreign Ministry, 30 June 1945, Asie/Indochine, file 31, MAE.

34. Bonnet to Foreign Ministry, 17 May 1945, Asie/Indochine, file 50, MAE; "Revue des événements politiques et militaires en Extrême-Orient et dans le Pacifique," 22 May 1945, Amérique, file 132, MAE; "Compte-Rendu des Nouvelles Reçues dans la Journée du 14 Mai," 14 May 1945, Asie/Indochine, file 30, MAE.

35. Foreign Ministry to Hoppenot, 29 May 1945, Asie/Indochine, file 30, MAE; Berard to Foreign Ministry, 23 July 1945, Amérique, file 199, MAE. For Franco-U.S. tensions in mid-1945, see Julian G. Hurstfield, *America and the French Nation, 1939–1945* (Chapel Hill: University of North Carolina Press, 1986), 214–215, and Wall, *The United States and the Making of Postwar France*, 30–39. On Viet Minh hopes for U.S. aid, see especially Bradley, *Imagining Vietnam and America*, 125–133.

36. Poynton to Sterndale Bennett, 23 July 1945, FO 371, file 46322, PRO; Halifax to Foreign Office, 5 July 1945, ibid.

37. Dening to Foreign Office, 23 March 1945, FO 371, file 46305, PRO.

38. Minute by Sterndale Bennett, 22 May 1945, FO 371, file 46307, PRO. For background on the theater dispute, see Thorne, *Allies of a Kind*, 300–301, 454.

39. Mountbatten to Eden, 8 May 1945, FO 371, file 46307, PRO; Wedemeyer to War Department, 28 May 1945, RG218, box 31, NA; Wedemeyer to Mountbatten, 25 May 1945, RG218, box 31, NA.

40. Blaizot to Juin, 25 July 1945, Asie/Indochine, file 31, MAE; "Note pour le Ministre," 31 July 1945, ibid.

41. Attlee to Chiang Kai-shek, 1 Aug. 1945, PREM 8, vol. 33, PRO; Bonnet to Foreign Ministry, 29 Sept. 1945, Asie/Indochine, file 44, MAE. For further discussion of the Potsdam decisions on Southeast Asia, see Thorne, *Allies of a Kind*, 627–628.

42. See especially Archimedes L. A. Patti, *Why Vietnam? Prelude to America's Albatross* (Berkeley: University of California Press, 1980), but also accounts of OSS activities in Bradley, *Imagining Vietnam and America*, 125–128; Duiker, *Ho Chi Minh*, 288–345; and Marr, *Vietnam, 1945*, 279–291, 482–490.

43. Sainteny is quoted in Michael Charlton and Anthony Moncrieff, *Many Reasons Why: The American Involvement in Vietnam* (New York: Hill and Wang, 1978), 6. For French accusations about military assistance, see Thomas's comments in Maurer, *Strange Ground*, 35; Jean Sainteny, *Histoire d'une Paix Manquée: Indochine, 1945–47* (Paris: Amoit-Dumont, 1953), 62–70; and Philippe Devillers, *Histoire du Viêt-Nam de 1940 à 1952* (Paris: Editions du Seuil, 1952), 116, 133, 150–151, 202–203. Some of this literature is reviewed in Gary R. Hess, "United States Policy and the Origins of the French–Viet Minh War, 1945–46," *Peace & Change* 3, nos. 2 and 3 (summer–fall 1975): 21. The film *Apocalypse Now* parodies this view in the famous French plantation scene.

44. Allison Thomas stressed this point in an interview published in 1989. See Maurer, *Strange Ground*, 35. For scholarly confirmation, see especially Marr, *Vietnam, 1945*, 286–291.

45. "Note pour le Ministre," 10 July 1945, Asie/Indochine, file 31, MAE; Bonnet to Bidault, 30 June 1945, Amérique, file 128, MAE.

46. "Note sur la mission de M. Siriex à Londres," 14 May 1945, Europe/Grande Bretagne, file 40, MAE; "Note pour le Ministre," 15 June 1945, Asie/Indochine, file 38, MAE; Massigli to Foreign Ministry, 27 July 1945, Asie/Indochine, file 53, MAE.

47. Pechkoff to Foreign Ministry, 31 May 1945, Y-International/Affaires Politiques, Asie et Extrême-Orient, file 25, MAE; Cadogan to Massigli, 6 July 1945, Asie/Indochine, file 46, MAE; Mountbatten to Chiefs of Staff, 8 Aug. 1945, WO 203, file 4452, PRO.

48. "Exposé du Général Sabattier à la réunion du Comité de l'Indochine," 21 June 1945, Asie/Indochine, file 50, MAE.

49. Pleven to de Gaulle, 10 May 1945, Amérique, file 119, MAE; Kunming to State Department, 17 May 1945, RG226, OSS Intelligence Reports, box 500, NA; memcon, Bonnet with Grew, 21 May 1945, Asie/Indochine, file 45, MAE; Bidault to Massigli, 10 Aug. 1945, Asie/Indochine, file 31, MAE; Bonnet to Foreign Ministry, 13 June 1945, Amérique, file 132, MAE.

50. "Rapport de la Sous-Commission des Mandats," 15 May 1945, Y-International, file 656, MAE; Berard to Foreign Ministry, 23 July 1945, Amérique, file 119, MAE; "Entretiens de Washington," 20 Aug. 1945, Secrétaire Général/Conférences, 1943–1945, file 7, MAE; Kunming to State Department, 17 May 1945, RG226, OSS Intelligence Reports, box 500, NA.

51. "Compte-Rendu de la Réunion tenue le 19 juillet 1945," 19 July 1945, Asie/Indochine, file 42, MAE.

52. "Note pour le Conseil des Ministres: Futur statut économique de l'Indochine," 13 Aug. 1945, Bidault papers, box 127, AN.

53. Ibid.

54. Kahn to Culbertson, 5 Sept. 1945, RG59, PSA, reel 8, NA.

55. OSS report, "Comment on 'French Intentions in French Indochina,'" 6 Aug. 1945, RG59, PSA, reel 12, NA; "SEA Draft," 20 Aug. 1945, RG59, PSA, reel 12, NA.

56. Note by Direction d'Asie-Océanie, "Attitude des principales puissances dans la question de l'Indochine," 24 Aug. 1945, Asie/Indochine, file 32, MAE.

57. Ibid.

58. Ibid.

59. Chungking to Foreign Ministry, 11 Aug. 1945, Bidault papers, box 127, AN; London to High Commissioner, 15 Sept. 1945, Archives de l'Indochine/10H, box 140, CV; Leclerc to Defense Ministry, 22 Aug. 1945, Bidault papers, box 127, AN; Leclerc to Colonial Ministry, 23 Aug. 1945, Asie/Indochine, file 32, MAE.

60. De Gaulle to Bidault, 14 Aug. 1945, Asie/Indochine, file 32, MAE.

61. Bonnet to Foreign Ministry, 20 Aug. 1945, Asie/Indochine, file 32, MAE; Caffery to Bidault, 15 Aug. 1945, Asie/Indochine, file 32, MAE.

62. Duiker, *The Communist Road to Power in Vietnam*, 95.

63. For Ho's speech, see Gareth Porter, ed., *Vietnam: The Definitive Documentation of Human Decisions*, Vol. 1: *The First Indochina War and the Geneva Agreements, 1941–1955* (Stanfordville, N.Y.: Coleman Enterprises, 1979), 64–66. For details of the August Revolution, see especially Duiker, *Ho Chi Minh*, 307–345; Duiker, *The Communist Road to Power in Vietnam*, 95–109; Marr, *Vietnam, 1945*, 347–539; Huynh, *Vietnamese Communism*, 290–338.

64. Bradley, *Imagining Vietnam and America*, 123–133; Marr, *Vietnam, 1945*, 483–490.

65. Donovan to Byrnes, 22 Aug. 1945, RG59, PSA, reel 11, NA. For later appeals to Washington, see Bradley, *Imagining Vietnam and America*, 127–128.

66. Foreign Ministry to Bonnet, 31 March 1945, Asie/Indochine, file 147, MAE; Bonnet to Foreign Ministry, 21 April 1945, Asie/Indochine, file 47, MAE.

67. Memcon, Moffat with Lacoste, 31 Oct. 1945, RG59, 851G.00/10-3145, NA; Lacoste to Foreign Ministry, 31 Oct. 1945, Asie/Indochine, file 138, MAE.

68. Memo by d'Argenlieu, "Note sur le Viet Minh," 28 Sept. 1945, Asie/Indochine, file 138, MAE; Foreign Ministry report, "Agissements américains contre le rétablissement de la souveraineté française en Indochine," 10 Oct. 1945, Asie/Indochine, file 148, MAE; memcon, Vincent with Lacoste, 3 Oct. 1945, RG59, PSA, reel 8, NA. Ironically, there were very few Americans in Tonkin around this time. On September 27 one State Department document placed the number at nineteen—nine OSS officers and ten others. See "The Situation in Indochina," annex to memo by Vincent, 27 Sept. 1945, RG59, 851G.00/9-2845, NA.

69. D'Argenlieu to de Gaulle, 25 Sept. 1945, Asie/Indochine, file 34, MAE; Baudet to Bonnet, 29 Sept. 1945, Asie/Indochine, file 138, MAE; Ministry of Information to Leclerc, 17 Sept. 1945, F60, box 3035, AN; "Minutes of SAC's 28th Miscellaneous Meeting," 23 Sept. 1945, WO 203, file 2173, PRO. The number of Japanese troops who assisted the Viet Minh is difficult to pin down. Henri Laurentie of the French Colonial Ministry, speaking to reporters, put the number at ten thousand, but the Foreign Office believed the number was much lower. Reuter dispatch, 14 Sept. 1945, FO 371, file 46308, PRO. For a historian's appraisal, see Christopher E. Goscha, "Belated Asian Allies: The Technical and Military Contributions of Japanese Deserters, 1945–1950," in Marilyn B. Young and Robert Buzzanco, eds., *A Companion to the Vietnam War* (Malden, Mass.: Blackwell, 2002).

70. Caffery to State Department, 22 Sept. 1945, RG59, 851G.00/9-2245, NA; Baudet to Bonnet, 29 Sept. 1945, Asie/Indochine, file 138, MAE.

71. OSS report, "French Intentions in French Indochina," 10 July 1945, RG59, PSA, reel 12, NA; memcon, Moffat with UPI correspondent, 18 Aug. 1945, RG59, PSA, reel 9, NA.

72. Donovan to Byrnes, 5 Sept. 1945, RG59, 851G.00/9-545, NA; Gallagher to McClure, 20 Sept. 1945, in Porter, ed., *Vietnam: The Definitive Documentation of Human Decisions*, 78.

73. State Department report, "American Interests in Southeast Asia," Sept. 1945, RG59, PSA, reel 5, NA; Moffat to Vincent, "SEAC Actions in Allied Name without American Concurrence," 22 Sept. 1945, ibid.
74. Vincent to Acheson, 26 Sept. 1945, RG59, 851G.00/9-2845, NA.
75. State Department draft report, "United States Policy toward the Netherlands Indies and Indochina," 20 Nov. 1945, RG59, PSA, reel 6, NA; Vincent to Acheson, 26 Sept. 1945, RG59, CDF, 851G.00/9-2845, NA. On the parallel Indonesian case, see Robert J. McMahon, *Colonialism and Cold War: The United States and the Struggle for Indonesian Independence, 1945–1949* (Ithaca: Cornell University Press, 1981).
76. Bonbright to Matthews, 2 Oct. 1945, RG59, 851G.00/10-245, NA.
77. Donovan to Byrnes, 22 Aug. 1945, PP (DoD), 46–48; OSS memo, 6 Sept. 1945, Rose Conway File, box 15, HSTL; Kennan to State Department, 26 Sept. 1945, RG59, 851G.00/9-2645.
78. Trachtenberg, *A Constructed Peace*, 37–38.
79. Bonnet to Foreign Ministry, 24 Sept. 1945, Etats-Associés, file 135, MAE.
80. Text of speech by Vincent, 20 Oct. 1945, FO 371, file 46353, PRO.
81. Bonbright to Acheson, 29 Sept. 1945, RG59, PSA, reel 8, NA; Acheson to Robertson, 5 Oct. 1945, *FRUS 1945*, 6:313; memcon, Vincent with Lacoste, 3 Oct. 1945, RG59, PSA, reel 8, NA.

3. ILLUSIONS OF AUTONOMY

1. Report by Direction d'Asie-Océanie, "Attitudes des principales puissances dans la question de l'Indochine," 24 Aug. 1945, Asie/Indochine, file 32, MAE.
2. Dening to Foreign Office, 10 Sept. 1945, WO 203, file 4453, PRO; report by Headquarters, Supreme Allied Commander, South East Asia, 18 Aug. 1945, Gracey papers, file 4/1, LHCMA.
3. "Welfare in FIC [French Indochina]," undated, Gracey papers, 4/1, LHCMA; "Medical History, Allied Land Forces, French Indochina, Sept. 1945–Feb. 1946," undated, Gracey papers, file 4/7, LHCMA.
4. Mountbatten to Chiefs of Staff, 23 Sept. 1945, FO 371, file 46308, PRO.
5. For detailed descriptions of these events, see Devillers, *Histoire du Viêt-Nam*, 158–161; Duiker, *The Communist Road to Power in Vietnam*, 117–120; Dunn, *The First Vietnam War*, 184–207.
6. Gracey to Mountbatten, 9 Nov. 1945, Gracey papers, file 4/13, LHCMA; Graziani to Gracey, 20 Nov. 1945, Archives de l'Indochine/10H, box 138, CV. For an account of French operations, see Dunn, *The First Vietnam War*, 257–312.
7. Memcon, Sterndale Bennett with John Allison, 6 Feb. 1946, FO 371, file 54052, PRO.
8. See especially Kenneth O. Morgan, *Labour in Power, 1945–1951* (New York: Oxford University Press, 1984), 232–242.
9. Article by Rita Hindon, "Imperialism Today," April 1945, Fabian Colonial Bureau Papers, box 31, Rhodes House, Oxford University.

10. Earnest Bevin, 24 Oct. 1945, *Parliamentary Debates*, Commons, 5th ser., vol. 414 (London: His Majesty's Stationery Office, 1945), 2149–2150. For other instances, see ibid., vol. 398, 1151–1154, 1863–1864; vol. 415, 1727–1729; vol. 416, 12–14, 302, 867–872; vol. 417, 1052; and vol. 418, 526–527.

11. "Reply by Noel-Baker to Parliamentary Question," 28 Jan. 1946, FO 371, file 53958, PRO.

12. Morgan, *Labour in Power*, 63.

13. Harold Laski, 20 Nov. 1945, *Parliamentary Debates*, Commons, 5th ser., vol. 416, (1945), 302; "Pacific Intervention Condemned by Laski," *New York Times* (15 Nov. 1945), 5.

14. Viet Minh leaflet, undated, Gracey papers, file 4/20, LHCMA; D. R. SarDesai, *Indian Foreign Policy in Cambodia, Laos, and Vietnam, 1947–1964* (Berkeley and Los Angeles: University of California Press, 1968), 10; Commander-in-Chief, India, to Mountbatten, 18 Sept. 1945, WO 203, file 2235, PRO; Commander-in-Chief, India, to South East Asia Chief of Staff, 19 Sept. 1945, WO 203, file 4249, PRO.

15. Colombo to Foreign Ministry, 20 Oct. 1945, Archives de l'Indochine/10H, box 162, CV; Mountbatten to Chiefs of Staff, 29 Nov. 1945, FO 371, file 46310, PRO; Delhi to War Office, 8 Dec. 1945, WO 203, file 5067, PRO; report by Joint Planning Staff, "SACSEA's Plan for Reduction of Forces to Peacetime Strengths," 5 Feb. 1946, FO 371, file 54038, PRO.

16. Bevin to Secretary of State for India, 14 Nov. 1945, FO 371, file 46424, PRO.

17. Joint Planning Staff paper no. 216, "Organization of Command in the Far East," 19 Nov. 1945, WO 203, file 4373, PRO; report by Foreign Office Civil Planning Unit, 31 Dec. 1945, FO 371, file 54052, PRO.

18. Ministry of Production report, "Economic Coordination in South East Asia," 30 Nov. 1945, FO 371, file 46325, PRO.

19. Draft White Paper by minister of food, 29 March 1946, CAB 129, vol. 3, PRO.

20. Ibid.; Meiklereid to Foreign Office, 4 Dec. 1945, FO 371, file 46310, PRO; Kirkwood to Service Economique, French High Commission, 9 Nov. 1945, Archives de l'Indochine/10H, box 138, CV.

21. Report by Foreign Office Civil Planning Unit, 31 Dec. 1945, FO 371, file 54052, PRO.

22. Mountbatten to Cabinet Office, 24 Sept. 1945, FO 371, file 46308, PRO.

23. British leaflet, no date, Gracey papers, box 4/13, LHCMA; Mountbatten to Gracey, 31 Oct. 1945, ibid.

24. Mountbatten to SEAC commanders, 30 Sept. 1945, WO 203, file 2173, PRO; "Minutes of Ad Hoc Ministers' Meeting," 18 Oct. 1945, FO 371, file 46329, PRO; "Minutes of SACSEA's 28th Miscellaneous Meeting," 23 Sept. 1945, WO 203, file 2173, PRO; Gracey to Mountbatten, 28 Sept. 1945, WO 203, file 4431, PRO; Brain to Mountbatten, 25 Sept. 1945, WO 203, file 4431, PRO; Brain to Dening, 25 Sept. 1945, WO 203, file 5023, PRO; Dening to Foreign Office, 26 Oct. 1945, FO 371, file 46309, PRO; "Minutes of SACSEA's

31st Miscellaneous Meeting," 28 Sept. 1945, WO 203, file 5023, PRO; Browning to Mountbatten, 10 Oct. 1945, WO 203, file 5024, PRO.

25. 24 Oct. 1945, *Parliamentary Debates,* Commons, 5th ser., vol. 414 (1945), 2149–2150.

26. Joint Planning Staff Paper No. 201, "Handover of FIC to French," 21 Sept. 1945, WO 203, file 2151, PRO; Mountbatten to Chiefs of Staff, 25 Sept. 1945, WO 203, file 2173, PRO.

27. Commander in Chief, India, to Mountbatten, 9 Oct. 1945, WO 203, file 4846, PRO.

28. Historians critical of the United States for backing French colonialism in 1945 have sometimes emphasized the role of Americans in ferrying French troops back to Indochina aboard these ships. See, for example, Marilyn B. Young, *The Vietnam Wars, 1945–1990* (New York: Harper, 1991), 1–2, and Michael Gillen, "The Roots of Opposition: The Critical Response to U.S. Indochina Policy, 1945–1954" (Ph.D. diss., New York University, 1991), 99–150. In fact, a lengthy paper trail in U.S. and British archives, though difficult to piece together, suggests that these ships were under British control. The British government leased the ships and their crews in October 1945 and immediately assigned them the task of transporting troops to Indochina. On December 8 Field Marshall Wilson, responding to a U.S. query about this episode, told the U.S. Navy that no American ships were being used or would be used for this purpose. U.S. concern may have been sparked by a report in the *Chicago Tribune* quoting U.S. merchant marine sailors protesting their assignment. The navy's response—puzzlement and requests for further information—suggests that no senior navy official had formally approved Britain's use of the U.S. ships. See War Office memo for Chiefs of Staff, 13 Oct. 1945, FO 371, file 46309, PRO; Colombo to State Department, 23 Nov. 1945, RG59, PSA, reel 8, NA; "Extract from SAC's 300th Meeting," 6 Dec. 1945, WO 203, file 5067, PRO; Vittrup (War Department) to Moffat, "Use of U.S. Liberty Ships by SACSEA for Move of Troops," 8 Dec. 1945, RG49, PSA, reel 5, NA; report by Southeast Asia Division, "U.S. Prestige in Southeast Asia," 7 Feb. 1946, RG59, PSA, reel 7, NA.

29. "Minutes of SAC's 300th Meeting," 6 Dec. 1945, Archives de l'Indochine/ 10H, box 140, CV; Mountbatten to Chiefs of Staff, 17 March 1946, WO 203, file 4455, PRO.

30. Meiklereid to Foreign Office, 21 Feb. 1946, WO 203, file 4349, PRO; memo by Joint Planning Staff, 13 Dec. 1945, FO 371, file 46310, PRO; Chiefs of Staff to Mountbatten, 17 Dec. 1945, FO 371, file 46310, PRO; Mountbatten to Chiefs of Staff, 28 Jan. 1946, WO 203, file 2463, PRO; Commander in Chief, Allied Land Forces, South East Asia, to Maunsell, 10 Feb. 1946, WO 203, file 2463, PRO; Mountbatten to Maunsell, "Operations Instruction No. 2," 25 Feb. 1946, WO 203, file 2579, PRO.

31. Allied Land Forces, South East Asia, to War Office, 20 Jan. 1946, FO 371, file 54038, PRO; Mountbatten to Chiefs of Staff, 26 Jan. 1946, FO 371, file 54046, PRO; Chiefs of Staff to Mountbatten, 28 Jan. 1946, FO 371, file 54046, PRO; "Extract from SAC's 311th Meeting," 29 Jan. 1946, WO 203, file 5026, PRO.

32. "Extract from Chiefs of Staff Meeting," 28 Jan. 1946, FO 371, file 54046, PRO; Maunsell to SEAC, 3 Feb. 1946, WO 203, file 2463, PRO; Dening to Meiklereid, 2 March 1946, WO 203, file 5026, PRO; Meiklereid to Foreign Office, 2 March 1946, FO 371, file 53959, PRO; Chiefs of Staff to Joint Staff Mission, 20 Feb. 1946, FO 371, file 53959, PRO.

33. Chiefs of Staff to Mountbatten, 31 Dec. 1945, FO 371, file 53957, PRO; Cabinet Office to Wilson-Young, 17 Dec. 1945, FO 371, file 46310, PRO; Meiklereid to Bevin, 1 Feb. 1946, FO 371, file 53959, PRO; Dening to Meiklereid, 2 March 1946, WO 203, file 5026, PRO.

34. Mountbatten to Chiefs of Staff, 17 March 1946, WO 203, file 4455, PRO.

35. Mountbatten to Rear SACSEA, 27 Nov. 1945, WO 203, file 4349, PRO; Chiefs of Staff to Mountbatten, 30 Nov. 1945, WO 203, file 4431, PRO; Juin to Bidault, 3 Nov. 1945, Asie/Indochine, file 35, MAE; Clarac to Baudet, 8 Dec. 1945, Asie/Indochine, file 40, MAE; "Note pour le ministre, Conseil de la Défense Nationale du samedi 22 Décembre," Asie/Indochine, file 35, MAE; "Extract from SAC's 296th Meeting," 20 Nov. 1945, WO 203, file 5025, PRO.

36. D'Argenlieu to Mountbatten, 17 Nov. 1945, Archives de l'Indochine/ 10H, box 140, CV; Mountbatten to Chiefs of Staff, 19 Nov. 1945, ibid.; memcon, d'Argenlieu and Mountbatten, 30 Nov. 1945, ibid.; "Synthèse journalière," 10 Nov. 1945, Asie/Indochine, file 43, MAE; d'Argenlieu to Foreign Ministry, Amérique, file 128, MAE.

37. Paris to Foreign Office, 21 Sept. 1945, FO 371, file 46308, PRO; d'Argenlieu to Interministerial Committee, 7 Oct. 1945, Asie/Indochine, file 34, MAE; Mountbatten to Foreign Office, 1 Nov. 1945, FO 371, file 46309, PRO; Bonnet to Foreign Ministry, 12 Sept. 1945, Amérique, file 128, MAE; "Entretien entre Général de Gaulle et M. T. V. Soong," 19 Sept. 1945, Asie/Indochine, file 210, MAE; d'Argenlieu to Foreign Ministry, 9 Jan. 1946, Asie/Indochine, file 40, MAE; Leclerc to Bidault, 7 Sept. 1945, Bidault papers, box 127, AN; Pechkoff to Foreign Ministry, 7 Dec. 1945, Asie/Indochine, file 40, MAE.

38. Leclerc to Bidault, 7 Sept. 1945, Bidault papers, box 127, AN.

39. "Notes on Overall Situation in FIC by Major General D. Gracey," 28 Jan. 1946, WO 203, file 4349, PRO; report by SEAC director of intelligence, "Situation in French Indo-China," 17 Dec. 1945, WO 203, file 4432, PRO..

40. Massigli to Bidault, 12 Nov. 1945, Asie/Indochine, file 138, MAE; military attaché in Chungking to Chiefs of Staff, 2 March 1946, Asie/Indochine, file 48, MAE; Reed to State Department, 1 March 1946, *FRUS 1946*, 8:31.

41. "Note pour le Ministre," 20 Feb. 1946, Asie/Indochina, file 40, MAE.

42. Giacobbi to Bidault, 8 Nov. 1945, Asie/Indochine, file 35, MAE; Maunsell to SEAC, 3 Feb. 1946, WO 203, file 2463, PRO; Meiklereid to Foreign Office, 22 Feb. 1946, FO 371, file 53959, PRO; "Extract from Minutes of SAC's 321st Meeting," 22 Feb. 1946, WO 203, file 5026, PRO; minute by Sterndale Bennett, 27 Feb. 1946, FO 371, file 53959, PRO.

43. For details, see Devillers, *Histoire du Viêt-Nam,* 236–239, and Duiker, *Ho Chi Minh,* 365.

44. Mountbatten to Chiefs of Staff, 17 March 1946, FO 371, file 53961, PRO; Juin to Giacobbi, 20 Feb. 1946, Archives de l'Indochine/10H, box 162, CV.

45. For analysis of the relationship between de Gaulle and Laurentie, see Shipway, *The Road to War*, 140–147.
46. Quoted in ibid., 143.
47. Duiker, *Ho Chi Minh*, 358.
48. Shipway, *The Road to War*, 142–146.
49. Ibid., 105.
50. Juin to Giacobbi, 20 Feb. 1946, Archives de l'Indochine/10H, box 162, CV.
51. Leclerc is quoted in R. E. M. Irving, *The First Indochina War: French and American Policy, 1945–1954* (London: Croom Helm, 1975), 15.
52. Shipway, *The Road to War*, 96.
53. Irving, *The First Indochina War*; Shennan, *Rethinking France*, 163–164; Alain Ruscio, *Les communistes français et la guerre d'Indochine, 1944–1954* (Paris: L'Harmattan, 1985), 33–49, 122–125; Irwin Wall, *French Communism in the Era of Stalin: The Quest for Unity and Integration, 1945–1962* (Westport, Conn.: Greenwood, 1983), 32–47.
54. For discussion of the background and details of the March 6 accord, see Devillers, *Histoire du Viêt-Nam*, 205–226; Duiker, *The Communist Road to Power in Vietnam*, 122–124; Duiker, *Ho Chi Minh*, 356–365; Sainteny, *Histoire d'une paix manquée*, 177–202.
55. Quoted in Stanley Karnow, *Vietnam: A History*, rev. ed. (New York: Penguin, 1991), 169.
56. Quoted in Shipway, *The Road to War*, 168.
57. For Ho Chi Minh's calculations, see Duiker, *Ho Chi Minh*, 358–362.
58. Memo by Minerva (French intelligence), "Opinion d'une haute personnalité américaine, sur l'emprunt français aux Etats-Unis," 8 Feb. 1946, Bidault papers, box 81, AN; report by Haut Commission, 2 Sept. 1946, Asie/Indochine, file 255, MAE; d'Argenlieu to Interministerial Committee, 19 Nov. 1946, Asie/Indochine, file 255, MAE; d'Argenlieu to Defense Ministry, 4 May 1946, Asie/Indochine, file 255, MAE; Juin to d'Argenlieu, 14 May 1946, Asie/Indochine, file 255, MAE; London to Foreign Ministry, 17 May 1946, Amérique, file 61, MAE.
59. Naggiar to Foreign Ministry, 20 Feb. 1946, Asie/Dossiers Généraux, file 51, MAE; Bonnet to Bidault, 22 March 1946, Europe/Grande Bretagne, file 23, MAE.
60. Juin to d'Argenlieu, 14 May 1946, Asie/Indochine, file 255, MAE; London to Foreign Ministry, 17 May 1946, Amérique, file 61, MAE.
61. Moffat to Wallner, 23 Oct. 1946, RG59, 751G.00/10-2346, NA.
62. For details of the Dalat and Fontainebleau talks, see Devillers, *Histoire du Viêt-Nam*, chaps. 15, 17; Shipway, *The Road to War*, 177–221.
63. Minerva memo (French intelligence, Saigon), "Le catholicisme américain et l'Indochine," 14 Jan. 1946, Bidault papers, box 132, MAE; Meiklereid to Foreign Office, 8 March 1946, FO 371, file 53960, PRO; "Exposé du M. Baudet à Fontainebleau," 20 July 1946, Asie/Indochine, file 54, MAE; memo for the president, 12 Aug. 1946, Bidault papers, box 127, AN; "Projet de déclaration du Gouvernement Provisoire," 12 Aug. 1946, Bidault papers, box 127, AN.

64. Caffery to State Department, 28 June 1946, *FRUS 1946*, 8:47; O'Sullivan to State Department, 5 June 1946, ibid., 8:46; Reed (Hanoi) to State Department, 31 Aug. 1946, RG59, 851G.oo/8-3146, NA.

65. Reed to State Department, 17 Sept. 1946, *FRUS 1946*, 8:59; "Note pour le Président concernant Ho Chi Minh," 3 July 1946, Bidault papers, box 127, AN.

66. Foreign Ministry to Washington, 11 March 1947, Asie/Indochine, file 353, MAE; report by Far Eastern command, "Fiche concernant les violences et exactions imputées aux troupes du corps expéditionnaire," 5 Nov. 1946, Bidault papers, box 127, AN.

67. Foreign Ministry to Bonnet, 20 Aug. 1946, Etats-Associés, file 123, MAE; d'Argenlieu to Interministerial Committee, 10 Oct. 1946, Etats-Associés, file 137, MAE; Foreign Ministry to Interministerial Committee, 11 Oct. 1946, Etats-Associés, file 135, MAE.

68. Memo by d'Argenlieu, "Activités américaines," 27 Feb. 1946, Amérique, file 128, MAE.

69. Memcon, Moffat with Lt. J.R. Withrow, Dec. 1945, RG59, PSA, reel 11, NA; memcon, Moffat, et al. with Gallagher, 30 Jan. 1946, *FRUS 1946*, 8:15–20; Landon to Vincent, 14 March 1946, RG59, PSA, reel 7, NA.

70. Byrnes to Caffery, 4 Feb. 1946, *FRUS 1946*, 8:23; Caffery to Byrnes, 6 Feb. 1946, ibid., 8:24–25.

71. See, for example, John Lewis Gaddis, *The United States and the Origins of the Cold War, 1941–1947* (New York: Columbia University Press, 1972), chap. 9; Leffler, *A Preponderance of Power*, chap. 3; Trachtenberg, *A Constructed Peace*, chap. 2.

72. Trachtenberg, *A Constructed Peace*, 41.

73. Report by Southeast Asia Division, "United States Prestige in Southeast Asia," 7 Feb. 1946, RG59, PSA, reel 7, NA.

74. Caffery to State Department, 25 June 1946, RG59, 851G.oo/6-2546, NA; Clayton to Saigon, 9 Sept. 1946, RG59, 851G.oo/9-946, NA.

75. Report by Strategic Services Unit, War Department, 7 Aug. 1946, RG59, 851G.oo/8-746, NA; Moffat to Vincent, 9 Aug. 1946, *FRUS 1946*, 8:52–54.

76. At the end of 1945, Leclerc noted that the British were willing to supply even lethal goods like ammunition as long as it could be done without attracting notice. The scheme called for deliveries over a period of seven months, followed by six months of inactivity. See Leclerc to Allied Land Forces, South East Asia (ALFSEA), 7 Dec. 1945, Archives de l'Indochine/10H, box 161, CV; orders for ALFSEA forces, "Administration des Forces Françaises," 16 Nov. 1945, Archives de l'Indochine/10H, box 138, CV.

77. Lacoste to Bidault, 15 Nov. 1945, Amérique, file 40, MAE; memo for Mr. Berry, "Interview with George Allen," 30 Nov. 1945, RG59, PSA, reel 9, NA; "Memorandum of the Press and Radio News Conference," 24 Oct. 1945, Byrnes papers, box 554, STI.

78. Matthews to Acheson, 18 Jan. 1946, RG263, box 101, NA; Acheson to Matthews, no date, RG263, box 101, NA.

79. D'Argenlieu to Defense Ministry, 8 Jan. 1946, Archives de l'Indochine/ 10H, box 162, CV; memo by Andlauer, 10 Jan. 1946, RG59, PSA, reel 8, NA;

Vidal to Kahn, 29 Nov. 1945, RG59, 11-2945, NA; Giacobbi to New York consulate, 18 Dec. 1945, Asie/Indochine, file 41, MAE; Leclerc to d'Argenlieu, 15 Nov. 1945, Archives de l'Indochine/10H, box 161, CV; d'Argenlieu to Defense Ministry, 22 Nov. 1945, Asie/Indochine, file 43, MAE; d'Argenlieu to Washington, October 1945, Archives de l'Indochine/10H, CV.

80. OSS memo from Saigon, 6 Dec. 1945, RG263, box 101, NA.

81. See, for example, Truslow to Kennedy, 4 Oct. 1945, RG59, 851G.6176/10-445, NA; memo by Walter Kahn, "Trucks for Indo-China," 26 Nov. 1945, RG59, 851G.24/11-2645, NA; memcon, Moffat with Lt. J. R. Withrow, Dec. 1945, RG59, PSA, reel 11, NA.

82. Report by Office of Intelligence and Research, "Economic Reconstruction in the Far East," 10 Aug. 1946, RG59, OIR Reports, NA.

83. Fetter to Thurston, 26 Nov. 1945, RG59, 851G.24/11-2645, NA.

84. Bonnet to Foreign Ministry, 3 Aug. 1946, Asie/Indochine, file 41, MAE.

85. Lacy to Ringwalt, 3 July 1946, RG59, PSA, reel 8, NA; State Department memo, 24 June 1946, RG59, PSA, reel 8, NA; Nophan to Scobey, 2 Oct. 1946, RG59, 851G.00/10-246, NA; memo by Office of Foreign Liquidation Commissioner, 18 Oct. 1946, RG59, 851G.00/10-1846, NA.

86. Quantities of equipment and total costs are extremely difficult to piece together, especially once the flow of French purchases becomes more routinized in mid-1946. This glimpse of U.S. sales has been compiled from the following sources: de Langlade to d'Argenlieu, 13 Jan. 1946, Archives de l'Indochine/10H, box 125, CV; Calcutta to High Commission, 30 Jan. 1946, ibid.; Manila purchasing mission to d'Argenlieu, 15 Feb. 1946, ibid.; d'Argenlieu to Manila purchasing mission, 26 Feb. 1946, ibid.; State Department to French embassy, 27 March 1946, RG59, PSA, reel 8, NA; Bonnet to Bidault, 17 April 1946, Asie/Indochine, file 41, MAE. U.S. equipment was obtainable at sharp discounts. For example, a Dakota transport aircraft sold for $20,000 in October 1946 and could be rented for $5,000 per year. See "Fiche: Achat d'avions Dakota pour l'Indochine," 3 Oct. 1945, Nouveau Fond Indochine, box 134, AOM.

87. Reed to State Department, 27 May 1946, RG59, 851G.00/5-2746, NA; aide mémoire, French embassy to State Department, 21 June 1946, RG59, 851G.00/6-2146, NA.

88. Chungking to High Commission, 23 April 1946, Archives de l'Indochine/10H, box 126, CV; Acheson to various posts, 30 April 1946, *FRUS 1946*, 8:38; State Department to French embassy, 1 July 1946, *FRUS 1946*, 8:47; Acheson to Marshall, 15 May 1946, *FRUS 1946*, 8:42.

89. State Department memo, "French and Siamese Positions on the Disputed Territories," 17 April 1946, RG59, PSA, reel 7, NA; d'Argenlieu to Interministerial Committee, 15 Aug. 1946, Bidault papers, box 127, AN; Bidault to Bonnet, 20 July 1946, Bidault papers, box 127, AN; Caffery to State Department, *FRUS 1946*, 8:47; Interministerial Committee to d'Argenlieu, 3 Aug. 1946, Etats-Associés, file 135, MAE. For detail on the Thai border issue during 1946, see especially Ellen J. Hammer, *The Struggle for Indochina* (Stanford: Stanford University Press, 1954), 254-256.

90. Foreign Ministry to Washington, 17 Nov. 1946, Nations Unies et Organisations Internationales, file 197, MAE.

4. CRISIS RENEWED

1. D'Argenlieu to Leclerc, 8 May 1946, Archives de l'Indochine/10H, box 162, CV.
2. Moutet, Pignon, and d'Argenlieu are quoted in Shipway, *The Road to War,* 215, 206, 209.
3. Shipway, *The Road to War,* 211.
4. "Note pour le Ministre," August 1946, Bidault papers, box 127, AN.
5. See Devillers, *Histoire du Viêt-Nam,* 304–310; Duiker, *Ho Chi Minh,* 379–380; Shipway, *The Road to War,* 217–221.
6. Duiker, *The Communist Road to Power in Vietnam,* 129.
7. Shipway, *The Road to War,* 235–237.
8. Quoted in Shipway, *The Road to War,* 250, and Stein Tønnesson, *1946: Le déclenchement de la guerre d'Indochine: Les vêpres tonkinoises du 19 décembre* (Paris: l'Harmattan, 1987), 139.
9. Memo for prime minister, "Entretien des effectifs du CEFEO et Organisations des Armées locales en Indochine," 23 Sept. 1946, F60, box 3035, AN. The military staff approved a force of seventy-five thousand for Indochina in 1947, rather than the forty-six thousand envisioned in the budget.
10. Memo by Humbert, 30 Nov. 1946, in Devillers, *Paris, Saigon, Hanoi,* 257–258.
11. Quoted in Shipway, *The Road to War,* 256.
12. Blum statement in *Le Populaire,* 10 Dec. 1946, in Devillers, *Paris, Saigon, Hanoi,* 285–286.
13. Valluy is quoted in Karnow, *Vietnam: A History,* 172. On the December 16 meeting, see Shipway, *The Road to War,* 261.
14. Rapport du Conseiller Politique, 17 Dec. 1946, in Devillers, *Paris, Saigon, Hanoi,* 293.
15. Duiker, *Ho Chi Minh,* 395–396. For Giap's view, see Vo Nguyen Giap, *Unforgettable Days,* 3d ed. (Hanoi: GIOI Publishers, 1994), 381–382.
16. Assemblée Nationale, *Journal Officiel,* Débats Parlementaires, Année 1946, no. 125, 24 Dec. 1946, 320–321.
17. Quoted in Lansing Warren, "Moutet Rules Out Indo-China Parley," *New York Times* (5 Jan. 1947).
18. MRP press release, "La France et le Problème Indochinois," 12 Dec. 1946, F60, box 3035, AN; *L'Aube* (14 Dec. 1946).
19. *L'Humanité* (24 Dec. 1946). See also Wall, *French Communism in the Era of Stalin,* 47.
20. Irving, *The First Indochina War,* 140–141.
21. "Intervention de Maurice Schumann," *L'Aube,* 19 March 1947.
22. Quoted in Lansing Warren, "French Reds Urge Indo-China Peace," *New York Times* (20 March 1947).
23. Pierre Courtade, "Il faut négocier avec Ho Chi Minh!" *L'Humanité* (8 Feb. 1947).
24. Assemblée Nationale, *Journal Officiel,* 18 March 1947, 905.
25. Quoted in Irving, *The First Indochina War,* 44.
26. Assemblée Nationale, *Journal Officiel* (15 March 1947), 854.

27. Irving, *The First Indochina War*, 44.

28. For discussion of the surprising consistency and stability within the French bureaucracy during a time known best for political upheaval, see Hitchcock, *France Restored*.

29. Poll results cited in Robert Trumbull, "France Preparing to Strengthen Her Armed Forces in Indo-China," *New York Times* (4 Feb. 1947).

30. Paris to State Department, 4 March 1947, RG59, 851G.00/3-447, NA.

31. Ruscio, *Les communistes français et la guerre d'Indochine*, 165.

32. Shipway, *The Road to War*, 263. For the Vietnamese perspective on the early fighting, see Duiker, *The Communist Road to Power in Vietnam*, 133-139.

33. Robert Trumbull, "French Are Facing Long, Costly Drive against Viet Nam," *New York Times* (19 Jan. 1947); "Indo-China Disease Crippling French," *New York Times* (28 Jan. 1947).

34. Acheson to Caffery, 24 March 1947, *FRUS 1947*, 6:81; Caffery to Marshall, 27 March 1947, *FRUS 1947*, 6:81-82.

35. Quoted in Hammer, *The Struggle for Indochina*, 206.

36. For the Mus mission, see Duiker, *The Communist Road to Power in Vietnam*, 134; Duiker, *Ho Chi Minh*, 403; Hammer, *The Struggle for Indochina*, 204-207; Karnow, *Vietnam: A History*, 174-275.

37. Notes by Ségalat, 29 Nov. 1946, in Devillers, *Paris, Saigon, Hanoi*, 257.

38. Interministerial Committee to Moutet, 14 Jan. 1947, Asie/Indochine, file 55, MAE.

39. Singapore to Foreign Ministry, 3 Feb. 1947, Asie/Indochine, file 373, MAE; Calcutta to Foreign Ministry, 14 Jan. 1947, Asie/Indochine, file 372, MAE; "Calcutta Riots Continue," *New York Times*, 23 Jan. 1947; note by Asia-Oceania Division, 3 Jan. 1947, Asie/Indochine, file 55, MAE; SarDesai, *Indian Foreign Policy in Cambodia, Laos, and Vietnam*, 13; "Viet Nam Urges India to Bring Case to U.N.," *New York Times* (10 Oct. 1947).

40. Report by High Commissioner in India, "India and Events in Indo-China," 24 Jan. 1947, FO 371, file 63451, PRO.

41. "Vietnam Predicts a Twenty-Year War," *New York Times* (12 Jan. 1947); Governor of Burma to Secretary of State for Burma, 8 Feb. 1947, FO 371, file 63460, PRO; Governor of Burma to Secretary of State for Burma, 22 March 1947, M/4, box 2802, OIOC.

42. SarDesai, *Indian Foreign Policy in Cambodia, Laos, and Vietnam*, 11-16.

43. Ramadier to Bidault, 9 Jan. 1947, Asie/Indochine, file 132, MAE; Coulson (Paris) to Anderson (Foreign Office), 14 Jan. 1947, FO 371, file 63459, PRO; Calcutta (Fouchet) to Foreign Ministry, 21 Jan. 1947, Asie/Inde, file 62, MAE; Air Headquarters-India to Air Attaché-Paris, 4 Feb. 1947, FO 371, file 63460, PRO; Air Ministry to Air Attaché-Paris, 10 Feb. 1947, FO 371, file 63460, PRO.

44. Report by Pignon, "Le Parti Communiste Chinois au Tonkin," 22 Nov. 1946, Etats-Associés, file 144, MAE.

45. Note by Asia-Oceania Division, "Répercussions aux Indes et en Chine des événements de l'Indochine," 3 Jan. 1947, Asie/Indochine, file 55; Bonnet to Foreign Ministry, 10 Jan. 1947, Bidault papers, box 128, AN; Nanking (Meyrier) to Foreign Ministry, 21 Jan. 1947, Asie/Indochine, file 372, MAE.

46. Killearn to Foreign Office, 26 Jan. 1947, FO 371, file 63542, PRO; minute by Bevin for Attlee, 10 Feb. 1947, FO 371, file 63542, PRO. It is difficult to calculate the value of equipment quietly provided for the French military during this period of British wariness about French policy. In March 1947 anonymous French officials told the Reuters news service that British support over the previous sixteen months totaled more than £17.5 million. G. H. Thompson, the British ambassador in Bangkok, dismissed that figure as "French propaganda" designed to create the impression of active foreign support for French policy, but the Foreign Office in March 1947 still placed the figure at £10 million, with most coming since the outbreak of fighting in December. Thompson to Foreign Office, 10 March 1947, M/4, box 2802, OIOC; minute by Anderson, 12 March 1947, FO 371, file 63453, PRO.

47. "Malayan Force Banned," *New York Times* (21 April 1947); Paris (Duff Cooper) to Foreign Office, 19 Feb. 1947, M/4, box 2802, OIOC; minute by Anderson, 23 Jan. 1947, FO 371, file 63459, PRO; Dening to Foreign Office, 7 Feb. 1947, FO 371, file 63547, PRO.

48. "Disappointed Hopes?" *Empire: Journal of the Fabian Colonial Bureau* 9, no. 1 (May–June 1946), in Papers of the Fabian Colonial Bureau, Rhodes House Library, Oxford University; minute by Anderson, 31 Jan. 1947, FO 371, file 53970, PRO.

49. 12 Feb. 1947, *Parliamentary Debates,* Commons, 5th ser., vol. 433 (1947), 361; Bevin to Hicks, 25 Feb. 1947, FO 371, file 63453, PRO; 24 March 1947, *Parliamentary Debates,* Commons, 5th ser., vol. 435, (1947), 827.

50. Killearn to Foreign Office, 19 Aug. 1946, M/4, file 3052, OIOC. For details of Killearn's operation, see Killearn to Bevin, "South-East Asia: Work of the Special Commission during 1946," 6 May 1947, M/4, file 3053, OIOC.

51. Dening to Killearn, 20 Feb. 1947, FO 371, file 63518, PRO; Colonial Office (Seel) to Dening, 21 June 1947, ibid.

52. D'Argenlieu to Bidault, 21 Sept. 1946, Amérique, file 128, MAE.

53. Foreign Office to Meiklereid, 4 Dec. 1946, FO 959, file 14, PRO; Killearn to Foreign Office, 30 Jan. 1947, FO 371, file 63452, PRO; Meiklereid to Foreign Office, 9 Nov. 1946, FO 371, file 53968, PRO; Killearn to Orme-Sargent, 3 Feb. 1947, FO 371, file 63451, PRO.

54. Moscow to Foreign Office, 31 Dec. 1946, FO 371, file 63451, PRO; Ashley-Clarke to Allen, 12 Dec. 1946, FO 371, file 59968, PRO.

55. Meiklereid to Bevin, 17 Jan. 1947, FO 959, file 14, PRO.

56. Bonnet to Foreign Ministry, 5 Dec. 1946, Etats-Associés, file 135, MAE; report by Asia-Oceania Division, "Attitude des Etats-Unis sur la question d'Indochine," 10 Jan. 1947, Asie/Indochine, file 372, MAE; Bonnet to Foreign Ministry, 24 Dec. 1946, Etats-Associés, file 135, MAE.

57. Landon to Vincent, "Proposed U.S. action in Indochina dispute," 14 Jan. 1947, RG59, 751G.00, box 4002, NA; Landon to Vincent, "Critical situation in Indochina and possible developments," 14 Jan. 1947, RG59, PSA, reel 10, NA.

58. Wallner to Byrnes, 15 Jan. 1947, RG263, CIA/Murphy files, box 102, NA.

59. Memo by Wallner, "Relations with the Soviet Union," 17 Jan. 1947, RG59, lot file 1, Acheson Undersecretary file, box 9, NA; Acheson to Saigon, 5 Dec. 1946, RG59, 851G.00/12-346, NA.
60. Schaller, "Securing the Great Crescent," 392-395.
61. Moffat (Saigon) to State Department, 21 Dec. 1946, RG59, 851G.00/12-2146, NA; Moffat to Byrnes, 7 Jan. 1947, *FRUS 1947*, 6:54.
62. Landon to Vincent, 14 Jan. 1947, RG59, PSA, reel 10 NA; Reed to Marshall, 7 March 1947, RG263, Murphy papers/CIA, box 102, NA.
63. Intelligence memo, "Communist Influence in Indochina," 10 Feb. 1947, RG263, Murphy papers/CIA, box 102, NA; Landon to Vincent, 14 Jan. 1947, RG59, PSA, reel 10, NA.
64. "Outlook in Indochina," *New York Times* (22 Jan. 1947); "Trouble in Indo-China," *Washington Post* (29 Jan. 1947).
65. Byrnes to Caffery, 24 Dec. 1946, *FRUS 1946*, 8:77-78; d'Argenlieu to Foreign Ministry, 29 Dec. 1946, Bidault papers, box 127, AN; High Commission report, "Note sur la visite de M. Abbott Moffat," 9 Jan. 1947, Etats-Associés, file 135, MAE; Bonnet to Foreign Ministry, 28 Dec. 1946, Etats-Associés, file 135, MAE; Vincent to Acheson, 8 Jan. 1947, *FRUS 1947*, 6:58-59.
66. Marshall to Caffery, 3 Feb. 1947, PP (DoD), 8:98-99.
67. Ibid.
68. Caffery to Bidault, 6 Feb. 1947, Bidault papers, box 128, AN; Marshall to O'Sullivan, 25 Feb. 1947, RG59, 851G.00/2-2547, NA.
69. Foreign Ministry to Washington, Jan. 1947, Asie/Indochine, file 129, MAE; Bonnet to Foreign Ministry, 27 Nov. 1946, Etats-Associés, file 137, MAE; Byrnes to Paris, 8 Jan. 1947, PP (DoD), 8:97.
70. Ogburn to Wallner, 18 March 1947, RG59, PSA, reel 8, NA; Moffat to Ruck, 25 Feb. 1947, RG59, PSA, reel 11, NA.
71. Ramadier to Finance Ministry, 14 Jan. 1947, Asie/Indochine, file 129, MAE; military attaché (Washington) to Chiefs of Staff, 16 Jan. 1947, Asie/Indochine, file 129, MAE.
72. Coulson (Paris) to Foreign Office, 25 June 1947, FO 371, file 63455, PRO; Caffery to State Department, 3 March 1947, RG59, 851G.00/3-447, NA; Moutet to High Commission, 26 March 1947, Archives de l'Indochine/10H, box 166, CV.
73. Bernard B. Fall, *Street without Joy* (New York: Schocken Books, 1972), 27-31; report by Military Liaison Officer, Saigon, 21 Oct. 1947, FO 371, file 63456, PRO.
74. Memo by Chauvel, "L'Indochine," 10 Feb. 1947, Bidault papers, 128.
75. O'Sullivan to State Department, 4 Dec. 1946, RG59, 851G.00/12-346, NA; Meiklereid to Bevin, 17 Jan. 1947, FO 959, file 14, PRO.
76. "Instructions pour M. le Haut Commissaire de France pour l'Indochine," 23 March 1947, F60, box 2035, AN; Caffery to Marshall, *FRUS 1947*, 6:80; "Discours prononcé par M. Bollaert à Hanoi," 15 May 1947, Asie/Indochine, file 55, MAE.
77. Foreign Ministry to Ministry of Overseas France, 16 May 1947, Asie/Indochine, file 374, MAE; Foreign Ministry to Ministry of Overseas

France, 17 July 1947, Asie/Indochine, file 375, MAE; Defense Ministry report, "Les réactions étrangères devant le conflit franco-vietnamien," 14 March 1947, Asie/Indochine, file 373, MAE; Moffat to Vincent, 7 March 1947, RG59, 851G.918/2-1947, NA; Robert Trumbull, "Indo-China Curbs on News Assailed," New York Times (22 Feb. 1947); Lacoste to Foreign Ministry, 25 Feb. 1947, Asie/Indochine, file 353, MAE; Foreign Ministry to Washington, 17 April 1947, Asie/Indochine, file 374, MAE; Bonnet to Foreign Ministry, 1 May 1947, Asie/Indochine, file 374, MAE; Ministry of Overseas France to Foreign Ministry, 7 May 1947, Amérique, file 123, MAE; Lacoste to Foreign Ministry, 20 March 1947, Amérique, file 123, MAE.

78. Bonnet to Foreign Ministry, 28 March 1947, Etats-Associés, file 136, MAE; New York to Foreign Ministry, 15 Feb. 1947, Bidault papers, box 128, AN; State Department to Saigon, 29 Sept. 1947, RG59, 851G.00/9-2947, NA; memo for cabinet, "L'Activité Extérieure du Gouvernement Viet Minh," 28 March 1947, Asie/Indochine, file 168, MAE; Hanoi to State Department, 18 Sept. 1947, RG59, 851G.01/9-1847, NA.

79. Ministry of Overseas France memo, "Note pour M. le Directeur des Affaires Politiques," 24 April 1947, Etats-Associés, file 135, MAE; O'Sullivan to State Department, 29 July 1947, RG59, 851G.00/7-2947, NA; report by Direction de la Police et de la Sûreté Fédérale en Indochine, "Rapport sur l'Activité des Etrangers," 26 Sept. 1947, Asie/Indochine, file 346, MAE; aide-mémoire by Division d'Asie-Océanie, 1 July 1947, Bidault papers, box 128, AN; Washington to Foreign Ministry, 20 March 1947, Y-International/Affaires Politiques, Asie et Extrême-Orient, file 28, MAE.

80. High Commission report, "Etude sur les Activités Américaines en Indochine," 30 Oct. 1947, Amérique, box 128, MAE; Lacoste to Bidault, 8 Sept. 1947, Asie/Dossiers Généraux, file 31, MAE; Lacoste to Bidault, 19 March 1947, Y-International, file 655, MAE.

81. Reed to State Department, 13 Oct. 1947, RG59, 851G.00/10-1347, NA; Kunming to Nanking, 28 June 1947, Etats-Associés, file 135, MAE; Kunming to Bollaert, 2 Aug. 1947, Asie/Indochine, file 168, MAE; Hong Kong to Foreign Ministry, 26 Dec. 1947, Asie/Indochine, file 103, MAE; Bangkok to State Department, 5 Jan. 1948, RG59, 851G.00/1-548, NA; Landon to Penfield, 17 Feb. 1948, RG59, PSA, reel 8, NA. On Pham Ngoc Thach's activities, see Duiker, Ho Chi Minh, 404-406.

82. Memo by Bollaert, 31 Jan. 1948, Etats-Associés, file 138, MAE; Research and Analysis report, "Implications of the European Recovery Program for Indochina," 11 Feb. 1948, RG59, OIR reports, NA; Landon to Butterworth, 16 Sept. 1947, RG59, PSA, reel 10, NA.

83. Mock radio interview, "PL draft of SEA Radio Interview," no date, RG59, PSA, reel 4, NA; Foreign Ministry memo, "Acquisition d'armes pour l'Indochine," 13 Jan. 1948, Asie/Indochine, file 129, MAE; memcon, Lawson, Landon, et al., 29 Aug. 1947, RG59, PSA, reel 8, NA; State Department memo, "Transport of Munitions to Indochina on U.S. Vessels," 8 Oct. 1947, RG59, PSA, reel 9, NA; Landon to Saugstad, 16 Oct. 1947, RG59, PSA, reel 9, NA.

84. Foreign Office report, "Economic Conditions in Indochina: Foreign Trade," 22 Nov. 1947, FO 371, file 63461, PRO; War Office to Foreign Office,

7 July 1947, FO 371, file 63455, PRO; Foreign Office to Massigli, 11 July 1947, FO 371, file 63455, PRO; Duff Cooper to Foreign Office, FO 371, file 63455, PRO.

85. Cabinet memo, "Note sur la solution par une entente avec Bao Dai du problème indochinois," 7 Dec. 1947, Bidault papers, file 128, AN.

86. For early French contacts with Bao Dai, see, for example, Saigon to Foreign Office, 27 Dec. 1946, M/4, file 2802, OIOC; Paris to State Department, 26 Feb. 1947, RG59, 851G.00/2-2647, NA; Caffery to State Department, 27 March 1947, RG59, 851G.00/3-2747, NA.

87. Interview with Bollaert by R. E. M. Irving, in Irving, *The First Indochina War*, 48-49.

88. "Discours prononcé par M. E. Bollaert," 11 Sept. 1947, RG59, 851G.00/9-1147, NA.

89. Trevor-Wilson to Gibbs, 12 Sept. 1947, M/4, file 2802, OIOC.

90. Irving, *The First Indochina War*, 51.

5. DOMESTIC DIVIDES, FOREIGN SOLUTIONS

1. For biographical details, see Devillers, *Histoire du Viêt-Nam*, 61-64, 124-127; Irving, *The First Indochina War*, 54-55, 65; Kahin, *Intervention*, 24-26; Karnow, *Vietnam: A History*, 54-55; and Philip Shenon, "Bao Dai, 83, the Last Emperor of Long-Colonized Vietnam," *New York Times* (2 Aug. 1997).

2. R. E. M. Irving argues, for example, that the Bao Dai policy was implemented in "such a dilatory, backhanded manner that the 'solution' was discredited before it was properly implemented." Irving, *The First Indochina War*, 56.

3. Ibid., 56-58.

4. CIA report, "Prospects for De Gaulle's Return to Power," 15 Oct. 1948, NSC records/CIA file, box 2, HSTL.

5. CIA report on Indochina, 10 Dec. 1947, RG59, 851G.00/12-1047, NA; Abbott to State Department, 7 June 1948, RG59, 851G.00/6-748, NA.

6. Report by Trevor-Wilson, "Political and Military Intelligence, French Indochina," 10 April 1948, FO 371, file 69654, PRO; Trevor-Wilson to Gibbs, 7 June 1948, FO 959, file 19, PRO; report by British Military Liaison Officer, 7 June 1948, FO 371, file 69656, PRO.

7. Report by Bollaert for cabinet, 24 March 1948, Asie/Indochine, file 103, MAE; Foreign Ministry report, "Note pour la Direction d'Asie-Océanie, Question de l'Indochine et Assemblée de l'ONU," 1 Sept. 1948, Asie/Indochine, file 202, MAE.

8. "Entretien avec le Général Valluy," 18 Feb. 1948, Asie/Indochine, file 103, MAE; "Procès Verbal du Conseil de Défense," 27 March 1948, Archives de l'Indochine/10H, box 157, CV; report by Valluy, "Point de la Situation Militaire en Indochine," 22 Nov. 1948, ibid.

9. Gibbs to Foreign Office, 15 Dec. 1948, FO 959, file 20, PRO; Alessandri to Valluy, Aug. 1948, Archives de l'Indochine/10H, box 169, CV. Because of the fragmentary nature of the archival record, it is difficult to determine many details of the poison-gas plan. General Latour, French commander in Cochinchina,

appears to have initially proposed the idea. "There is every reason to believe," he wrote, "that if the decision [to use gas] were made at the beginning of a general conflict, that is at the moment when world opinion was focused on the Western theater, the protests that would accompany the use of these methods in a remote territory would attract little notice." Latour to Alessandri, 24 July 1948, Archives de l'Indochine/10H, box 169, CV.

10. Foreign Ministry report, "Les Etats-Unis et l'Indochine Française," 20 Nov. 1948, Asie/Indochine, file 255, MAE.

11. Coste-Floret to Schuman, 14 June 1948, Asie/Indochine, file 129, MAE; Foreign Ministry report, 17 Dec. 1948, Asie/Indochine, file 55, MAE.

12. Memcon, Abbott with M. Frances (Sûreté), 18 Oct. 1948, RG59, PSA, reel 6, NA; Abbott to State Department, 13 Jan. 1949, RG59, 851G.00/1–1349, NA; Lovett to Saigon, 1 Oct. 1948, RG59, 851G.00/10–148, NA.

13. "Note pour le Ministre, Entrée des Communistes chinois en Indochine," 29 Sept. 1948, Etats-Associés, file 144, MAE.

14. Qiang Zhai, *China and the Vietnam Wars, 1950–1975* (Chapel Hill: University of North Carolina Press, 2000), 11–12; Chen Jian, *Mao's China and the Cold War* (Chapel Hill: University of North Carolina Press, 2001), 119–120.

15. Report by Commander of Armed Forces in the Far East, "Evolution de la Situation Militaire en Indochine pendant le Mois de Janvier," 11 Feb. 1949, Archives de l'Indochine/10H, box 170, CV.

16. Military intelligence report, 28 Feb. 1949, FO 371, file 75960, PRO; Bonnet to Foreign Ministry, 10 July 1948, Etats-Associés, file 136, MAE; Caffery to State Department, 17 Oct. 1948, RG59, 851G.01/10–1748, NA; Saigon to State Department, 21 April 1949, RG59, 851G.00/4–2149, NA; State Department to Saigon, 27 May 1949, RG59, 851G.00/5–2749, NA; "Note pour le Cabinet du Ministre, Visa pour l'Indochine de M. Harold Isaacs," 22 Jan. 1949, Asie/Indochine, file 346, MAE.

17. Canberra (Auge) to Foreign Ministry, 17 Nov. 1948, Asie/Indochine, file 55, MAE; request for ECAFE membership, 22 Nov. 1948, FO 371, file 69659, PRO; Hanoi to State Department, 14 Sept. 1948, RG59, 851G.00/9–1448, NA; Directeur de la Police et de la Sûreté Fédérale to Bollaert, 19 May 1948, Asie/Indochine, file 255, MAE; Sûreté memo for commander of French land forces, "Activités suspectes d'étrangers en collusion avec les rebels indochinois," 5 April 1948, Asie/Indochine, file 346, MAE. On the DRV's growing diplomatic network, see Christopher E. Goscha, *Thailand and the Southeast Asian Networks of the Vietnamese Revolution, 1885–1954* (London: Curzon, 1999).

18. Memcon, Reed with Daridan, 1 Sept. 1948, *FRUS 1948*, 6:40–41; Paris to State Department, 14 Sept. 1948, RG59, 851G.00/9–1448, NA; Abbott to State Department, 26 May 1948, RG59, 851G.00/5–2648, NA.

19. Report by Direction d'Amérique, "La Politique Américaine en Extrême Orient," Feb. 1949, Amérique, file 134, MAE; Foreign Ministry to Tokyo, 17 Dec. 1946, Asie/Indochine, file 327, MAE; note by Robert Ducrest, 7 Nov. 1948, Asie/Indochine, file 143, MAE; Abbott to State Department, 6 Dec. 1948, RG59, 851G.00/12–648, NA.

20. Guibaut to Foreign Ministry, 5 Feb. 1949, Asie/Dossiers Généraux, file 31, MAE; memo by Division d'Asie-Océanie, "Indochine," 8 Jan. 1949, Asie/Indochine, file 143, MAE; Roux to Queuille, 16 March 1949, Asie/Indochine, file 56, MAE.

21. For Rotter's meticulous attention to the dollar shortage and the importance of Malayan exports, see his *The Path to Vietnam,* esp. chap. 3, and Rotter, "The Triangular Route to Vietnam," 404–423.

22. Note by Foreign Secretary, "Rice Supplies—South East Asia," 8 Sept. 1948, CAB 129, vol. 29, PRO.

23. Report by Hopson, "French Indo-China: Annual Review for 1948," 25 May 1949, FO 371, file 75958, PRO; Gibbs to Scrivener (Singapore), 19 Oct. 1948, FO 959, file 23, PRO; Hopson (Saigon) to Foreign Office, 16 Nov. 1948, FO 959, file 20, PRO.

24. Brief for Secretary of State, 26 July 1948, FO 371, file 69657, PRO; Foreign Office to Washington, 14 April 1948, FO 371, file 69654, PRO; Thompson to Foreign Office, 14 Dec. 1948, FO 371, file 69684, PRO.

25. Scott to Allen (Washington), 1 July 1949, FO 371, file 75991, PRO. For discussion of British pressure to expand the Brussels arrangement into the North Atlantic Treaty, see Leffler, *A Preponderance of Power,* 210–213.

26. Report by British military liaison officer, "The Military Situation in Tonkin," 18 March 1949, FO 371, file 75961, PRO.

27. Lloyd to War Office (Battye), 10 Sept. 1948, FO 371, file 69657, PRO; Gibbs to Foreign Office, 2 Nov. 1948, FO 371, file 69660, PRO.

28. Gibbs to Foreign Office, 7 Dec. 1948, FO 959, file 20, PRO; "Record of Meeting Held in the Foreign Office," 14 March 1949, FO 959, file 28, PRO.

29. C. R. Price to Dening, 14 Aug. 1948, FO 371, file 69702, PRO; Gibbs to Bevin, 21 March 1949, FO 371, file 75961, PRO; Foreign Office memo, "French Indo-China," 24 March 1949, ibid.

30. Minute by Grey, 29 Sept. 1948, FO 371, file 69695, PRO; Foreign Office report, "Communist Strategy in S.E. Asia," 8 Nov. 1948, ibid.; report by Grey, "Brief for Secretary of State's Visit to The Hague," 17 July 1948, FO 371, 69694, PRO.

31. SarDesai, *Indian Foreign Policy in Cambodia, Laos, and Vietnam,* 16–18.

32. Lloyd to Commonwealth Relations Office, 26 Aug. 1948, FO 371, file 69657, PRO.

33. See, for example, 27 Oct. 1948, *Parliamentary Debates,* Commons, 5th series, vol. 457 (1948), 148–149.

34. Minute by Mackworth-Young, 13 May 1948, FO 371, file 69656, PRO.

35. Memo by Grey, 20 Oct. 1948, FO 371, file 69684, PRO; brief by Grey for Bevin's visit to The Hague, 17 July 1948, FO 371, file 69694, PRO.

36. Brief for Bevin's talks with Schuman, 10 Jan. 1949, FO 371, file 76002, PRO; Dening to MacDonald, 24 Feb. 1949, FO 371, file 76031, PRO; Dening to MacDonald, Aug. 1948, FO 371, file 69702, PRO.

37. Gibbs to Foreign Office, 6 Nov. 1948, FO 959, file 23, PRO; Ashley-Clarke to Attlee, 28 March 1949, FO 959, file 28, PRO; military intelligence report by British military liaison officer, Saigon, 18 Dec. 1948, FO 371, file

69659, PRO; Saigon to Foreign Office, 30 Nov. 1948, FO 371, file 69659, PRO; minute by Dening, 16 Dec. 1948, ibid.

38. Foreign Office to Saigon, 2 Dec. 1948, FO 959, file 20, PRO; Dening to Graves (Washington), 14 Feb. 1949, FO 371, file 76003, PRO; Dening to Syers (Commonwealth Relations Office), 18 March 1949, FO 371, file 76023, PRO.

39. Bangkok to Foreign Office, 19 Feb. 1949, FO 371, file 76003, PRO; Dening to Graves (Washington), 14 Feb. 1949, ibid. On Thai politics, see Daniel Fineman, *A Special Relationship: The United States and Military Government in Thailand, 1947–1958* (Honolulu: University of Hawaii Press, 1997).

40. Study by Foreign Office Research Department, 15 March 1949, FO 371, file 76036, PRO; MacDonald to Bevin, 23 March 1949, FO 371, 76033, PRO; Dening to Graves (Washington), 14 Feb. 1949, FO 371, file 76003, PRO; cabinet memo, "Sir William Strang's Tour in South-East Asia and the Far East," 17 March 1949, CAB 129, vol. 33, PRO.

41. Minute by Graves, 23 Feb. 1949, FO 371, file 76003, PRO; State Department to Saigon, 2 Aug. 1948, RG263, Murphy papers, box 102, NA; Garner (Commonwealth Relations Office) to Dening, 25 April 1949, FO 371, file 76032, PRO; Bangkok to Foreign Office, 28 Feb. 1949, FO 371, file 76004, PRO; Dening to Syers (Commonwealth Relations Office), 18 March 1949, FO 371, file 76023, PRO; brief for Bevin's talks with MacDonald, 1 May 1949, FO 371, file 76031, PRO.

42. Minute by Lloyd, 11 June 1949, FO 371, file 76033, PRO; Bangkok to Foreign Office, 14 Dec. 1948, FO 371, file 69684, PRO.

43. British Information Services release, "Mr. Bevin at the National Press Club," 1 April 1949, FO 371, file 74184, PRO.

44. Aide-mémoire, "The Political Situation in China and the Communist Threat in South East Asia," 21 Jan. 1949, FO 371, file 76003, PRO.

45. Maux to Bollaert, 23 March 1948, Asie/Indochine, file 129, MAE; Bonnet to Foreign Ministry, 25 Feb. 1948, ibid.; Lovett to Manila, 21 Oct. 1948, RG59, PSA, reel 11, NA; Washington to Foreign Ministry, 22 Nov. 1948, Asie/Indochine, file 132, MAE; memcon, Reed with Daridan, 4 Oct. 1948, RG59, 851G.00/10-448, NA; Reed to Butterworth, 25 March 1949, RG59, PSA, reel 6, NA.

46. Bonnet to Foreign Ministry, 8 Sept. 1948, Asie/Indochine, file 255, MAE; Butterworth to Hickerson, 29 April 1948, RG59, 751G.00/4-2948, NA; "Note pour le Président: Indochine et crédits E.R.P.," 15 Sept. 1948, Asie/Indochine, file 322, MAE.

47. Summary of the Bangkok conference proceedings, "Regional Implications of the Emergence of Burma and Other Neighboring Countries as Independent States," 21–26 June 1948, RG59, PSA, reel 3, NA.

48. Saigon to State Department, 30 June, 1948, RG263, box 102, NA; paper by Abbott and Wallner for Bangkok conference, 21–26 June 1948, John W. Melby papers, Southeast Asia file, box 9, HSTL.

49. Butterworth to Hickerson, 25 May 1948, RG59, 759G.00/5-2548, NA.

50. Marshall to Caffery, 14 July 1948, *FRUS 1948*, 6:33; note by Secrétariat Général, 15 July 1948, Bidault papers, box 128, AN; Abbott to Marshall, 28

Aug. 1948, *FRUS 1948*, 6:39; Marshall to Caffery, 30 Aug. 1948, *FRUS 1948*, 6:40–41.

51. "Department of State Policy Statement on Indochina," 27 Sept. 1948, *FRUS 1948*, 6:43–49.

52. Ibid.

53. Acheson to Caffery, 25 Feb. 1949, *FRUS 1949*, 7:8–9; Caffery to Acheson, 6 March 1949, ibid., 7:9.

54. Bonnet to Foreign Ministry, 8 Sept. 1948, Asie/Indochine, file 255, MAE.

55. Bonnet to Foreign Ministry, 13 July 1948, Asie/Indochine, file 255, MAE; memcon, Caffery with Chauvel, 27 Sept. 1948, ibid. For Dutch policy, see McMahon, *Colonialism and Cold War*, esp. chap. 8.

56. Foreign Ministry to Washington, 7 Jan. 1949, Asie/Indochine, file 257, MAE; Foreign Ministry report, "Les Etats-Unis et l'Indochine Française," 20 Nov. 1948, Asie/Indochine, file 255, MAE; Bonnet to Foreign Ministry, 17 Jan. 1949, Asie/Indochine, file 257, MAE.

57. For details of these events, see Arthur J. Dommen, *The Indochinese Experience of the French and the Americans: Nationalism and Communism in Cambodia, Laos, and Vietnam* (Bloomington: University of Indiana Press, 2001), 188–189, and Rotter, *The Path to Vietnam*, 91–92.

58. Reuters dispatch, "Elephants Bow to Bao Dai to Signify Tribal Homage," *New York Times* (1 June 1949).

59. For details of the independence ceremony, see "Bao Dai Is Proclaimed as Emperor of Viet Nam," *New York Times* (15 June 1949). Hopson and Bodard, are quoted in Rotter, *The Path to Vietnam*, 92. Bodard's reminiscences come from his book *The Quicksand War: Prelude to Vietnam*, trans. Patrick O'Brian (Boston: Little Brown, 1967), 169.

60. Acheson to Abbott, 2 May 1949, *FRUS 1949*, 7:21–22; Acheson to Saigon, 10 May 1949, ibid., 7:23–25; memo by Ogburn, "Requirements for the Security of the Countries of Southeast Asia," 20 April 1949, RG59, PSA, reel 5, NA.

61. State Department draft policy statement, "Indochina," April 1949, RG59, PSA, reel 10, NA; Abbott, "Memorandum on Indochina for New Delhi Foreign Service Conference," 31 March 1949, RG59, 851G.00/3-3149, NA; Caffery to Saigon, 16 March 1949, RG59, 851G.01/3-1649, NA.

62. Office of Intelligence Research report, "Appraisal of Communist Efforts in Southeast Asia: 1948," 12 Oct. 1948, PP (DoD), 1:A50; memo by Davies, 28 Feb. 1949, RG59, PSA, reel 6, NA; Acheson to Hanoi, 20 May 1949, *FRUS 1949*, 7:29–30.

63. Paris to Foreign Office, 12 March 1949, FO 371, file 75961, PRO; Reed to Butterworth, 25 March 1949, RG59, PSA, reel 6, NA.

64. See Rotter, *The Path to Vietnam*, chap. 7.

65. ORE report 103, "The Strategic Importance of the Far East to the U.S. and the USSR," 4 May 1949, RG263, ORE Reports, box 3, NA; memo by Davies, 28 Feb. 1949, RG59, PSA, reel 6, NA.

66. Memcon, Lacy with Daridan, 10 May 1949, RG59, PSA, reel 6, NA; Caffery to State Department, 18 March 1949, RG59, 851G.00/3-1849, NA;

Washington to Foreign Ministry, 24 May 1949, Asie/Indochine, file 256, MAE; Paris to State Department, 13 May 1949, RG59, 851G.00/5-1349, NA.

67. "Note pour M. le Haut Commissaire de France en Indochine: Le communisme chinois et l'Indochine," May 1949, Asie/Indochine, file 213, MAE; Caffery to State Department, *FRUS 1949*, 7:14-15; Defense Ministry to Schuman, 9 May 1949, Asie/Indochine, file 129, MAE; Schuman to Defense Ministry, 13 May 1949, Asie/Indochine, file 129, MAE.

68. Pignon to Ministry of Overseas France, 27 May 1949, Etats-Associés, file 141, MAE; Nanking to Defense Ministry, 21 May 1949, ibid.; Schuman (New York) to Foreign Ministry, 13 April 1949, Asie/Indochine, file 256, MAE; memcon, Acheson with Schuman, 8 April 1949, RG59, PSA, reel 11, NA.

69. Hanoi to State Department, 21 March 1949, RG59, 851G.00/3-2149, NA; Paris to State Department, 16 March 1949, RG59, 851G.00/3-1649, NA; Bruce to State Department, 2 June 1949, RG59, 851G.01/6-249, NA; Foreign Ministry to High Commission, 3 June 1949, Asie/Indochine, file 56, MAE.

70. "Extrait d'une lettre de M. du Gardier," 4 April 1949, Asie/Indochine, file 132, MAE; Hanoi to State Department, 5 June 1949, RG59, 851G.00/6-549, NA; memcon, Reed with Graves, 26 April 1949, RG59, 851G.01/4-2649, NA; Gibson to State Department, 2 June 1949, RG59, 851G.00/6-249, NA.

71. "Memorandum by the Department of State to the French Foreign Office," 6 June 1949, *FRUS 1949*, 7:39-45.

72. Bruce to Acheson, 14 June 1949, *FRUS 1949*, 7:45-46; Bohlen to Acheson, 13 June 1949, RG59, 851G.00/6-1349, NA.

73. Bruce to State Department, 2 June 1949, *FRUS 1949*, 7:36-38; Bruce to State Department, 30 May 1949, ibid., 7:34-35; Bruce to State Department, 6 June 1949, RG59, 851G.00/6-649, NA; Abbott to State Department, 10 June 1949, *FRUS 1949*, 7:45.

74. For the statement, see "U.S. Backs Bao Dai's Rule," *New York Times* (22 June 1949). For Rotter's discussion of this episode, see Rotter, *The Path to Vietnam*, 97-99.

75. Stanton to State Department, 17 June 1949, *FRUS 1949*, 7:58-59.

76. Ogburn to Reed and O'Sullivan, 28 June 1949, RG59, PSA, reel 9, NA.

6. CLOSING THE CIRCLE

1. NSC-51, "A Report to the National Security Council by the Secretary of State on U.S. Policy toward Southeast Asia," 1 July 1949, RG273, NSC papers, box 7, NA.

2. Ibid.
3. Ibid.
4. Ibid.
5. Ibid.
6. ORE report, "Prospects for the Defense of Indochina against a Chinese Communist Invasion," 7 Sept. 1949, RG263, box 4, NA; Acheson to Abbott, 29 June 1949, *FRUS 1949*, 7:64. On the question of ministries, see, for example, Bruce to State Department, 13 Oct. 1949, RG59, 851G.00/10-1349, NA.

7. NSC-51, "A Report to the National Security Council by the Secretary of State on U.S. Policy toward Southeast Asia," 1 July 1949, RG273, NSC papers, box 7, NA; Bruce to Acheson, 29 June 1949, *FRUS 1949*, 7:65–66; Abbott to Acheson, 6 July 1949, RG59, 851G.01/7-549, NA.

8. Webb to Paris, 18 June 1949, RG59, 851G.00/6-1849, NA; Bruce to Acheson, 29 June 1949, *FRUS 1949*, 7:65–66.

9. Report by the Permanent Under-Secretary's Committee, "United Kingdom in South-East Asia and the Far East," 28 July 1949, FO 371, file 76030, PRO; brief for Bevin's talks with Nehru, 10 Nov. 1949, FO 371, file 76005, PRO; Foreign Office brief for Bevin, 12 Sept. 1949, FO 371, file 75969, PRO; Gibbs to Foreign Office, 9 April 1949, FO 371, file 75962, PRO.

10. Paper for Permanent Under-Secretary's Committee, "Regional Cooperation in South-East Asia and the Far East," 20 Aug. 1949, FO 371, file 76030, PRO.

11. Washington to Foreign Office, 6 Sept. 1949, FO 371, file 76033, PRO; memo by Ford (Washington), 8 Sept. 1949, FO 371, file 76005, PRO; Reed to Butterworth, 8 Sept. 1949, RG59, PSA, reel 7, NA.

12. Paper for Permanent Under-Secretary's Committee, "Regional Cooperation in South-East Asia and the Far East," 20 Aug. 1949, FO 371, file 76030, PRO.

13. Dening to MacDonald, 1 Oct. 1949, FO 371, file 76032, PRO; Franks to Foreign Office, 10 Nov. 1949, FO 371, file 75970, PRO; Scott to Hood (Paris), 9 Nov. 1949, FO 371, file 75969, PRO.

14. MacDonald to Foreign Office, 20 Dec. 1949, FO 371, file75983, PRO.

15. Memo by Ford, 8 Sept. 1949, FO 371, file 76005, PRO; 62nd Cabinet Conclusions, 27 Oct. 1949, CAB 128, vol. 16, PRO.

16. MacDonald to Dening, 2 Sept. 1949, FO 371, file 75967, PRO. For MacDonald's trip, see Massigli to Foreign Ministry, 21 Nov. 1949, Asie/Malaysie, file 15, MAE.

17. Foreign Office memo, 12 Nov. 1949, FO 371, file 75973, PRO; Bevin (Paris) to Foreign Office, 12 Nov. 1949, FO 371, file 75970, PRO.

18. Hopson to Scott, 24 May 1949, FO 371, file 75963, PRO; memo by Bevin, "South East Asia and the Far East—Conference of H.M. Representatives and Colonial Governors," 26 Nov. 1949, CAB 129, vol. 37, PRO.

19. High Commission to Commonwealth Relations Office, 13 June 1949, FO 371, file 75964, PRO; New Delhi to Dening, 1 Aug. 1949, FO 371, file 75966, PRO; Paris to Foreign Office, 15 Aug. 1949, FO 371, file 75966, PRO.

20. Acheson to New Delhi, 30 June 1949, RG59, 851G.01/6-3049, NA; Acheson to New Delhi, 5 July 1949, RG59, 851G.01/7-549, NA; Abbott to State Department, 23 Sept. 1949, RG59, 851G.01/9-2349, NA; memcon, Acheson and Nehru, 12 Oct. 1949, Acheson papers, memoranda of conversations, box 65, HSTL; memcon, Bajpai with Noel-Baker, 11 Dec. 1949, FO 371, file 76026, PRO.

21. UK high commissioner in Ceylon to Foreign Office, 13 Oct. 1949, FO 371, file 75969, PRO; State Department memo, "Problem: To determine U.S. policy in regard to proposals for an association of non-Communist Asian states," 12 Sept. 1949, RG59, PSA, reel 6, NA; memcon, Reed and Landon with Prince Wan, 21 Dec. 1949, RG59, 751G.00/12-2149, NA.

22. Reed to Jessup, 22 Aug. 1949, RG59, 851G.00/8-2249, NA; Reed to Hickman, Oct. 1949, RG59, PSA, reel 9, NA.

23. Memo for Carpentier, 30 Nov. 1949, Archives de l'Indochine/10H, box 1583, CV; "Procès-verbal de la Conférence Militaire du 15 Juin 1949," 15 June 1949, Archives de l'Indochine/10H, box 170, CV; Pignon to Letourneau, Dec. 1949, F60, box 3036, AN; Pignon to Bidault, 3 Dec. 1949, ibid.; Letourneau to Pignon, Nov. 1949, ibid.; Pignon to Ministry of Overseas France, 15 Dec. 1949, Etats-Associés, file 135, MAE; memo by Far Eastern Command, "Besoins des Forces Terrestres en Extrême-Orient en matériel américain," 21 Jan. 1950, Archives de l'Indochine/10H, box 1586, CV; "Fiche: Matériels Britanniques qui seraient necéssaires aux Forces Terrestres en Extrême-Orient," 21 Nov. 1949, Archives de l'Indochine/10H, box 144, CV.

24. "Indo-China Policy of Paris Assailed," *New York Times* (19 July 1949).

25. Foreign Ministry to multiple posts, 1 Aug. 1949, Asie/Indochine, file 209, MAE.

26. Du Gardier to Foreign Ministry, 24 Oct. 1949, Asie/Indochine, file 256, MAE; memo for Bidault, "Avis du Comité Juridique relatif au statut du Viet-Nam selon les Accords du 8 Mars 1949," 2 Nov. 1949, ibid.; Du Gardier to Baeyens, 28 July 1949, Asie/Indochine, file 209, MAE; "Reunion Interministerielle sur la Situation du Viet Nam par Rapport aux Organizations et Conventions Internationales," 26 Aug. 1949, Nations Unies et Organizations Internationales, file 110, MAE; Saigon to Foreign Ministry, 16 Nov. 1949, Asie/Indochine, file 156, MAE.

27. Pignon to Foreign Ministry, 2 July 1949, Asie/Indochine, file 377, MAE; Abbott to State Department, 5 July 1949, *FRUS 1949*, 7:67-68; Washington to Foreign Office, 19 Sept. 1949, FO 371, file 75968, PRO; Schuman to Bevin, 21 Dec. 1949, FO 371, file 83626, PRO.

28. Bevin (Paris) to Foreign Office, 12 Nov. 1949, FO 371, file 75970, PRO.

29. Bangkok to Foreign Office, 9 Sept. 1949, FO 371, file 75968, PRO.

30. "Note de M. Pignon au sujet de l'aspect politique du problème indochinoise," Dec. 1949, Asie/Dossiers Généraux, file 179, MAE; memcon, Dening and Butterworth, 14 Sept. 1949, FO 371, file 75976, PRO; State Department memo, "Indochina," 28 Sept. 1949, RG59, 851G.00/9-2849, NA.

31. Pignon to Ministry of Overseas France, 26 Nov. 1949, F60, box 3036, AN; Pignon to Ministry of Overseas France, 7 Nov. 1949, ibid.; Ashley-Clarke to Dening, 14 Oct. 1949, FO 371, file 75969, PRO.

32. Pignon to Ministry of Overseas France, 18 Oct. 1949, Asie/Indochine, file 213, MAE. Emphasis in original.

33. Pignon to Foreign Ministry, 27 Oct. 1949, Asie/Indochine, file 256, MAE; Hopson to Scott, 14 Nov. 1949, FO 959, file 33, PRO.

34. Washington to Foreign Ministry, 16 Sept. 1949, Asie/Indochine, file 256, MAE; Paris to Foreign Office, 12 Nov. 1949, FO 371, file 75970, PRO; "Note pour le Ministre," 16 Nov. 1949, Asie/Indochine, file 277, MAE; London to State Department, RG59, 851G.00/11-3049, NA; Pignon to Ministry of Overseas France, 27 Jan. 1950, Etats-Associés, file 138, MAE.

35. Pignon to Foreign Ministry, 26 Nov. 1949, Asie/Malaisie, file 15, MAE; Ashley-Clarke to Dening, 20 Oct. 1949, FO 371, file 75969, PRO.

36. Saigon to State Department, 5 Dec. 1949, RG59, 851G.00/12–549, NA; Bruce to State Department, 17 Jan. 1950, RG59, 751G.00/1–1750, NA; Foreign Office to Paris, 23 Nov. 1949, FO 371, file 75977, PRO.

37. Reuters dispatch, "Dock Halt Voted at Dunkerque," *New York Times* (21 Aug. 1949); AP dispatch "French to Strike Arms Ships," *New York Times* (30 Oct. 1949); UPI dispatch, "Marseilles Dockers Strike," *New York Times* (8 Dec. 1949); "Marseilles Strikers Clash with Police," *New York Times* (11 Jan. 1950); "French Leftists Ask Indo-China Plebiscite," *New York Times* (27 Dec. 1950).

38. MacDonald to Foreign Office, 28 Nov. 1949, FO 371, file 75977, PRO; Holmes to State Department, 5 Dec. 1949, RG59, 851G.01/12–549, NA.

39. Foreign Office to Paris, 16 Dec. 1949, PREM 8, file 1221, PRO; Massigli to McNeil, 2 Jan. 1950, PREM 8, file 1221, PRO.

40. On December 31, for example, the *New York Times* reported that London would recognize Bao Dai and Mao "concurrently." "Accord with French Gives Viet Nam Virtual Freedom," *New York Times* (31 Dec. 1949).

41. "Extracts from minutes of China and South-East Asia Committee of Cabinet," 16 Dec. 1949, PREM 8, file 1221, PRO; "Aide-mémoire," 26 Nov. 1949, Archives de l'Indochine/10H, box 144, CV; Ministry of Overseas France to Foreign Ministry, 27 Dec. 1949, Asie/Indochine, file 129, MAE.

42. Far Eastern Command to Chiefs of Staff (London), 13 Jan. 1950, FO 371, file 83648, PRO; minute by Scott, 22 Dec. 1949, FO 371, file 75990, PRO.

43. London to State Department, 9 Nov. 1949, PP (DoD), 8:223–224.

44. For Acheson's views, see, for example, Acheson testimony before Congress, 12 Oct. 1949, RG59, PSA, reel 11, NA.

45. Memcon, Reed with Graves, 28 Nov. 1949, RG59, 851G.01/11–2849, NA.

46. Bruce to State Department, 11 Dec. 1949, RG59, 851G.00/12–1149, NA.

47. Butterworth to Fosdick, 17 Nov. 1949, RG59, 751G.00/11–1749, NA; Acheson to Bangkok, 23 Dec. 1949, RG59, 851G.01/12–2349, NA.

48. Gibson to State Department, 19 Nov. 1949, 851G.00B/11–1949, NA; PPS memo, "East and South Asia," 6 June 1950, RG59, lot 64D563, Records of the Policy Planning Staff, box 26, NA.

49. Kennan to Robert G. Hooker, 17 Oct. 1949, RG59, lot file 1, Acheson Undersecretary file, box 9, NA; Abbott to Folsom, 17 Dec. 1949, RG59, 751G.00/12–1749, NA.

50. Bruce to State Department, 22 Dec. 1949, RG59, 851G.00/12–2249, NA.

51. NSC-48/1, "A Report to the President by the National Security Council on the Position of the United States with Respect to Asia," 30 Dec. 1949, PP (DoD), 8:265–272.

52. Abbott to State Department, 27 Dec. 1949, RG59, 851G.01/12–2749, NA.

53. Paris to Foreign Office, 2 Feb. 1950, FO 371, file 83599, PRO.

54. Foreign Ministry to Ministry of Overseas France, 25 Jan. 1950, Asie/Indochine, file 209, MAE; Paris to Foreign Office, 25 Jan. 1950, FO 371, file 83599, PRO.

55. Note by Division d'Asie-Océanie, "Attitude des principales puissances vis-à-vis du gouvernement vietnamien," 14 Jan. 1950, Asie/Indochine, file 205, MAE; note for Bao Dai, 27 Jan. 1950, FO 371, file 83599, PRO; Gibbs to Foreign Office, 3 Feb. 1950, FO 371, file 83599, PRO.

56. Zhai, *China and the Vietnam Wars*, 13–16; Chen Jian, *Mao's China and the Cold War*, 120–121.

57. Zhai, *China and the Vietnam Wars*, 15; Acheson press statement, 1 Feb. 1950, FO 371, file 83604, PRO; "U.S. Recognizes Viet Nam, Two Other Indo-China States," *New York Times* (8 Feb. 1950).

58. Foreign Ministry to Washington, 13 Feb. 1950, Asie/Indochine, file 257, MAE.

59. Pleven to Schuman, 20 Feb. 1950, Archives de l'Indochine/10H, box 1586, CV; Reed (Paris) to ECA Administrator, 18 Feb. 1950, RG59, Griffin Mission, box 5, NA; circular by Division d'Amérique, 28 Feb. 1950, file 129, MAE.

60. "Note pour le Ministre de la Défense Nationale," 3 Feb. 1950, Asie/Indochine, file 257, MAE; "Note pour le Ministre: Aide Américaine à l'Indochine," 13 Feb. 1950, Etats-Associés, file 135, MAE; Carpentier to Bidault, 24 Feb. 1950, Archives de l'Indochine/10H, box 172, CV; Bonnet to Foreign Ministry, 16 Feb. 1950, Asie/Indochine, file 257, MAE; Bonnet to Foreign Ministry, 22 March 1950, Asie/Indochine, file 257, MAE; Foreign Ministry to Ministry of Overseas France, 27 March 1950, Asie/Indochine, file 56, MAE; "Entretien entre M. Jessup et M. Schuman," 13 March 1950, Asie/Indochine, file 257, MAE.

61. Bonnet to Schuman, "Du sentiment anticolonial américain appliqué à l'Extrême Orient," 22 March 1950, Amérique, file 106, MAE.

62. Pignon to Ministry of Overseas France, 28 March 1950, Asie/Indochine, file 214, MAE; Massigli to Parodi, 16 March 1950, Massigli papers, file 101, MAE.

63. Dening to Strang, 3 May 1950, FO 371, file 83013, PRO; Graves to Gibbs, 2 May 1950, FO 371, file 83645, PRO.

64. Minutes of 35th Chiefs of Staff meeting, 6 March 1950, FO 371, file 83648, PRO; Scott to Price, 30 March 1950, ibid.; brief for Bevin's talks with Schuman, 6 March 1950, FO 371, file 83600, PRO.

65. "Note pour le Secrétaire Général," 10 March 1950, Asie/Indochine, file 209, MAE; Washington to Foreign Office, 21 Feb. 1950, FO 371, file 83655, PRO.

66. Bonnet to Schuman, 11 April 1950, Asie/Indochine, file 262, MAE; memo by Jessup et al., "Interviews with French Officials," 13 March 1950, RG59, 751G.00/3-1450, NA; Saigon to State Department, 30 March 1950, RG59, 751G.00/3-3050, NA; Paris to Foreign Office, 4 May 1950, FO 371, file 83651, PRO.

67. Paris to Foreign Ministry, 21 Feb. 1950, FO 371, file 83655, PRO; Paris to Foreign Office, 23 Feb. 1950, ibid.; Massigli to Foreign Office, 4 March 1950, Asie/Indochine, file 257, MAE.

68. Paris to Foreign Office, 21 Feb. 1950, FO 371, file 83655, PRO; Pignon to Ministry of Overseas France, 18 March 1950, Asie/Indochine, file 257, MAE; Paris to Foreign Office, 3 May 1950, FO 371, file 83655, PRO.

69. State Department memo, "Depletion of the French Army in Indo-China," 6 April 1950, RG59, PSA, reel 9, NA; Lacy to Rusk, 30 March 1950, RG59, PSA, reel 8, NA; Paris to Foreign Office, 21 Feb. 1950, FO 371, file 83655, PRO; "Meeting of the Griffin Mission Held at USIS Offices," 7 March 1950, RG59, lot file M-46, ESMSA records, box 5, NA; "National Security Council Progress Report by the Under Secretary of State on the Implementation of 'The Position of the United States with Respect to Asia,'" 27 Feb. 1950, RG273, box 6, NA; Truman to Acheson, 10 March 1950, White House Central File, box 25, HSTL.

70. Acheson to Bruce, 7 March 1950, RG59, PSA, reel 9, NA; Griffin to State Department, 16 March 1950, RG59, lot file M-46, ESMSA records, box 5, NA.

71. Saigon to Foreign Office, 27 Feb. 1950, FO 371, file 83658, PRO; Acheson to Saigon, 7 March 1950, RG59, 851G.00/3-750, NA; Acheson to Saigon, 16 Feb. 1950, RG59, 751G.00/2-1550, NA; Acheson to Saigon, 31 March 1950, RG59, 751G.00/3-3150, NA; Foreign Ministry to Pignon, 14 Feb. 1950, Amérique, file 129, MAE; Bonnet to Foreign Ministry, 23 Feb. 1950, Asie/Indochine, file 163, MAE.

72. Memo by Carpentier, "Sur les conditions de délais et la mise sur pied des Forces des Etats Associés compte tenu de l'aide américaine," 1 June 1949, Archives de l'Indochine/10H, box 171, CV; "Note pour le Ministre," 16 June 1949, Asie/Indochine, file 256, MAE; memo by Ministry of Overseas France, "Aide mémoire à l'usage de M. le Ministre des Affaires Etrangères sur la situation à la frontière sino-tonkinoise," 9 Nov. 1949, Asie/Indochine, file 277, MAE.

73. Foreign Ministry memo, "Conséquences de la Ratification des Accords du 8 Mars sur le Plan Economique," March 1950, Asie/Indochine, file 262, MAE.

74. Griffin to State Department, 25 March 1950, RG59, lot file M-46, ESMSA records, box 5, NA; Saigon to State Department, 15 April 1950, RG59, 751G.00/4-1550, NA; Carpentier to Bidault, 24 Feb. 1950, Archives de l'Indochine/10H, box 172, CV.

75. Acheson to Paris, no date, RG59, lot file M-46, ESMSA records, box 5, NA; Griffin Mission memo, "Final Meeting between the Griffin Mission and the Representatives of the French High Commission," 15 March 1950, ibid.

76. Bonnet to Foreign Ministry, 13 March 1950, Asie/Indochine, file 257, MAE.

77. Scott to Graves, 26 April 1950, FO 371, file 83644, PRO; Bonnet to Foreign Ministry, 12 April 1950, Asie/Indochine, file 262, MAE.

78. Memo by Service de Coopération Economique, "Aide économique à l'Indochine," April 1950, Asie/Indochine, file 262, MAE; Foreign Ministry to Washington, 1 April 1950, Asie/Indochine, file 258, MAE; Foreign Ministry to Washington, 1 April 1950, ibid.

79. Gibaut to Baeyens, 21 April 1950, Asie/Dossiers Généraux, file 179, MAE; memo by Division d'Asie-Océanie, "Le problème d'Indochine et la Conférence de Londres," 3 May 1950, ibid.

80. Cabinet memo, "Note relative à la création d'Armées Nationales en Indochine," 5 May 1950, F60, box 3038, AN; Foreign Ministry memo, "Le problème d'Indochine et la Conférence de Londres," 3 May 1950, Asie/Dossiers Généraux, file 179, MAE; Foreign Ministry memo, "Fiche au sujet de l'Indochine," April 1950, Secrétaire Général, vol. 8/Conférence Tripartite de Londres, MAE; London to Foreign Ministry, 2 May 1950, MAE.

81. Foreign Ministry memo, "Le problème d'Indochine et la Conférence de Londres," 3 May 1950, Asie/Dossiers Généraux, file 179, MAE; "Note pour le Secrétaire Général," 22 April 1950, Secrétaire Général, vol. 8/Conférence Tripartite de Londres, MAE; "Note pour le Secrétariat des Conférences: Analyse succincte de la Politique Gouvernementale et de la Reglementation Relative aux Investissements de Capitaux Etrangers Privés dans l'Union Française," May 1950, Nations Unies et Organisations Internationales, file 110, MAE; minutes, "Réunion tenue à l'Ambassade de France," 29 April 1950, Secrétaire Général, vol. 8/Conférence Tripartite de Londres, MAE; "Compte-Rendu de la 5ème réunion des Ministres," 13 May 1950, ibid.

82. Foreign Ministry memo, "Conversations Franco-Américaines," 8 May 1950, Asie/Indochine, file 258, MAE; memo by Bevin, "Conversations with Mr. Acheson on 9th and 10th May," 19 May 1950, CAB 129, vol. 40, PRO.

83. Report by State Department's Policy Information Committee, "Weekly Review," 10 May 1950, White House Central File, box 59, HSTL; excerpts from Schuman's news conference, 15 May 1950, Asie/Indochine, file 278, MAE.

84. Harding to Carpentier, 6 May 1950, FO 959, file 56, PRO; Foreign Ministers' Conference memo, "Minute No. 1," Asie/Indochine, file 278, MAE; Massigli to Foreign Ministry, 3 May 1950, Asie/Indochine, file 278, MAE; "Compte-Rendu de la 5ème réunion des Ministres," 13 May 1950, Secrétaire Général, vol. 8/Conférence Tripartite de Londres, MAE.

CONCLUSION

1. Ronald H. Spector, *Advice and Support: The Early Years of the U.S. Army in Vietnam, 1941–1960* (New York: Free Press, 1985), 115–116.

2. Herring, *America's Longest War*, 21.

3. NSC 64/1, "A Report to the National Security Council by the Secretary of Defense on the Position of the United States with Respect to Indochina," 21 Dec. 1950, RG263, box 8, NA.

4. 4ème bureau memo, "Renseignements statistiques concernants l'aide U.S.," 31 May 1953, Archives de l'Indochine/10H, box 1585, CV; 4ème bureau memo, "Aide Américaine," Sept. 1953, ibid. Estimates vary slightly in other sources. See, for example, Spector, *Advice and Support*, 167–168.

5. Zhai, *China and the Vietnam Wars*, 19–38.

6. For military analysis, see especially Bernard Fall's classic, *Street without Joy*.

7. David Anderson, *Trapped by Success: The Eisenhower Administration and Vietnam, 1953–1961* (New York: Columbia University Press, 1991), 46.

8. For the 1950–1954 period, see Anderson, *Trapped by Success;* James R. Arnold, *The First Domino: Eisenhower, the Military, and America's Intervention in Vietnam* (New York: William Morrow, 1991); Melanie Billings-Yan, *Decision against War: Eisenhower and Dien Bien Phu, 1954* (New York: Columbia University Press, 1988); Duiker, *The Communist Road to Power in Vietnam,* chap. 7; Kathryn Statler, "From the French to the Americans: Intra-Alliance Politics, Cold War Concerns, and Cultural Conflict in Vietnam, 1950–1960" (Ph.D. diss., University of California, Santa Barbara, 1999); and Zhai, *China and the Vietnam Wars,* chaps. 1–2.

9. Anderson, *Trapped by Success,* 18.

10. For a guide to this vast scholarship, see Herring, *America's Longest War,* 322–340.

11. See Dallek, *John F. Kennedy;* Jones, *Death of a Generation;* Kaiser, *American Tragedy;* and especially Logevall, *Choosing War.*

12. Robert S. McNamara et al., *Argument without End: In Search of Answers to the Vietnam Tragedy* (New York: PublicAffairs, 1999), 47–48, 81.

13. Robert Latham, *The Liberal Moment: Modernity, Security, and the Making of the Postwar International Order* (New York: Columbia University Press, 1997).

14. For an important exception, see Leslie Bethell and Ian Roxborough, eds., *Latin America between the Second World War and the Cold War, 1944–1948* (Cambridge: Cambridge University Press, 1992), esp. 1–32. For other discussion of this period of flux, see especially McMahon, *Colonialism and Cold War.*

15. Quoted in Herring, *America's Longest War,* 22.

16. Arnold, *The First Domino,* 120.

17. "Récapitulation de la valeur du matériel pouvant être compris par le Gouvernement Britannique dans une aide gratuite," 15 Jan. 1953, Asie/Indochine, file 275, MAE.

18. Minutes of Foreign Office meeting, 4 Nov. 1950, FO 371, file 83630, PRO; "Brief for Attlee's Meeting with Pleven and Schuman," 1 Dec. 1950, ibid.

Bibliography

PRIMARY SOURCES

FRANCE

Archives Nationales, Paris
Série F60 (Archives du Président du Conseil)

Dépôt des Archives d'Outre Mer, Aix-en-Provence
Fonds Haut-Commissariat de France en Indochine
Fonds cabinet
    Fonds conseiller diplomatique
    Fonds conseiller economique
    Fonds conseiller politique
Indochine Nouveau Fonds

Archives du Ministère des Affaires Etrangères, Paris
Amérique, 1944–1952 (série)
    Etats-Unis (sous-série)
Asie, 1944–1955
    Dossiers Généraux
    Birmanie
    Ceylon
    Chine
    Inde
    Indochine

Malaisie
　　　Pacifique Sud
　　　Thaïland
　Cabinet du Ministre
　　　Cabinet George Bidault, 1944–1948
　　　Cabinet Robert Schuman, 1948–1953
　Europe, 1944–1960
　　　Grande-Bretagne
　　　Pays-Bas
　　　Portugal
　Etats-Associés, 1945–1957
　Guerre, 1939–1945, Londres-Alger
　　　Chine
　　　Etats-Unis
　　　Grande-Bretagne
　　　Indochine
　　　Japon
　　　Pays-Bas
　Nations Unies et Organisations Internationales
　Secrétaire Général
　Y-International, 1944–1949

Service Historique de l'Armée de Terre, Chateau de Vincennes, Paris
Série 10H, Guerre de l'Indochine
Série Q, Sous-série 4, Etat-Major Général de la Défense Nationale
Série T, Etat-Major de l'Armée de Terre

Personal Papers
Bidault, Georges (Achives Nationales)
Bollaert, Emile (Archives d'Outre Mer)
Bonnet, Henri (Ministère des Affaires Etrangères)
Massigli, René (Ministère des Affaires Etrangères)
Moutet, Marius (Archives d'Outre Mer)
Pereyra, Miguel Joaquim de (Archives d'Outre Mer)
Pignon, Léon (Archives d'Outre Mer)
Pleven, René (Archives Nationales)
Schuman, Robert (Ministère des Affaires Etrangères)

GREAT BRITAIN

Oriental and India Office Collections, British Library, London
Burma Office Records, 1932–1948
   M/4: Frontier and Foreign
India Office Records, 1880–1947
   L/P&S/12
   L/P&S/18
Military Department Records, 1708–1957
   L/Mil
   L/WS

Public Record Office, Kew
Cabinet Office Records
   CAB 65, War Cabinet Conclusions, 1944–1945
   CAB 66, War Cabinet Memoranda, 1944–1945
   CAB 128, Cabinet Conclusions, 1945–1950
   CAB 129, Cabinet Memoranda, 1945–1950
Colonial Office Records
   CO 852, Colonial Office, Economic Policy Correspondence
   CO 875, Colonial Office, Public Relations Department
Foreign Office Records
   FO 371, Foreign Office, General Correspondence
   FO 959, Consular files, French Indochina
   FO 1091, Commissioner-General's files, Singapore
Prime Minister's Office Records
   PREM 8, Correspondence and Papers, 1945–1951
War Office Records
   WO 203, South East Asia Command, 1943–1946

Rhodes House Library, Oxford University
Papers of the Fabian Colonial Bureau

Personal papers
Bevin, Ernest (Public Record Office)
Gracey, Douglas (Liddell Hart Centre for Military Archives, King's College, London)
Jones, Arthur Creech (Rhodes House Library, Oxford University)

UNITED STATES

Harry S. Truman Library, Independence, Mo.
Clayton-Thorpe File
Official File
Oral Histories
President's Secretary's File
Psychological Strategy Board Files
Records of the National Security Council
Rose Conway File
White House Central File

National Archives and Records Administration, College Park, Md.
Record Group 59, Records of the Department of State
    Central Decimal File
    Office of Intelligence Research Reports
    Lot File 1, Acheson Files
    Lot File 54D190, Philippine and Southeast Asia Division, 1944–1952
    Lot File 64D563, Policy Planning Staff
    Lot File M-46, Economic Survey Mission to Southeast Asia
Record Group 169, Records of the Foreign Economic Administration
    Files of the Bureau of Areas, European Branch, French Division
    Geographic File of the Administrator
Record Group 218, Records of the Joint Chiefs of Staff
    Geographic Files
Record Group 226, Records of the Office of Strategic Services
    Intelligence Reports, 1941–1945
Record Group 263, Records of the Central Intelligence Agency
    Estimates of the Office of Research Evaluation, 1946–1950
    Murphy Collection on International Communism, 1917–1958
Record Group 273, Records of the National Security Council
    Meeting Minutes
    Policy Papers

Personal Papers
Acheson, Dean (Yale University, Truman Library)
Byrnes, James (Strom Thurmond Institute, Clemson University)

Connelly, Matthew J. (Truman Library)
Elsey, George M. (Truman Library)
Grew, James (Harvard University)
Leahy, William (Library of Congress)
Melby, John W. (Truman Library)
Patterson, Robert (Library of Congress)

PUBLISHED DOCUMENT COLLECTIONS

Assemblée Nationale. *Journal Officiel de la République Française: Debats Parlementaires*. Paris: editions for 1946–1950.
Devillers, Philippe, ed. *Paris, Saigon, Hanoi: Les archives de la guerre, 1944–1947*. Paris: Editions Gallimard/Julliard, 1988.
Gettleman, Marvin E., et al., eds. *Vietnam and America: A Documented History*. New York: Grove Press, 1985.
Porter, Gareth, ed. *Vietnam: A History in Documents*. New York: New American Library, 1979.
———, ed. *Vietnam: The Definitive Documentation of Human Decisions*. Vol. 1, *The First Indochina War and the Geneva Agreements, 1941–1955*. Stanfordville, N.Y.: Coleman Enterprises, 1979.
United Kingdom. *Parliamentary Debates*. Commons, 5th ser., various vols. London: His Majesty's Stationery Office, 1945, 1947–1948.
U.S. Congress. Senate. Committee on Foreign Relations. *The United States and Vietnam, 1944–1947: A Staff Study Based on the Pentagon Papers*. 92d Cong., 2d sess. Washington, D.C.: U.S. Government Printing Office, 1972.
U.S. Department of Defense. *United States–Vietnam Relations, 1945–1967: Study Prepared by the Department of Defense*. 12 vols. Washington, D.C.: U.S. Government Printing Office, 1971.
U.S. Department of State. *Foreign Relations of the United States*. Washington, D.C.: U.S. Government Printing Office, volumes for 1944–1950.
Williams, William Appleman, et al., eds. *America in Vietnam: A Documentary History*. New York: Norton, 1975.

NEWSPAPERS

L'Aube (Paris)
L'Humanité (Paris)
Manchester Guardian
The Nation (New York)
New York Times
The Times (London)
Washington Post

SECONDARY SOURCES AND PUBLISHED MEMOIRS

Acheson, Dean. *Present at the Creation: My Years in the State Department.* New York: Norton, 1969.
Ageron, Charles-Robert. *La décolonisation française.* Paris: Armand Colin, 1991.
———. *France coloniale ou parti colonial?* Paris: Presses Universitaires de France, 1978.
Agulhon, Maurice. *La République.* Paris: Hatchette, 1990.
Anderson, David L. *Trapped by Success: The Eisenhower Administration and Vietnam, 1953–1961.* New York: Columbia University Press, 1991.
Arnold, James R. *The First Domino: Eisenhower, the Military, and America's Intervention in Vietnam.* New York: William Morrow, 1991.
Attlee, Clement. *As It Happened.* London: Heinemann, 1954.
Bao Dai. *Le dragon d'Annam.* Paris: Plon, 1980.
Barnett, Correlli. *The Collapse of British Power.* London: Eyre Methuen, 1972.
Bethell, Leslie, and Ian Roxborough, eds. *Latin America between the Second World War and the Cold War, 1944–1948.* Cambridge: Cambridge University Press, 1992.
Bidault, Georges. *D'une résistance à l'autre.* Paris: Presses du Siècle, 1965.
Billings-Yan, Melanie. *Decision against War: Eisenhower and Dien Bien Phu, 1954.* New York: Columbia University Press, 1988.
Bills, Scott A. *Empire and Cold War: The Roots of U.S.–Third World Antagonism, 1945–1947.* New York: St. Martin's Press, 1990.
Blum, Robert M. *Drawing the Line: The Origin of the American Containment Policy in East Asia.* New York: Norton, 1982.
Bodard, Lucien. *La guerre d'Indochine: l'Enlisement.* Paris: Gallimard, 1963.
———. *The Quicksand War: Prelude to Vietnam.* Translated by Patrick O'Brian. Boston: Little, Brown, 1967.
Borden, William S. *The Pacific Alliance: United States Foreign Economic Policy and Japanese Trade Recovery, 1947–1955.* Madison: University of Wisconsin Press, 1984.
Borg, Dorthy, and Waldo Heinrichs, eds. *Uncertain Years: Chinese-American Relations, 1947–1950.* New York: Columbia University Press, 1980.
Bradley, Mark P. *Imagining Vietnam and America: The Making of Postcolonial Vietnam.* Chapel Hill: University of North Carolina Press, 2000.
Brands, H. W. *The Specter of Neutralism: The United States and the Emergence of the Third World.* New York: Columbia University Press, 1989.
Bullock, Alan. *Ernest Bevin: Foreign Secretary, 1945–1951.* New York: Norton, 1983.
Cesari, Laurent. "The Declining Value of Indochina: France and the Economics of Empire, 1950–1955." In Lawrence and Logevall, *The First Vietnam War.*
Chang, Gordon H. *Friends and Enemies: The United States, China, and the Soviet Union, 1948–1972.* Stanford: Stanford University Press, 1990.
Chen Jian. *Mao's China and the Cold War.* Chapel Hill: University of North Carolina Press, 2001.
Cohen, Warren I. *America's Response to China: A History of Sino-American Relations.* 4th ed. New York: Columbia University Press, 2000.

Colbert, Evelyn. "The Road Not Taken: Decolonization and Independence in Indonesia and Indochina." *Foreign Affairs* 51 (1973): 608–628.

Costigliola, Frank. *France and the United States: The Cold Alliance since World War II.* New York: Twayne, 1992.

Cullather, Nick. *Illusions of Influence: The Political Economy of United States–Philippines Relations, 1942–1960.* Stanford: Stanford University Press, 1994.

Dallek, Robert. *Franklin D. Roosevelt and American Foreign Policy, 1932–1945.* New York: Oxford University Press, 1979.

———. *An Unfinished Life: John F. Kennedy, 1917–1963.* Boston: Little, Brown, 2003.

Dalloz, Jacques. *La guerre d'Indochine, 1945–1954.* Paris: Editions du Seuil, 1987.

de Folin, Jacques. *Indochine, 1940–1955: La fin d'un rêve.* Paris: Perrin, 1993.

de Gaulle, Charles. *Discours et messages: Pendant la guerre, 1940–1946.* Paris: Plon, 1970.

———. *The War Memoirs of Charles de Gaulle: Salvation, 1944–1946.* Translated by Richard Howard. New York: Simon and Schuster, 1960.

Devillers, Philippe. *Histoire du Viêt-Nam de 1940 à 1952.* Paris: Editions du Seuil, 1952.

Dommen, Arthur J. *The Indochina Experience of the French and the Americans: Nationalism and Communism in Cambodia, Laos, and Vietnam.* Bloomington: Indian University Press, 2001.

Drachman, Edward R. *United States Policy toward Vietnam, 1940–1945.* Rutherford, N.J.: Fairleigh Dickinson University Press, 1970.

Dreifort, John E. "Japan's Advance into Indochina, 1940: The French Response." *Journal of Southeast Asian Studies* 13 (September 1982): 279–295.

Duiker, William J. *The Communist Road to Power in Vietnam.* 2d ed. Boulder: Westview Press, 1996.

———. *Ho Chi Minh: A Life.* New York: Hyperion, 2000.

———. *U.S. Containment Policy and the Conflict in Indochina.* Stanford: Stanford University Press, 1994.

Dunn, Peter M. *The First Vietnam War.* New York: St. Martin's, 1985.

Edmonds, Robin. *Setting the Mould: The United States and Britain, 1945–1950.* New York: Norton, 1986.

Elgey, Georgette. *La république des illusions, 1945–1951, ou la secrète de la IVe République.* Paris: Fayard, 1965.

Fall, Bernard B. *Street without Joy.* New York: Schocken Books, 1972.

Fifield, Russell H. *Americans in Southeast Asia: The Roots of Commitment.* New York: Crowell, 1973.

Fineman, Daniel. *A Special Relationship: The United States and Military Government in Thailand, 1947–1958.* Honolulu: University of Hawaii Press, 1997.

FitzGerald, Frances. *Fire in the Lake: The Vietnamese and the Americans in Vietnam.* Boston: Little, Brown, 1972.

Fleury, Georges. *La guerre de l'Indochine, 1945–1954.* Paris: Plon, 1994.

Franchini, Philippe. *Les Guerres d'Indochine.* Paris: Pygmalion, 1988.

Gaddis, John Lewis. "New Conceptual Approaches to the Study of American Foreign Relations: Interdisciplinary Perspectives." *Diplomatic History* 14 (summer 1990): 403–425.
———. *The United States and the Origins of the Cold War, 1941–1947*. New York: Columbia University Press, 1972.
———. *We Now Know: Rethinking Cold War History*. New York: Oxford University Press, 1997.
Gardner, Lloyd C. *Approaching Vietnam: From World War II through Dienbienphu*. New York: Norton, 1988.
Gelb, Leslie H., with Richard K. Betts. *The Irony of Vietnam: The System Worked*. Washington, D.C.: Brookings Institution, 1979.
Georges, Alfred. *Charles de Gaulle et la guerre d'Indochine*. Paris: Nouvelles Editions Latines, 1974.
Gibbons, William Conrad. *The U.S. Government and the Vietnam War: Executive and Legislative Roles and Relationships, Part I: 1945–1960*. Princeton: Princeton University Press, 1986.
Gibbs, David N. *The Political Economy of Third World Intervention: Mines, Money, and U.S. Policy in the Congo Crisis*. Chicago: University of Chicago Press, 1991.
Giles, Frank. *The Locust Years: The Story of the Fourth French Republic, 1946–1958*. New York: Carroll and Graf, 1991.
Gillen, Michael. "The Roots of Opposition: The Critical Response to U.S. Indochina Policy, 1945–1954." Ph.D. diss., New York University, 1991.
Goscha, Christopher E. "Belated Asian Allies: The Technical and Military Contributions of Japanese Deserters, 1945–1950." In Marilyn B. Young and Robert Buzzanco, eds., *A Companion to the Vietnam War*, 37–64. Malden, Mass.: Blackwell, 2002.
———. *Thailand and the Southeast Asian Networks of the Vietnamese Revolution*. London: Curzon, 1999.
Gras, Yves. *Histoire de la guerre d'Indochine*. Paris: Plon, 1979.
Hammer, Ellen J. *The Struggle for Indochina*. Stanford: Stanford University Press, 1954.
Herring, George C. *America's Longest War: The United States and Vietnam, 1950–1975*. 4th ed. New York: McGraw-Hill, 2002.
———. "The Truman Administration and the Restoration of French Sovereignty in Indochina." *Diplomatic History* 1, no. 2 (spring 1977): 97–117.
Hess, Gary R. "The First American Commitment in Indochina: The Acceptance of the 'Bao Dai Solution,' 1950." *Diplomatic History* 2 (1978): 331–350.
———. "Franklin Roosevelt and Indochina." *Journal of American History* 59 (September 1972): 353–368.
———. *The United States' Emergence as a Southeast Asian Power, 1940–1950*. New York: Columbia University Press, 1987.
———. "United States Policy and the Origins of the French–Viet Minh War, 1945–46." *Peace and Change* 3, nos. 2 & 3 (summer–fall 1975): 21–33.
Hill, John S. "American Efforts to Aid French Reconstruction between Lend-Lease and the Marshall Plan." *Journal of Modern History* 64 (September 1992): 500–524.

Hitchcock, William I. *France Restored: Cold War Diplomacy and the Quest for Leadership in Europe, 1944–1954*. Chapel Hill: University of North Carolina Press, 1998.
Ho Chi Minh. *Ho Chi Minh: Selected Articles and Speeches, 1920–1967*. Edited and translated by Jack Woddis. New York: International Publishers, 1969.
Hogan, Michael J. *A Cross of Iron: Harry S. Truman and the Origins of the National Security State, 1945–1954*. New York: Cambridge University Press, 1998.
Hull, Cordell. *The Memoirs of Cordell Hull*. Vol. 2. New York: Macmillan, 1948.
Hunt, Michael H. *Ideology and U.S. Foreign Policy*. New Haven: Yale University Press, 1987.
Hurstfield, Julian G. *America and the French Nation, 1939–1945*. Chapel Hill: University of North Carolina Press, 1986.
Huynh Kim Khanh. *Vietnamese Communism, 1925–1945*. Ithaca: Cornell University Press, 1982.
Iriye, Akira. *The Cold War in Asia: A Historical Introduction*. Englewood Cliffs, N.J.: Prentice Hall, 1974.
Irving, R. E. M. *The First Indochina War: French and American Policy, 1945–1954*. London: Croom Helm, 1975.
Jennings, Eric T. *Vichy in the Tropics: Pétain's National Revolution in Madagascar, Guadeloupe, and Indochina, 1940–1944*. Stanford: Stanford University Press, 2001.
Jones, Howard. *Death of a Generation: How the Assassinations of Diem and JFK Prolonged the Vietnam War*. New York: Oxford University Press, 2003.
Kahin, George McT. *Intervention: How America Became Involved in Vietnam*. New York: Anchor Books, 1986.
Kahn, E. J., Jr. *The China Hands: America's Foreign Service Officers and What Befell Them*. New York: Viking, 1972.
Kaiser, David. *American Tragedy: Kennedy, Johnson, and the Origins of the Vietnam War*. Cambridge, Mass.: Harvard University Press, Belknap, 2000.
Karnow, Stanley. *Vietnam: A History*. Revised ed. New York: Penguin, 1991.
Kolko, Gabriel. *Anatomy of a War: Vietnam, the United States, and the Modern Historical Experience*. New York: Pantheon, 1985.
———. *Confronting the Third World: United States Foreign Policy, 1945–1980*. New York: Pantheon, 1988.
———. *The Politics of War: The World and United States Foreign Policy, 1943–1945*. New York: Pantheon, 1968.
———. *The Roots of American Foreign Policy: An Analysis of Power and Purpose*. Boston: Beacon, 1969.
Kolko, Joyce, and Gabriel Kolko. *The Limits of Power: The World and United States Foreign Policy, 1945–1954*. New York: Harper and Row, 1972.
Kuisel, Richard F. *Seducing the French: The Dilemma of Americanization*. Berkeley and Los Angeles: University of California Press, 1993.
Lacouture, Jean. *De Gaulle: The Ruler, 1945–1970*. Translated by Alan Sheridan. New York: Norton, 1993.
LaFeber, Walter. "Roosevelt, Churchill, and Indochina, 1942–1945." *American Historical Review* 80 (December 1975): 1277–1295.

Latham, Robert. *The Liberal Moment: Modernity, Security, and the Making of the Postwar International Order.* New York: Columbia University Press, 1997.

Lawrence, Mark Atwood. "Selling Vietnam: The European Colonial Powers and the Origins of the U.S. Commitment to Indochina, 1944–1950." Ph.D. diss., Yale University, 1999.

———. "Transnational Coalition-Building and the Making of the Cold War in Indochina, 1947–1949." *Diplomatic History* 26 (summer 2002): 453–480.

Lawrence, Mark, and Fredrik Logevall, eds. *The First Vietnam War.* Cambridge, Mass.: Harvard University Press, forthcoming.

Leffler, Melvyn P. *A Preponderance of Power: National Security, the Truman Administration, and the Cold War.* Stanford: Stanford University Press, 1992.

Leffler, Melvyn P., and David S. Painter, eds. *Origins of the Cold War: An International History.* London: Routledge, 1994.

Logevall, Fredrik. *Choosing War: The Lost Chance for Peace and the Escalation of War in Vietnam.* Berkeley and Los Angeles: University of California Press, 1999.

Louis, William Roger. *Imperialism at Bay: The United States and the Decolonization of the British Empire, 1941–1945.* New York: Oxford University Press, 1978.

Lundestad, Geir. "Empire by Invitation? The United States and Western Europe, 1945–1952." In Charles S. Maier, ed., *The Cold War in Europe: Era of a Divided Continent.* New York: Markus Wiener, 1991.

Madjarian, Grégoire. *La question coloniale et la politique du Parti communiste français, 1944–1947: Crise de l'impérialisme et mouvement ouvrier.* Paris: Librairie François Maspero, 1977.

Maison Rouge, Olivier de. *La guerre d'Indochine, 1945–1954.* Paris: La Bruyère, 1989.

Mann, Robert. *A Grand Delusion: America's Descent into Vietnam.* New York: Basic Books, 2001.

Marr, David G. *Vietnam, 1945: The Quest for Power.* Berkeley and Los Angeles: University of California Press, 1995.

———. *Vietnamese Tradition on Trial, 1920–1945.* Berkeley and Los Angeles: University of California Press, 1981.

Marshall, D. Bruce. *The French Colonial Myth and Constitution-Making in the Fourth Republic.* New Haven: Yale University Press, 1973.

Maurer, Henry. *Strange Ground: Americans in Vietnam, 1945–1975: An Oral History.* New York: Henry Holt, 1989.

McClellan, David S. *Dean Acheson: The State Department Years.* New York: Dodd, Mead, 1976.

McCormick, Thomas J. *America's Half-Century: United States Foreign Policy in the Cold War.* 2d ed. Baltimore: Johns Hopkins University Press, 1995.

McDougal, Walter L. *Promised Land, Crusader State: The American Encounter with the World since 1776.* New York: Houghton Mifflin, 1997.

McMahon, Robert J. "Anglo-American Diplomacy and the Reoccupation of the Netherlands East Indies." *Diplomatic History* 2 (1978): 1–23.

———. "The Cold War in Asia: Toward a New Synthesis?" *Diplomatic History* 12 (1988): 307–327.

———. *Colonialism and Cold War: The United States and the Struggle for Indonesian Independence, 1945–1949*. Ithaca: Cornell University Press, 1981.

———. *The Limits of Empire: The United States and Southeast Asia since World War II*. New York: Columbia University Press, 1999.

———. "The Study of American Foreign Relations: National History or International History?" in Michael J. Hogan and Thomas G. Paterson, eds., *Explaining the History of American Foreign Relations*, 11–23. New York: Cambridge University Press, 1991.

McNamara, Robert S., et al. *Argument without End: In Search of Answers to the Vietnam Tragedy*. New York: PublicAffairs, 1999.

———. *In Retrospect: The Tragedy and Lessons of Vietnam*. New York: Times Books, 1995.

Melby, John F. "Vietnam—1950." *Diplomatic History* 6 (winter 1982): 97–109.

Miller, Robert Hopkins. *The United States and Vietnam, 1787–1941*. Washington, D.C.: National Defense University Press, 1990.

Morgan, Kenneth O. *Labour in Power, 1945–1951*. New York: Oxford University Press, 1984.

Morley, James William, ed. *The Fateful Choice: Japan's Advance into Southeast Asia, 1939–1941*. New York: Columbia University Press, 1980.

Nathanson, Charles E. "The Social Construction of the Soviet Threat: A Study in the Politics of Representation." *Alternatives* 13 (1988): 443–483.

Ngo Vinh Long. *Before the Revolution: Vietnamese Peasants under the French*. New York: Columbia University Press, 1991.

Nitz, Kiyoko Kurushu. "Japanese Military Policy towards French Indochina during the Second World War: The Road to *Meigo Sakusen* (9 March 1945)." *Journal of Southeast Asian Studies* 14 (September 1983): 328–350.

Offner, Arnold A. *Another Such Victory: President Truman and the Cold War, 1945–1953*. Stanford: Stanford University Press, 2002.

Olson, James S., and Randy Roberts. *Where the Domino Fell: America and Vietnam, 1945–1995*. 3d ed. St. James, N.Y.: Brandywine, 1999.

Ovendale, Ritchie. "Britain, the United States, and the Cold War in South-East Asia." *International Affairs* 58 (summer 1982): 447–464.

———, ed. *The Foreign Policy of the British Labour Governments, 1945–1951*. Leicester: Leicester University Press, 1984.

Patti, Archimedes L. A. *Why Vietnam? Prelude to America's Albatross*. Berkeley and Los Angeles: University of California Press, 1980.

Pelling, Henry. *The Labour Governments, 1945–51*. New York: St. Martin's Press, 1984.

Reynolds, David, ed. *The Origins of the Cold War in Europe: International Perspectives*. New Haven: Yale University Press, 1994.

Risse-Kappen, Thomas. *Cooperation among Democracies: The European Influence on U.S. Foreign Policy*. Princeton: Princeton University Press, 1995.

Rotter, Andrew J. *The Path to Vietnam: Origins of the American Commitment to Southeast Asia*. Ithaca: Cornell University Press, 1987.

———. "The Triangular Route to Vietnam: The United States, Great Britain, and Southeast Asia, 1945–1950." *International History Review* 6 (August 1984): 404–423.

Ruscio, Alain. *Les communistes français et la guerre d'Indochine, 1944–1954.* Paris: L'Harmattan, 1985.

———. *La guerre française d'Indochine.* Paris: Editions Complexes, 1992.

Said, Edward W. *Orientalism.* New York: Vintage, 1979.

Sainteny, Jean. *Histoire d'une paix manquée: Indochine, 1945–47.* Paris: Amiot-Dumont, 1953.

Sanger, Clyde. *Malcolm MacDonald: Bringing an End to Empire.* Montreal: McGill-Queen's University Press, 1995.

SarDesai, D. R. *Indian Foreign Policy in Cambodia, Laos, and Vietnam, 1947–1964.* Berkeley and Los Angeles: University of California Press, 1968.

Sbrega, John J. *Anglo-American Relations and Colonialism in East Asia, 1941–1945.* New York: Garland, 1983.

———. "'First Catch Your Hare': Anglo-American Perspectives on Indochina during the Second World War." *Journal of Southeast Asian Studies* 14 (March 1983): 63–78.

Schaller, Michael. *The American Occupation of Japan: The Origins of the Cold War in Asia.* New York: Oxford University Press, 1985.

———. "Securing the Great Crescent: Occupied Japan and the Origins of Containment in Southeast Asia." *Journal of American History* 69 (September 1982): 392–414.

Schulzinger, Robert D. *A Time for War: The United States and Vietnam, 1941–1975.* New York: Oxford University Press, 1997.

Shaplen, Robert. *The Lost Revolution: The U.S. in Vietnam, 1946–1966.* Revised ed. New York: Harper, 1966.

Shennan, Andrew. *Rethinking France: Plans for Renewal, 1940–1946.* New York: Oxford University Press, 1989.

Shipway, Martin. *The Road to War: France and Vietnam, 1944–1947.* Providence: Berghahn, 1996.

Short, Anthony. *The Origins of the Vietnam War.* London: Longman, 1989.

Smith, Ralph B. "The Japanese Period in Indochina and the Coup of 9 March 1945." *Journal of Southeast Asian Studies* 9 (September 1978): 268–301.

Smith, Tony. "New Bottles for New Wine: A Pericentric Framework for the Study of the Cold War." *Diplomatic History* 24 (fall 2000): 551–565.

Spector, Ronald H. *Advice and Support: The Early Years of the U.S. Army in Vietnam, 1941–1960.* New York: Free Press, 1985.

Statler, Kathryn. "From the French to the Americans: Intra-alliance Politics, Cold War Concerns, and Cultural Conflict in Vietnam, 1950–1960." Ph.D. diss., University of California, Santa Barbara, 1999.

Thomas, Martin. "Free France, the British Government and the Future of French Indo-China, 1940–1945. *Journal of Southeast Asian Studies* 28 (March 1997): 137–160.

———. *The French Empire at War, 1940–1945.* Manchester: University of Manchester Press, 1998.

Thompson, Virginia. *French Indo-China.* New York: Macmillan, 1937.

Thorne, Christopher. *Allies of a Kind: The United States, Britain, and the War against Japan, 1941–1945*. New York: Oxford University Press, 1978.
———. "Indochina and Anglo-American Relations, 1942–1945." *Pacific Historical Review* 45 (February 1976): 73–96.
———. *The Issue of War: States, Societies, and the Far Eastern Conflict of 1941–1945*. New York: Oxford University Press, 1985.
———. *The Limits of Foreign Policy*. New York: Putnam's Sons, 1972.
Tønnesson, Stein. *1946: Le déclenchement de la guerre d'Indochine: Les vêpres tonkinoises du 19 décembre*. Paris: L'Harmattan, 1987.
———. *The Vietnamese Revolution of 1945: Roosevelt, Ho Chi Minh, and de Gaulle in a World at War*. London: Sage, 1991.
Trachtenberg, Marc. *A Constructed Peace: The Making of the European Settlement, 1945–1963*. Princeton: Princeton University Press, 1999.
Truman, Harry S. *The Memoirs of Harry S. Truman*. 2 vols. New York: Da Capo, 1955–1956.
Turpin, Frédéric. "Le Mouvement Républicain Populaire et la guerre d'Indochine (1944–1954)." *Revue d'histoire diplomatique* (1996): 157–190.
Valette, Jacques. *La guerre d'Indochine*. Paris: Armand Colin, 1994.
Vo Nguyen Giap. *Unforgettable Days*. 3d ed. Hanoi: GIOI Publishers, 1994.
Wall, Irwin M. *French Communism in the Era of Stalin: The Quest for Unity and Integration, 1945–1962*. Westport, Conn.: Greenwood Press, 1983.
———. *The United States and the Making of Postwar France, 1945–1954*. New York: Cambridge University Press, 1991.
Wendt, Alexander. "Constructing International Politics." In Michael E. Brown et al., eds., *Theories of War and Peace*. Cambridge, Mass.: MIT Press, 1998.
———. *Social Theory of International Politics*. Cambridge: Cambridge University Press, 1999.
Williams, Philip M. *Crisis and Compromise: Politics in the Fourth Republic*. Garden City, N.Y.: Anchor, 1966.
———. *The Tragedy of American Diplomacy*. New ed. New York: Norton, 1988.
Young, John W. *France, the Cold War, and the Western Alliance, 1944–49: French Foreign Policy and Post-War Europe*. Leicester: Leicester University Press, 1990.
Young, Marilyn B. *The Vietnam Wars, 1945–1990*. New York: Harper, 1991.
Zhai, Qiang. *China and the Vietnam Wars, 1950–1975*. Chapel Hill: University of North Carolina Press, 2000.
Zinn, Howard. *A People's History of the United States, 1492–Present*. Revised and updated ed. New York: Harper, 1995.
Zubok, Vladislav, and Constantine Pleshakov. *Inside the Kremlin's Cold War: From Stalin to Khrushchev*. Cambridge: Harvard University Press, 1996.

Index

Abbott, George M., 195, 200, 218, 224, 231, 238, 239, 251–52, 257, 259
Acheson, Dean: American assistance and, 1–2, 140, 213, 262, 263, 267, 270, 272–75, 284; American opinion and, 101, 171; Bao Dai solution and, 220, 224, 228, 231, 232, 238, 242, 244, 247, 250, 255, 256, 259, 261, 268; Chinese occupation and, 143; French threat of withdrawal and, 294n21; Soviet threat and, 172, 173, 176
Alanbrooke, Lord, 116
Alessandri, Marcel, 196
Alphand, Hervé, 273
American aid: 1945 and, 61–66, 89; 1946 and, 138–42; 1948 and, 197–201; 1949 and, 244; 1950 and, 74–91, 262–64, 268–71; amount of, 276–77, 284; to Asian nationalists, 213, 229; during British occupation, 112–13; clash with France over details of, 268–71; economic aid and, 221–22; military aid and, 60, 61–66, 89; momentum toward direct aid and, 227–32, 262–75; Netherlands and, 222; policy loopholes and, 139–41; Tonkin resistance and, 60, 61–62, 63–66, 76, 90; transfer of equipment and, 140–42, 178–79, 185–86
Anglo-French Protocol of Mutual Aid, 37

anticolonialism, U.S.: Bao Dai solution and, 283–84; British policy in 1944 and, 40–45; economic motives for, 24–25; French impatience with, 130, 184, 263–64, 268; geostrategic priorities and, 11–12, 25–26, 282; "liberal moment" and, 282; policy under Roosevelt and, 23–26, 33, 40, 41, 46, 64, 80; postwar critique and, 46–52; relations with European allies and, 12, 39–41, 283–84; rhetoric of, 40, 287
anticolonial movements: nationalism vs. communism and, 206–7, 210, 241, 268; U.S. postwar response to, 11–12. *See also* Asian nationalists; Third World; Viet Minh; Vietnamese nationalism
Ashley-Clarke, J. O., 169, 210–11, 251
Asian nationalists: anticommunist resistance among, 216–17, 239, 240; Bao Dai state and, 238, 239, 240, 248, 253–53, 259, 261–62; British support for French and, 166, 170, 186, 191, 211–12; opposition to French policy, 163–64, 166, 207, 212, 282; U.S. relations with, 49–50, 52, 92, 174, 228–29; Western recognition of Bao Dai and, 247–52
Associated Press, 133–34, 199
Atlantic Charter, 24
Attlee, Clement, 208, 253, 259, 264

347

August Revolution, 92, 129; American response to, 96–101; Franco-British suppression and, 102–3, 104–5, 113; French response to, 92–96
Auriol, Vincent, 127, 222, 226, 252, 266–67

Bajpai, Sir Girja, 244
Bao Dai: character of, 190–91; constraints on autonomy of, 246, 250; demands of, 189, 193; as emperor, 60, 190–91; foreign pressure for French concessions to, 195, 218–19, 220, 229–31, 237, 245–46, 248; French concessions to, 222–23, 226–27, 251, 252–53, 254, 255, 256, 257, 259, 260, 261, 262, 263, 264, 265, 267, 268; French negotiations with, 187, 193, 206, 207, 220; French promotion of, 187, 189, 192–93, 197, 200, 221; installation of, 223–24, 231, 233; as nationalist leader, 195–96, 219, 220, 224, 230, 237, 239, 247–50, 253, 256–57; regional support for, 232, 238, 239, 243–44; return to Vietnam, 217, 223–24; Vietnamese independence under Japan and, 60. *See also* Bao Dai state; French Bao Dai solution
Bao Dai solution, 60, 187–89, 283; American support for, 216–17, 218–19, 225, 228–29, 230, 232, 234, 235, 242, 287; British support for, 210–11, 240; Cochinchina and, 222, 223; failure of, 191; foreign skepticism of, 194–96, 206, 210, 216; Ha Long Bay agreement and, 193, 195, 217, 218; independence issue in, 193, 206, 207, 222, 237, 238; as success, 191, 221, 234, 261. *See also* Elysée accords
Bao Dai state, 269; events leading to, 179–89; French constraints on, 234; recognition and, 227, 231–32, 239–40, 247–62; relations with other nations, 228–29, 248–49; Western contact with, 260, 269
Barjot, Pierre, 153
Battambang-Seamreap question, 116–17
Baudet, Philippe, 7, 95, 96, 180
Bevin, Ernest: Bao Dai solution and, 242, 247, 249, 253–54; British occupation and, 106–7, 112; British policy and, 204, 206, 208, 213, 214, 265, 273, 274, 275; war matériel and, 166
Bidault, Georges, 74, 83, 160, 164, 178, 193, 194, 266

Bishop, Max, 51, 64, 65
Blaizot, Roger: information sharing and, 205–6; mission in Kandy, 37, 61, 68, 83; views on U.S. cooperation, 76
Blum, Léon, 130, 154–55, 156
Bodard, Lucien, 223–24
Bohlen, Charles, 262
Bollaert, Emile, 182, 187–89, 193, 199, 200
Bonbright, James, 98–99, 101
Bonnet, Henri: Bao Dai solution and, 221, 222, 227; conservative continuity and, 160; foreign perceptions and, 66, 93, 134, 199; French role in Pacific War and, 61, 83, 85, 91; mediation and, 170–71, 176; Thai government and, 144; Tonkin resistance and, 61; U.S. support and, 100, 130, 142, 170–71, 216, 221, 262, 265, 270, 271
Bose, Sarat Chandra, 163, 164
Bo Yan Naing, 163
Bradley, Mark, 51
Brain, Harry, 111, 114
Brazzaville Conference (1944), 21, 66–67, 123–25
British diplomatic efforts: American public opinion and, 40–41, 44–45; as influence in U.S., 13, 242, 284–86; pressure on France (1948), 210–11; success of, 285–86; U.S. policy and (1944), 41–45; U.S. policy and (1945), 62–63, 67–68; U.S. policy and (1947), 168–70; U.S. policy and (1948–49), 202, 209–10, 212, 240–43
British government: aid to France and, 67, 83–84, 204–7, 254, 264–65, 270, 271; Bao Dai solution and, 191, 195, 210–15, 251, 252–55; Chiefs of Staff and, 37–38, 116, 205–6; Commonwealth governments and, 240, 243, 254; dissent within, 191–92, 282 (*See also* Asian nationalists; Labour party); European defense and, 204; Franco-American clash over aid and, 270–71; frustrations with U.S., 77–78; international coalition against communism and, 209–15; Japanese takeover in Indochina and, 60–61; need for U.S. support and, 38–41, 68, 84, 115; occupation policies and, 106–8, 109–10; regional imperative of, 33–45; withdrawal from occupied Vietnam and, 115. *See also* British occupation of Vietnam; colonial concerns of Britain

Index

British occupation of Vietnam, 80, 103, 104–15; American material support and, 112–13; British-American relations during, 105–6, 112–13; criticism of activities in, 105–8; French autonomy and, 103; opposition within Britian to policies during, 105–8; revision of policy in, 108–13; suppression of nationalists and, 8–9, 102–3, 104–5, 113; withdrawal and, 113–15
Bruce, David: Bao Dai solution and, 229, 230–31, 232, 239, 250, 255–56; French concessions and, 260; French recovery and, 258; French threats of withdrawal and, 252, 266, 267
Brussels Treaty (1948), 196, 204, 205. *See also* North Atlantic Treaty
Burma, 202, 213; British policy concerns and, 202–3, 240; Franco-Viet Minh war and, 163–64, 166
Butler, Neville, 39
Butterworth, Walton, 217, 227, 256
Byrnes, James, 69, 91, 130

Cadogan, Alexander, 33, 40, 42
Caffery, Jefferson: Bao Dai solution and, 218, 220, 221–22, 224, 227, 229; communist expansion in Indochina, 137; French colonialism and, 176, 177, 178, 182; French moderation and, 136; Soviet threat in France and, 62; Viet Minh and, 96
Cambodia, 116–17, 119, 261, 270, 278
Capra, Frank, 184
Caribbean Council, 42
Carpentier, Marcel, 263, 266, 268, 269, 271
Castries, General Christian de, 281
casualties: British, 105; French, 156, 179–80; Viet Minh, 180
Catroux, Georges, 18
censorship, 133, 182–83
Central Intelligence Agency (CIA), 3, 4, 194
Chamberlain, Ronald, 167
Chauvel, Jean, 181, 273
Chen Jian, 198
Chiang Kai-shek, 203, 224, 244. *See also* China; British officials and, 77; French sovereignty and, 23, 90; government of, 143, 165; trusteeship plan and, 27, 54
China: communist regime in, 1, 5, 198–99, 214–15, 216, 234, 236, 240–41, 253, 254; evacuation of occupation troops and, 142–43; Franco-Viet Minh war and, 165;

French negotiations with, 103, 117–18, 120–21, 142; postwar occupation in Vietnam, 90–91, 94, 117–18, 120–21, 127–29, 143; postwar role of, 41, 55, 56, 90–91, 117–18, 120–21; as threat to French Indochina, 17, 23, 34, 90–91, 255; Viet Minh and, 198–99, 260, 277, 279
Churchill, Winston, 24, 41, 63
Civil-affairs accord, 83–84
Clarac, Pierre, 132, 133
Clayton, Will, 137
Cochinchina, 17, 118, 128, 132; French atrocities in, 133; negotiations on status of, 150–52; Republic of, 117, 132, 150–52, 189, 223; Vietnamese reunification and, 189, 217, 218, 222–23
Cold War: containment policy and, 136, 236; French diplomacy in 1950s and, 265–67; French domestic politics and, 157–58; nuanced view on waging of, 281–82; recasting of Vietnam situation and, 8, 9–10, 13–14, 282–85; tensions in Europe and, 89, 170, 172, 196, 220; Third-World extension of paradigm for, 9, 10–11; U.S. fears about Indochina and, 2–3, 265, 281; U.S. neutrality in Indochina and, 136–38; Western partnership against, 261. *See also* communist threat
colonialism: communist threat as result of repression by, 149, 174–75, 206, 234, 237, 257–58; transnational debate over, 7–8. *See also* anticolonialism, U.S.; anticolonial movements
colonial world. *See* Third World
Comité Français de la Libération Nationale, 22
communism: in Europe, 89, 170, 172, 196, 220; as failed device for consensus building, 149, 175; puppet nationalist regimes and, 117; regional cooperation in Southeast Asia and, 200–204, 206–7, 209–15; as result of colonial repression, 149, 174–75, 206, 234, 237, 257–58; Truman administration and, 4, 100, 136, 235, 241, 266, 291n9; U.S. Indochina policy and (1949), 226–27, 235–39; Vietnamese nationalism and, 3, 95–96, 99–101, 133, 137, 198, 224–25, 237, 279, 286–87. *See also* China; Cold War; French Communist Party; Soviet Union

Confédération Générale du Travail, 252
Congress, 130, 266
conservative, as term, 52
conservative policymakers. *See* British diplomatic efforts; conservative policymakers, U.S.; D'Argenlieu, Thierry; Gaullists; hawkish French policymakers; High Commission in Saigon; Ministry of Foreign Affairs; Ministry of Overseas France
conservative policymakers, U.S.: Bao Dai solution and, 217, 230–31; European pressures and, 69; Franco-Viet Minh war and, 172–74; French colonial reform and, 87–88; in Roosevelt administration, 52–58, 63–65, 68–69; in Truman administration, 69–71, 72, 74, 79, 87, 255–59, 286. *See also* Truman administration; U.S. government, Joint Chiefs of Staff
"construction," as term, 10
containment strategy, 136, 236
Cooper, Duff, 186
Corps Léger d'Intervention, 28
Coste-Floret, Paul, 160, 189, 193, 194, 197, 231

Dalat conference, 151–52
D'Argenlieu, Thierry, 126; American motives and, 94, 130, 144; American support and, 134–35, 141; British support and, 116, 117; Cochinchina and, 189, 223; communist threat and, 175; "Japanese nuisance" and, 95; negotiation and, 147–48; "politique de force" and, 147, 150, 151–52, 152, 153, 154, 159; replacement of, 181–82
Daridan, Jean, 226
Decoux, Jean, 18, 59, 61, 190
De Gaulle, Charles, 66; American ambivalence and, 62, 63; foreign perceptions and, 96; Free French policymaking and, 27–28, 123–26; Indochina debate and, 19, 20, 22, 28, 31, 33; Rassemblement du Peuple Français (RPF) and, 157; resignation of, 126, 136, 149, 150; Roosevelt's dislike of, 46, 53; sense of unity and, 124–25; visit to Washington, 85–87, 88
De Langlade, François, 19, 28
Democratic Republic of Vietnam (DRV), 103; Bao Dai alternative and, 217, 219, 220, 221, 224, 225, 234, 236–37; Bao Dai as advisor to, 191;

British policy in 1948 and, 203, 207, 210; China as threat to, 165; diplomatic efforts of, 129, 183, 199; foreign support for, 93–94, 183; Franco-British suppression and, 8–9, 102–3, 104–5, 113; French drift toward war with, 149–55; French military efforts against, 160–61; French policy toward and, 123–29, 132, 135; French vilification of, 132–33, 198; Ho Chi Minh as head of, 60; independence and, 92, 93, 96; Sino-Soviet recognition of, 260–61; Soviet influence and, 173, 176, 177, 199, 224–25, 260–61, 268; U.S. contact with, 81–82, 93–94, 130. *See also* August Revolution; Franco-Viet Minh war; Ho Chi Minh; Viet Minh; Vietnamese nationalism
Dening, M. Esler: British occupation and, 104; British support for France and, 104, 166, 168, 239–40; resistence against communism and, 208–9, 211, 212; U.S. anticolonialism and, 42–43, 78; U.S. support and, 241, 264, 211l3
Devinat, Paul, 227
Dien Bien Phu, 278, 294n21
dissent. *See* British government, dissent within; foreign-policy bureaucracies, dissent within; France, dissent within; liberal policymakers, U.S.
Divide and Conquer, 184
domino theory, 279
Donovan, William J., 99
DRV. *See* Democratic Republic of Vietnam (DRV)
Du Gardier, Robert, 250, 251, 252
Duiker, William J., 92
Dulles, John Foster, 294n21
Dunn, James Clement, 63, 72, 74, 81
Dutch East Indies, 106–7

ECAFE. *See* Economic Commission for Asia and the Far East (ECAFE)
Economic Commission for Asia and the Far East (ECAFE), 199, 246
economic interdependence of Far East: American involvement and, 140–41, 201; British assistance in 1950 and, 264–65; British policy and, 109, 167–68; Commonwealth mechanisms and, 243; ECAFE and, 199, 246; French policy on aid and, 270, 271. *See also* Japan, reindustrialization of

Index 351

economic interests of U.S.: anticolonialism and, 24–25, 47–48; as basis for intervention, 4–5, 235–36; French policy and, 67, 86–88, 130, 201; liberal vs. conservative views of, 53–54; postwar order and, 293n18; trade barriers in Indochina and, 2, 17, 32, 47, 130

Eden, Anthony, 37–38, 41, 42, 43

Eisenhower administration, 279, 280, 284

Elysée accords: demands for ratification of, 238–39, 242, 245, 247, 249, 252–53; implementation of, 222, 223, 224, 226–27, 245, 265, 270; ratification of, 259–60; restrictive provisions in, 230, 231–32, 246–47, 250, 255–56, 269

European Defense Community (EDC), 284

Fabian Colonial Bureau, 166
Fabian Colonial Society, 106
Fall, Bernard, 180
Farouk (King of Egypt), 196
FEA. *See under* U.S. State Department
Fenard, Raymond, 66, 69
"Field Liquidation Commissions," 140–41
Folsom, Robert S., 258
Fontainebleau conference, 151, 152
Ford, J.F., 242
Foreign Office (Britain): communist threat in Asia and, 203–6; Franco-American clash and, 270–71; French requests and, 84, 166, 168; problems with French policy and, 206–7, 208; U.S. anticolonialism and, 42
Foreign-policy bureaucracies, dissent within, 7, 9, 281–82. *See also* British government, dissent within; France, dissent within; liberal policymakers, U.S.
Foulds, L.H., 36
France: debates between reformers and hardliners in, 123–28, 135–36; dissent within, 21, 22, 123–26, 135–36, 191–92, 193–94, 225–26, 245, 251–52, 281, 282, 283; fears of communist influence in, 62, 63, 70, 89, 100, 136, 29 1n9; Franco-Japanese understanding and, 17–18, 21, 22, 59; need for U.S. support, 30–31; politics in, 127, 149–62, 225, 238, 245, 255; postwar importance of, 35–36, 53–55, 88–89, 220, 238–39, 258; recovery of Indochina and, 19–33, 22; World War II defeat and, 17–18. *See also* Franco-Viet Minh war; Free France; French government; French Indochina policy; French sovereignty, restoration of

Franco-Chinese agreement, 142

Franco-Viet Minh war: amount of U.S. aid to, 276–77, 284; Asian opposition to, 163–64; British aid and, 83–84, 165–68, 170, 186, 254, 264–65; British efforts to involve U.S. and, 168–70; Cold War recasting of, 148–49; domestic unity and, 155–56; emergence of Bao Dai solution and, 187–89; French dissent and, 281, 282, 283; French domestic politics and, 157–59; French need for aid and, 148–49, 158, 164, 165–66, 180–81; lack of U.S. control and, 277–78; 1950–1954 events and, 276–78, 279; outbreak of, 147; reasons for French failure in, 277–78; reasons for U.S. decision to support, 1–2, 3, 8, 276, 278, 281–86; shift from negotiation to force and, 147–48, 150–62; surrender at Dien Bien Phu and, 278; U.S. dilemma after aiding, 277–78; U.S. policy and, 170–79, 184–86

Franks, Oliver, 241

Free France: British support and, 37–38; divisions among leaders of, 123–26; tensions between U.S. and, 49; war on Japan and, 22. *See also* French government

French Communist Party (PCF): anticommunist propaganda and, 133; French politics and, 156, 157–58, 159; power of, 70, 89, 95, 136, 157, 255, 266; reform and, 127; Southeast Asia and, 137, 169, 170

French military: American ships and, 309n28; in British-occupied Vietnam, 105, 112; casualties and, 156, 179–80; drift toward war in 1946 and, 151, 153–54, 160–61; Franco-Viet Minh war efforts and, 160–61, 164; French autonomy in 1946 and, 120–23; French confidence in, 121–22, 153–54; hawkish leadership and, 150; persistent crises in, 195, 196–97, 204–5, 244–45, 267; role in Pacific war and, 22, 23, 27–29, 37, 42–43, 61, 66, 68, 76, 80, 83, 85, 89–91; Tonkin resistance and, 60, 61–62, 63–67, 76, 79–80

French diplomatic efforts: with Britain (1944), 30; with Britain (1945–46), 115–20; with Britain (1947), 186; with Britain (1948), 201–15; failure to win ongoing support and, 148; foreign demands (1949) and, 245–47; Franco-Viet Minh war and, 180–84; with other colonial powers, 29–30; recognition of Bao Dai and, 247–52; in Soviet Union (1944), 29; successes of, 75, 285–86; threats of withdrawal and, 251–52, 266–67; with U.S. (1944), 28–29, 30–33; with U.S. (1945), 61–62, 63, 66–67, 85–87; with U.S. (1946), 129–44; with U.S. (1948), 197–201; with U.S. (1949), 226–27; with U.S. (1950), 262–64, 265–67

French government: continuity of ministries in, 159–60; debates on colonial reform within, 21, 123–28, 156, 160; frustrations with U.S., 75–77; hawkish influences within, 196–97, 244–45, 283–84 (*See also* Bao Dai solution); leverage over U.S. policy, 13, 32–33, 89–90, 251–52, 263–64, 266–67, 284, 285; limits on American support and, 74–77; management of U.S. neutrality and, 79–83, 129–44; 1945 negotiations with Ho Chi Minh and, 97–98; 1946 negotiations with Ho Chi Minh and, 103, 127–28, 132, 138, 147, 150–52, 153, 155, 219; 1947–49 negotiations with Ho Chi Minh and, 158, 161–62, 171, 181, 186, 187–88, 189, 192, 193, 234, 245; 1954 negotiations with Ho Chi Minh and, 153; political crisis within, 127, 149–62, 225, 238, 245, 255; U.S. interest in postwar strengthening of, 291n9. *See also* Free France; French Indochina policy; French sovereignty, restoration of

French Indochina policy: August Revolution and, 92–96; British rejection of, 208–9; doubts about Bao Dai and, 192–201; following British occupation, 115–29; Free France and, 19–33; global hostility to French war and, 162–79; Haiphong harbor incident and, 147–49, 154; as issue for political parties, 156–62; Japanese takeover and, 60–61; moderates vs. hawks and, 123–28, 135–36, 149–53, 154–55, 156–62; reorientation of, in 1945, 115–29; roots of Bao Dai solution and, 179–89; steps toward liberalization, 66–67, 71–72, 85–87, 125, 126–28, 192–201. *See also* French sovereignty, restoration of; hawkish French policymakers

French intelligence: Bao Dai and, 196, 228–29; communist influences in Hanoi and, 133, 174–75, 198; U.S. and, 32–33, 131, 183–84

French sovereignty, restoration of: Britain's regional imperative and, 33–45; British assistance and, 83–84, 104–5; British occupation and, 80–81, 102–3, 104–15; British withdrawal and, 115–29; ending of Chinese occupation and, 117–18, 120–21, 127–29; failures of French policy and, 119–20; Free France policies and, 19–33, 123–26; importance to France, 19–20, 22; Japanese coup in Indochina and, 60–61; liberal U.S. alternative to trusteeship and, 58, 70, 71–72, 73–74; military vs. political support for, 63–65, 71, 80, 208–9; period of autonomy in Vietnam and, 103, 115, 121–23, 127–28, 129–44; U.S. postwar dilemma regarding, 45–58, 177

French Union, 67, 128, 155, 188, 193, 260

Gallagher, Phillip E., 94, 96, 135
Gaullists: debate over Indochina and, 21–33; Franco-Viet Minh war and, 157; tensions with U.S. and, 49. *See also* Rassemblement du Peuple Français (RPF)
geostrategic priorities of U.S.: anticolonial rhetoric and, 11–12, 282; British diplomacy and, 43–44; economic exploitation and, 48–49; importance of France to, 88–89, 220, 281; as reason for intervention, 4, 8, 234–35, 281. *See also* Cold War; military bases in Southeast Asia
Germany, rearming of, 284
Giacobbi, Paul, 61–62, 121, 160
Gibbs, Frank, 206, 210, 240, 260
Gibson, William M., 229, 257
Gide, André, 252
Gracey, Douglas D.: Allied strategy and, 112–13; British withdrawal and, 114, 115, 118; criticism of, 110–11; pro-French activities of, 102–3, 104–5, 111

Index

Graves, Hubert Ashton, 213, 264
Great Britain. *See* British government
Grew, Joseph, 61, 72, 85
Grey, Paul, 206, 208, 209
Griffin, R. Allen, 267, 268, 269, 270
guerrilla warfare, 18, 28, 175, 277. *See also* Franco-Viet Minh war; Viet Minh
Gullion, Edmund, 267

Haiphong incident, 147–49, 154, 170
Halifax, Lord, 40, 41, 43, 46, 77
Ha Long Bay agreement, 193, 195, 217, 218
Hanoi government. *See* Democratic Republic of Vietnam; Ho Chi Minh; Viet Minh
Harriman, W. Averell, 57
hawkish French policymakers, 150: drift to war and, 147–49, 150–55; 1947 anxieties among, 158–62; policy domination by, 158–60; political polarization and, 156, 157, 158, 159; status of Cochinchina and, 150–52; U.S. position on Franco-Viet Minh war and, 178–79. *See also* D'Argenlieu, Thierry; French army; High Commission in Saigon; Valluy, Jean
Henderson, J. Thyme, 44
Hiaphong harbor incident, 147
Hicks, G.E., 167
High Commission in Saigon (French): control of foreign opinion and, 182–84, 199–200; unilateral actions of, 150–52, 154–55. *See also* D'Argenlieu, Thierry
Hoang Minh Giam, 161
Ho Chi Minh: French negotiations (1945) and, 97–98; French negotiations (1946) and, 103, 127–28, 132, 138, 147, 150–52, 153, 155, 219; French negotiations (1947–49) and, 158, 161–62, 171, 181, 186, 187–88, 189, 192, 193, 234, 245; French negotiations (1954) and, 153; "modus vivendi" agreement and, 152–53; nationalism-communism blend in, 133, 169, 207, 243, 283; nationalist support for, 18–19, 92–93, 195, 220, 230, 234, 237, 253, 263, 268; vilification of, 9, 132–33, 159, 247, 263, 268; Western alternative to, 9, 263, 283 (*See also* Bao Dai solution). *See also* Democratic Republic of Vietnam; Viet Minh
Hoppenot, Henri, 26

Hopson, Donald, 243
Humbert, Georges, 154
Hurley, Patrick, 31, 32

India: British risk of backlash in, 186; British training centers in, 84; food crisis in, 236; forces in Vietnam and, 104–5, 107–8; Franco-Viet Minh war and, 163–64, 166; French policy and, 130, 207, 212, 240, 243, 261; independence for, 24
"Indo-Burma Volunteer Force," 163–64
International Labor Organization, 246, 265
International Monetary Fund, 246
Irving, R.E.M., 157
Isaacs, Harold, 199

Japan, 52, 116; coup in Indochina and, 59–61; end of war with, 88, 89–91, 125; French understanding with, 17–18, 21, 22, 59; reindustrialization of, 173–74, 201, 226, 236; repatriation of troops from, 112, 116; as U.S. ally, 173–74
JCS. *See* U.S. government, Joint Chiefs of Staff
Jessup, Philip, 251, 260
Johnson administration Vietnam policy, 281
Joint Chiefs of Staff (JCS), 64–65, 68, 80, 85, 91, 114
journalists. *See* media reporting
Juin, Alphonse, 29, 116, 122, 126, 153

Kahn, Walter, 87–88
Kandy, French mission in, 37, 61, 68, 83
Kennan, George, 99–100, 258
Kennedy administration, 280, 281
Killearn, Lord, 166, 168, 169
Knight, Melvin, 51–52
Knox, Frank, 55
Korean War, 276
Kuomintang, 99, 117, 165, 224

Labour party (Britain), 166–67, 170; Cold War concerns and, 207–8; Franco-Viet Minh war and, 166–67, 170; occupation policies and, 106–7
Lacoste, François, 63, 94, 101, 139, 176, 184
Lacy, William, 271
Landon, Kenneth P., 51, 135, 171, 174, 175
Laos, 261, 270, 278
Laski, Harold, 107
Latham, Robert, 282
Laurentie, Henri, 21, 67, 123, 125, 151, 306n69

Leahy, William D., 64
Lebanon, 76, 97
Leclerc, Jacques Philippe: British aid and, 312n76; Chinese occupation and, 118, 122, 143; Cochinchinese campaign, 120, 121–22; as head of French forces, 95, 112, 153, 154; negotiation and, 126–29; occupation of Hanoi, 121–22, 143; support for military and, 105, 116, 141
Lend-Lease program, 80, 84, 139, 140
Letourneau, Jean, 244–45, 260
liberal, as term, 46–47
"liberal internationalism," 47
"liberal moment," 282
liberal policymakers. *See* Asian nationalists; Labour party; liberal policymakers, U.S.; reformist French policymakers; Socialist party
liberal policymakers, U.S.: alternative to trusteeship and, 58, 70, 71–72, 73–74; August Revolution and, 97–98, 100; Bao Dai solution and, 216–17, 229–31, 232; concerns about communism and, 99, 136–37; economic recovery and, 141; Franco-Viet Minh war and, 174–76; French colonialism and, 237, 286; "liberal moment" and, 282; "liberal viewpoint" and, 46–52; neutrality policy and, 135–38, 174; under Roosevelt administration, 46–52, 56–58, 64–66, 68; shift away from views of, 56–58, 68–69; Stettinius compromise and, 64–66; under Truman administration, 79, 80, 81–83, 88, 89, 136–37, 138, 286. *See also* Roosevelt administration; U.S. State Department
liberal tradition. *See* anticolonialism, U.S.
Life (magazine), 199
Lloyd, J.O., 205
Lovett, Robert, 69
Lu Han, 117–18

MacArthur, Douglas, 143
MacDonald, Malcolm, 242; British policy in 1948 and, 202, 205, 212–13; support for Bao Dai, 253, 256
MacKenzie, Colin, 67
Mackworth-Young, Gerard, 208
MacLeish, Archibald, 66
Malaya: economic value of, 202, 226; insurgency in, 201, 202, 207, 216, 226, 233; opposition to French in, 163, 166

Mao Zedong, 198, 215, 233, 241, 254, 267; victory in China, 1, 3, 234, 236, 253, 258, 260–61. *See also* China
March 6 accord, 127–29, 132, 142, 150, 153, 188
March 24 declaration, 67, 125; British occupation and, 102, 106–7; French concessions and, 86–87, 125; U.S. views of, 71
Marie, André, 194
Marshall, George, 58, 143, 176–77, 218–19
Marshall Plan funds, 185, 197, 216, 262
Massigli, René, 21, 30, 33, 41
Matthews, H. Freeman, 73, 176
Maunsell, M.S.K., 121
Mayer, David, 159
McCarthy, Joseph, 287
McCloy, John J., 63
McNeil, Hector, 167
media reporting: Franco-Viet Minh war and, 175–76; French censorship and, 133–34, 182–83
Meiklereid, Ernest W., 113, 114, 122, 169, 170, 181
Messmer, Pierre, 152
Middle East, 76, 97
military bases in Southeast Asia: acceptance of colonialism and, 55, 72; British diplomacy and, 42; French concerns about, 25–26, 32, 76, 130, 131; U.S. Indochina policy and, 79, 226, 241
Ministry of Foreign Affairs (France): American aid and, 262; conservative domination of, 160; foreign perceptions and, 133; relations with U.S. and, 199–200; responsibility for Indochina and, 238, 265
Ministry of Overseas France, 149, 265; conservative domination of, 160; Fontainbleau negotiations and, 151–52. *See also* Moutet, Marius; reformist French policymakers
Moffat, Abbot Low: censorship and, 182–83; compromise and, 64; importance of Southeast Asia and, 49; mediation and, 174, 176; military vs. political support and, 65; State Department conflicts and, 72; U.S. prestige and, 98; Viet Minh and, 94, 96, 97, 138, 175
Morgan, Kenneth O., 107
Mountbatten, Lord Louis: Battambang-Seamreap question and, 117; British occupation policy and,

Index

110–11, 112; British withdrawal and, 113–15; Franco-British cooperation and, 36, 38, 84; theater boundaries and, 78
Moutet, Marius, 128, 136, 151, 152, 154, 155, 159, 160
Mouvement Républicain Populaire (MRP), 124, 156, 157, 158, 159, 194, 245
MRP. *See* Mouvement Républicain Populaire (MRP)
Mus, Paul, 162

The Nation, 199
National Security Council, 235–39, 258–59
Nehru, Jawaharlal, 108, 163–64, 207, 243–44
Netherlands, 29–30, 222, 239
New York Times, 175–76, 183
Ngo Dinh Diem, 184, 191
Nguyen Phan Long, 269
Nguyen Van Xuan, 193, 195, 228
Noel-Baker, Philip, 107
Norodom Sihanouk, King of Cambodia, 60
North Atlantic Treaty Organization (NATO), 1, 196, 204, 214
NSC-48/1 (National Security Council study), 258–59

Oakes, Hawley, 48, 50–51
Office of Strategic Services (OSS), 25, 32–33, 47, 81–82, 83, 94, 96, 134
Ogburn, Charlton, 224, 232
"Operation Lea," 180
OSS. *See* U.S. government, Office of Strategic Services
O'Sullivan, James, 130, 134, 178, 181

"Pacific Pact," 212, 213, 240, 243
Parodi, Alexandre, 266
Parti Communiste Français (PCF). *See* French Communist Party
Patti, Archimedes L. A., 82, 134, 144
PCF. *See* French Communist Party
Pechkoff, Zinovi, 30, 75, 85, 86, 90, 118; French policy and, 23, 25, 26, 30
People's Liberation Army (Viet Minh), 60
People's Republic of China. *See* China
Perkins, George W., 222
Peter, Georges, 85
Pham Ngoc Thach, 185
Pham Van Dong, 152
Pignon, Léon, 151, 223, 228, 244, 246, 249, 250–51, 266, 271
Platon, Charles, 20

Pleven, René, 32, 74–75, 85, 266
"Point IV" program, 213
poison gas plan, 196, 319n9
political order in Vietnam: recasting of, as Cold War front, 8, 9–10, 13–14, 149, 221, 282–85; U.S. interests in, 3, 183–85, 277–78, 279–80. *See also* Vietnamese nationalism
"politique de force." *See* D'Argenlieu; hawkish French policymakers
Potsdam agreement, 80–81, 91
Pownall, Sir Henry, 39
Poynton, A. H., 77
progressive advocacy of change, 287. *See also* liberal policymakers, U.S.
propaganda: by British, 44–45, 114–15; by French, 66–67, 85, 93–96, 131–34, 170–71, 181–84; by Viet Minh, 107–8, 183
public opinion, French: antiwar protests and, 251–52; reformist program and, 156, 160
public opinion, U.S.: 1949 shifts in, 240; anticolonialism and, 24, 40, 50–51; British diplomacy and, 40–41, 44–45; Franco-Viet Minh war and, 162, 171, 181–84; French propaganda and, 66–67, 85, 93–96, 131–34, 170–71, 181–84; Indochina as market and, 48; skepticism about France and, 66–67, 88; Vietnamese people and, 256–57
puppet regimes, 117, 158, 165. *See also* Bao Dai solution

Qiang Zhai, 198
Queuille, Henri, 201, 227, 230, 231
Quirino, Elpidio, 244

Ramadier, Jean, 187
Ramadier, Paul, 158–59, 164, 179
Rassemblement du Peuple Français (RPF; Gaullists), 157, 194
Reed, Charles S., 120, 131, 133, 134, 137–38, 143, 175, 215, 225–26, 255
reformist French policymakers, 149–50; failure of negotiation and, 147–48, 152–53; ineffectiveness of, against hawks, 154–55; political polarization and, 156, 157, 158–59. *See also* Leclerc, Jacques Philippe; Moutet, Marius; Socialist Party
"regional councils," 42
regional pact. *See* "Pacific Pact"
regional stability in the Far East: anticolonial resentments and, 49–50; British Indochina policy and, 33–45, 202–7, 213–14, 239, 242–43;

regional stability in the Far East: anticolonial resentments and *(continued)* British occupation policies and, 109–10; colonialism and, 55, 56, 208–9; communist expansion and, 200–207, 214–15; economic concerns of U.S. and, 226, 236; French attempts to involve U.S. and, 200–201; Indochinese importance for, 109–10; insurgencies of 1948–49 and, 233; Japan as postwar ally and, 173–74
Revers, Georges, 229
Rhineland, 76
rice, 109, 140, 202–3
Ritchie, Sir Neil, 205–6
Roosevelt, Franklin D.: anticolonialism and, 23–26, 40, 41, 46, 56, 64, 82–83; anti-French stance of, 29, 31, 46, 53, 68, 80, 82, 300n68; death of, 68, 74; Stettinius proposal and, 63–64; trusteeship idea and, 26, 40, 46, 57–58, 68, 70
Roosevelt administration: conservative policymakers in, 52–58, 63–65, 68–69; liberal policymakers in, 46–52, 56–58, 64–66, 68
Rotter, Andrew, 202, 232
RPF. *See* Rassemblement du Peuple Français (RPF)
rubber, 33, 140, 141, 202
Rubber Development Corporation, 141

Sabattier, Gabriel, 84
Sainteny, Jean, 82, 127, 155
SarDesai, S.R., 164
Schaller, Michael, 173
Schuman, Robert, 160, 189, 260, 266; talks with Acheson and, 2, 228, 242, 247, 250, 272, 273, 274, 275
Schumann, Maurice, 158
Scott, R.H., 204, 241–42, 253, 254, 270
SEAC. *See* South East Asia Command (SEAC)
Section Française de l'Internationale Ouvrière (SFIO). *See* Socialist party
Seel, G.T., 168
self-determination: British Labour rhetoric and, 106; conflicted U.S. stance on, 11; European partnership with U.S. and, 12; French views on, 21; Vietnamese capabilities for, 35, 256–57. *See also* anticolonialism, U.S.; anticolonial movements; Asian nationalists; Vietnamese nationalism
Seymour, Sir Horace, 41
SFIO. *See* Socialist party

Shipway, Martin, 21, 127, 151
Singapore, 163
Sisavong Vong, King of Laos, 60
Socialist party (Britain). *See* Labour party
Socialist party (France), 127, 158, 161, 193–94, 245, 259–60
South East Asia Command (SEAC), 77; British withdrawal and, 114; support for French troops and, 83–84; theater issue and, 77–78, 80–81, 84; U.S. prestige in Asia and, 97. *See also* Kandy, French mission in
Southeast Asia Treaty Organization, 279
Soviet Union: British diplomacy and, 43–44, 169; containment policy and, 136; French diplomacy and, 28; French rhetoric and, 250–51; Ho Chi Minh and, 169, 199, 224–25, 260, 261, 268; unrest in Southeast Asia and, 34, 99–100, 235–36; U.S. relations with, 57. *See also* communist threat
Stalin, Josef, 27, 55, 57, 261
Stanton, Edwin, 72, 216, 232
Sterndale Bennett, J.C., 62, 68, 78, 106
Stettinius, Edward R., 63–64, 74, 80, 81
Stimson, Henry L., 55, 96
Strang, Sir William, 213
Syngman Rhee, 244
Syria, 76, 97

Taussig, Charles, 58, 68
Thailand, 116–17, 183, 185, 212, 248; border question and, 143–44, 163
Third World: origins of Cold War in, 10–11; U.S. goal of compliant nationalisms in, 287
Thomas, Allison K., 82
Thompson, G.H., 204, 213–14
Thompson, Virginia, 2, 35
Tonkin province: aid to French "resistance" in, 60–67; American aid and, 61–62, 63–66, 76, 90; Chinese occupation and, 90–91, 94, 118; French propaganda and, 85; Japanese suppression of, 79–80; "Operation Lea" in, 180; Viet Minh "liberated zone" in, 60, 180
Trachtenberg, Marc, 100, 136, 293n17
Trevor-Wilson, A.G., 195
tripartisme, 158
Truman, Harry S., 5, 85, 140, 213
Truman administration, 149; aid commitments in 1950 and, 262, 264, 267, 268–71, 274–75, 276–77; Bao Dai solution and, 215–16, 218, 221,

222, 228, 229, 232, 239, 249, 255, 261; communist expansion and, 4, 100, 136, 235, 241, 266, 291n9; domestic politics and, 5; leverage over France and, 69–74, 87, 224, 255, 267, 286, 294n21; neutrality policy and, 78–83, 88–89, 119–20; policy shift on Indochina and, 69, 74–76, 75, 79; range of factors in decisionmaking by, 3–6; views on aid for Indochina and, 197, 204, 214, 259

Truman Doctrine of 1947, 4, 169, 184

trusteeship idea, 57–58; abandonment of, 70, 73–74, 79; liberal alternative to, 58, 70, 71–72, 73–74; resistence to, 27, 54–56; Roosevelt and, 26, 40, 46, 57–58, 68, 70

Tsuchihashi, Yūichi, 59

United Nations: Bao Dai government and, 196, 229, 245, 246, 255, 265; DRV government and, 163, 199; Franco-Viet Minh war and, 170–71; inaugural meeting of, 74

U.S. aid. *See* American aid

U.S. Department of State: American aid to Indochina and, 241–42, 244; April 1949 debate within, 69–73; Bao Dai solution and, 219–20, 224–25; British policy and, 212–15; communism in Viet Minh and, 175; Far Eastern Affairs office, 58, 69–70, 71–72, 73, 97–98, 100, 174, 224; Foreign Economic Administration (FEA), 48; Japanese and Korean Affairs division, 173–74; Marshall Plan funds, 185, 197, 216, 262; mediation approach and, 97–98, 100, 101, 144, 171, 174, 176, 178; news agency protest and, 134; policy paper on Bao Dai (1949), 229–31, 232; policy paper on Indochina (1945), 69–74; policy paper on Indochina (1948), 219–20; Southeast Asia division, 88, 137–38; strategic value of Indochina and, 48–49; transfer of military equipment and, 141–42, 178–79, 185–86; West European division of, 54–55, 69–71, 98–100, 172

U.S. policy: ambiguities in, 26, 27, 73–74, 79, 217–18; ambivalence in, 26–27, 37–38, 40–41, 63, 77, 81–82, 176–78, 224–25, 263–64, 271–72; assumed autonomy of, 5–6; Bao Dai solution and, 215–32, 234, 255–61, 287; contingency vs. continuity in, 280; decision to aid France and, 1–2, 3, 8, 276, 278, 281–86; European leverage over, 13, 32–33, 79–80, 251–52, 263–64, 266–67, 284, 285; factors in, 3–6; Franco-Viet Minh war and, 170–79, 184–86; French politics and, 225–26; ignorance of colonial issues and, 40–41; internal debates over, 69–74, 171–77, 216–19, 282 (*See also* conservative policymakers, U.S.; liberal policymakers, U.S.); leverage over France and, 69–74, 87, 224, 255, 267, 286, 294n21; liberal-conservative split in, 45, 53, 69–74, 79, 171–77; mediation proposals and, 97–98, 100, 101, 144, 171, 174, 176, 178; military vs. political support and, 63–65, 71, 80, 208–9; neutrality and, 78–83, 88–89, 92–101, 119–20, 129–44, 174, 221; 1945 shift in, 61–74; position on Franco-Viet Minh war, 178–79; postwar dilemma and, 45–58, 177; reorientation of, 255–59; response to August Revolution, 96–101; review of, under Truman, 69–74; Stettinius proposal and, 63–66; transnational debate and, 6–8; vision of, 3, 279–80, 286–87; before World War II, 2. *See also* American aid; anticolonialism, U.S.; communist threat; conservative policymakers, U.S.; economic interests of U.S.; geostrategic priorities of U.S.; liberal policymakers, U.S.; political order in Vietnam

Valle d'Aosta, 76
Valluy, Jean, 153, 154, 155, 159, 188, 196
Vatican, 217, 248
Viet Minh: August Revolution and, 92–96; bases for success of, 286–87; British concerns about communist influence in, 169–70, 234–35; Chinese cooperation with, 165, 198–99, 204, 260, 277, 279; Committee of the South, 105; economic destruction and, 180; French claims of communist influence in, 95–96, 133, 174–75, 198–99; French hostility to, 95–96, 158–59, 161, 198; Japanese troops and, 306n69; lack of evidence for communist influence in, 172–73; military assistance for, 163–64; military capabilities of, 163, 195, 277, 278;

Viet Minh: August Revolution and *(continued)*
nationalist support for, 92–96, 163, 166, 169, 177, 207, 212, 230, 243–44; origin of, 18–19; risks in repression of, 92, 177; U.S. sensitivity to communist influence in, 99–101, 169, 173, 174, 177, 234–35; Western contact with, 94, 130, 169, 178, 199–200; Western sympathy and, 177, 178, 237. *See also* Democratic Republic of Vietnam; Franco-Viet Minh war; Ho Chi Minh; Vietnamese nationalism

Vietnam: Chinese occupation and, 90–91, 94, 117–18, 120–21, 127–29, 143; division of, 278–79; as early anticolonial movement, 11; Franco-Japanese understanding and, 17–18, 21, 22, 59; Geneva Accords and, 278–79; independence under Bao Dai and, 193, 206, 207, 222, 237, 238; independence under Japan and, 60; independence within French Union and, 128, 155, 188, 193, 260; postwar division of, 80–81, 90–91; reunification of, 147, 189, 217, 218, 222–23. *See also* Bao Dai state; British occupation of Vietnam; Cochinchina; Democratic Republic of Vietnam; Franco-Viet Minh war; political order in Vietnam; Tonkin province; Vietnamese nationalism

Vietnam, French war in. *See* Franco-Viet Minh war

Vietnamese-American Friendship Association, 183

Vietnamese leaders, current, and 1950 events, 280–81

Vietnamese National Army (VNA): French failure to develop, 270, 277–78; French requests for aid and, 227–28, 229; planned role in defense and, 227–28, 270

Vietnamese nationalism: British sensitivity to, 111–12; communist influence in, 3, 279, 286–87; concerns about alienation of, 9, 97, 281–82; conservative pessimism about, 56, 98–99, 135; foreign opinion and, 183; Franco-British suppression of, 8–9, 102–3, 104–5, 113; Franco-Viet Minh war and, 174; French views of, 92–96, 125; liberal optimism about, 51–52; postwar opportunity for, 18–19, 83; transnational debate over, 8, 9; Western responses to August Revolution and, 92–100. *See also* anticolonial movements; Ho Chi Minh; Viet Minh

Vietnamese people, 35, 51, 256–57

Vincent, John Carter, 97–98, 100–101, 176, 216

Vo Nguyen Giap, General, 153, 155, 278

Wallner, Woodruff, 172, 173, 185, 217
Washington Post, 176
Webb, James, 231–32, 239
Wedemeyer, Albert, 58, 64–65, 78, 81, 90, 91, 134, 144
Williams, Tom, 110
Williams, William Appleman, 293n18
Wilson, Sir Henry Maitland, 63
Wilson, Woodrow, 40, 53
World Bank, 246
World Health Organization, 246, 265
World War II: Allied operations in Indochina and, 22–23; defeat of France in, 17–18; Japanese coup in Indochina and, 59–61; role of French military in Pacific and, 22, 23, 27–29, 37, 42–43, 61, 66, 68, 76, 80, 83, 85, 89–91; theater boundaries in Far East and, 77–78, 80–81. *See also* Southeast Asia Command
Wright, Michael, 169
Wyatt, Woodrow Lyle, 167

Compositor:	International Typesetting & Composition
Text:	10/13 Sabon
Display:	Sabon
Printer and binder:	Integrated Book Technology